EXPANDED EDITION

ONE BOOK
RIGHTLY DIVIDED

The Key to Understanding the Bible

EXPANDED EDITION

ONE BOOK
RIGHTLY DIVIDED

The Key to Understanding the Bible

By Dr. Douglas D. Stauffer

Publisher's Note:
Scripture quotations are from the Authorized King James Bible (A.V. 1611). For clarity, all scripture is in italics with reference and any emphasis in bold print. Any deviations from the King James Bible are not intentional.

ISBN 0-9677016-1-9
Library of Congress Catalog 99-722539

First printing. February, 2000
Second printing. November, 2000 (second edition)
Third printing. July 2003
Fourth printing. August 2005
Fifth Printing. October, 2006 (expanded edition)

For information, address:

McCowen Mills Publishers
Dr. Douglas D. Stauffer
P.O. Box 1611
Millbrook, AL 36054
(334) 285-6650
www.rightlydivided.com
Doug@BibleDoug.com
dougstauffer@rightlydivided.com

Acknowledgments

The author would like to express his deepest appreciation to the following:

Most preeminently, the precious Lord Jesus Christ for His saving and sustaining grace.

Those who pioneered the study of Right Division. They cross this nation and the globe and God knows who they are. May God give them their rewards and recognition.

My devoted helpmeet Judy for her support, encouragement, and understanding through our many years of marriage and ministry together.

Justin and Heather, our two children, for their understanding when daddy could not always come play ball, ride a bike, or just plain have fun with them. Now, our Justin has grown up and joined the Marines, while Heather is attending college and preparing for marriage.

My parents, Richard and Marianne Stauffer, who instilled in me the work ethic and the fortitude to never quit. Thank you for the character building foundation the Lord used to convict and convince me to repent of my sins and accept the Saviour.

Dr. Bill Grady, my cattle prod in the Lord. Thank you for pushing me when I got bogged down and being the person who first convinced me to write this book.

Mr. James Yow, for his hard work on the charts through the many revisions.

Mr. Hugh Taylor for his contribution, especially chapters fifteen and sixteen which he drafted.

Miss Michelle Goree, Mrs. JoAnn Jernigan, Mrs. Frances Eller, and Mrs. Wanda Brantley for their many hours of proofreading, grammatical suggestions, encouragement, and prayer.

Mr. Tommy Trucks for his persistent encouragement, assistance and prayers.

Mr. Tommy Ray and his wife, Lori, with the Aslan Group for their creativity reflected in their impressive cover design.

Dr. Craig Lampe of Jonathan Byrd's Rare Books and Bibles in Greenwood, Indiana for the use of the antique Bible on the cover of this book.

Finally, Pastor Steve Sanders and Victory Baptist Church of Millbrook, Alabama, for providing a learning, growing, and teaching environment for these last twenty-two years. Also, a special thanks to Dr. Dave Reese who taught me the principles of right division.

ISBN 0-977016-1-9
Author's Photo by: Terry Jones • Bill Miller Photographers
Cover Photo by: Ron Dobbs • Ron E. Dobbs Photography

To my loving wife, Judy, who has been without a husband at times during this time of attempting to obey the
Saviour. Although God's work is never done, your sacrifice will be rewarded in the life to come. I could never
have done it without you!

*". . . but as his part is that goeth down to the battle,
so shall his part be that tarrieth by the stuff: they
shall part alike."* **(I Samuel 30:24)**

Table of Contents

Synopsis
Introduction

1. Why This Book? 1
2. God's Spokesmen 13
3. Whose Mail? 21
4. Reconciling the Scriptures I 33
5. Reconciling the Scriptures II 47
6. God's Chosen Vessel 61
7. Fulfilling the Word of God 67
8. Following Paul 79
9. To the Jew First? 87
10. The Gospel—Rightly Divided 105
11. Signs & Wonders—Historical Background 117
12. Signs & Wonders—To Whom/For What? 127
13. Apostles and Prophets 137
14. Hyper-Dispensationalism 149
15. Dispensational Ages (Old Testament) 169
16. Dispensational Ages (New Testament) 184
17. Questions and Answers 194
18. What Must I Do? 211

Appendix A
Appendix B
Appendix C
Glossary
Index
Scripture Index

Synopsis

One Book Rightly Divided tackles one of the most pressing theological debates of our time—how to properly interpret the scriptures. Unlike most hermeneutical works, this book empowers the student by presenting the Bible's own internal method of self-interpretation.

The teaching of right division is not a new concept designed by the author, but rather the scriptural mandate of God.

Study to shew thyself approved unto God, a workman that needeth not to be ashamed, **rightly dividing the word of truth. (II Timothy 2:15)**

By allowing the Bible to interpret itself, alleged contradictions and cultic heresies lose their power to confuse. Likewise, difficult passages (the ones evaded in the commentaries) are suddenly reconcilable by rightly dividing the word of truth.

Unique in its versatility, *One Book Rightly Divided* serves as a Christian's study guide, a Bible college textbook, or a pastor's homiletical aid. The reader will be helped by the many illuminating charts and the absence of technical language.

This volume will enhance the Christian's personal walk with God by providing him with **the biblical key** to Bible study.

> *"Any person is a dispensationalist who trusts the blood of Christ rather than bringing an animal sacrifice, and any person is a dispensationalist who observes the first day of the week rather than the seventh."*
> Lewis Sperry Chafer, *Dispensationalism* (Dallas: Dallas Seminary Press, 1936), p. 9.

Introduction

Since becoming a Christian in 1980, I have heard many negative statements regarding the word of God. These include allegations that the Bible contains contradictions; suggestions that you can make the Bible say whatever you want it to say; and assertions that we should not take the Bible so literally. As a seasoned preacher, I have thankfully come to realize that these statements are not insurmountable. God clearly states that He wants us to know what is right. *"And ye shall know the truth, and the truth shall make you free" (John 8:32)*.

Although the statements in the first paragraph seem to contain some validity, none can be accepted without further consideration. The truth is that the Bible contains *no* contradictions; therefore, every alleged contradiction can be explained. Likewise, a person attempting to make the Bible say whatever he wants it to say can do so only by disregarding proper scriptural context. Finally, the Bible should be taken literally whenever God expresses a truth that He wishes us to apply literally.

My purpose in writing *One Book Rightly Divided* is to give the student a better understanding of how to properly interpret God's word. The book of Nehemiah clearly expresses my desire, *"So they read in the book in the law of God distinctly, and gave the sense, and caused them to understand the reading" (Nehemiah 8:8)*. Every teacher and preacher should hunger and thirst for a greater comprehension of "what saith the scripture," thus enabling him to correctly teach others *(II Timothy 2:2)*.

Proper interpretation is the key that unlocks the scriptures. Consequently, the student must allow the Bible to interpret itself naturally without forcing his own private rendering into the text. *"Knowing this first, that no prophecy of the scripture is of any private interpretation" (II Peter 1:20)*. To avoid abusing a passage, one must discover and employ the Bible's own built-in hermeneutical formula as revealed in Paul's letter to Timothy.

Study to shew thyself approved unto God, a workman that needeth not to be ashamed, rightly dividing the word of truth (II Timothy 2:15).

The study of right division focuses on determining the correct doctrinal application of any particular passage. Having determined this application, the supposed contradictions lose their capacity to confuse. Without the discipline of right division, it is impossible to obey the scriptural injunction to *". . . be ready always to give an answer to every man that asketh you a reason of the hope that is in you with meekness and fear" (I Peter 3:15)*. You cannot be prepared to give an answer if you do not know how to handle the "contradictory" statements found in the Bible.

Preachers appear to be weary of having to evade the hard questions because they do not have the answers. For this reason, many have prodded, prayed, and pushed this book into existence. Three distinct groups spurred the writing of this treatise. First, the *pastors* desired a tool to enable them to teach the Bible dispensationally to their congregations. Secondly, the *faculty members* of Bible colleges and seminaries grew tired of skipping or spiritualizing the difficult passages, as do their commentaries. Thirdly, *church members* wanted a Bible study tool for their personal use. Thus in December, 1996, at the prompting of Dr. Bill Grady, I began collating the information to publish *One Book Rightly Divided.*

Due to the aforementioned controversy surrounding God's word, some people may be tempted to judge this book without reading it. Such a disposition reflects a failure to heed the scriptural admonition found in **Proverbs 18:13**, *"He that answereth a matter before he heareth it, it is folly and shame unto him."* Before you pass judgment on this book, open to page one and begin reading.

Because of the advanced material contained in the latter half of this book, the individual chapters were designed to be studied in sequential order. Without the foundational principles supplied in the earlier chapters, the student will have difficulty grasping the more advanced concepts.

This book is not recommended for the spiritually weak in heart. Although the study of right division will open the word of God to you, unexpected consequences will also be encountered. For every question that is answered by applying these principles, other questions are certain to arise. Thus, the student will be compelled to continually search the scriptures for further answers *(Acts 17:11).* The same verse that commands us to study and to rightly divide also calls us workmen.

It is my sincere prayer that *One Book Rightly Divided* will bring glory to the Lord Jesus Christ by *"endeavouring to keep the unity of the Spirit in the bond of peace" (Ephesians 4:3).* I have found that if the brethren do not "rightly divide" the book, the book will divide the brethren. May the Lord richly bless you as you seek to serve Him.

Douglas D. Stauffer
December 10, 1999

1
Why This Book?

Have you ever considered why different churches disagree on many of the major doctrines, yet most of these churches use the same Bible to prove their respective doctrinal beliefs? For instance, consider the following contradictory teachings made by various churches, with scriptures cited to "prove" each position:

- The New Testament begins immediately following Malachi *(Matthew 1:1).*
  versus
  The New Testament does not begin until after Christ's death *(Hebrews 9:17).*

- A person can lose the Holy Spirit through sin *(I Samuel 16:14, Psalm 51:11)*
  versus
  The Holy Spirit seals the Christian and will never leave him *(Ephesians 5:30).*

- Water baptism bestows the gift of the Holy Spirit *(Acts 2:38)*
  versus
  Baptism identifies Christians with the death, burial and resurrection *(Colossians 2:12).*

By reading these seemingly contradictory scriptures, some have concluded, "You can make the Bible say whatever you want it to say." The truth is, that conclusion is correct! You *can* make the Bible say whatever you *want* it to say, **simply by ignoring context**. However, the Bible is not self-contradictory, as this work will endeavor to illustrate.

People desiring spiritual truth can only acquire this truth through a diligent search of the scriptures *(John 5:39)*. However, *how* they search the scriptures will determine the extent of truth derived from this search. Many different denominations and churches exist, each claiming to be correctly interpreting the Bible and attaining spiritual truth. Each claims that searching the scriptures, *using their methods*, is the only way to arrive at the truth. Can they all be right and still contradict one another?

Purpose: **This book presents the scriptural system (i.e., approach to Bible study) by which anyone can determine the proper context when reading various Bible passages and establish sound doctrine from these passages.** When the student takes the scriptural approach—the *right division approach*—he can reconcile what may first appear to be contradictory scriptures. He can easily recognize and explain the reasons for the differing beliefs or positions of the various churches and denominations. Once he reconciles these scriptures, a person can know and stand firm on the truth.

Command: The biblical **command** to study and instruction for **how to study** the Bible are found in the same verse. This verse is the key to understanding how the Bible is laid out and how it is to be applied. Ignoring this verse will hinder Christian growth and the knowledge of scriptural truth. This verse is:

> **II Timothy 2:15 Study** *to shew thyself approved unto God, a workman that needeth not to be ashamed,* **rightly dividing the word of truth.**   (A.V. 1611—King James Bible)

The preceding scripture quotation comes from the King James Bible (KJB). The KJB is the *only* version of the scriptures on the market today that gives both commands—to study and to rightly divide the Bible. Yes, the Bible is to be "stud(ied)" and must be "divid(ed)" as scripturally commanded. If a person follows this direct command and approach to Bible study, he will be able to reconcile the various church and scriptural doctrines, and come to the right doctrinal position every time.

Caution: As with all extremes, dividing the Bible to an extreme is also negative. Dividing the Bible does not imply that some verses are not important or that they lack relevance. The guiding verse when dividing the Bible is *II Timothy 3:16*: *"All scripture is given by inspiration of God, and is profitable for doctrine, for reproof, for correction, for instruction in righteousness."* The reader must never forget that ALL scripture is profitable and it is profitable for doctrine! None of it needs to be ignored. None of it needs to be given any lesser degree of importance. It all must be read, studied, believed and taught verse by verse.

Time-line (of 'Division'): This study uses the following time-line as a tool to help obey the command given to us in *II Timothy 2:15*. The time-line will be explained and developed in detail throughout this chapter and will be expanded throughout this book.

Semi-Chronological time-line

[The Beginning]   **[The End]**

Genesis 1:1
In the beginning God created the heaven and the earth.

Revelation 21:1
And I saw a new heaven and a new earth

Chart 1.1 - Basic Time-line

Basic Time-line: God laid out the Bible in a "semi-chronological" order from the beginning to the end. A time-line helps to more easily visualize the chronology of events and the related books of the Bible. The far left of the chart shows "the beginning," as recorded in the beginning of the Bible (Genesis). The far right of the chart shows the new heaven and new earth, referred to at the end of the Bible (Revelation). As our study progresses, the intervening books of the Bible are added to the time-line.

Book Groupings: Saying that the Bible is "*semi*-chronological" simply means that the Bible follows a generally chronological format, but that not everything in the Bible is in an *absolute* chronological order. What is meant by *generally* chronological may be best understood by considering the events as they are recorded in the four books of Matthew, Mark, Luke and John, commonly called the "Gospels." To be perfectly chronological, each one of these books would have to begin at a point where the previous book ended. For example, the book of Mark would continue at the point where Matthew ended. It is necessary to group these four books together, when looking at the Bible on a time-line, because they are not absolutely chronological. Other sequential books of the Bible, that are not strictly chronological, are also divided into groups of books. These other groupings are discussed later.

Rightly Dividing: The books of the Bible are divided into categories based upon the **primary** group of people *to whom* God is speaking. Consider this: does every doctrine in the Bible apply equally to each of the following groups.

- The Jews under the law?
- The Gentiles?
- The Christian living today?
- The Tribulation saint?
- The person living in the Millennium?

No! Therefore, as you read a passage, ask yourself this question: "*to whom* does *this doctrine primarily* apply?" For example, the Bible deals differently with the Old Testament saint living under the law; the Spirit-filled Christian's attempts to live the will of God today; and the Tribulation saint's avoiding the Mark of the Beast. There is no disputing the fact that the Bible contains scriptures which fundamentally apply to groups of people in other time periods, but which do not *directly* apply to the child of God today.

As you will see in detail later, to "rightly divide" your Bible is simply to divide it into sections based upon the **primary** group of people God addresses in each section. You must remember that the entire Bible is **for** you, but not all of it is written **to** you. Now that this foundation has been established, it is time to add a little more detail to the basic time-line chart.

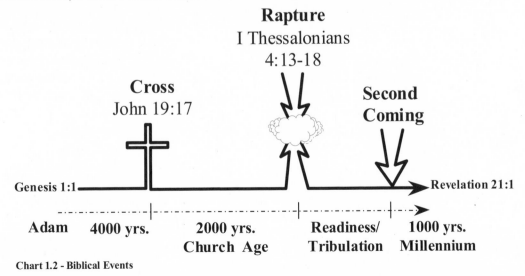

Chart 1.2 - Biblical Events

Explanation of symbols:

1.   **Cross**: The first symbol (on the left of the chart) signifies the crucifixion of the Lord, which occurred about **4,000 years** *after Adam* and *about* 2,000 years ago. *(Combining our calendars with the Bible's chronology and genealogy shows that about 6,000 years have transpired from the creation of **Adam** to the present day.)* The period after the cross and prior to the Rapture is known as the **Church Age. NOTE:** Although the charts reflect some very fine lines drawn on them, they are not meant to reflect pinpoint precision as to the exact timing of each event. Additionally, the groupings simply cannot reflect all of the transitions from one period to the next. The book of John is a prime transitional example. **The fine lines drawn on the charts are not meant for the reader to miss the transitional nature of books like the gospel of John. It is equally unwise to allow the chart divisions to effectively eliminate from the church today the many important applications found in the book Hebrews.**

2.   **Rapture**: The next symbol is the "catching out of the saints" commonly referred to as the Rapture of the Church. The two arrows meeting in the clouds signify the Rapture. The arrow pointing up indicates a future time when the resurrected bodies of the saved are "caught up together" in the clouds to meet the Lord. The arrow coming down represents the Lord's descending from heaven to meet the saints "in the air." Although the word *Rapture is not* found in the Bible, its use to describe a true biblical concept is as acceptable as using the word *Trinity* (also not in the Bible) to describe the three persons of the Godhead. Here is the Rapture:

> *I Thessalonians 4:13 But I would not have you to be ignorant, brethren, concerning them which are asleep, that ye sorrow not, even as others which have no hope. 14 For if we believe that Jesus died and rose again, even so **them also which sleep in Jesus will God bring with him.** 15 For this we say unto you by the word of the Lord, that **we which are alive and remain unto the coming of the Lord** shall not prevent them which are asleep. 16 **For the Lord himself shall descend from heaven** with a shout, with the voice of the archangel, and with the trump of God: **and the dead in Christ shall rise first:** 17 **Then we which are alive and remain** shall be caught up together with them in the **clouds**, to meet the Lord in the air: and so shall we ever be with the Lord. 18 Wherefore comfort one another with these words.*

The period following the Rapture is known as the Readiness Age which includes the **Great Tribulation**. *(Note: the time-line is NOT to scale, for this period is but seven years.)*

3.   **Second Coming**: The third symbol, the single arrow coming down, indicates the Lord's Second Coming. The arrow touches the bottom line signifying that the Lord will return to the earth at the Second Coming (unlike the Rapture where Christians meet Him in the clouds). *The Second Coming is also known as the Second Advent.* All dispensationalists refer to the period following the Second Coming as the 1,000-year Millennium or **Kingdom Age**.

> *Revelation 20:6 Blessed and holy is he that hath part in the first resurrection: on such the second death hath no power, but they shall be priests of God and of Christ, and **shall reign with him a thousand years.***

During the Millennium, the Lord Jesus Christ will reign on the earth. Following the Millennium, the Great White Throne Judgment will take place. After the judgment of the lost and those saints that came through the Tribulation and Millennium, the heaven and earth will be destroyed by fire and God will create a new heaven and a new earth *(Revelation 21:1)*.

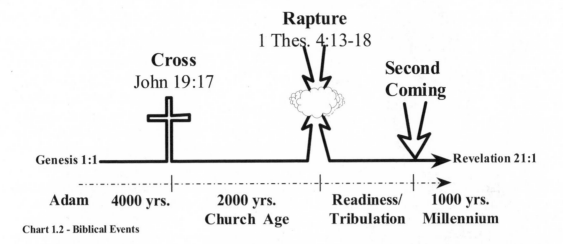

Chart 1.2 - Biblical Events

Where am I located on this time-line?

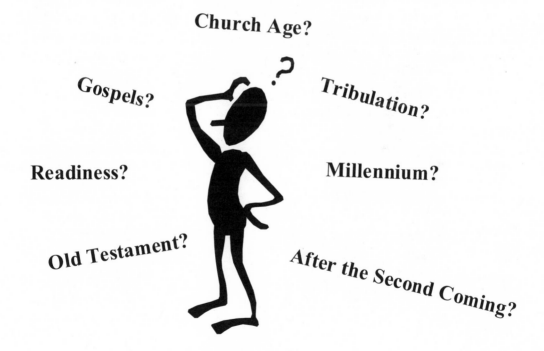

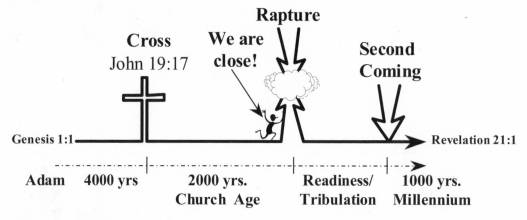

Chart 1.3 - The Question

Where are we on the time-line?

The Church finds itself on the charts after the cross and very close to the Rapture in the period which is called the Church Age. The Church is made up of the Body of Christ, which consists of only saved believers *in Christ*. The following verses clearly indicate why this period is called the Church Age. The verses also make it equally clear that the Church consists of the Body of Christ. Like Israel of the Old Testament, God has chosen the local church of the New Testament as His fighting arm to put forth His message and bring His will to pass.

> *Ephesians 1:22 And hath put all things under his feet, and gave him to be the head over all things to **the church**, 23 **Which is his body**, the fulness of him that filleth all in all.*

> *Colossians 1:18 And **he is the head of the body, the church**: who is the beginning, the firstborn from the dead; that in all things he might have the preeminence.*

> *Colossians 1:24 Who now rejoice in my sufferings for you, and fill up that which is behind of the afflictions of Christ in my flesh for **his body's sake, which is the church**:*

The Church Age will last approximately 2,000 years. This amount of time is derived through the study of biblical and natural patterns. Seven is God's number of completion (seven days of creation, seven days in a week, seven years of Tribulation, seven colors of the light spectrum and rainbow, seven notes of the scale, etc.). God uses the number *seven* to indicate completion; the eighth is generally a "new beginning." Assuming that God's pattern of seven as completeness holds true concerning God's dealings with man, the approximate length of the Church Age can be easily computed as follows.

Genealogical lists verify that approximately 4,000 years transpire from Adam to the time of the Lord Jesus Christ. The Millennium is given as a 1,000-year period yet to come. If 5,000 years (4,000 plus 1,000) is subtracted from a "completion" total of 7,000 years, around 2,000 years remain for the Church Age. *Note: This is not an attempt to date the Rapture or the Second Coming. It is simply a means to illustrate the lengths of time in God's dealings with man and the approximate length of time of the Church Age.*

Our calendar places us nearly 2,000 years after Christ's birth, and at a point very close to the Rapture on our time-line. Most serious Bible students would *not* disagree with the events and times depicted in *chart 1.3*, nor would they disagree that the "last days" are upon us. This is the period just prior to the Rapture of the Church.

Where are the books of the Bible on the time-line?

The next chart reflects the placement of the sixty-six books of the Bible on our time-line. Note: Although the books neatly fit on the next chart, **some of the actual divisions occur within the books themselves.** Generally, although a division may occur within a book, a transition is occurring from one period to the next.

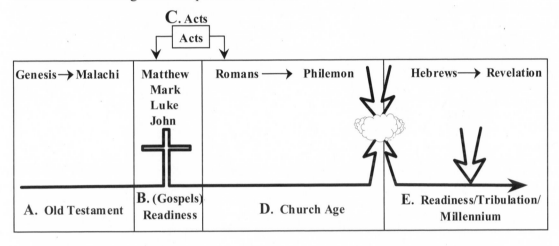

Chart 1.4 - Book Divisions

First, an overview of the sections of *chart 1.4* is presented. Then each section will be studied in further detail.

Section A—Old Testament: *Thirty-nine Books,* **Genesis through Malachi**, cover the period of time from the beginning (far left) to a time before the cross. The Lord Jesus Christ is not born until after the close of the period defined as the "Old Testament" in our Bible, and He goes to the cross at the age of thirty-three. Note: The New Testament did not actually begin or take effect until after the death of the Lord Jesus Christ (the testator) *(Hebrews 9:16-18)*.

Section B—The Gospels: *Four Books,* **Matthew through John**, cover approximately thirty-three years of events preceding the cross through the events immediately following the cross. The theme of these books is the teaching of how to be prepared for the coming of the Kingdom when the Lord Jesus Christ will rule on earth as King of Kings and Lord of Lords. Thus, its name "Readiness." (See *Luke 1:17, 12:40, Matthew 24:44, 25:10,* discussed later.)

Section C—Acts: *One Book,* **Acts**, covers the time period immediately following the cross until the time of Paul's imprisonment in Rome. This book covers the actions of the apostles historically and is commonly referred to as a transitional book because it **continues** the transition from one time period into the next. *Note: Although the entire Bible is the history of a King and His Kingdom, some books emphasize history over doctrine. Acts is one such book; whereas, Romans and Galatians are best characterized as doctrinal books.*

Section D—The Church Age: *Thirteen Books,* **Romans through Philemon**, cover the writings of the Apostle Paul as presented to the Body of Christ—the Church. Paul's name is the first word in each of these epistles. Church Age doctrine comes predominantly, yet not exclusively from these thirteen epistles. They should be the starting point for any serious Bible student wanting to learn his or her Bible.

Section E—Readiness, Tribulation and Millennium: *Nine Books,* **Hebrews through Revelation** also cover future events, including the Readiness and Tribulation period, Second Coming, Millennium, Great White Throne Judgment and Eternity; in addition to having significant Church Age application.

The five periods of time (A through E) cover all sixty-six books of the Bible.

Section	Number of Books
A. Old Testament	39
B. Gospels	4
C. Acts	1
D. Church Age	13
E. Readiness/Tribulation/Millennium	9
Total Books	**66**

Each of these five sections will be discussed in more detail, beginning with Section A below.

Section A: Old Testament

The Old Testament records God's dealings predominantly with the Jews and *through* the Jews. Through Moses, God gives the law to the Jews and calls them out as His chosen people.

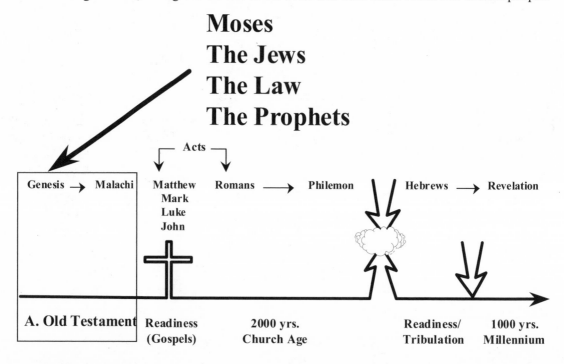

Chart 1.5 - Old Testament

Section B: Gospels

The Gospels are the first four books following the thirty-nine "Old Testament" books of the Bible. The books of Matthew through John cover a period of time of approximately 33 years prior to the cross and through the resurrection and ascension of the Lord Jesus Christ. These books cover the following:

The *forerunner* of the Lord Jesus Christ (John the Baptist), the *birth* of the Lord Jesus Christ, the *life* of the Lord Jesus Christ, the *ministry* of the Lord Jesus Christ, the *death* of the Lord Jesus Christ, the *resurrection* of the Lord Jesus Christ, and the *ascension* of the Lord Jesus Christ.

Not any one of the four Gospel books covers all of the events mentioned above, but it is very easy to see that each book contains a great number of each of these events. It is also easy to recognize that these four books are logically and theologically grouped together as a unit.

> *"The Gospels do not unfold the doctrine of the Church. The word occurs in Matthew only. ...'I will build my church' (Mt. 16.16,18). It was, therefore, yet future; but His personal ministry had gathered out the believers who were, on the day of Pentecost, by the baptism with the Spirit, made the first members of 'the church which is his body.' (1 Cor. 12.12,13; Eph.1.23)"*
>
> **Scofield Reference Bible, "The Four Gospels," pages 990, section IV.**

For this reason, the four Gospel books should be studied as a unit when considering how the Bible is applied doctrinally and historically to various peoples and individuals. However, God never intended for the application of Systematic Theology to the Bible to indicate that some books lack any application outside of their primary focus. This erroneous method is almost as dangerous as the haphazard exegesis that many preachers call Bible study.

Gospels
All Agree   (birth/life/ministry/death/resurrection/ascension)

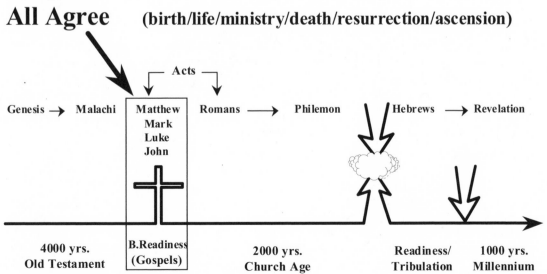

Chart 1.6 - The Gospels

Section C: Acts

Acts follows the book of John. As has been said, Acts is a historical and transitional book. It begins with the ascension of the Lord Jesus Christ, which is the last major event recorded in the Gospels *(Luke 24:51)*. Grouping the four Gospels, Matthew through John, fits them perfectly just prior to the beginning of the book of Acts which opens with an account of the ascension *(Acts 1:9).*

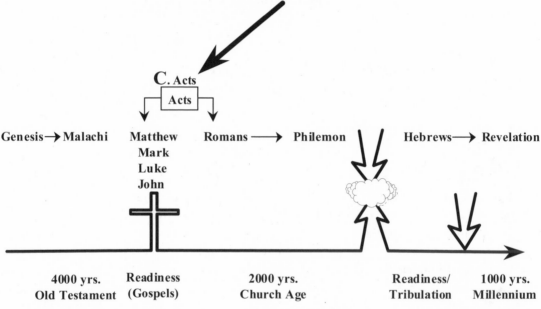

Actions of the apostles

History book

Transition from Peter to Paul

Chart 1.7 - The book of Acts

As a historical book, Acts tells us about the **Act**(ion)**s** of the apostles: their acts. The student will notice that Acts in *not* primarily a book of doctrine but, instead, is predominantly historical. Acts also serves as a transition from the Gospels (The Lord Jesus Christ, Peter and the other eleven apostles ministering to the Jews only) to Paul and his writings. Acts features a definite transition from one spokesman (Peter) to another (Paul). The Gospel books record Peter as the leader of the apostles. The early chapters of the book of Acts depict his leadership also. Later chapters in Acts (13 through 28) cover the missionary journeys of the Apostle Paul. Thereafter, in the first thirteen epistles following the book of Acts, Paul serves as God's primary spokesman.

Section D: Church Age

The *primary* Church Age books are the thirteen books following the book of Acts, from Romans to Philemon. **Paul's name is the first word in each of these thirteen books.** (The improbability of Pauline authorship of Hebrews will be examined in Chapter 4 of this work. For now, compare the dissimilarity of the "confirmed unto us" of *Hebrews 2:3* with Paul's "neither was I taught it" and "by revelation" of *Galatians 1:11-12, 16, 2:6, Ephesians 3:3,* etc.).

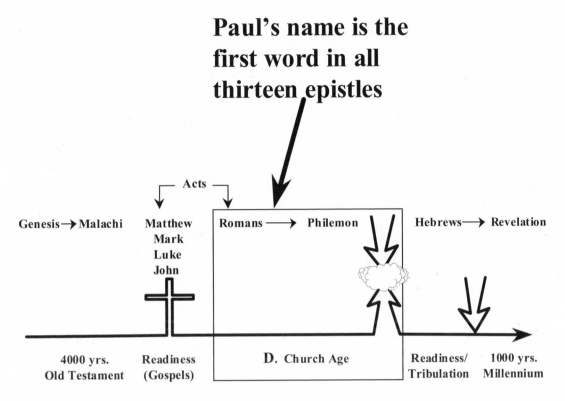

Chart 1.8 - Paul's Epistles

All of Paul's writings *must* have occurred after the cross. He is not mentioned by name prior to the cross, and his salvation occurred when he met the Lord in Acts chapter 9. These thirteen books cover the revelations of the Gospel of the Grace of God and of God's expectations of the Church Age saints. These books cover Paul's early ministry to the "Jew first" through the period of the Rapture (yet to come). The Rapture ends the Church Age, as members of the Body of Christ are caught out together to meet the Lord in the air.

Section E: Readiness/Tribulation/Millennium

The nine books following Philemon (Hebrews through Revelation) include the Readiness/ Tribulation/Millennium periods. These nine books include five major events or time periods. They are the Readiness period, Tribulation period, the Second Coming of the Lord Jesus Christ, the Millennium and Eternity. The reason that aspects of Hebrews through Revelation effectively apply to these periods rather than *exclusively* to the Church Age will be explained later. One simple point to consider is that God is speaking primarily through the Gentile during the Church Age, but will once again begin speaking through the Jew (Hebrew) during the Readiness/Tribulation period. Thus, the first book addresses the Jews in its title—*Hebrews*. (The Readiness period will be discussed in depth as part of Chapter 16.)

As stated above, the Tribulation period compromises a total of seven years occurring sometime after the Rapture of the Church. The Tribulation ends with the return of the Lord Jesus Christ (His Second Coming). When He returns, He will set up His Kingdom and reign for 1,000 years as King on this earth. At the end of this time, God will destroy the heaven and earth by fire and create a new heaven and a new earth for Eternity *(II Peter 3:10-12)*.

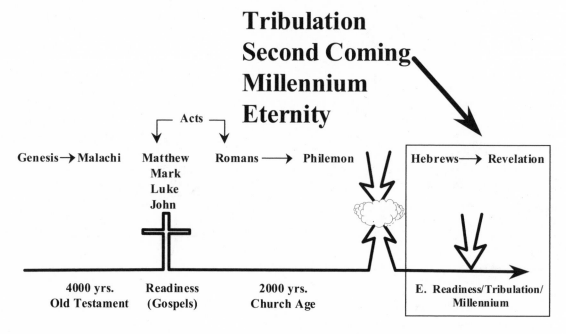

Chart 1.9 - Events to Come

Summary: These five sections give us the *basic* divisions needed to understand the biblical approach of studying and rightly dividing the Bible. The remainder of this book deals with how to practically apply this knowledge after mastering these basic principles.

While reading and studying this book, always keep in mind ***Chart 1.4***—"Book Divisions." In the next chapter, the divisions are presented from another perspective. The basic book groupings serve as dividing points based upon whom they feature as God's spokesman. Yet, most of the divisions are not absolutely distinct (i.e., a precise division without any overlapping transitional features or dual applications). **The charts are not intended to completely compartmental-ize the books in such a manner as to disallow or disavow personal application of those books designated as outside the "Church Age."**

For instance, the Lord tells His apostles to go to "the Jews only" during His earthly ministry *(Matthew 10:5)*. However, following His ascension (and Calvary), His commission to the apostles includes all nations *(Matthew 28:19)* and every creature *(Mark 16:15)*. Failing to recognize these periods of transition within certain epistles can cause much confusion when attempting to "rightly divide" the word of truth. For example, many overzealous Bible students fail to recognize God's overwhelming desire concerning world missions by rightly dividing the "great commis-sion" out of any spiritual significance to the Church. Christianity does not need any more hyper-dividing, hypercritical, know-it-alls who fail to comprehend God's love for world missions. What it desperately does need are Christians that are both soul conscious and ardent Bible students willing to admit that *mastery* of the Bible is an unattainable feat.

2
God's Spokesmen

The careful Bible student observes that God gives His message to a spokesman *(Hebrews 1:1)*. The spokesman, in turn, gives God's message to the world. God requires the world to listen to the spokesman He has chosen for each time period. A spokesman during one period does not necessarily carry God's entire message for any other time period. ***Thus, following the wrong spokesman during any time period is as dangerous as ignoring the right one.***

God's spokesmen are presented in the following order based on the five basic divisions given in Chapter 1. Take note that Section E is discussed out of order and has two distinct parts.

- Spokesmen of the Old Testament *(Section A)*
- Spokesmen of the Gospels *(Section B)*
- Spokesmen of the: Readiness/Tribulation *(Section E)* & Millennium *(Section E)*
- Spokesmen during the book of Acts *(Section C)*
- Spokesman during the Church Age *(Section D)*

The sections are presented in this manner in order to establish that God has one or more spokesmen during every period. Once this truth is established, the primary spokesman for the Church Age can be clearly identified. Hopefully, discussing the Church Age *last* will leave a more lasting impression as you continue reading through the book. Thus, the Christian can easily recognize God's particular commands and directions for him to follow. We begin with the Old Testament.

A. Spokesmen of the Old Testament

Some examples of the Old Testament spokesmen include: Noah, Abraham, Isaac, Jacob, Joseph, Moses, Joshua, etc. Each of these men received a particular God-given message and, as God's spokesman, presented that message to the world. The Bible says the Holy Ghost led the spokesmen.

> ***II Peter 1:21*** *For the prophecy came not in old time by the will of man: but holy men of God **spake as they were moved by the Holy Ghost***.

Those living during the Old Testament economy had to listen to God's chosen spokesman in order to know His expectations of humanity. If a man or a woman did not listen to God's spokesman, that individual neglected to do so at his own risk. The next chart lists a few of the Old Testament spokesmen, both before and after the law was given.

What would have been the wisest thing you could have done if you had lived when one of these persons lived? Two choices exist—either you could have ignored the spokesman or you could have *followed* him! Of course, any time a man follows God's spokesman he displays his willingness to obey God and His leadership (although through a man). It is always best to have listened to God's spokesman. A few of these Old Testament spokesmen are considered in detail.

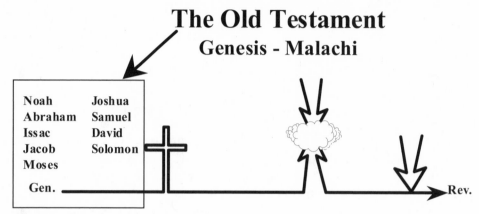

Chart 2.1 - O.T. Spokesmen

Noah: Noah is one of the earliest spokesmen in the Bible. He preached about a coming flood. If you had been on the earth when *Spokesman Noah* warned others about a flood, what would you have done? You would either have listened to God's spokesman and the message that God gave him for you, and entered the ark; or you would have rejected the message of God's messenger! *The Bible reveals clearly that most people rejected the message of God's spokesman and perished in the flood.* Eight persons entered the ark, including Noah! The continual rejection of God's spokesmen throughout time clearly indicates that man does not learn from history.

Moses: The Bible emphasizes Moses as another of God's spokesmen. When *Spokesman Moses* returned to Egypt with a message from God for Israel, what would you have done? You should have considered what Moses said concerning the blood on the door posts and *followed* him when he announced it was time to leave Egypt. Furthermore, in order to have been spiritually right with God, you would have been required to obey the "book of the law of Moses" *(Joshua 8:31)* in its entirety *(Galatians 5:3)*. Failure to obey required the offering of an animal sacrifice *(Leviticus 4:26)*. Considering how clearly these truths do *not* directly apply to us today, it is inconceivable how anyone could claim to be a student of the Bible and simultaneously claim to be a non-dispensationalist in practice.

Joshua: God insured that Joshua would pick up the mantle when Moses died. Joshua was present at Mt. Sinai when Moses received the Ten Commandments. How would you have responded when *Spokesman Joshua* took the mantle from Moses *(Joshua 1:1-2)* and said it was time to go into the Promised Land? Need the answer be given considering the forty years of wandering? The same scenarios and questions apply to Abraham, Isaiah and many others. God always chooses a spokesman to announce His message to a particular group of people during a particular period of time.

Having made this general statement, we must consider the exception to the rule. In the book of Judges, the Bible records a time when God did *not* have a particular spokesman. The tragic result of the world without a spokesman is described in the final verse of the book of Judges.

*Judges 21:25 In those days **there was no king in Israel**: every man did that which was right in his own eyes.*

Israel had Moses and the prophets (in written form), but no king and no judge. Each time the children of Israel turned away from the Lord, God would deliver them into the hands of their enemies. The children of Israel would then cry unto the Lord, and God would raise up a deliverer known as a judge *(Judges 3:9, 3:15)*. Clearly, when God did *not* appoint a spokesman, man was in a state of utter confusion. When God does not provide a spokesman or when the spokesman's message is rejected, people generally do whatever *they think* is right. The same problem occurs when people ignorantly refuse to acknowledge their spokesman today.

B. Spokesmen of the Gospels

Chart 2.2 moves over into the beginning of the "New Testament" books. God's spokesman throughout the four Gospels is initially John the Baptist preparing the way for the Lord. However, the main spokesmen throughout the books are the Lord and His apostles. The Bible reveals the Lord's earthly ministry until we get to the beginning of the book of Acts. Once the Lord ascends into heaven (Acts chapter 1), God focuses on Peter, the leader of the apostles, to reveal His message.

> *"The doctrines of grace are to be sought in the Epistles* (of Paul), *not in the Gospels; but those doctrines rest back upon the death and resurrection of Christ, and upon the great germ-truths to which He gave utterance, and of which the Epistles are the unfolding."*
>
> **Scofield Reference Bible, "The Four Gospels," p. 989, section III.**

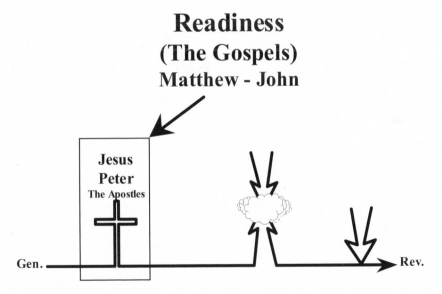

Readiness
(The Gospels)
Matthew - John

Jesus
Peter
The Apostles

Gen.

Rev.

Chart 2.2 - Gospel Spokesmen

The Readiness/Tribulation and Millennium periods are discussed next, saving the book of Acts and the Church Age for last. Therefore, the two periods designated as "C" and "D" are postponed for discussion until after the two periods designated as "E" are studied.

E. Spokesmen of the Readiness/Tribulation

The Tribulation will occur sometime after the Church is removed from the earth and taken to heaven. During the Tribulation, God will use spokesmen, just as at other times. God's spokesmen will be the two Witnesses mentioned in the book of the Revelation. Any person who wants to know the directives of God must listen to His two Witnesses who will give God's specific messages for that time period.

*Revelation 11:3 And I will give power unto my **two witnesses**, and they shall prophesy a thousand two hundred and threescore days, clothed in sackcloth.*

The two Witnesses, who are Moses and Elijah, will prophesy for 1,260 days (one half of the Tribulation period or three and one half years). (See Appendix A at the end of the book for a discussion of the identity of the two Witnesses). In addition to the two Witnesses, the 144,000 Jewish male virgins *(Revelation 14:1, 4)* will also be God's spokesmen on this earth during the Tribulation.

*Revelation 7:4 And I heard the number of them which were sealed: and there were sealed **an hundred and forty and four thousand** of all the tribes of the children of Israel.*

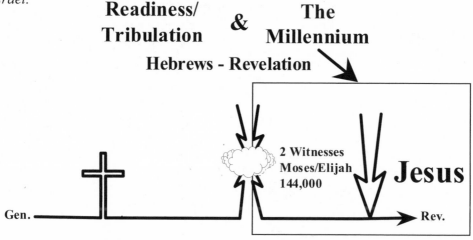

Chart 2.3 - Future Spokesmen

E. Spokesman of the Millennium

The return of the Lord at His Second Coming will end the Tribulation and begin the Millennium. There can be no question as to the identity of God the Father's Spokesman during this time. The Lord Jesus Christ Himself will be the Spokesman, King and Ruler during His literal, physical and visible 1,000-year reign on earth.

*Revelation 19:15 And out of his mouth goeth a sharp sword, that with it he should smite the nations: and **he shall rule them with a rod of iron**: and he treadeth the winepress of the fierceness and wrath of Almighty God. 16 And he hath on his vesture and on his thigh a name written, **KING OF KINGS, AND LORD OF LORDS**.*

The next chapter (Revelation 20) tells about the Millennium—the 1,000-year reign of King Jesus on this earth. Those living in the Millennium had better listen to Him. He will be ruling with a rod of iron as a King who knows every thought, every action and every secret thing *(Isaiah 66:23-24)*. There will be no excuses for failing to *follow* the dictates of King Jesus.

Summation: *God chooses to give His message through a spokesman. When there has been no spokesman, everyone has "done his own thing" or "that which was right in his own eyes."*

The world without a spokesman is not God's desired method of interacting with man. However, if man ignores God long enough, God will show man the result of his chosen direction by allowing him to choose his own direction with heavenly silence.

With God's method of communicating to man through a spokesman clearly established, focus will be directed toward the book of Acts and the Church Age. This will enable the reader to determine exactly whom God has designated as our *primary* spokesman. Some groups would try to convince you that today's spokesman is Peter. The Bible clearly points to another spokesman for today. Today's primary message is certainly not Peter's early Acts dialog.

C. Spokesmen during the Book of Acts

As recorded in the Gospels and in the book of Acts, Peter serves as the main spokesman immediately after the departure of the Lord in Acts chapter 1. During this time period, an individual desiring to know the will of God would have listened to the words of Peter and the other apostles. Peter remains the main speaker *until Acts chapter 12*. Peter appears as speaker only one more time in the book of Acts. In *Acts 15:7* we find him speaking concerning the Gentiles. There, he simply affirms the ministry given to Paul. *Acts 2:14* is a typical verse reflecting Peter's position as spokesman in the early part of Acts.

> *Acts 2:14 But **Peter**, standing up **with the eleven**, lifted up his voice, and said unto them, Ye men of Judaea, and all ye that dwell at Jerusalem, be this known unto you, and hearken to **my words**:*

Peter remains the spokesman until shortly after the conversion of the Apostle Paul. *From Acts chapter 13* forward, Paul becomes the main character and spokesman. God gives His complete revelation to Paul and he travels around the world testifying the message God had given him for individuals living in the Church Age. This point leads into the next and final period covered. The next thirteen books of the Bible, written by the Apostle Paul, are the books that predominantly cover this period called the Church Age.

D. Spokesman during the Church Age

The only period not discussed in detail thus far covers a period of time after the cross up to the Rapture of the Church—the period in which we live today. By determining who our spokesman is, we will know where in the Bible to find our primary instructions for living today.

Unquestionably, our chief spokesman is the Apostle Paul. We are first introduced to Paul (Saul) at the end of Acts chapter 7 and read about his conversion two chapters later. As previously demonstrated, Peter was God's main spokesman until the time of Paul's conversion. Shortly thereafter, Peter virtually disappears from the scene. One of the few times Peter reappears is in *Galatians 2:11*, when Paul rebukes him for his hypocrisy concerning the Gentiles.

Beginning in Acts chapter 13, we read about Paul's missionary journeys. In the last chapter of the Book of Acts, we read about Paul's placement in a Roman prison. When we turn the page to the next book in the Bible (Romans), the first word reveals much . . . *Paul*. His name is recorded as the first word in the next thirteen consecutive books (Romans through Philemon). God emphasizes the author in each of these thirteen books to show us the importance of our knowing exactly who penned each epistle. He also establishes these books as a unit to be studied together *(II Timothy 2:15)* **and the place where we find the bulk of Church Age doctrine.**

These thirteen books address a specific group (the Body of Christ) during a specific period of time (the Church Age). God's use of Paul as the messenger of today parallels His use of Noah to speak to those individuals alive before the flood. God's use of Paul also relates to His future use of the two Witnesses speaking during the Tribulation and to the Lord Jesus Christ speaking during the Millennium. **Throughout history, God's message has generally been conveyed in this same manner.**

> *"...the truth concerning the Church was never made known until the beginning of Paul's Apostleship (Eph. 3). We must not, therefore, except in types and symbols, expect to find it in Matthew."*
> **William L. Pettingill, *Simple Studies in Matthew* (Wilmington: Just a Word, Inc., n.d.) p. 121-122.**

God gives us many scriptures expressing Paul's unique ministry to the Church. As introductory material, we will specifically look at just seven of these beginning in the book of Romans.

I. The Apostle Paul's writings *minister* the Lord Jesus Christ and His gospel to the Gentile world so that we may be acceptable and sanctified.

    Romans 15:16 That I should be the minister of Jesus Christ to the Gentiles, *ministering the gospel of God, that the offering up of the Gentiles might be acceptable, being sanctified by the Holy Ghost.*

II. In order to obey the following command, one must consider *who* authored First Corinthians and *follow* the writings of this author. God led the Apostle Paul to write First Corinthians, thus we are to follow him as he followed the Lord Jesus Christ.

    I Corinthians 4:16 *Wherefore I beseech you,* ***be ye followers of me****.*

III. Later in the same epistle, the Apostle Paul informs us that he is the one who *declares* the gospel to us. He also defines the gospel as the death, burial and resurrection of Christ.

    I Corinthians 15:1 *Moreover, brethren,* ***I declare unto you the gospel*** *which I preached unto you, which also ye have received, and wherein ye stand;*

IV. The Apostle Paul declares the gospel and also instructs us how to live as Christians. He instructs us to *do* those things we have learned, received, heard, and seen in him. Without considering the scriptures that Paul has penned, how can the Church Age saint obey this command?

    Philippians 4:9 *Those things, which ye have both learned, and received, and heard, and seen in me,* ***do****: and the God of peace shall be with you.*

V. Paul's particular position as the primary spokesman of the Church Age also included a calling to serve as the example for the Church Age Christian. For this reason, Paul tells us that we receive from him instructions concerning *how* we should walk and please God.

    I Thessalonians 4:1 *Furthermore then we beseech you, brethren, and exhort you by the Lord Jesus, that as ye have* ***received of us how ye ought to walk and to please God****, so ye would abound more and more.*

VI. The reader should readily recognize how important Paul's writings are to the Church. He beseeches us to be followers of him. He declares the Gospel of the Grace of God. He even tells us how to walk so that we may please God. It should come as no surprise when Paul tells those who want to understand all things to *consider* what he says.

*II Timothy 2:7 Consider what I say; and the Lord give thee **understanding in all things**.*

VII. In order to understand *all things*, we must consider what the Apostle Paul has said through his writings. Obviously, this understanding of *all things* includes gaining an understanding of the Bible too! Do you want to understand the differences associated with the various instructions given in the scriptures (sometimes referred to as "contradictions")? Consider what Paul says—any instructions that seem to contradict his writings apply to a group other than the Church. This would include, among other things, such issues as the observance of Sabbath Days, the eating of certain meats and the sacrificial system. Paul even claims that by him the preaching is fully known so that the Gentiles might hear God's instructions to them.

*II Timothy 4:17 Notwithstanding the Lord stood with me, and strengthened me; that **by me the preaching might be fully known, and that all the Gentiles might hear**: and I was delivered out of the mouth of the lion.*

Much of the confusion within Christianity can be cleared up through systematic Bible study. Each of these scriptures will be more fully developed and many others will be provided in subsequent chapters. Simply, the student should recognize that Peter ministered primarily to the Jews while Paul's ministry was primarily to the Gentiles (specifically to those of us living in the Church Age). This truth should make a difference in how you walk, talk, and think.

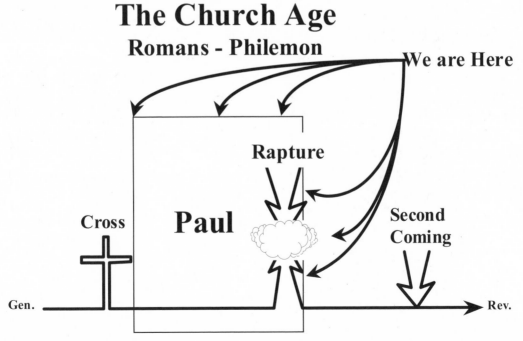

Chart 2.4 - Church Age Spokesman

The Bible can be viewed very simply in the fashion shown in this book. We must determine the period in which we live and the corresponding God-designated spokesman for our present age. For ease of reference, examine the previous chart. If you are reading these words prior to the Rapture of the Church (and obviously following the cross), you must place yourself within the Church Age. (This locates you to the right of the cross and to the left of the Rapture). The books written by the Apostle Paul (those bearing his name as the first word) are the *primary* books covering this period of time. All other scripture is profitable too *(II Timothy 3:16)*, but must be studied in light of what our apostle (Paul) has been led to reveal to us.

> *"The Apostle Paul was principally, though not exclusively, the agent of the revelation of the grace of God for this dispensation. Christ himself brought the grace of God to mankind in His incarnation (Titus 2:11), but Paul was the one who expounded it. To be sure, the dispensationalist does not say that there was no grace ever displayed before the coming of Christ (any more than he says there is no law after His coming), but the Scriptures do say that His coming displayed the grace of God in such brightness that all previous displays could be considered as nothing."*
>
> **Charles C. Ryrie, *Dispensationalism*, (Chicago, IL: Moody Press, 1995), p. 56.**

Many people wonder how they can know if a particular scripture, epistle or doctrine outside of Paul's thirteen Church Age epistles applies to the Child of God today. The answer comes only after diligent Bible study. Once the student learns the truths presented to the Church in Paul's thirteen epistles, the answer is readily apparent *(II Timothy 2:7)*. Quite simply, the scripture, epistle or doctrine in question cannot violate the explicit truths, instructions and doctrines given to us by our Apostle. If it does seemingly contradict the Apostle Paul's guidelines, the passage should *not* be pulled out of its context and twisted to fit where it does not belong.

Consider the general epistles of Hebrews through Revelation, which contain truths following the resurrection. Although they contain much Church Age application, they cannot be arbitrarily applied in total to the Church without *considering* what the Apostle Paul has written. Paul says:

II Timothy 2:7 Consider what I say; and the Lord give thee understanding in all things.

Before we proceed, a common misconception must be dispelled. Some people claim to do *everything* the Bible says to do. Have you ever read some of the requirements in the Old Testament? If you attempt to do everything in the Bible, you are going to have a very difficult time keeping your sanity. We must obey the commands given by *our* spokesman in order to comprehend exactly what it is that God would have us do.

*II Timothy 2:15 Study to shew thyself approved unto God, a workman that needeth not to be ashamed, **rightly dividing the word of truth**.*

When one rightly divides the Bible, he is naturally allowing the Bible to interpret itself when considering any particular command or scripture. Now that we have seen God's appointed spokesman for the Church, we will look at an application of this truth in the next chapter. In later chapters, we will develop these points in even greater detail.

3
Whose Mail?

As expressed in the two preceding chapters, not every commandment in the Bible is *directed* to us who live in the Church Age. We cannot, and should not, follow or attempt to follow *every* commandment contained in the scriptures. For example, in **Genesis 6:14** we find the commandment to "*make thee an ark of gopher wood.*" If we are to obey every commandment in the Bible, why not this one? The obvious answer is that God was speaking to *Noah* when He told *him* to build the ark.

God was speaking to Noah and not to us! It is scripturally incorrect for someone to apply to himself biblical commands addressed to someone else. We should not attempt to follow every commandment in the Bible. This simple example of Noah provides a starting point that will help determine the extent of this truth. If every command written in the Bible is to be followed and obeyed, consider the following:

> **Leviticus 4:20** *And he shall do with the bullock as he did with the bullock for a sin offering, so shall he do with this: and **the priest shall make an atonement for them, and it shall be forgiven them.***

Are we to follow this example and bring a sin offering to the priest for atonement? Obviously not! However, prior to the crucifixion of the Lord Jesus Christ, one of the priestly functions was to make atonement for sin. *Whose mail are you reading in the book of Leviticus?*

The Lord did not abolish this practice during His earthly ministry. Instead, He commanded the leper whom He had healed to show himself to the priest. The leper was to abide by the Law of Moses *for a testimony* to the religious leaders and make an offering for his cleansing.

> **Mark 1:44** *And saith unto him, See thou say nothing to any man: but go thy way, shew thyself to the priest, and **offer for thy cleansing those things which Moses commanded, for a testimony unto them***

Whose mail are you reading in Mark chapter one? The priestly duties were *not* abolished until after Christ's final blood sacrifice on Calvary. From that point forward, there is no basis for any further sacrifices. No instructions are given for involving an earthly priest in atoning or forgiving anyone's sin today. In fact, Christ is specifically pointed to as our *High Priest*.

> **Hebrews 3:1** *Wherefore, holy brethren, partakers of the heavenly calling, **consider the Apostle and High Priest** of our profession, **Christ Jesus;***

Hebrews points to the Lord Jesus Christ as our High Priest. Romans further reveals that through Christ's functioning as our High Priest and sacrifice, we NOW have the *atonement*. It is a present possession. Consider whose mail you are reading in the next verse.

*Romans 5:11 And not only so, but we also joy in God **through our Lord Jesus** **Christ, by whom we have now received the atonement.***

No longer do we follow the formula of Leviticus chapter 4 or even **Mark 1:44**. Our High Priest provided the atonement (payment) for sin through the offering of Himself. Through His bodily sacrifice we are sanctified for ever. The Old Testament priest could never accomplish this feat through his multitude of sacrifices offered year after year.

*Hebrews 10:10 By the which will **we are sanctified through the offering of the** **body of Jesus Christ once for all**. 11 And every priest standeth daily ministering and offering oftentimes the same sacrifices, which can never take away sins: 12 **But this man, after he had offered one sacrifice for sins for ever, sat down on the** **right hand of God;***

Thus, once a person receives the atonement mentioned in Romans, there is no further need for priestly sacrifices. Christ ended all of the sacrifices by offering Himself one time on the cross for our sins, and sat down at the right hand of the Father for ever.

All those that think that the church must be patterned after verses like those from Leviticus **should bring their bullock to the altar for sacrifice**. If an offering or blood sacrifice is still necessary for atonement or forgiveness, wouldn't this indicate that Christ's sacrifice of Himself was insufficient? This position is not only incorrect, but blasphemous!

The two examples, one from Genesis (the command given to Noah) and the other from Leviticus (concerning the priestly offering) may seem obvious to most Bible students. However, these two examples are presented to reveal the importance of considering the distinctions that must be made in other passages as well. An individual can certainly learn from reading scripture doctrinally applicable to another group. However, that individual is not commanded to keep every command contained in the Bible. This is especially true of those commands that God intended to apply only to a specific group of people during a particular period of time.

The different spokesmen in different ages gave different instructions from God. Whose "mail" (instructions) should we read and heed? Every Bible student must determine *where* to find God's applicable direction in His word. Is God's direction for the Church found as clearly in Matthew, Mark, Luke or John, when the Lord said He was *"not sent but unto the lost sheep of the house of Israel" (Matthew 15:24)*? Is God's direction for the Church found as clearly in Revelation where John plainly discusses the Tribulation period, Second Coming and Millennial rest? The answer is a resounding "no"! This mail primarily applies to others in the future.

Fortunately, God did not leave things up to chance for the student of His word. God's specific directions for the Church are found predominantly in the thirteen epistles that God used Paul to pen for the Church Age; each of these epistles or books (Romans through Philemon) begins with Paul's name. Ignore the instructions in these books at your own peril!

To further the point, consider the following question: what scriptures are most often used when trying to lead someone to trust Christ as Saviour? Many people have "instinctively" used the verses from the book of Romans first because they give a complete, concise picture of what one must know and believe in order to be saved. These verses have become so common in soul-winning discussions that they have been referred to as the "Roman's Road" to salvation. It is not coincidental that these verses occur in Paul's first epistle. Nor is it in fact simply *instinct* that has led people to this book, but rather the guiding hand of the Holy Spirit of God *(Romans 8:14, Galatians 5:18)*.

The Romans Road—Your Mail

Romans chapter 2—the goodness of God leadeth thee to repentance *(2:4-5)*
Romans chapter 3—all have sinned *(3:23)*
Romans chapter 5—while we were yet sinners, Christ died for us *(5:8)*
Romans chapter 6—the wages of sin is death, but the gift of God is eternal life *(6:23)*
Romans chapter 10—whosoever shall call upon the name of the Lord shall be saved *(10:13)*

Why do you suppose that so many soul winners are led by the Spirit of God to go to the epistles of the Apostle Paul? The answer is rather simple. Many preachers, teachers, and evangelistically-minded persons follow the precepts of right division in practice without considering why. *While reading everyone's mail (Genesis through Revelation), the soul winner gravitates toward Paul's epistles through supernatural prodding.*

Romans provides the clearest, most concise presentation of the gospel. It is not only important that Christ died on the cross, but essential that the *lost* person *(II Corinthians 4:3)* understand exactly what this means to him. Romans provides the individual with a basis for his belief. For this reason, the next of Paul's epistles emphasizes the *how* of Christ's sacrifice as an important aspect of the gospel.

> *I Corinthians 15:1 Moreover, brethren, I declare unto you **the gospel...how** that Christ died for our sins according to the scriptures; 4 And that he was buried, and that he rose again the third day according to the scriptures:*

According to Paul, the gospel includes the *how* of Christ's death. Yet, the whys and wherefores of Christ's death were not completely revealed until after His death. Only then did the first century world find out that Christ specifically died *for our sins (I Corinthians 15:3), became sin for us (II Corinthians 5:21)* and that we must *trust* in Him for forgiveness of sins.

> *Ephesians 1:13 **In whom ye also trusted**, after that ye heard the word of truth, the gospel of your salvation: in whom also after that ye believed, ye were sealed with that holy Spirit of promise,*

In addition to realizing the importance of trusting in Christ, Paul's epistles explain that the sealing of the Spirit follows one's trusting in the person and work of Christ. Many of these truths could not have been *revealed* prior to the cross. With full knowledge of what would follow, Satan would not have become God's pawn in the betrayal and crucifixion of God's Son. The truth about the crucifixion had to remain a mystery until *after* the cross; therefore, you will find no one apart from the Lord with a full understanding of it prior to the cross. A mystery only remains a mystery until revealed. Had the princes of this world known the mystery, they would not have crucified Christ!

> *II Corinthians 2:7 But we speak the wisdom of God in a **mystery**, even the hidden wisdom, which God ordained before the world unto our glory: 8 **Which none of the princes of this world knew: for had they known it, they would not have crucified the Lord of glory.***

The detailed truths of Christ's death had to be hidden until the appointed time. Had the full implications of Christ's sacrifice been understood by Satan prior to the cross, he would never have instigated Christ's betrayal. No one understood the full implications of the cross prior to the cross. It was still a mystery, or else *II Corinthians 2:7* is simply incorrect.

The Apostle Paul Reveals the Mysteries

If, over 5,000 years ago, a person or group was commanded to follow Noah and, much later, others were to follow Moses, why should it seem odd that God would have a specific spokesman for the Christian believer of today? God deals through a spokesman and we had better listen and take heed to what our primary spokesman has been led to say to us. The Apostle Paul wrote that they were *stewards of the mysteries of God (I Corinthians 4:1)*. God even called Paul His *chosen vessel (Acts 9:15)* for this Church Age.

From his epistles we find out that Paul was chosen to reveal mysteries *kept secret since the world began.* He was to make *"known unto us the **mystery** of his will" (Ephesians 1:9)*; that is, God's will. God's will is to give His Son a Body and a Bride to work out His will on this earth. These few verses clearly emphasize the mysteries in Paul's epistles.

> *Romans 11:25 For I would not, brethren, that ye should be ignorant of this **mystery**, lest ye should be wise in your own conceits; that **blindness in part is happened to Israel, until the fulness of the Gentiles be come in.***

> *Romans 16:25 Now to him that is of power to **stablish you** according to my gospel, and the preaching of Jesus Christ, **according to the revelation of the mystery**, which was kept secret since the world began,*

> *1 Corinthians 15:51 Behold, I shew you a **mystery;** We shall not all sleep, but we shall all be changed,*

> *Ephesians 3:3 How that **by revelation he made known unto me the mystery**; (as I wrote afore in few words, 4 Whereby, **when ye read, ye may understand my knowledge in the mystery of Christ**) 5 Which in other ages was not made known unto the sons of men, as it is now revealed unto his holy apostles and prophets by the Spirit;*

> *Ephesians 3:9 And to make all men see what is the **fellowship of the mystery**, which from the beginning of the world hath been hid in God, who created all things by Jesus Christ:*

> *Ephesians 5:32 This is a great **mystery**: but I speak concerning Christ and the church.*

> *Ephesians 6:19 And for me, that utterance may be given unto me, that I may open my mouth boldly, to make known **the mystery of the gospel**,*

Paul is our primary God-given spokesman. He is used of God to teach *us* that we are saved and sealed forever by the Holy Spirit. He reveals the various truths that had remained a *mystery* prior to the penning of his epistles. The mystery program today concerns *spiritual blessings in heavenly places (Ephesians 1:3, 2:6; Colossians 3:1-3)*. For further study of the mysteries of Paul's epistles, consider: *Colossians 1:26-27, 2:2, 4:3; I Timothy 3:9, 3:16*.

The final mysteries after the Church Age will be fully revealed by the seventh angel of the Tribulation. The Bible states that he will *finish* the mystery program at that time *(Revelation*

10:7). With so many mysteries existing prior to the revelations given to the Apostle Paul, why do so many preachers still teach that those living prior to the cross were simply looking forward to the cross?

Looking Forward to the Cross?

When one reads the Old Testament, it is sometimes hard for the New Testament Christian to comprehend how those in the first century refused to accept Jesus as Messiah. The Bible student quickly encounters and easily identifies numerous Old Testament pictures and types of Christ. How could Israel have missed truths so evident to the Church today? The answer is rather simple. The pictures and types are clearly recognizable only in light of the revelation of the New Testament obscured prior to that time. God chose Paul to reveal these mysteries.

Without question, David, Joseph and Isaac are magnificent pictures and types of Christ. However, it is very unwise to teach that the Old Testament saints grasped the same truths so visible to the Christian today. In fact, the Bible teaches that the Jews read the Old Testament with spiritual blinders on. Therefore, contrary to the teaching of the majority of seminaries, those living prior to the cross could not simply have been *looking forward to the cross.* In fact, the Bible says that there was a veil over their minds preventing their seeing the very truths we hold so dear.

> *II Corinthians 3:14 But their minds were blinded: for until this day remaineth the same vail untaken away in **the reading of the old testament; which vail is done away in Christ.***

The veil is only removed *in Christ.* The Bible also plainly teaches that the veil was *not* taken away until after the cross. For this reason, the dishonest Bible "scholar" is hard-pressed to reconcile the truth with his teaching of Old Testament saints *looking forward to the cross for salvation.* Consider these four points which prove that not even the leader of the twelve disciples was looking forward to the cross for his salvation.

- Peter **rebuked** the Lord when He foretold His death, burial and resurrection *(Luke 8:32).*
- Peter fought to stop the soldiers from taking Jesus ultimately to the cross *(John 18:10).*
- Peter thought that the resurrection account was an "idle tale" *(Luke 24:11).*
- Peter wondered as he looked in the sepulchre what had happened to Jesus' body *(Luke 24:12).*

Could the other apostles have been looking forward to and trusting in the cross for their salvation if even their leader Peter was not? Absolutely not! If a person wishes to somehow make all of the Bible to apply equally to all generations throughout history without exception, then the following verse would mean that everyone who ever had the gospel *hidden* from him would be spiritually lost. Right?

> *II Corinthians 4:3 But if **our gospel** be hid, it **is hid to them that are lost**:*

There is no arguing with this truth! The Bible says that the lost have the gospel *hidden* from them. Consistent Bible application using the method of Bible study most seminaries employ would mean that all of the apostles were lost! Yet, it is a grave doctrinal and historical error to claim that any of the apostles apart from Judas Iscariot (the son of perdition) was ever lost. Otherwise, Jesus was a liar or the Bible contains contradictions and errors.

*John 17:12 While I was with them in the world, I kept them in thy name: those that thou gavest me I have kept, and **none of them is lost, but the son of perdition**; that the scripture might be fulfilled.*

If the pastor, preacher and teacher allows the "scholars' union" or his own *alma mater* to determine what to believe and teach, complete spiritual infidelity will result. It is impossible to teach the traditional "everyone was looking forward to the cross" doctrine without explaining away the seemingly contradictory information. In the next passage, Jesus clearly communicates the gospel to the twelve. He tells them that He is going to be put to death and rise again three days later. That is, the Gospel as defined in the first four verses of First Corinthians chapter 15).

*Luke 18:31 Then he took unto him the **twelve**, and said unto them, Behold, we go up to Jerusalem, and all things that are written by the prophets concerning the Son of man shall be accomplished. 32 For he shall be delivered unto the Gentiles, and shall be mocked, and spitefully entreated, and spitted on: 33 And they shall scourge him, and **put him to death: and the third day he shall rise again**.*

No one can argue that this passage fails to record Christ's prophesying His own death, burial and resurrection. He foretells the gospel that would be the basis for everyone's salvation. However, notice how the passage continues below. The writer says that the twelve apostles did not understand what He was saying. In fact, the Bible says that the gospel (the death, burial and resurrection) was HIDDEN from them.

*Luke 18:34 And they understood none of these things: and **this saying was hid from them**, neither knew they the things which were spoken.*

Were all of the twelve apostles in fact lost? Was Jesus a liar? Does the Bible contain contradictions? No, on all three accounts. If the so-called biblical scholars retroactively apply ***II Corinthians 4:3*** (quoted earlier) to the apostles situation, they have just created a glaring contradiction in the Bible. This should be unacceptable for all those that love the word of God. Because many Bible teachers and preachers refuse to apply the Bible passages dispensationally, they pile error upon error and the world remains in a state of utter confusion. Christians become increasingly disillusioned with Bible study because it becomes impossible to believe in something that teachers continually spiritualize (that is, something they fail to apply literally).

Anyone that teaches that those prior to the cross were simply looking forward to the cross for salvation may be unwittingly calling Jesus a liar. It is impossible to be honest and claim that everyone before the cross is looking forward to the cross. Consistent application requires that one rightly divide the word of truth. Bible teachers need to be consistent and honest by studying the Bible using God's method of Bible study or else risk the disdain of God Almighty.

Although nobody gets to heaven apart from the blood of the Lord Jesus Christ, how this blood is applied differs from one period (or age) to the next. We cannot apply how God deals with man today to all other periods of time. As we have seen, the period covered by the four Gospels is a prime example.

The Kingdom Gospel

The subject of the Kingdom Gospel, introduced here, will be more fully developed in Chapter 4. Let us consider Peter for a moment. During the earliest part of Peter's ministry, his primary focus was *not* to preach the Gospel of the Grace of God. Rather, he preached about the future

Kingdom of Jesus Christ. The Lord Jesus Christ and John the Baptist preached the kingdom message also. They were announcing the promised kingdom *to the Jewish nation*. One cannot read the next verse and be ignorant of this truth without simply rejecting the plain truth.

Matthew 4:17 From that time Jesus began to preach, and to say, Repent: for the kingdom of heaven is at hand.

The Lord Jesus Christ preached about the kingdom. He preached that the "kingdom of heaven is at hand." *At hand*, in this context, means within reach. Israel did not accept the Lord while the kingdom was within their reach. Instead, they crucified their future King. Therefore, the kingdom will not be established until after the present Church Age and future Tribulation. The kingdom is a synonymous designation for the 1,000-year (Millennial) reign of the Lord Jesus Christ, and it is yet to come *(Revelation 20:4).*

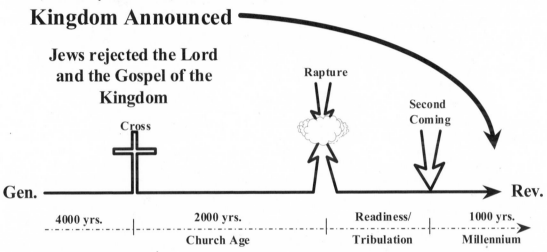

Chart 3.3 - Kingdom

The chart depicts how the Gospel of the Kingdom was preached. However, the actual beginning of the kingdom would not occur until thousands of years later, following the Second Coming. We know that almost 2,000 years have transpired since the Lord's first coming. Jesus preached *the Gospel of the Kingdom* during His earthly ministry. He instructed His apostles and disciples to do the same.

> *"The story of the kingdom was called 'the gospel,' that is, good news or tidings, while the kingdom was said to be at hand. Jesus preached 'the gospel of the kingdom' (Matt. 4:23; Matt. 9:35) as long as the kingdom was at hand."*
>
> John R. Rice, *The Coming Kingdom of Christ* (Murfreesboro: Sword of the Lord, 1945), p. 76.

Matthew 4:23 And Jesus went about all Galilee, teaching in their synagogues, and preaching the gospel of the kingdom, and healing all manner of sickness and all manner of disease among the people.

No Bible-believing preacher today preaches the Gospel of the Kingdom. He preaches instead the Gospel of the Grace of God. In later studies, the critical distinctions between these two gospels will be examined. The differing features between the Gospel of the Kingdom and the Gospel of the Grace of God *(Acts 20:24)* are sometimes readily apparent.

Understanding the difference between the Kingdom Gospel and the gospel preached today would clarify many other issues as well. For instance, the Kingdom Gospel included the healing of all manner of sickness and disease as a sign to the nation of Israel.

*Matthew 9:35 And **Jesus went about** all the cities and villages, teaching in their synagogues, and **preaching the gospel of the kingdom**, **healing** every sickness and every disease among the people.*

*Mark 1:14 Now after that John was put in prison, **Jesus came** into Galilee, **preaching the gospel of the kingdom of God**, 15 And saying, The time is fulfilled, and the **kingdom of God is at hand**: repent ye, and **believe the gospel**.*

The Kingdom Gospel preached in Matthew, Mark, Luke and John will go back into effect after the Church Age. These four gospel books proclaim the Kingdom's various features as do portions of the last nine books of the Bible (Hebrews through Revelation). Anytime we read from a doctrinal perspective, we *must* consider to whom the passage is being addressed. We *must* consider what period of time is being covered. The Church is taken out of this world at the Rapture, prior to the time when the Kingdom Gospel (as referred to in *Hebrews 2:3-5*) goes back into effect. This Gospel (of the Kingdom) must be preached "in all the world" before the end comes.

> *"However, the gospel of the kingdom is to be preached again during the tribulation period and just before Christ returns to set up His kingdom...IN THOSE DAYS OF THE GREAT TRIBULATION, THE GOSPEL OF THE KINGDOM WILL BE PREACHED AGAIN!"* **(Emphasis in original).**
>
> John R. Rice, *The Coming Kingdom of Christ* (Murfreesboro: Sword of the Lord, 1945), p. 77.

*Matthew 24:14 And **this gospel of the kingdom shall be preached in all the world** for a witness unto all nations; **and then shall the end come**.*

This "end" refers to the Second Coming, not the Rapture. This "end" is contingent upon the full preaching of the Gospel of the Kingdom and *not* to the preaching of the Gospel of the Grace of God. Therefore, the whole world will hear the Gospel *of the Kingdom* prior to the end (of the Tribulation). When God's revived Jewish nation finds itself in the midst of the Tribulation searching for answers, what is the first New Testament book that might arouse their interest?

The Message of Hebrews

Obviously, a book that contains their name would interest the *Hebrews* the most. The book of Hebrews begins by referring to "the fathers" and "the prophets" (of the nation of Israel). When reading the book of Hebrews, a person living in the present Church Age should initially liken it to reading mail that is *not* directly addressed to him. You can certainly learn from reading someone else's mail, but you should not attempt to treat the message it contains as though it were *all* expressly intended for you.

*Hebrews 1:1 God, who at sundry times and in divers manners spake in time past **unto the fathers** by the prophets, 2 Hath **in these last days** spoken unto us by his Son...*

One might wonder why the message of Hebrews is addressed to the nation of Israel when the previous thirteen epistles emphasize the Gentiles (and the Church). Shortly after the cross, the nation of Israel was cast away *(Romans 11:15)* and broken off *(Romans 11:17)* because of unbelief. The Gentiles were grafted in, thus ending God's dealings almost *exclusively* with and through the Jews. After the Church Age following the Rapture, the Hebrews (Jews) will be God's tool to once again bring His message to the world.

The Jews did not accept their Messiah at His first coming. Soon after the Rapture of the Church, God will again be dealing with and through the Hebrew *(Deuteronomy 15:12)* nation of Israel (thus the assumption for God's titling the *first* of future New Testament prophecy books "Hebrews" and calling out the 144,000 Hebrews to preach during the Tribulation). Today, God has chosen to use the Gentile nations rather than Israel, expressing His command and guidance to the Gentiles primarily through the Apostle Paul's books that contain his name as the first word.

Many people including Bible publishers believe that Paul authored the book of Hebrews because of the mentioning of bonds *(Hebrews 10:34),* Timothy *(Hebrews 13:23)* being in the body *(Hebrews 13:3)* and Italy *(Hebrews 13:24)*. But the evidence against Pauline authorship of Hebrews is demonstrably stronger. For instance, the statement about being *in the body* appears to be a reference to a physical body rather than a reference to the Body of Christ. See *Hebrews 13:11* reference to the "bodies of those beasts" and the physical body referenced in *Hebrews 10:5*.

The book of Hebrews is distinctively unique from the other New Testament books. Attempting to equate the distinctive features of Hebrews with those epistles which are unquestionably authored by the Apostle Paul is an exercise in futility. Paul points to his salutation (the opening of each of his letters) as a characteristic or token of every one of his epistles, something not found in the book of Hebrews.

*II Thessalonians 3:17 The salutation of Paul with mine own hand, **which is the token in every epistle**: so I write.*

The thirteen epistles which are indisputably attributed to Paul each contain his peculiar salutation in the very first verse. However, Hebrews does not have Paul's customary *salutation* (or greeting) of his name as the first word of this epistle. Consider the five following additional points which support Hebrews authorship by someone other than Paul.

1. Paul claims supernatural revelation *(Ephesians 3:3)*, while the writer of Hebrews emphasizes how his message was *confirmed* to him by others.

*Hebrews 2:3 How shall we escape, if we neglect so great salvation; which at the first began to be spoken by the Lord, and was **confirmed unto us by them that heard him**; 4 God also bearing them witness, both with signs and wonders, and with divers miracles, and gifts of the Holy Ghost, according to his own will?*

Paul wrote in Galatians that the gospel that he preached was *"not after man...For I neither received it of man, neither was I taught it, but by the revelation of Jesus Christ" (Galatians 1:11-12)*. Paul goes on to point out that he did not immediately go up to Jerusalem after his conversion to meet with the other apostles. Instead he writes that he *"conferred not with flesh and blood" (Galatians 1:16)*. When he finally did meet with the other apostles in

Jerusalem he boldly proclaims that *"in conference* (they) *added nothing to me" (Galatians 2:6)*. This hardly sounds like the writer of Hebrews whose message *was* confirmed by him.

2. When Paul describes the last days, he refers to it a future time (***II Timothy 3:1***—*"in the last days..."* certain things will transpire). The writer of Hebrews seems to have been given visions of the future much like John in the book of Revelation.

> ***Revelation 1:10 I was in the Spirit on the Lord's day***, *and heard behind me a great voice, as of a trumpet,*

The Apostle John wrote Revelation as an eyewitness of the events. The writer of Hebrews seems also to have been spiritually present in "these" last days as he penned his epistle.

> ***Hebrews 1:2*** *Hath* **in these last days** *spoken unto us by his Son, whom he hath appointed heir of all things, by whom also he made the worlds;*

3. The writer of Hebrews says that he is speaking about *the world to come*. *"For unto the angels hath he not put in subjection* **the world to come, whereof we speak** *(Hebrews 2:5)*. This phrase refers to the Millennium (the 1,000-year reign of Christ) as can be seen from the following verses:

> ***Matthew 12:32*** *And whosoever speaketh a word against the Son of man, it shall be forgiven him: but whosoever speaketh against the Holy Ghost, it shall not be forgiven him,* **neither in this world, neither in the world to come**.

> ***Mark 10:30*** *But he shall receive an hundredfold now in this time, houses, and brethren, and sisters, and mothers, and children, and lands, with persecutions; and in* **the world to come eternal life.**

> ***Luke 18:30*** *Who shall not receive manifold more in this present time, and in* **the world to come life everlasting.**

> ***Hebrews 6:5 And have tasted*** *the good word of God, and* **the powers of the world to come,**

4. The references to "the world to come" are not the only direct correlation to the Gospel books. Matthew chapter 24 is one of the most obvious prophecies concerning Israel and the Great Tribulation. The context refers to the Gospel of the Kingdom, the abomination of desolation, Judaea fleeing into the mountains, and the Sabbath day, and culminates in the Great Tribulation.

> ***Matthew 24:14*** *And* **this gospel of the kingdom** *shall be preached in all the world for a witness unto all nations; and then shall the end come. 15 When ye therefore shall see* **the abomination of desolation,** *spoken of by Daniel the prophet, stand in the holy place, (whoso readeth, let him understand:) 16 Then let them which be in* **Judaea flee into the mountains:** *20 But pray ye that your flight be not in the winter, neither on the* **sabbath day:** *21 For then shall be* **great tribulation,** *such as was not since the beginning of the world to this time, no, nor ever shall be.*

Another of the distinct characteristics of the Tribulation is the need to *endure to the end*. Getting weary in well doing will have unimaginable consequences during that future time. There is no hope for those that take the Mark of the Beast, thus failing to endure to the end (of the Tribulation).

*Matthew 24:13 But he that shall **endure unto the end**, the same shall be saved.*

The believers in the Tribulation will face intense persecution—unlike any during any other period in the history of the world. Matthew says that it will be a requirement for them to endure to the end. At no time can they become weary or impatient and take the Mark of the Beast. This doctrine sounds very similar to that found in the book of Hebrews.

*Hebrews 6:4 For **it is impossible** for those who were once enlightened, and have tasted of the heavenly gift, and were made partakers of the Holy Ghost, 5 And have tasted the good word of God, and the powers of the world to come, 6 **If they shall fall away, to renew them again unto repentance**; seeing they crucify to themselves the Son of God afresh, and put him to an open shame.*

Here, the writer of Hebrews offers no hope of renewal. This hardly sounds like the Apostle Paul who wrote that no matter how great the offense, grace is greater than all of our sin.

*Romans 5:20 Moreover the law entered, that the offence might abound. **But where sin abounded, grace did much more abound:***

5. Another interesting observation is the emphasis in Hebrews placed on entering into the **Lord's millennial rest** as found at the end of chapter 3 and *the majority* of chapter 4.

*Hebrews 4:1 Let us therefore **fear**, lest, a promise being left us of **entering into his rest**, any of you should seem to **come short of it**....4 For he spake in a certain place of the seventh day on this wise, And **God did rest the seventh day** from all his works....11 **Let us labour therefore to enter into that rest**, lest any man **fall** after the same example of unbelief.*

The reader should study the entire context of these two chapters. The writer of Hebrews is warning the reader not to come short of entering into his rest. The *rest* is clearly associated with the *seventh* day of creation. Combining this truth *with **II Peter 3:8*** (one day is with the Lord as a thousand years), the context clearly appears to be the seventh millennium.

Also take note that the first verse in Hebrews Chapter 4 encourages the reader to *fear* his relationship with God; whereas, the Church Age saint is never told to fear in this same context. In fact, he is told that his adoption means that he has not "received the spirit of bondage again to fear" *(Romans 8:15)*. Paul also tells Timothy that Christians have been given the spirit of power, love and sound mind and not the "spirit of fear" *(II Timothy 1:7)*.

One must rightly divide the scriptures or be forever confused. To further drive home the point, take note that the Apostle Paul never refers to the "rest," nor does he refer to Israel's entering into the Kingdom promised FROM the foundation of the world.

*Hebrews 4:3 For we which have believed do enter into rest, as he said, As I have sworn in my wrath, if they shall **enter into my rest**: although the works were finished **from the foundation of the world**.*

*Matthew 25:34 Then shall the King say unto them on his right hand, Come, ye blessed of my Father, **inherit the kingdom prepared for you from the foundation of the world**:*

Israel's promise is in the earth (the land promise) "from the foundation" of the world. The Church's blessings are said to be "before the foundation" of the world.

*Ephesians 1:4 According as he hath chosen us in him **before the foundation of the world**, that we should be holy and without blame before him in love:*

The examples abound. Some preachers would correctly point out that Hebrews refers to the *Church* in chapters 2 and 12. For this reason, they assume that this proves that the entire book applies directly to the Church Age. However, neither of these usages refers to Church in the sense of the Body of Christ, removed from the earth at the Rapture. Instead, both of these Hebrews references refer to the congregation of the seed of Jacob and Israel.

*Hebrews 2:12 Saying, **I will declare thy name unto my brethren, in the midst of the church will I sing praise unto thee.***

This verse from Hebrews is an Old Testament quotation found originally in Psalm chapter 22. The direct parallel of ***Hebrews 2:12*** is found in ***Psalm 22:22***. The context of the quotation is briefly provided in verses ***Psalm 22:23, 27 and 28***.

*Psalm 22:23 Ye that fear the LORD, praise him; all ye **the seed of Jacob**, glorify him; and fear him, all ye **the seed of Israel**...27 **All the ends of the world shall remember and turn unto the LORD: and all the kindreds of the nations shall worship before thee.** 28 **For the kingdom is the LORD'S**: and he is the governor among the nations.*

The context is indisputably the Millennium—when the *ends of the world shall...turn unto the LORD*: and all the nations shall worship before the LORD. This is the Millennial reign of Jesus Christ on the earth—verse 28 says that *the kingdom is the LORD's **(Revelation 11:15).*** This kingdom will be in place when Jesus rules as *King of kings* in the Millennium ***(Revelation 19:16)***. The second reference in Hebrews to *church* is found in chapter 12. Its context is also Israel when one compares scripture with scripture.

*Hebrews 12:23 **To the general assembly and church of the firstborn**, which are written in heaven, and to God the Judge of all, and to the spirits of just men made perfect,*

The LORD tells Moses to tell Pharaoh that Israel is the LORD's *firstborn*. It is complete spiritually infidelity to make the church of the firstborn refer to the Body of Christ.

*Exodus 4:22 And thou shalt say unto Pharaoh, Thus saith the LORD, **Israel is my** son, even my **firstborn:***

To claim that Hebrews contains Church Age doctrine simply because of these references to "church" would be as wise as stating that the whole Old Testament applies directly to the Church Age because of the reference to *the church in the wilderness* under Moses.

*Acts 7:37 This is that **Moses**, which said unto the children of Israel, A prophet shall the Lord your God raise up unto you of your brethren, like unto me; him shall ye hear. 38 This is he, **that was in the church in the wilderness with the angel which spake to him in the mount Sina**, and with our fathers: who received the lively oracles to give unto us:*

We need more systematic theology rather than arbitrary misapplication of scripture. Applying these particular passages to the Church Age is analogous to reading another person's mail.

4

Reconciling the Scriptures I

The next two chapters compare *Paul's thirteen Church Age epistles* with the remainder of the scriptures. As various passages are compared, the key to understanding the scriptures will further unfold, and our need to rightly divide the Bible will be reinforced. The comparisons will reconcile seemingly contradictory verses. The student of God's word must find the answers to these "contradictions" and always be ready to give an answer to anyone seeking the truth *(I Peter 3:15)*. Rather than moving directly into the comparisons using the charts, the point concerning future application of the book of Hebrews must be further impressed upon the reader.

The Course of the New Testament

The New Testament follows an identifiable course covering approximately 3,000 years. The New Testament books begin with the birth of Jesus in the Gospels and end with the book of Revelation foretelling the new heaven and new earth following the 1,000-year reign of Christ. Each of the books systematically grouped together naturally records the flow of time. However, if the books of Hebrews and James lack any direct Tribulation application, then the New Testament course stays on track from beginning to end, but goes askew when the reader arrives at these two books addressing the nation of Israel. This 3,000 year sequence can be viewed as follows:

Matthew through John cover Christ's earthly ministry to the Jews, culminating with His passing of the helm to the apostles. The book of *Acts* then transitions the reader from the apostles' ministry (predominantly to the nation of Israel) to the ministry of the Apostle Paul (predominantly to the Gentiles and directly to the Church).

The next book, *Romans*, takes place during Paul's Acts missionary journeys. He goes to the Jews first during these journeys until the Jewish remnant is reached by the time he lands in prison. Paul's epistles written from prison (Ephesians forward) reveal how the middle wall of partition between Jew and Gentile was broken down during the current Church Age *(Ephesians 2:14)*. He then proclaims Jew and Gentile to be one in the Body of Christ.

It would be incompatible for Hebrews to again magnify the distinctions between Jew and Gentile during the Church Age. If Hebrews reestablishes this division between Jew and Gentile during the Church Age it would be the only regressive portion of scripture in the New Testament. However, if its application applies to the nation of Israel in their yet future renewed capacity, these books too continue the pattern of continuity. Since we know that the Tribulation and Millennium again focus on the nation of Israel, it would make infinitely more sense if the obvious Tribulational material found in these books pointed to that yet future event.

The New Covenant

Possibly one additional example from Hebrews concerning the *new* covenant would benefit the unyielding skeptic immensely. Galatians reveals that there is no difference between the Jew and Greek (Gentile) in the Body of Christ.

Galatians 3:28 There is neither Jew nor Greek, there is neither bond nor free, there is neither male nor female: for ye are all one in Christ Jesus.

Since Galatians explicitly points out the elimination of any distinction between the Jew and non-Jew, why does Hebrews resurrect these very same distinctions by again pointing to Israel's unique status as a nation?

*Hebrews 8:8 For finding fault with them, he saith, Behold, the days come, saith the Lord, when **I will make a new covenant with the house of Israel and with the house of Judah**:*

Paul went to great lengths to point out the necessity for all to be one in the Body of Christ. It seems contradictory for Hebrews to reestablish these same distinctions unless these distinctions apply to a period after the Body of Christ is no longer on the earth. This *new* covenant applies to a yet future period of time when Israel will once again come into national prominence. There is no other plausible explanation for the book of Hebrews to draw attention to the new covenant to be made with Israel. The new covenant with Israel and Judah prophesied in the Old Testament is clearly delineated in Jeremiah chapter 31.

*Jeremiah 31:31 Behold, the days come, saith the LORD, that I will **make a new covenant with the house of Israel, and with the house of Judah:** ...33 But this shall be the covenant that I will make with the house of Israel; **After those days,** saith the LORD, **I will put my law in their inward parts, and write it in their hearts**; and will be their God, and they shall be **my people**. 34 And **they shall teach no more** every man his neighbour, and every man his brother, saying, Know the LORD: for they shall all know me, from the least of them unto the greatest of them, saith the LORD: for I will forgive their iniquity, and I will remember their sin no more.*

These references to the new covenant certainly do not sound like the Apostle Paul as he wrote about Israel's being cast away in Romans chapter 11. Once Paul reaches the remnant (covered in chapters 9-11 of this book), he turns his attention to making no further distinction between Jew and Gentile. To reapply these distinctions to the Body of Christ is quite counter-productive to everything that the Apostle Paul wrote.

God's unchanging character

Some may wonder why God "allows" us to misunderstand the scriptures. Confusion occurs when man fails to realize that God often requires something of man during one period of time, which He does not require during another period of time. To *rightly* divide the Bible, one must consider God's changing commissions. Many people have misapplied *Hebrews 13:8* to justify their rejection of God's changing expectations of man.

Hebrews 13:8 Jesus Christ the same yesterday, and to day, and for ever.

Instead of realizing that this verse refers to *God's unchanging character*, many assume that *Hebrews 13:8* refers to God's plan for man. God's character never changes. His message to mankind, however, is dynamic. Those who fail to make a distinction in God's *messages* will end up confused and sometimes completely bewildered.

The Lord Jesus Christ is the same, but God's interaction with man has not remained *constant* throughout time. For example, we are not required to make animal sacrifices that were required under the Old Testament law. To restate: *Jesus is the same yesterday, today and forever, but God's plan and how He relates it to man is not the same throughout all ages.* This chapter will distinguish Paul's epistles, as they relate to us today, from the other scriptures that **directly** relate to man in other periods of time.

In this comparative chapter, the following chart will be presented in various forms to help you visualize the points being made. For some points, only portions of the chart will be used, but the primary Church Age epistles are "boxed." Of course, these are the epistles containing the bulk of material for this present age, but in no way do they exclude the Church Age material found elsewhere. As you read and study, refer back to this chart for a complete representation of the chart's contents.

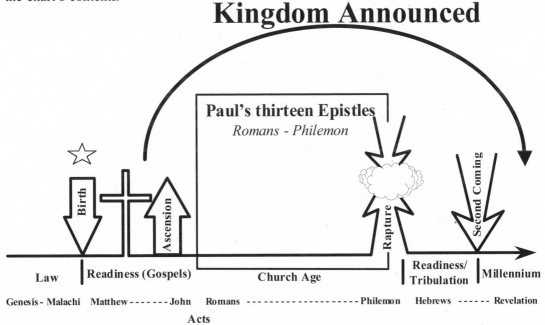

Chart 4.1 - Kingdom Postponed

Our basic chart, presented in previous chapters, has three major additions that are pertinent to the next few chapters:

1. Arrow with a star: Represents the birth of the Lord Jesus Christ occurring thirty-three years prior to the cross. It designates the record of an event clearly at the beginning of the "Gospel" books.

2. Arrow pointing up: Follows shortly after the cross and denotes the ascension of the Lord Jesus Christ, Who is now seated at the right hand of God the Father. This event occurred following the resurrection.

3. Paul's Thirteen Epistles (boxed): Covers the time period sometime prior to Paul's conversion until the Rapture of the Church (or Body of Christ).

One of the following chart designations will introduce most of the verses in our comparisons:

"Pre-law"—Verses prior to the giving of the law in Exodus chapter 20

"Law"—Verses from the Old Testament (Exodus 20 to Malachi)

"Gospels"—Verses from the four Gospels (Matthew to John)

"Church"—Verses from Paul's thirteen Church Age epistles

"Tribulation"—Verses from Hebrews through Revelation

"Millennium"—Verses from Hebrews through Revelation

This chapter will compare the following six teachings in Paul's epistles with the seemingly contradictory teachings from the remainder of the Bible:

I.   An eye for an eye -or- living peaceably

II.   Giving unreservedly to others -or- requiring work or responsibility of others

III.   Salvation for Jews only -or- salvation for Gentiles

IV.   Tithing -or- giving abundantly

V.   The Gospel of the Kingdom of Heaven -or- the Gospel of the Grace of God

I. An Eye for an Eye -or- Living Peaceably

The first of the comparisons deals with the responsibility each of us has when dealing with others, especially under adverse conditions. The law said the Jews were to respond in a spirit of vengeance with an "eye for an eye." On the other hand, the Lord said, "turn the cheek." Paul instructed one to "live peaceably." This comparison will ultimately reveal God's instruction to the Christian living during the Church Age without ignoring or spiritualizing the other teachings. In other words, each passage will be interpreted in a literal context.

The first instruction period discussed covers the period of time *under the law*, in Exodus chapter 21.

> **"Law"** *Exodus 21:23 And if any mischief follow, then thou shalt give life for life, 24 **Eye for eye**, tooth for tooth, hand for hand, foot for foot, 25 Burning for burning, wound for wound, stripe for stripe.*

In the previous chapter (Exodus chapter 20), God gave the Ten Commandments to the Jews. The law clearly prescribed what punishment to give for each sin. The law required not only the punishment of an eye for eye but also a "life for life." The death penalty was also imposed for many other infractions under the law. One could be stoned to death under the law for:

- Gathering sticks on the Sabbath *(Numbers 15:32-36)*.

- Blasphemy *(Leviticus 24:11-14)*.

- Serving other gods *(Deuteronomy 13:6-10)*.

- Being a disobedient, unrepentant child *(Deuteronomy 21:18-21)*.

One need only imagine for a moment the sharp decline in the average life expectancy in the United States (and around the world) if God imposed the same penalties for the same infractions on everyone today. The Lord Jesus Christ put an end to many of the punishments required under the law. He clearly restates God's position in the next passage.

"Gospels" *Matthew 5:38 Ye have heard that it hath been said, An eye for an eye, and a tooth for a tooth: 39 But I say unto you, That ye resist not evil: but whosoever shall smite thee on thy right cheek, turn to him the other also.*

The example from Matthew chapter 5 shows the Lord quoting the law (as given in Exodus chapter 21). He then gives God's *new* plan and direction. Although man has no business attempting to change God's laws or His word, God can and has done so here as well as in other places *(Jeremiah 36:32)*!

One should take note of the ramifications of this change. The Lord changed the "eye for eye" punishment. Although capital punishment did not end *(Romans 13:4)*, other legal recourses did. **Jesus (God) remained the same**, but His dealings with man changed drastically!

Obviously, these two responses to an act or sin, an eye for an eye versus turning the cheek, are not identical. Nor are they compatible. The Lord Jesus Christ preached kingdom/readiness doctrine, which gave the rule of law effective during His kingdom. The Lord told Pilate that *"now is my kingdom not from hence" (John 18:36)*. It was not NOW, but would be later.

These two time periods—under the law (Exodus) and in the Kingdom (Matthew)—vary greatly from Paul's definitive writings to the Church. What is the guiding principle today during the Church Age? Do you take an eye for every eye . . . do you turn the cheek . . . or do you *follow Paul*? Paul says, *"Be ye **followers** of me, even as I also am of Christ." (I Corinthians 11:1)* So, if Paul has the authority to tell us to follow him, we should consider what his epistles say *to us*. For example:

"Church" *Romans 12:17 Recompense to no man evil for evil. Provide things honest in the sight of all men. 18 **If it be possible, as much as lieth in you, live peaceably with all men**.*

We are no longer *authorized* or *permitted* to take an "eye for an eye." We are to live peaceably. Yet we are not *required* to turn the cheek every time either; we are to live peaceably **if it be possible**. Putting it simply: Turn the cheek if you can, but you are under no obligation to do so under every circumstance. Thus, God allows self-defense during the Church Age.

Eye for an eye   - vs - Living peaceably

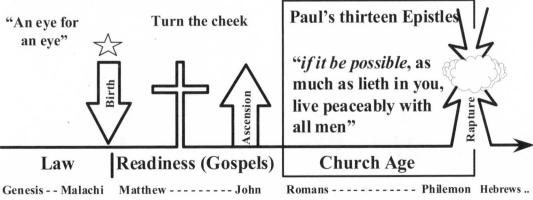

Chart 4.2 - Eye for an Eye

Paul instructs us that we are to live peaceably using everything that lies within us to do so—**if it be possible**! The Spirit of God lies within every believer. If a person submits to the leading of the Holy Spirit, he or she will be able to live peaceably in most instances . . . but not always. Sometimes it simply will not be possible! We should praise God for not leaving us as *helpless* sheep in a ravenous world *(Matthew 10:16)*.

You may wonder what this difference in standards might mean to you practically. The primary issue is whether you have the right to take an eye for an eye, or if you are required to turn the cheek in each and every case. Consider this: I might be able to live peaceably with a person who is hurting me, but not with one who is hurting my wife or children. Furthermore, I am duty bound to provide protection for my family *(I Timothy 5:8)*. Therefore, I may not always be able to find it possible to turn the cheek.

Most Bible teachers would agree that it would be wrong to instruct Christians by the Old Testament principle that gives them *a responsibility* to take an eye for eye. However, most persons never consider that it would be equally wrong in this sin-sick world *to require* that everyone turn the cheek. God is allowing a lot of things today that He will not permit when He is ruling as King of Kings and requiring everyone to turn the cheek. We need to rightly divide the Bible to know and obey the commands God has given **to us**.

Realizing that God does not always require a Christian to turn the cheek may encourage some readers to conclude they may do as they please. This conclusion is flawed. When you are willing to take the wrong done against you *(I Corinthians 6:7)*, you reflect your spiritual maturity. People who are lacking spiritual maturity will frequently respond in a carnal, vengeful way to those who have wronged them. Those who live trusting that God can and will take care of them will have a greater desire to live peaceably with others.

II. Giving Unreservedly to Others -or- Requiring Work or Responsibility of Others

As we have seen, a person's responsibility during the readiness period differs greatly from the Christian's responsibility in today's Church Age. For example, the Lord Jesus Christ preached readiness doctrine, making it clear that if a person asks for something or wants to borrow something, you are to give it to him. One has no right to turn him away.

"Gospels" *Matthew 5:42 Give to him that asketh thee, and from him that would borrow of thee turn not thou away.*

One can only imagine the abuse the Christian would endure if required to abide by this directive today. Can you imagine giving to any and every one who asks? People today would take advantage of us until we had nothing left to give. But when the Lord Jesus Christ rules on His throne during the future Millennial Kingdom, He will insure that no one gets away with taking advantage of anyone else.

If applying *Matthew 5:42* dogmatically to your Christian walk does not seem a problem for you, then you have not thoroughly considered its ramifications. For instance, if someone wanted to borrow your car or maybe your house for the weekend, would you turn him away? What would be your justification? It should be because you understand your Bible *rightly divided,* and realize that "giving to anyone who asks" is a doctrine that will apply to those living during the Millennium and not to us in this Church Age.

God gives us a different standard to follow today. He lets us know, through Paul, that we are under no obligation to give just because a person asks. For example, He goes so far as to say that those who are unwilling to work should not eat.

"Church" *II Thessalonians 3:10 For even when we were with you, this we commanded you, that **if any would not work, neither should he eat.***

The only way to know that our actions are right is by considering the commands given to us through our spokesman, the Apostle Paul *(Romans 11:13)*. If a person asks to borrow something, he can be asked to work for it. We are under no obligation to give anything to anyone just because he asks *(Matthew 5:42)*. Otherwise, we would be obligated to give every panhandler on the side of the road whatever handout he requests, whether it is food, money or personal belongings. Many times you are simply feeding his or her drug or cigarette habits.

Giving it Away - vs - Working for What You Get

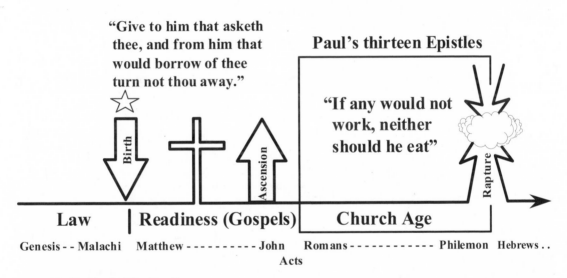

"Give to him that asketh thee, and from him that would borrow of thee turn not thou away."

Paul's thirteen Epistles

"If any would not work, neither should he eat"

Birth

Ascension

Rapture

Law | **Readiness (Gospels)** | **Church Age**

Genesis - - Malachi   Matthew - - - - - - - - - - John   Romans - - - - - - - - - - - - Philemon Hebrews . .
Acts

Chart 4.3 - Working for What You Get

Once again, we must emphasize caution. Our review of this subject should not be used as a justification to claim no responsibility to act in a Christian manner. However, if a person **will not** work, then we are doing them wrong by taking care of them in their sin. If they **cannot** work, we have a responsibility to help them. The devil is the "god of this world" right now *(II Corinthians 4:4)*; therefore, we are commanded to hold people accountable for their actions *(Galatians 1:4)*. Asking an able-bodied person to work is scriptural.

III. Jews Only -or- Gentiles Included

One of God's most blessed changes today concerns God's inclusion of the Gentiles in His direct dealings. Under the law and during the Gospel times (Matthew through John), the Gentiles had no way of approaching God, except by becoming a proselyte to Judaism *(Acts 2:10)*. For instance, consider the Lord's commands to His apostles. The Lord severely restricted the apostles' contact with the Gentiles.

"Gospels" *Matthew 10:5 These twelve Jesus sent forth, and commanded them, saying,* **Go not into the way of the Gentiles**, *and into any city of the Samaritans enter ye not: 6 But* **go rather to the lost sheep of the house of Israel***. 7 And as ye go, preach, saying, The kingdom of heaven is at hand.*

The Lord's ministry was to the Jews *only (Matthew 15:24)*. He sent His apostles out likewise. He commanded that they *not* go to the Gentiles. They were to preach the Gospel of the Kingdom the Jews only. One does not find out the extent of this changed directive until reading Paul's first epistle, the book of Romans, which coincides with the historical accounts concerning the Gentiles given in Acts chapters 10 through 28.

The Apostle Paul "contradicts" what the Lord told His followers. Unlike the twelve, Paul's ministry *includes* the Gentiles and is primarily directed toward them. He goes "to the Jew first" *(Romans 1:16)* during the early part of his ministry in order to reach the remnant *(Romans 11:5)*. Yet, God clearly called him to reach the Gentiles with the Gospel of God's Grace.

"Church" *Romans 11:13 For I speak to you Gentiles, inasmuch as* **I am the apostle of the Gentiles***, I magnify mine office:*

Either Paul disobeyed the command given in Matthew chapter 10 (and we are, too) or else God gave Paul (and us) a different set of instructions. There are many other passages that tell about Paul's ministry differing from that of the twelve apostles. If the Lord's command to the twelve prior to the cross applied to Paul and his ministry, then Paul was a disobedient and rebellious "follower."

Jews Only - vs - Gentiles Included

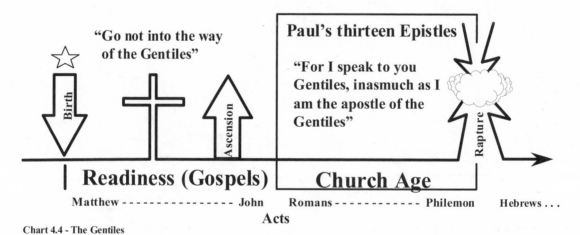

Chart 4.4 - The Gentiles

IV. Tithing -or- Giving Abundantly

Another extremely important issue concerns giving money to the Lord. Tithing (the giving of ten percent) was established prior to the law in the book of Genesis. The nation of Israel does not receive the law until the book of Exodus; therefore, tithing is a pre-law doctrine.

"Pre-law" *Genesis 14:18 And Melchizedek king of Salem brought forth bread and wine: and he was the priest of the most high God. 19 And he blessed him, and said,*

Blessed be Abram of the most high God, possessor of heaven and earth: 20 And blessed be the most high God, which hath delivered thine enemies into thy hand. **And he gave him tithes of all**.

Abram gave Melchizedek a tithe of everything that he had. The practice of tithing was in effect prior to the time of Moses and the law. With the example set by Abram, God said that ten percent of man's possessions belonged to Him.

"Law" **Leviticus 27:30** *And* **all the tithe of the land**, *whether of the seed of the land, or of the fruit of the tree,* **is the LORD'S**: *it is holy unto the LORD. 31 And if a man will at all redeem ought of his tithes, he shall add thereto the fifth part thereof. 32 And concerning the tithe of the herd, or of the flock, even of whatsoever passeth under the rod,* **the tenth shall be holy unto the LORD**.

The tithe was a **requirement** under the law for an individual to be right with the Lord. But what about today? Does God require us to simply tithe? Should a preacher tell his congregation that they must give 10% of their income to the church in order to be right with God? The answer is not a simple yes or no.

The problem arises when a person thinking that he must tithe under the same stipulations as that found under the law, gives out of **necessity**. He is not right with God! God is concerned with your heart being right about giving to Him. The Lord never tells the Church to tithe. Before a Christian thinks this fact releases him of his God-given responsibility to give to the Lord's work, review some of the guidelines for giving during the Church Age.

"Church" **II Corinthians 9:6** *But this I say, He which soweth sparingly shall reap also sparingly; and he which soweth bountifully shall reap also bountifully. 7 Every man according* **as he purposeth in his heart, so let him give; not grudgingly, or of necessity**: *for God loveth a cheerful giver. 8 And God is able to make all grace abound toward you; that ye, always having all sufficiency in all things, may abound to every good work:*

Tithing - vs - Giving Willingly

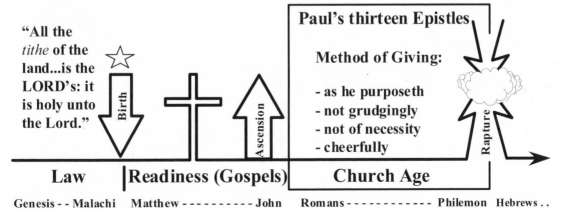

Chart 4.5 - Willingly Giving

God says that if you sow sparingly, you will also reap sparingly. If you sow bountifully, you will reap in like manner. God wants us to give as we purpose in our hearts. We are to give cheerfully, not with a frown on our faces and a heart that **grudgingly** parts with the money. We are to pray about this matter the same way we pray about other things. God promises peace to the Christian that goes before the throne of grace to determine the will of God *(Philippians 4:6-7)*. I have never seen a missions-minded church that limited their giving to a mere tithe.

You might ask, "What is a person to do?" Good question! Sometimes answering a question with a set of questions is the best approach. Here are a few to consider:

1. If God wanted man to tithe before the law, and under the law, how ought we to give?

2. If 10% was a *requirement* under the blood of bulls and goats, what ought we to give under the blood of the Lord Jesus Christ? Should it be less?

3. Just a thought: If you tip a waitress 15% for feeding you well and giving you good service . . . what should be the heart condition of every child of God in our local church when we feast on the manna from heaven that God has led the preacher to provide? Should we get a calculator out and try to compute how much to give or let the Holy Spirit lead?

An important point to remember is that God speaks to every Christian on an individual basis. Your responsibility is to be faithful to the Spirit's leading (even if this means giving 100%). For some people the idea of leaving the outcome in the hands of the Lord is a novel one. However, when God controls the giving, great and mighty things can and do happen. When people freely obey the Spirit's leading, they will generally not be limited to mechanically giving *a mere tithe*. I have seen this truth in action affecting the gospel around the world through faithful giving to missions and to the local church. Bear in mind that when a preacher overemphasizes money, the lost man tunes out everything else with it and may never hear the gospel message!

V. The Gospel of the Kingdom of Heaven -or- The Gospel of the Grace of God

Another *critical* distinction to consider concerns the difference between the messages preached at various times in history. Let us consider one very important distinction between the preaching of the Kingdom by John the Baptist, the Lord Jesus Christ, and the twelve apostles; versus the preaching of the Gospel of the Grace of God by the Apostle Paul.

1. The Preaching of John the Baptist

    "Gospels" *Matthew 3:1 In those days came John the Baptist, **preaching** in the wilderness of Judaea, 2 And saying, Repent ye: for **the kingdom** of heaven is at hand.*

    John the Baptist preached about the Kingdom. He preached that the Kingdom of Heaven was *at hand*. He preached this message because he was the forerunner of the Lord Jesus Christ. The future King was on earth and preparing His people for the time when He would set up His earthly reign. Thus the Lord also preached that the Kingdom of Heaven was *at hand*.

2. The Preaching of the Lord Jesus Christ

    "Gospels" *Matthew 4:17 From that time Jesus **began to preach**, and to say, Repent: for the **kingdom** of heaven is at hand.*

When the Lord Jesus Christ was here, He announced His kingdom to Israel. The Jews as a nation rejected their Messiah/King and this rejection ushered in the present Church Age. The apostles preached the same message.

3. The Preaching of the Twelve Apostles

    "Gospels" *Matthew 10:5 These **twelve** Jesus sent forth, and commanded them, saying, **Go not into the way of the Gentiles**, and into any city of the Samaritans enter ye not: 6 **But go rather to the lost sheep of the house of Israel**. 7 And as ye go, **preach**, saying, **The kingdom** of heaven is at hand.*

These twelve were to preach the same kingdom message as John the Baptist and the Lord —"The kingdom of heaven is at hand." They were to tell **the Jews** to repent and accept their Messiah. Although the transition away from Jewish exclusivity begins to take place at the end of each of the four Gospel books, the Bible records the most definitive shift occurring after Acts chapter 7. As the nation of Israel rejects Stephen's message and stones him to death, we are introduced to the major character of the rest of the book of Acts—the Apostle Paul. Two chapters later, the Bible records Paul's (Saul's) conversion

> *"Turn over Matthew's pages again: look up the many references to the 'kingdom of heaven' which speak of it as yet future, historical, visible. Then try to make them mean a purely spiritual kingdom identifiable with the church—and see how difficult it is."*
>
> J. Sidlow Baxter, *Explore the Book,* 6 vol. in one—volume 5 (Grand Rapids: Zondervan, 1960) p. 162.

to Christ on the road to Damascus. In order to delineate Paul's peculiar ministry, his name is placed as the first word in the next thirteen epistles.

4. The Preaching of the Apostle Paul

    If the gospel was intended to be preached to the Jews only (following the commission given to the apostles), this would mean that Paul was blatantly disobedient. Furthermore, his title would contradict the specific commands of the Lord. This holds true unless some changes occurred under the leadership of Paul during the period in which we find ourselves.

    "Church" *Romans 11:13 For I speak to you Gentiles, inasmuch as **I am the apostle of the Gentiles**, I magnify mine office:*

    Paul clearly states that he is going to the Gentiles and that God gave him this ministry and office. He is the one who plainly spells out the Gospel of the Grace of God. His second book (First Corinthians) explains the gospel during the Church Age.

    "Church" *I Corinthians 15:1 Moreover, brethren, **I declare** unto you **the gospel** which I preached unto you . . . by which also ye are saved . . . how that Christ **died** for our sins according to the scriptures; And that he was **buried**, and that he **rose** again the third day according to the scriptures:*

    God uses the Apostle Paul to **declare** and clearly define the Gospel of the Grace of God in writing. He reveals this gospel: how that the Lord Jesus Christ died for our sins (by shedding His blood), was buried and rose again. John the Baptist, the Lord Jesus Christ, and the twelve all preached the Gospel of the Kingdom. **No obedient, Spirit-led preacher since the first century has preached their message concerning the kingdom because it is not the message we are commanded to deliver during this Church Age.** The message applicable primarily to the nation of Israel, in this case, is *not* applicable to the Church.

We are to preach the Gospel of the Grace of God. We are to tell others that the Lord Jesus Christ will return and the Church will meet Him in the clouds *(I Thessalonians 4:17)*. Thus, our primary message differs greatly from the message represented in the books of Matthew through John. The Church will be taken out of this world prior to His return at the Second Coming to set up His kingdom. The Church will *not* herald in the return of the Lord due to our "diligent" efforts to evangelize the world.

As we have seen, the manner in which Paul came to know the gospel is interesting. One might think that Peter or one of the other apostles taught him. That is simply not the case. Paul received this gospel revelation directly from God. Nobody could reveal it to him or teach him because it was just that . . . a **new** revelation for all of them.

"Church" *Galatians 1:11 But I certify you, brethren, that the gospel which was preached of me is **not after man**. 12 For I **neither received** it of man, **neither was I taught it**, but by the revelation of Jesus Christ.*

Repeatedly, Paul emphasizes that the revelation of the mystery was given to him directly from God (as it was likewise then revealed to the other apostles by the Spirit—*Ephesians 3:5*). Ephesians contains another passage that clearly teaches about the revelation of the mystery given to Paul:

"Church" *Ephesians 3:1 For this cause I Paul, the prisoner of Jesus Christ for you Gentiles, 2 If ye have heard of **the dispensation of the grace of God** which is given me to you-ward: 3 How that **by revelation he made known unto me the mystery**; (as I wrote afore in few words,*

To understand why God had to reveal the mystery directly to Paul, we must examine the period prior to Paul's conversion. **During this time (covered by the vast majority of the four Gospels), no one understood this Gospel of God's Grace.** It was a mystery to all. Not even the twelve apostles understood when the Lord Jesus Christ told them about it. Their eyes (understanding) had to remain shut until *after* the cross. They could hear, but could not understand. For example, in Luke 18 the Lord explains to the twelve apostles about the coming crucifixion and resurrection. *(Be sure to read the next passage with the comments.)*

> *"The revelation of this mystery, which was foretold, but not explained by Christ (Mt. 16:18), was committed to Paul. In his writings alone we find the doctrine, position, walk, and destiny of the church."*
>
> Scofield Reference Bible, Ephesians 3:6 footnote, p. 1252.

"Gospels" *Luke 18:31 Then he took unto him the twelve, and said unto them, Behold, we go up to Jerusalem, and all things that are written by the prophets concerning the Son of man shall be accomplished. 32 For he shall be delivered unto* *the Gentiles, and shall be mocked, and spitefully entreated, and spitted on: 33 And they shall scourge him, and **put him to death: and the third day he shall rise again**.* (This is the gospel according to *I Corinthians 15:1-4*, right? . . . but the next verse says . . .) *34 **And they understood none of these things**: and this saying was **hid from them**, neither knew they the things which were spoken.*

Prior to the cross, the apostles did not understand the Gospel of the Grace of God (the death, burial and resurrection). Be sure not to miss this most important point. No one understood the significance or the necessity of the Lord's death, burial and resurrection. Thus, the apostles certainly did not preach something they did not understand. To understand why God could not clearly reveal the gospel at this time, one must consider that Satan would have tried to stop the cross rather than instigate it. Satan had no idea about the purpose or outcome of the cross.

"Church" *I Corinthians 2:7 But we speak the wisdom of God in a mystery, even the hidden wisdom, which God ordained before the world unto our glory: 8 Which **none of the princes of this world knew**: for had they known it, **they would not have crucified the Lord of glory**.*

The significance of the cross could not be revealed to anyone until **after** the cross. Had the Gospel of Grace *not* been hidden from the apostles, it would not have been hidden from Satan either. We read that the twelve apostles did **not** understand the gospel of God's grace in Luke 18 (above). But nine chapters *earlier* (Luke 9), we find them "preaching the gospel." The apostles certainly could not have been preaching a gospel they did not understand (the Gospel of the Grace of God).

> **"Jesus Himself did not give revelations concerning the course of this age with its rejection of the gospel, its wars, wickedness, and the worldliness of professing Christians, until after He ceased to preach that the kingdom of Heaven is at hand. To Paul the apostle was first given an understanding of some of the mysteries concerning the church in this age. Ephesians 3:1-10 tells us how Paul was given this grace to understand and teach how that Gentiles would be in the same body with Jews, the church. And Ephesians 3:5 expressly says that this mystery was not made known in other ages."**
>
> John R. Rice, *The Coming Kingdom of Christ* (Murfreesboro: Sword of the Lord, 1945), p. 71.

"Gospels" *Luke 9:1 Then he called his twelve disciples together, and gave them power and authority over all devils, and to cure diseases. ...6 And they departed, and went through the towns, **preaching the gospel**, and healing every where.*

The apostles could not preach a gospel they did not understand (as recorded in Luke chapter 18), or one that had not yet been fulfilled. The Lord Jesus Christ had not yet been crucified, so it was impossible for the apostles to preach the gospel as we know it *(I Corinthians 15:1-4)*. What's the answer? Simply this: the Lord came to fulfill the law. By fulfilling the law, He paved the way for the future establishment of His Kingdom. The gospel referenced in Luke chapter 9 is the *Gospel of the Kingdom*. The next verse refers to this gospel.

"Gospels" *Mark 1:14 Now after that John was put in prison, Jesus came into Galilee, preaching **the gospel of the kingdom** of God,*

The Apostle Paul tells us that the gospel we are to preach differs from that referred to in *Mark 1:14*. We are **not** to preach the Gospel of the Kingdom. Rather, we are to preach about what happened on the cross and the result of the cross. **This is not the same gospel as referenced in Mark (above).**

"Church" *I Corinthians 1:17 For Christ sent me not to baptize, but to **preach the gospel**: not with wisdom of words, lest the cross of Christ should be made of none effect. 18 For the **preaching of the cross** is to them that perish foolishness; but unto us which are saved it is the power of God.*

The cross emphasizes Christ's being crucified, buried and risen. The Lord Jesus Christ told the apostles about the cross so that they would believe *after* it happened, but His message (and theirs) was one about the kingdom. Yet, both of these messages (that of the cross and that of the kingdom) are different from the gospel to be preached in the future. The book of Revelation gives a gospel that *the angels* will be preaching to the inhabitants of the earth.

"Tribulation" *Revelation 14:6 And I saw another angel fly in the midst of heaven, having **the everlasting gospel to preach** unto them that dwell on the earth, and to every nation, and kindred, and tongue, and people, 7 Saying with a loud voice, **Fear God, and give glory to him; for the hour of his judgment is come**: and worship him that made heaven, and earth, and the sea, and the fountains of waters.*

This angel will be preaching **the everlasting gospel**. He will be telling people to fear God because His judgment is come to this earth. The next verse gives us the time frame . . . once Babylon has fallen.

*Revelation 14:8 And there followed another angel, saying, **Babylon is fallen,** is fallen, that great city, because she made all nations drink of the wine of the wrath of her fornication.*

Kingdom - vs - Grace

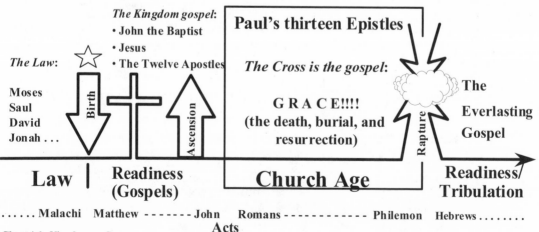

Chart 4.6 - Kingdom vs. Grace

5

Reconciling the Scriptures II

During today's Church Age, a major point of contention among various groups of professing Christians concerns the application of books such as Hebrews and James. The dual application of the book of Hebrews by now should be quite evident to the Bible student. Some of the Tribulational aspects of this book were covered in chapters 3 and 4. Now focus is directed to the book of James.

The Book of James

The book following Hebrews—the book of James—also contains some definite Tribulation features. For this reason, the astute Bible student immediately recognizes the identity of those to whom the book of James is addressed.

"Tribulation" *James 1:1 James, a servant of God and of the Lord Jesus Christ, **to the twelve tribes which are scattered abroad**, greeting.*

The importance of determining the primary application of the books of the Bible has already been established. By simply reading the address, it is easy to see whose "mail" we are reading in the book of James. If this is primarily *your mail*, to which of the **twelve tribes** do you belong? The book of James is addressed to the twelve tribes of the nation of Israel with a message that has some distinctly Tribulational components.

Since Israel as a nation is broken off *(Romans 11:17)* during the Church Age, which of the twelve tribes an individual belongs today is of little consequence. It certainly mattered in the past and it certainly will again be important in the future *(Revelation 7:4),* but it is of no consequence today since national distinctions are eliminated in the Body of Christ. The Apostle Paul writes that there is no difference today between the Jew and non-Jew…whosoever calls upon Christ shall be saved.

"Church" *Romans 10:12 For there is no difference between the Jew and the Greek: for the same Lord over all is rich unto all that call upon him. 13 **For whosoever shall call** upon the name of the Lord shall be saved.*

In fact, the Apostle Paul points out that "in Christ Jesus" there is no longer any distinction between Jew and Greek, bond and free, male and female. We are all one in Christ Jesus.

"Church" *Galatians 3:28 **There is neither Jew nor Greek**, there is neither bond nor free, there is neither male nor female: **for ye are all one in Christ Jesus**.*

Obviously, Galatians refers to the lack of distinctions in a spiritual sense since it certainly matters on a mere physical level whether a person falls into these distinct categories. The point is that Paul's latter epistles uniquely eliminate the distinctions between Jew and Gentile. Only the dishonest or biblically illiterate would seek to claim that there never existed any distinction between Jew and Gentile *(Matthew 2:6, 15:24)*.

These truths are developed even further in the book of Ephesians. The Apostle Paul reminds Gentiles that "in time past" we were without Christ because we were not a part of God's chosen nation. He then points out BUT NOW (verse 13) "in Christ Jesus" the wall that separated us has been broken down.

> "Church" *Ephesians 2:11 Wherefore remember, that ye being in time past Gentiles in the flesh, who are called Uncircumcision by that which is called the Circumcision in the flesh made by hands; 12 That at that time ye were without Christ, being aliens from the commonwealth of Israel, and strangers from the covenants of promise, having no hope, and without God in the world: 13 But now in Christ Jesus ye who sometimes were far off are made nigh by the blood of Christ. 14 For he is our peace, who hath made both one, and hath broken down the middle wall of partition between us;*

The Apostle Paul repeatedly stresses that there is no longer any difference between the Jew and the non-Jew. It would be counterproductive for the books of Hebrews and James to reestablish these distinctions during the Church Age. Paul wrote that he was *"Endeavouring to keep the unity of the Spirit in the bond of peace" (Ephesians 4:3)*. With Hebrews and James addressed to the nation of Israel, the Body of Christ would be divided rather than united. For this reason, these books obviously address the same 144,000 addressed in the book of Revelation.

> "Tribulation" *Revelation 7:3 Saying, Hurt not the earth, neither the sea, nor the trees, till we have sealed the servants of our God in their foreheads. 4 And I heard the number of them which were sealed: and there were sealed an hundred and forty and four thousand of all the tribes of the children of Israel.*

Some commentators place later first century dates to the authorship of these books. However, it seems more likely that James was not familiar with the inspired writings of Paul when he addressed these national distinctions. This would make infinitely more sense if the writings of James preceded those of the Apostle Paul. The note in the introduction to the book of James in the Scofield Reference Bible is quite interesting concerning the possible date of the book of James:

Tradition fixes the martyrdom of James in the year 62, but his Epistle shows no trace of the larger revelations concerning the church and the distinctive doctrines of grace made through the Apostle Paul, nor even of the discussions concerning the relation of Gentile converts to the law of Moses, which culminated in the first council (Acts 15.), over which James presided. This presumes the very early date of James, which may confidently be set down as "the first Epistle to Christians." —Weston.

Scofield Reference Bible, Introduction to James, p. 1306.

It is believed that the Acts chapter 15 council referenced above took place in A.D. 45, which could place the date of this writing prior to Paul's epistles. The emphasis of the book of James is all wrong when attempting to apply its full teaching to the Church during this Age.

Regardless of whether a person agrees with Scofield's supposition or not, the peculiarity of the book of James remains. Studying the Bible dispensationally (biblically) links various emphases of James with the obvious doctrines of the Tribulation. For instance, the book of James mentions the patience of the prophets, specifically mentioning Job by name. James offers Job as an example of someone that patiently suffered affliction.

"Tribulation" *James 5:10 Take, my brethren, the prophets, who have spoken in the name of the Lord, for an example of suffering affliction, and of patience. 11 Behold, we count them happy which endure.* **Ye have heard of the patience of Job,** *and have seen the end of the Lord; that the Lord is very pitiful, and of tender mercy.*

Job pictures how the tribulation saints must endure until they lose their life at the hands of the Antichrist. Job was rich, and he lost everything, at least temporarily. The forty-two chapters of Job have been likened to the forty-two months repeatedly mentioned as the halfway point of the Tribulation.

"Tribulation" *Revelation 11:2 But the court which is without the temple leave out, and measure it not; for it is given unto the Gentiles: and the holy city shall they tread under foot* **forty and two months**. *3 And I will give power unto my two witnesses, and they shall* **prophesy a thousand two hundred and threescore days**, *clothed in sackcloth.*

"Tribulation" *Revelation 13:4 And they worshipped the dragon which gave power unto the beast: and they* **worshipped the beast**, *saying, Who is like unto the beast? who is able to make war with him? 5 And there was given unto him a mouth speaking great things and blasphemies;* **and power was given unto him to continue forty and two months.** *....7 And it was given unto him to make war with the saints, and to overcome them: and power was given him over all kindreds, and tongues, and nations.*

The Beast will have power for one-half of the Tribulation. He will kill the saints of God who refuse to take the Mark of the Beast. In the next passage, the *patience of the saints* is directly associated to the Mark of the Beast and those that die for refusing his Mark. Patience is more than a virtue in the Tribulation.

"Tribulation" *Revelation 14:11 And the smoke of their torment ascendeth up for ever and ever: and they have no rest day nor night, who worship the beast and his image, and* **whosoever receiveth the mark of his name.** *12* **Here is the patience of the saints**: *here are they that keep the commandments of God, and the faith of Jesus. 13 And I heard a voice from heaven saying unto me, Write,* **Blessed are the dead which die in the Lord henceforth:** *Yea, saith the Spirit, that they may rest from their labours; and their works do follow them.*

There are eternal consequences associated with patience during the Tribulation. An individual cannot simply give up, deciding that he or she has waited long enough for the Lord's return. From beginning to end, the book of James communicates the necessity of having endur-ing patience *(Matthew 24:13)*.

"Tribulation" *James 1:2 My brethren, count it all joy when ye fall into divers tempta-tions; 3 Knowing this, that **the trying of your faith worketh patience.** 4 **But let pa-tience have her perfect work**, that ye may be perfect and entire, wanting nothing.*

Those in the Tribulation are to "count as joy" their temptations because tribulation tries their faith and strengthens their patience. The final chapter of James commands the Tribulation saint to be patient until the *coming of the Lord,* promising that the Lord's return draws near. The Holy Spirit will obviously use passages like these to encourage the Tribulation saints to endure to the end during this future period of time.

"Tribulation" *James 5:7 **Be patient therefore, brethren, unto the coming of the Lord.** Behold, the husbandman waiteth for the precious fruit of the earth, and hath long patience for it, until he receive the early and latter rain. 8 **Be ye also patient**; stablish your hearts: for **the coming of the Lord draweth nigh**. 9 Grudge not one against another, brethren, lest ye be condemned: behold, **the judge standeth be-fore the door.***

Although the emphasis on patience described herein is quite obvious, the other Tribulation expressions in the passage are equally revealing. The *early and latter rain* (verse 7 above) refers to promises made to Israel concerning the timing of their future blessings. Many scrip-tures reveal this great prophecy.

The Early and Latter Rain

The Bible relates the seasonal rains that revive the earth to the reviving of God's chosen people. James refers to the early and latter rain and the fact that the husbandman patiently waits for these rains to come.

*James 5:7 Be patient therefore, brethren, unto the coming of the Lord. Behold, the **husbandman waiteth** for the precious fruit of the earth, and hath long patience for it, **until he receive the early and latter rain.***

Ten verses later in James, the Bible mentions Elijah's prayer that stopped the rain for three and one-half years.

*James 5:17 Elias was a man subject to like passions as we are, and he prayed earnestly that it might not rain: and **it rained not on the earth by the space of three years and six months.***

This same period of time (3½ years, forty-two months, or 1,260 days) is repeatedly men-tioned in Revelation as associated with events during the Tribulation *(Revelation 11:2-3, 13:4-5)*. The next passage refers to "After two days" which marks the end of the Tribulation. "The third day" refers to the beginning of the final Millennium—the thousand year reign of Christ on the earth.

*Hosea 6:2 **After two days** will he revive us: in **the third day** he will raise us up, and we shall live in his sight. 3 Then shall we know, if we follow on to know the LORD: his going forth is prepared as the morning; and **he shall come unto us as the rain, as the latter and former rain unto the earth.***

Hosea refers to a literal resurrection of the nation of Israel. *After two days* (the end of the Tribulation), the Lord will revive the nation of Israel. He will raise up this nation to the prominence that it once held. The book of Psalms says that God sends a plentiful rain to confirm His inheritance.

Psalm 68:9 *Thou, O* **God, didst send a plentiful rain, whereby thou didst confirm thine inheritance,** *when it was weary.*

Hebrews 6:7 *For the earth which drinketh in the rain that cometh oft upon it,* **and** *bringeth forth herbs meet for them by whom it is dressed,* **receiveth blessing from God:**

All of these truths are best summed up in the book of Second Samuel which provides a beautiful picture of these truths.

II Samuel 23:4 *And he shall be as the light of the morning, when the sun riseth, even a morning without clouds; as the tender grass springing out of the earth by clear shining* **after rain**.

Condemnation of the Rich in the Tribulation

During the Tribulation, the satanic powers in control of the whole earth will compel the world to take the Mark of the Beast. No one will be permitted to buy or sell any thing unless he accepts this Mark. The Bible describes the Beast's control of the world systems during this time as absolute.

"Tribulation" **Revelation 13:16 And he causeth all, both small and great, rich and poor,** *free and bond, to receive a mark in their right hand, or in their foreheads: 17 And that* **no man might buy or sell, save he that had the mark,** *or the name of the beast, or the number of his name. 18 Here is wisdom. Let him that hath understanding count the number of the beast: for it is the number of a man; and* **his number is Six hundred threescore and six** (666).

Being rich in the Tribulation means one of two things. Either the individual has taken the Mark allowing him to buy and sell or he is hoarding his goods during these final days, refusing to share with those in dire need. For this reason, God unconditionally condemns the rich during the Tribulation period.

"Tribulation" **James 1:10 But the rich, in that he is made low:** *because as the flower of the grass he shall pass away. 11 For the sun is no sooner risen with a burning heat, but it withereth the grass, and the flower thereof falleth, and the grace of the fashion of it perisheth:* **so also shall the rich man fade away in his ways**.

The rich who abide by the rules during the Tribulation will have a financial stake in seeing others take the Mark. For this reason, James says that the rich men oppress and draw God's people before the judgment seats (attempting to compel them to take the Mark).

"Tribulation" **James 2:6** *But ye have despised the poor.* **Do not rich men oppress you, and draw you before the judgment seats?** *7 Do not they blaspheme that worthy name by the which ye are called?*

These rich people are anti-Christ. They blaspheme the name of Christ. The book of Matthew reveals the heartrending conditions during this time. Family members will deliver up their "loved ones" causing those who refuse the Mark to be put to death.

"Tribulation" *Matthew 10:19 But when they deliver you up*, *take no thought how or what ye shall speak: for it shall be given you in that same hour what ye shall speak. 20 For it is not ye that speak, but the Spirit of your Father which speaketh in you. 21 **And the brother shall deliver up the brother to death**, and the father the child: and the children shall rise up against their parents, and cause them to be put to death. 22 And ye shall be hated of all men for my name's sake: **but he that endureth to the end shall be saved.***

Only those believers who withstand the spiritual onslaught will be spared. The last chapter of James, like the first, also warns the rich during the Tribulation. The rich are to weep and howl as they reap what they sow. James warns those hoarding their belongings. They will find their riches corrupted, moth-eaten, cankered and rusted. The Bible says that their riches will witness against them during this time because of their refusal to share them with the brethren.

"Tribulation" *James 5:1 Go to now,* ***ye rich men, weep and howl for your miseries that shall come upon you. 2 Your riches are corrupted, and your garments are motheaten. 3 Your gold and silver is cankered; and the rust of them shall be a witness against you,*** *and shall eat your flesh as it were fire. Ye have heaped treasure together for the last days.*

It is important not to miss the full implications of these statements. The book of James condemns the rich for being rich. However, the Apostle Paul simply charges the rich to use their wealth wisely. He tells the rich to be ready and willing to use those riches for the work of God. In doing so, they will be storing up treasures in heaven.

*I Timothy 6:17 **Charge them that are rich in this world,*** *that they be not highminded, nor trust in uncertain riches, but in the living God, who giveth us richly all things to enjoy; 18 **That they do good, that they be rich in good works, ready to distribute, willing to communicate;*** *19 Laying up in store for themselves a good foundation against the time to come, that they may lay hold on eternal life.*

Contrasting Paul's charge to the rich with the outright condemnation of the rich by James is a real eye opener to the astute Bible student. However, not everyone reads the book of James in this manner. Frequently, the doctrinal application of the book of James is obscured by the preconceived assumptions brought to one's Bible study.

Those who struggle with a future application of these books

> **"Again, it is not unreasonable to recognize that these kingdom teachings should directly apply to a future age…Certain revelations are of the coming tribulation period and are in no sense applicable to the present time. Who has ever prayed that his flight should not be on a Sabbath day? Yet Christ commanded that prayer to be prayed (Matt. 24:20)"**
>
> L.S. Chafer, *Systematic Theology*, Volume 4, (TX: Dallas Seminary Press, 1947) p. 224-225.

usually wonder to whom these particular doctrines directly applied when the books were origi-nally written. If these books applied to the earliest of first century churches, the record would be found in the early part of the book of Acts. And it is. During this time, there were to be no rich Christians either. None whatsoever. The early converts to Christ sold all of their possessions and turned their money over to the apostles. The apostles then distributed the money according to each individual's particular needs. All possessions were to be given up for the common good, leaving no obedient rich Christian in the early church.

*Acts 2:44 And all that believed were together, and **had all things common**; 45 And **sold their possessions and goods, and parted them to all men, as every man had need**.*

Verse 14 of this same chapter reveals the spokesman (Peter) and the identity of those to whom he was speaking ("Ye men of Judaea, and all ye that dwell at Jerusalem"). Peter, like all faithful Christians in the first century, obediently forfeited all of his belongings. Peter's words to the lame man in the very next chapter literally meant that he had no money.

*Acts 3:6 Then Peter said, **Silver and gold have I none**; but such as I have give I thee: In the name of Jesus Christ of Nazareth rise up and walk.*

Peter did not own anything! However, he was far from unique in this regard. None of the other faithful followers of the Lord Jesus Christ *at that time* retained any of their possessions. All of the believers had all things common and did not claim any personal ownership of the things which he had previously possessed. Everyone who followed Christ was on economic common ground.

*Acts 4:32 And **the multitude of them that believed** were of one heart and of one soul: neither said any of them that ought of the things which he possessed was his own; but they **had all things common**. 33 And with great power gave the apostles witness of the resurrection of the Lord Jesus: and great grace was upon them all. 34 Neither was there any among them that lacked: for as many as were **possessors of lands or houses sold them**, and brought the prices of the things that were sold, 35 And laid them down at the apostles' feet: and **distribution was made unto every man according as he had need**.*

During this time, none of the believers lacked for any of the necessities since the rich gave up their riches. God even provides an example of a couple that wanted to keep back part of their riches. Ananias and Sapphira were two who lied about their "faithful" service in an attempt to look spiritual.

These two kept back part of the price of a possession they sold, bringing only a portion of the money to the apostles. As a result of their lying, each of them literally dropped dead *(Acts 5:5, 10)*. They died because they claimed to have sold their land for a certain price but actually sold it for more. The early church reading the book of James would have understood and accepted the condemnation of the rich during the first century. The application of these passages in this way to the church today would be twisting them. Everything changed once the nation of Israel refused to repent and turn to God—stoning God's messenger to death *(Acts 7:58)*.

The Bible student must recognize another distinction concerning the gospel and the end of time. Those that fail to acknowledge this next point cannot legitimately claim to believe in the imminent return of Christ. In fact, many of the a-millennialists and post-millennialists believe their erroneous positions because of misunderstandings regarding the following truth.

Gospel Preached in all the World?

The Lord Jesus Christ said the end would come when the Gospel (**of the Kingdom**) was preached throughout the entire world. This has not happened yet, but it will occur when the two Witnesses *(Revelation 11:3)* and the 144,000 *(Revelation 7:4)* preach this gospel to every creature.

"Gospels" *Matthew 24:14 And **this gospel of the kingdom** shall be preached in all the world for a witness unto all nations; and **then shall the end come**.*

It is grave error not to make a distinction between "this gospel" of the Kingdom in Matthew chapter 24 and "my gospel" of the Grace of God in Romans chapter 16. The Apostle Paul points out that *"my gospel...now is made manifest, and made known to all nations."*

"Church" *Romans 16:25 Now to him that is of power to stablish you according to **my gospel**, and the preaching of Jesus Christ, according to the revelation of the mystery, which was kept secret since the world began, 26 But **now is made manifest, and** by the scriptures of the prophets, according to the commandment of the everlasting God, **made known to all nations** for the obedience of faith:*

These two gospels (from Matthew and the book of Romans) cannot be the same. The gospel of Matthew chapter 24 is not the one to which Paul refers in the book of Colossians. Paul refers to a gospel that has already come into all the world by the time he writes his latter epistles. If it is the same gospel, then the end should have come already. During Paul's ministry **in the first century** the Gospel of the Grace of God was spread over the entire world.

"Church" *Colossians 1:5 For the hope which is laid up for you in heaven, whereof ye heard before in the word of the truth of **the gospel**; 6 Which is **come unto you, as it is in all the world**; and bringeth forth fruit, as it doth also in you, since the day ye heard of it, and knew the grace of God in truth:*

A few verses later in the same book, Paul goes on to tell us that the Gospel (of God's Grace) has been preached to every creature under heaven too.

"Church" *Colossians 1:23 If ye continue in the faith grounded and settled, and be not moved away from the hope of the gospel, which ye have heard, **and which was preached to every creature which is under heaven**; whereof I Paul am made a minister;*

During Paul's missionary journeys, we read that all those who dwelt in Asia "heard the word of the Lord Jesus" *(Acts 19:10)*.

A distinction must be made between the Gospel of the Kingdom and the Gospel of the Grace of God. Failing to do so will cause one to attribute contradictions to the word of God. Obviously, Paul was not referring to the same gospel preaching that the Lord Jesus Christ was referring to in Matthew chapter 24 when He said the end would come as soon as that gospel went out into all of the world. The gospel of Matthew chapter 24 will go out into the entire world during the Tribulation.

Jews Only - vs - Gentiles Included

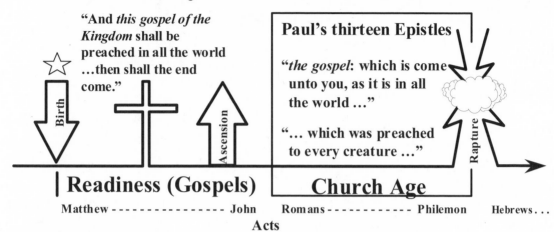

"And *this gospel of the Kingdom* shall be preached in all the world ...then shall the end come."

Birth

Ascension

Paul's thirteen Epistles

"*the gospel*: which is come unto you, as it is in all the world ..."

"... which was preached to every creature ..."

Rapture

Readiness (Gospels) | **Church Age**

Matthew - - - - - - - - - - - - - - - John   Romans - - - - - - - - - - - Philemon   Hebrews...

Acts

Chart 4.7 - Gospel in all the World

Losing the Spirit of God -or- Sealed by the Spirit until Redemption

The teaching that everyone during **all** ages received the Holy Spirit in an identical fashion is ludicrous. For instance, David received the Spirit of the Lord at *his anointing as King* of Israel. It would seem obvious that David did *not* have the Holy Spirit prior to this time. Otherwise, why would the Bible record that he received the Spirit at his anointing?

"Law" *I Samuel 16:13 Then Samuel took the horn of oil, and **anointed** him in the midst of his brethren: and **the Spirit of the LORD came upon David** from that day forward. So Samuel rose up, and went to Ramah.*

If everyone has received the Spirit in the same way throughout the ages, then why would the Bible record that David received the Spirit of God at his anointing? **Every** Christian receives the Spirit of God the moment when he believes on the Lord Jesus Christ. However, receiving the Holy Spirit in this manner differs greatly from what is recorded in the Old Testament. These differences can be easily reconciled. Once again, the student of the Bible must rightly divide it and consider that the method of God's dealings today varies considerably from His method of dealing with Israel in the past (and yet in the future). In this case, the difference is both easy to recognize and easy to reconcile when simply compared to the Church Age epistles.

"Church" *Ephesians 1:13 In whom ye also **trusted**, after that ye heard the word of truth, the gospel of your salvation: in whom also **after that ye believed, ye were sealed with that holy Spirit of promise**,*

During the Church Age, a person receives the Spirit of God when he believes on the Lord Jesus Christ at salvation. *Ephesians 1:13* gives a clear sequence of events: You hear the word of truth (the gospel) and trust in Christ when you believe. At that moment, the Holy Spirit seals the Christian until his body is finally redeemed *(Ephesians 4:30, Romans 8:23)*.

As we have already seen, many passages clearly reveal that the Old Testament saints did not receive the Spirit of God in the same manner as the Christian today. Not only did they receive the Holy Spirit in a different way, but they could also *lose* the Spirit. One example is the record of Saul's losing the Spirit of the Lord and receiving an evil spirit in its place.

"Law" *I Samuel 16:14 But the **Spirit of the LORD departed from Saul**, and an evil spirit from the LORD troubled him.*

Because of disobedience, God took the Spirit of the LORD from King Saul. Saul also lost the mercy of God.

"Law" *II Samuel 7:15 But my **mercy** shall not depart away from him (David), **as I took it from Saul**, whom I put away before thee.*

Praise the Lord, a Christian in the Church Age does not have to fear losing God's mercy or His Spirit. Yet, David was fearful of the same thing happening to him after his sin with Bathsheba. His prayer in Psalm chapter 51 should seem foreign to those of us who understand the promises given to the Church. David did not want God to take the Holy Spirit from him in the same fashion that the Holy Spirit was taken from King Saul. Why else would David pray the following prayer?

"Law" *Psalms 51:10 Create in me a clean heart, O God; and renew a right spirit within me. 11 Cast me not away from thy presence; and **take not thy holy spirit from me**.*

Losing Spirit of God - vs - Sealed until Redemption

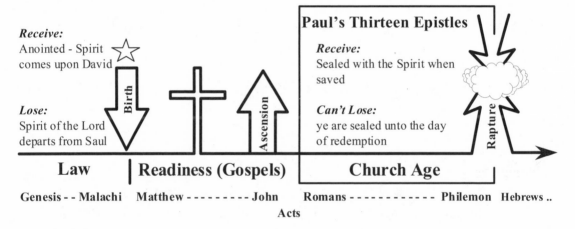

Chart 5.5 - Losing the Spirit

David earnestly prayed because he did not have the same promise given to the Church Age saint in *Ephesians 4:30*. He had witnessed Saul lose the Spirit of the Lord and knew that he could lose it too. Not so today—the Bible plainly teaches that a Christian cannot lose the Holy Spirit. A Christian would be scripturally incorrect to pray the same thing as David did in Psalm chapter 51.

"Church" *Ephesians 4:30 And grieve not the holy Spirit of God, whereby **ye are sealed unto the day of redemption**.*

The Holy Spirit seals the Christian until the day of redemption. The day of redemption is the day that our mortal bodies are *redeemed* and changed into glorified bodies *(Philippians 3:21)*. In Psalm chapter 51, David appealed to the Lord not to take away His Holy Spirit. He had committed adultery; he killed Uriah; he numbered the people. David had good reason to be concerned! Should a preacher apply these same truths to a Christian losing the Holy Spirit today? If not, why not? The Bible student's answer should come from an understanding of the teaching and application of *II Timothy 2:15*—rightly dividing the word of truth.

David needed to ask God to be merciful to him beyond a strict application of the law. God could have taken the Holy Spirit and condemned David, but God extended grace instead. In contrast, God **guarantees** us the grace we need to keep the Holy Spirit, no matter what our actions *(Romans 5:20)*. It is inconceivable that anyone would desire to place himself "under the law" today *(Galatians 4:21, 5:18)*.

The just shall live by *his* faith -or- By faith (the faith of the Lord Jesus Christ)

Even the concept of faith has a peculiar application specific to the Church Age. Take note of the distinct differences regarding faith in the next two references. The first scripture refers to a person under the law.

"Law" *Habakkuk 2:4 Behold, his soul which is lifted up is not upright in him: but the just shall live by **his** faith.*

Under the law *(Romans 6:14)*, a person was to live by his own faith. During that time, an individual's personal faith frequently wavered and was found lacking. For this reason, faith is only mentioned twice in the entire Old Testament. This faith differs from the faith of the child of God today who lives by the *faith of* the Lord Jesus Christ. Paul does not emphasize the individual's personal faith, but something far greater and vastly more effectual.

Take note of the one little word *his* in the previous verse. As God leads Paul to exclude this one word from his quotation of Habakkuk, the whole meaning changes when quoted by him in the book of Romans. The child of God is no longer limited to living by his *own* faith, but by something far greater.

"Church" *Romans 1:17 For therein is the righteousness of God revealed from **faith to faith**: as it is written, The just shall live **by faith**.*

The Old Testament saints did not have the permanently indwelling Lord Jesus Christ as we Church Age saints do *(Colossians 1:27)*. We are to live by the faith of the Lord Jesus Christ. Therefore, when Paul quotes Habakkuk in *Romans 1:17*, God changes the meaning by removing that one word—*his*. Christians are to use their small faith to tap into His great faith. The Bible emphasizes God, His faith and His faithfulness; whereas, man tends to emphasize his own self-sufficiency. Contrary to popular teachings, no one is saved by producing sufficient faith to be accepted of God.

The Romans verse also distinguishes between the different faiths when it says **from faith to faith**. The Lord Jesus Christ died for each of us and was faithful unto the end. Thank the Lord we are saved by *His* faith. The faith of the Lord Jesus Christ saves us and it keeps us day by day. Daily, the child of God is to live by *His* (Christ's) faith and not his own personal measure of faith. Galatians clearly indicates the faith we are to live by.

*Galatians 2:20 I am crucified with Christ: nevertheless I live; yet not I, but Christ liveth in me: and the life which I now live in the flesh **I live by the faith of the Son of God,** who loved me, and gave himself for me.*

We are *not* to live by our own faith during the Church Age . . . praise God! We have something far greater than our own faith . . . something which never falters or wavers . . . something that is absolutely dependable one hundred percent of the time. As we have seen, the faith of the Lord Jesus Christ differs from the Old Testament faith. Hebrews also seems to give a different perspective in the age yet to come.

"Tribulation" *Hebrews 10:38 Now the just shall live by faith: but if any man draw back, my soul shall have no pleasure in him.*

The *context* of the verse here in Hebrews indicates that the faith mentioned is the individual's faith. Compare the outcome of this faith (one can draw back) with the following four points on the faith of the Lord Jesus Christ.

Living by his faith - vs - Living by the faith of Christ

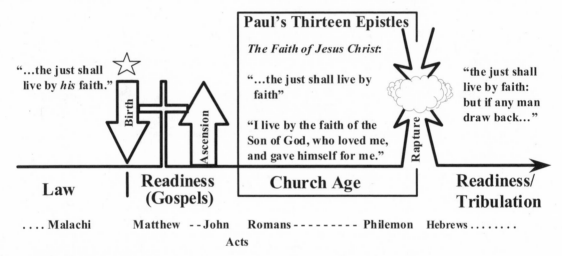

Chart 5.8 - The just Shall Live by

I. Righteousness comes through the faith of the Lord Jesus Christ

*Philippians 3:9 And be found in him, not having mine own **righteousness**, which is of the law, but that **which is through the faith of Christ**, the righteousness which is of God by faith:*

The law reveals that we are all condemned and under the curse of sin and its consequences. After the law convicts us concerning our sinful condition, we sense our need for a Saviour and look to Jesus, the author and finisher of our faith *(Hebrews 12:2)*, who was made a curse in our place *(Galatians 3:13)*.

The promise (BY FAITH OF JESUS CHRIST) is given to all of them that *believe*. Before this saving faith came, we were *"kept under the law"* and its condemnation *(John 3:18)*. Because of our new state, Christians are no longer *"under the law, but under grace" (Romans 6:14)*. Thankfully, the law served as our schoolmaster to bring us unto Christ and His saving faith. It is the law that schools us concerning sin and condemnation, directing us toward Him, and the faith of Jesus Christ that justifies, cleanses and saves us from our sin.

The Bible says that Christ became sin to take away our sin and give us His righteousness in its place. Once a person trusts in Christ, the pre-Adamic spiritual relationship is reinstituted. Once again man has the opportunity to "walk" in complete fellowship with God *(1 Thessalonians 4:1)*. It is only *the faith of Jesus Christ* that enables us to live the life God intended for us. In fact, He lives in us and through us.

II. The promise (the Holy Spirit) is given by the faith of the Lord Jesus Christ

*Galatians 3:22 But the scripture hath concluded all under sin, that **the promise by faith of Jesus Christ might be given to them that believe.** 23 But before faith came, we were kept under the law, shut up unto the faith which should afterwards be revealed.*

The Bible refers to the Spirit as coming by promise *(Galatians 3:14)* because of the faith of Jesus Christ. We were kept under the law "before faith **came**." What faith came? The faith of Jesus Christ! Where did it come from? Jesus Christ!

III. We are justified (saved) by the faith of the Lord Jesus Christ

*Galatians 2:16 Knowing that a man is not **justified** by the works of the law, but **by the faith of Jesus Christ,** even we have believed in Jesus Christ, that we might be **justified by the faith of Christ**, and not by the works of the law: for by the works of the law shall no flesh be justified.*

God does not force the faith of Jesus Christ upon anyone. It comes as a result of obediently following the scriptural admonition to *believe* on the Lord Jesus Christ. There is no such thing as irresistible grace (or faith)—everyone has the free will to make these choices. Every man is given enough faith of his own to put faith in Jesus Christ *(Romans 12:3)*. Our simple belief and faulty faith is made perfect by the faith given to us freely by God.

God does not save anyone apart from his or her decision to believe. We believe in order to be *justified by the faith of Jesus Christ (Galatians 2:16)*. Our simple belief in Christ allows us to be saved by *the faith of Jesus Christ*. We must believe but the justification comes from His faith, not simply our own!

IV. We have boldness and access by the faith of the Lord Jesus Christ

*Ephesians 3:12 In whom we have **boldness and access with confidence by the faith of him.***

We live by His faith. The Christian need never timidly approach God through prayer. The faith of the Lord Jesus Christ gives boldness and access to the divine throne room. Without the faith of the Lord Jesus, we would not have this access and certainly would lack the boldness in approaching Him having no basis for any such relationship.

God demands holiness *(Ephesians 1:4, I Peter 1:16)*, purity, righteousness and perfection. Fortunately, that which an infinitely holy God has demanded, He Himself also supplies through His love and by His grace. God's Son took upon Himself the form of human flesh. That which man could not do because of the weakness of the flesh *(Romans 8:3)*, God sent His own Son to conquer for us, bearing in His own body the sin of all mankind. God imputes Christ's attributes to those who choose Christ during this lifetime.

The law was given to function as our schoolmaster *prior to salvation* to bring us unto Christ. God's law warns against evil, places His standards before us, and reveals how far short of His righteous standards we come *(Romans 3:23)*. The natural man lacks the capacity within himself to attain to the standards of God's law. This is one of the main reasons that God gives us His Spirit after we trust in His Son, enabling us to live for Him and fulfill His law *(Romans 13:8, Galatians 5:14)*.

An understanding of *justification* is very important. A person that is justified is regarded and treated as if innocent. Since the Christian has been effectively acquitted by God, the Lord now sees the saint in light of the righteousness of His Son. The sinner's acquittal is *not* based on the sinner's own works, in whole or in part, but completely upon the atoning work and merits of Jesus Christ. Christ was treated as a sinner that we may be treated as righteous *(II Corinthians 5:21)*.

Salvation is not what *we do,* but what we trust *Him to have done* for us. For this reason, the scripture never tells the lost person that his personal faith alone must save him. The Bible simply commands him to *believe* on the Lord Jesus Christ *(Romans 10:14)*, having repented of trusting in anything else *(Acts 20:21)*. We are saved by faith, and **that faith** is a gift from God. No one can create or muster the faith sufficient for salvation, regardless of how fervently he works at it. Salvation is the work of God purchased by the blood of Christ and the power of His resurrection. We believe, but He does the full work of salvation.

Saving faith is the gift referred to in the second chapter of Ephesians. There is nothing that a person can do to earn or deserve the faith to be saved. Receiving Jesus Christ as one's personal Saviour leaves no room for pride or the self-satisfaction that comes from doing something to earn heaven. If only one believes, **God freely gives him the faith to be saved**!

*Ephesians 2:8 For by grace are ye saved through **faith**; and **that not of yourselves**: it is the gift of God: 9 Not of works, lest any man should boast.*

Faith saves! Whose faith? Notice that the verse says that *"that* (faith) *is not OF yourselves."* Praise God! Saving faith is a gift from God. This particular faith is almost exclusively found in Paul's epistles. The books of the Old Testament mention faith only twice. Nowhere does the word of God reveal that the Old Testament saints were ever promised or given the same faith that we receive today.

> *"...the Lord is dealing with thee on terms of grace, and does not say, 'I will not smite thee because thou dost not believe,' but he saith, 'I will give thee faith,' for faith is 'not of yourselves, it is the gift of God.'"*
>
> Sermon by Charles Haddon Spurgeon, *Salvation All of Grace,* p. 5.

Shamefully, most Bible colleges and seminaries have completely overlooked or ignored these important truths. Doctrines like *the faith of Jesus Christ* reveal the importance of recognizing the special significance of Paul's thirteen Church Age epistles. He wrote to and for the Church and no other group. Unlike the other apostles, Paul was not saved until the Church Age had already begun *(Romans 16:7, I Corinthians 15:9, Galatians 1:13, 23, Philippians 3:6)*. The three succeeding chapters reveal the Apostle Paul's unique ministry to the Church.

6

God's Chosen Vessel
(Who Paul is)

The importance placed upon Paul and his epistles in the preceding five chapters may disturb the observant reader. This emphasis on his ministry may lead the reader to assume that Paul is somehow being improperly elevated in this book. The scriptural proof included in the next three chapters will help the reader to determine whether this emphasis of the Apostle Paul is biblically sound. Through prayer and the leading of the Holy Spirit, the reader should come to the right conclusion.

Throughout the Old Testament, God used many different prophets to deliver His word to the world. Paul's epistles shift this emphasis to one man. They also reveal God's focus redirected from the nation of Israel *to the Gentiles*. Since the middle of the first century, the Gentile nations have been God's chosen New Testament instruments to evangelize the world *(Romans 11:25)*.

In this chapter, the scriptural evidence proving Paul's position as the apostle to the Gentiles will be examined. The Bible states that Paul was ordained and appointed a preacher and an apostle of the Gentiles. It also states that he was the minister of the Lord Jesus Christ *to the Gentiles*. In these capacities, Paul obediently laid the foundation for us and supplied the pattern for the Church to follow.

But first a little review . . .

A modified time line best represents the chronology of the Bible. Bible believers agree that the chronology of time, as man experiences it, starts in Genesis and ends in the book of Revelation. During most of the Old Testament, the Lord operated almost exclusively through the nation of Israel. The Gentile nations' contacts with God were generally incidental or occurred through the Jews.

The four Gospel books follow the thirty-nine Old Testament books. In these four books (Matthew, Mark, Luke and John) we read of the Lord Jesus Christ and his twelve apostles delivering God's message to the *Jews only*. The next book (Acts) is known as a transition book where God moves:

- From the Jews to the Gentiles

- From law to grace

- From Peter and the other apostles to the Apostle Paul

Prior to Paul's conversion to the Lord Jesus Christ, the scriptures reveal that God had a plan and purpose for him. God picked Paul to be His chosen vessel to bear the name of Christ to the

Gentiles, to kings, and to the children of Israel *(Acts 9:15)*. Although we may take it for granted, God's inclusion of the Gentiles in this list is highly significant. For thousands of years prior to this time, God dealt almost exclusively through and with His chosen people, the Jews. The Gentiles had access to God only through the Jews.

Although Paul initially ministered to the *Jew first* during the early part of his ministry *(Romans 1:16)*, the primary direction of his ministry was ultimately to be as the *apostle of the Gentiles*. Scripture proves and reinforces this truth. From the beginning when Paul (Saul) is introduced in the book of Acts, the Bible shows that his life and calling were unique. Even his conversion experience was unprecedented and clearly occurred on the heels of a pivotal time in the New Testament. The impact of Paul's conversion was so important that the book of Acts records his conversion three times in Acts chapters 9, 22, and 26. His unusual conversion was just a foreshadowing of his unique ministry.

> *Acts 9:15   But the Lord said unto him* (Ananias)*, Go thy way: for he* (Paul) *is **a chosen vessel unto me**, to bear my name before the Gentiles, and kings, and the children of Israel:*

Any Bible student with a thorough understanding of Paul's ministry agrees that his ministry was unlike any other. Following Paul's conversion in the book of Acts, he authored the following thirteen books of the Bible to the Body of Christ. The Apostle Paul reveals aspects about God's grace that are *not* revealed anywhere else in the scriptures.

The book of Acts is located in the Bible prior to Paul's epistles. God placed this book between two distinct groupings of books. Basically, the book of Acts begins where the Gospel books leave off (the ascension) and transitions into Paul's ministry and writings to the Church. Thus, Bible students recognize the book of Acts as a transition book. Acts transitions the Bible student *from* the four Gospel books covering the Jewish ministry of the Lord Jesus Christ *to the book of Romans* (named after a Gentile people).

The book of Romans is the first book, in a series of thirteen consecutive books, beginning with the word *Paul*. The Apostle Paul addresses these thirteen books to the Church (the Body of Christ—*Colossians 1:18, 24*). Paul clearly states that he is *not* sent to the "Jews only" as were the Lord Jesus Christ, Peter and the other apostles *(Matthew 15:24, 10:6)*. Even Paul's God-given title clearly reflects that his ministry differed considerably from the ministries of all others that preceded him.

Apostle to the Gentiles

The Lord appears to Paul while he is unmercifully killing Christians. The Lord saves him and sends him forth to minister Christ *to the Gentiles*. Thus, Paul's title becomes the *apostle to the Gentiles*. Paul was obedient to his calling. God instructed him to magnify his particular office so that others could learn about his calling. God led him to write verses like *Romans 11:13* for this purpose.

> *Romans 11:13   For I speak to you Gentiles, inasmuch as **I am the apostle of the Gentiles**, I magnify mine office:*

Paul obediently magnified his office, thus enabling others to recognize this office. Every Christian should understand how his office differs from all others. Unlike the Lord and the twelve who were sent to the Jews *(Matthew 15:24)*, Paul clearly stated that he was sent to the Gentiles. Too many "scholars" are either ignorant of or ignore the significance of Paul's office and position. In fact, many of the schisms in the Body of Christ find their roots here. These "scholars" incorrectly teach the preachers, and preachers then incorrectly instruct their congregations. The congregations do not know what to believe and are convinced that no one can be absolutely sure of the correct doctrine.

We should magnify Paul's office in the same fashion that he did. Once an individual recognizes the existence of Paul's office, he might wonder how Paul obtained this particular position. No other person held this office before him, and no one replaced him. So, why Paul? The Bible says that God ordained Paul to this position.

Ordained a preacher and an apostle

*I Timothy 2:7 Whereunto I am **ordained a preacher, and an apostle**, (I speak the truth in Christ, and lie not;) a teacher **of the Gentiles** in faith and verity.*

Clearly, the scriptures teach that Paul was *ordained* a preacher and an apostle *of the Gentiles*. Yet, his ordination was unlike any other ordination recorded in the scriptures. God personally ordained this apostle to his position; this fact alone should further magnify the significance of Paul's office.

Appointed a preacher, apostle and teacher

In addition to being ordained, the scriptures state that the Apostle Paul was *appointed* to his position. His appointment was also not man-made and included the position of teacher.

*II Timothy 1:11 Whereunto I am appointed a **preacher**, and an **apostle**, and a **teacher** of the Gentiles.*

Recognizing Paul's office can be the single most enlightening Church Age issue for any serious Bible student today. The significance of his position should not be ignored or minimized. He was appointed by God to be a preacher, apostle and teacher of the Gentiles. No other man could make a scriptural claim to this same appointment.

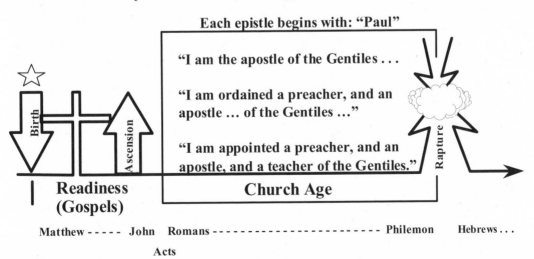

Chart 6.1 - Paul: Apostle, Ordained, Appointed

As we have seen, God ordained and appointed Paul to be a preacher, an apostle, and a teacher *of the Gentiles*. Since the scriptures record these facts, every Christian must determine exactly what doctrinal and practical application this holds. The remainder of this chapter is devoted to doing just that. By spending a little time in Bible study, the student can clearly determine what effect Paul's writings should have on those people living *today*.

Minister of Jesus Christ

Repeatedly, the Holy Spirit led Paul to emphasize his peculiar ministry. In the next verse, Paul indicates that he is *the minister* of Jesus Christ to the Gentiles. The verse also reveals *what* he is ministering. He is ministering the gospel of God. The Church should definitely listen to the man chosen of God to minister His Son to us.

> **Romans 15:16** *That I should be **the minister of Jesus Christ to the Gentiles**, ministering the gospel of God, that the **offering up of the Gentiles** might be acceptable, being sanctified by the Holy Ghost.*

Paul ministers Jesus Christ to us (the Church). He reveals the truth, thus enabling the Gentiles to be an acceptable offering to God when presented to Him. Furthermore, as the apostle to the Gentiles, he is the God-called vessel to lay the foundation.

Our Foundation

Our foundation is clearly the gospel that Paul preached *(I Corinthians 15:1-4)* . . .

- How that the Lord Jesus Christ died for our sins
- That He was buried
- That He arose again

To claim any other foundation means rejection of the shed blood of the Lord Jesus Christ. *God accepts no other foundation!* Paul establishes this foundation, expounding upon it beginning in the book of Romans and continuing through each of his other epistles.

> *I Corinthians 3:10 According to the grace of God which is given unto me, as a wise masterbuilder, **I have laid the foundation**, and another buildeth thereon. But let every man take heed how he buildeth thereupon. 11 For other **foundation** can no man lay than that is laid, which **is Jesus Christ**. 12 Now if any man **build upon this foundation** gold, silver, precious stones, wood, hay, stubble;*

Paul's responsibility was to reveal the foundation to the Church. The Christian's responsibility is to take heed **how** he individually builds upon the foundation already settled and established *in Paul's epistles*. Some Christians will build *works* (likened to gold, silver and precious stones) that will be rewarded; others will build *works* (likened to wood, hay and stubble) that will be burned up at the Judgment Seat of Christ *(II Corinthians 5:10)*.

> *I Corinthians 3:13 Every man's work shall be made manifest: for the day shall declare it, because it shall be revealed by fire; and **the fire shall try every man's work of what sort it is**. 14 If any man's work **abide** which he hath built thereupon, he shall **receive a reward**. 15 If any man's work shall be **burned**, he shall **suffer loss**: but he himself shall be saved; yet so as by fire.*

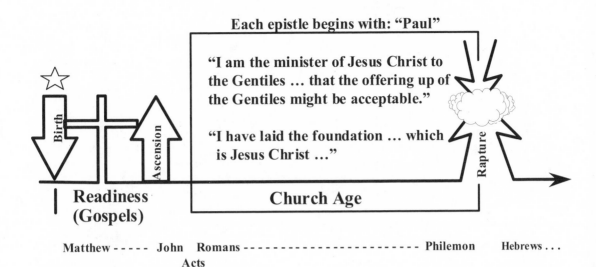

Each epistle begins with: "Paul"

"I am the minister of Jesus Christ to the Gentiles ... that the offering up of the Gentiles might be acceptable."

"I have laid the foundation ... which is Jesus Christ ..."

Birth

Ascension

Rapture

Readiness (Gospels)

Church Age

Matthew - - - - - John   Romans - Philemon   Hebrews . . .

Acts

Chart 6.2 - Paul: Minister to the Gentiles

Salvation settles the believer's foundation; then the process of building begins. Yet, no matter the magnificence of the structure, **the** most crucial component of any structure remains its foundation. A faulty foundation indicates certain trouble in the future. As the song states: "My hope is *built* on nothing less than Jesus' blood and righteousness." Attempting to build (work) prior to laying a foundation is an exercise in futility.

Spiritually, *I Corinthians 15:1-4* reveals the only acceptable foundation. Efforts to build upon anything other than this foundation will be to no avail. The end result will be eternal damnation as a result of lacking the only acceptable foundation—our Lord and Saviour Jesus Christ.

Read the specifics of *I Corinthians 3:10* again . . . "**I have** laid the foundation." God leads the Apostle Paul to eliminate debate concerning the importance of his ministry to us. Nevertheless, the devil vehemently attacks this truth. Paul laid the foundation for the Church Age.

Any group that builds their "church" by following someone other than Paul in this Church Age has the wrong foundation, even if they claim their foundation to be the Lord. Many cults claim that Christ is their rock when, in fact, their doctrines are built on the sinking sand of man-made dogmas. Those responsible for the schisms generally overlook or ignore the *abundance of the revelations* given to us by the Apostle Paul *(II Corinthians 12:7)*.

Our pattern

The scriptures establish that the Apostle Paul was appointed and ordained by God. As previously demonstrated, Paul is the minister of the Lord Jesus Christ to the Gentiles and actually lays the very foundation for the believer to build his life upon. The Bible further points out that God gives us a pattern to follow. Paul sets a pattern for all others during this age to follow.

*I Timothy 1:16 Howbeit for this cause I obtained mercy, that **in me first** Jesus Christ might shew forth all longsuffering, for a **pattern** to them which should hereafter believe on him to life everlasting.*

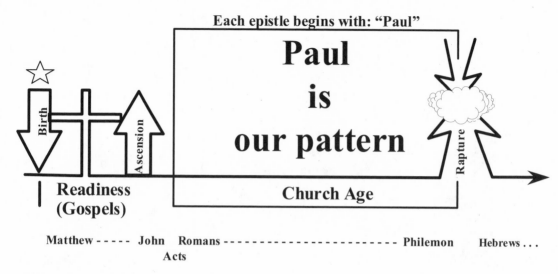

Chart 6.3 - Paul: Our Pattern

Since the scriptures plainly state that Paul is our pattern, the emphasis many religious organizations today place on following Peter (to the exclusion of Paul) is unsubstantiated and confusing. Who benefits from this confusion *(I Corinthians 14:33)*? It is certainly not those in search of truth.

Religious groups that use the early preaching of the Apostle Peter to substantiate their particular beliefs and teachings are incorrectly applying truths intended for others. Could it be that Satan benefits from a world ignorant of the differences between Paul's and Peter's ministries? Since the Apostle Paul sets the pattern for this age, Satan uses every tool in his spiritual arsenal to keep the world blind to this fact *(II Corinthians 4:3-4)*.

Paul received an abundance of revelations that had been kept *secret since the world began (Romans 16:25)*. For this reason, God used Satan to keep Paul's pride in check. The Bible does not specify the exact physical infirmity Paul suffered, but it does reveal the purpose for the affliction.

*II Corinthians 12:7 And lest I should be exalted above measure through **the abundance of the revelations**, there was given to me a thorn in the flesh, the messenger of Satan to buffet me, lest I should be exalted above measure.*

It is inconceivable that Bible believing preachers can simply claim ignorance of the Apostle Paul's God-given position for the Church Age. Yet, the so-called *stewards of the mysteries* in this Age seem more concerned with acceptance by their peers than with being faithful stewards of God's truths *(I Corinthians 4:1-2)*. The Church and the world desperately need Bible believing preachers willing to withstand the onslaught of criticism that comes when one stands firm for the truth.

The truth is not popular, nor is the Christian who unapologetically stands for it. The words of the man who fulfilled the word of God express the sentiments of those who care enough to suffer the reproach of others in order to share to truth.

*II Corinthians 12:15 And I will very gladly spend and be spent for you; though **the more abundantly I love you, the less I be loved.***

7

Fulfilling the Word of God
(What Paul Does)

One of the foremost objectives of this book is to demonstrate Paul's unique ministry. In addition to his ministry, his conversion and life were also unprecedented. Yet, some preachers attempt to match their own personal life experiences with those of the Apostle Paul. Such comparisons simply cannot be legitimately made! No one can equate Paul's life to his own. Any person that attempts to match his life experiences with Paul's must account for the following in his own life:

- Where is his road to Damascus *(Acts 9:3)*?
- When did the Lord Jesus Christ visibly appear to him, and make him blind *(Acts 9:8)* and then miraculously heal him of his blindness?
- When did the chains fall off his wrists while in prison and every door open to free him and all of the other prisoners *(Acts 16:26)*?
- Where are the divinely inspired scriptures he has penned *(Galatians 6:11)*?

Most students of scripture are familiar with the Lord's appearance to Paul (Saul) on the road to Damascus in Acts chapter 9. However, many of these same students fail to realize that the Lord appeared to Paul on more than that one occasion *(Acts 26:16)*. During those appearances, the Lord revealed His word (including the Gospel of the Grace of God). Paul was chosen as God's instrument to reveal His word to the world. Most of what each of us learns comes from what others teach us. Yet, the Lord supernaturally revealed His word directly to the Apostle Paul, and the Bible records the unique way in which Paul received it.

The gospel received by revelation

Paul declares that the gospel preached by him was *not* taught to him by anyone else. How did he learn about the gospel if no one taught him? The Bible says that God revealed the gospel *directly* to him.

> *Galatians 1:11 But I certify you, brethren, that the gospel which was preached of me is **not after man**. 12 For I **neither received it of man, neither was I taught it**, but by the revelation of Jesus Christ.*

Paul states that he did *not* receive and was *not* taught the gospel by anyone else. One should logically conclude from these statements that the other apostles could have had *absolutely nothing* to do with the Apostle Paul's receiving the gospel revealed in his epistles. Why do you suppose God chose to supernaturally reveal the gospel to the Apostle Paul? The answer may astonish you. Paul could not receive something *from man* that God had hidden from all men *(Luke 18:34)*. Neither Peter nor the other apostles completely understood the death, burial and resurrection (that is, the gospel) until after they had already been following Christ for over three years. Nor did they readily accept God's changing plans concerning the Gentiles.

For instance, Peter rebuked the Lord when the death, burial, and resurrection were mentioned *(Mark 8:31-32)*. Peter ran to the sepulcher after the resurrection to see what had happened and did not understand what had transpired *(Luke 24:12)*. Then the Bible records Peter's reaction to the changes God was instituting concerning the relationship between the Jews and Gentiles. Peter had a very difficult time accepting God's changing plans. These events occur toward the end of his recorded ministry (in Acts chapter 10). Peter learned that God was beginning to minister directly to the Gentiles. Initially, he defiantly refused to obey the Lord on three different occasions when the sheet with the "unclean" animals was let down *(Acts 10:8-10)*. God used this sign to signify to Peter His change of direction concerning the Gentiles.

God told Peter to go to Cornelius *(Acts 10:20)*. However, Cornelius was a Gentile! Reluctantly, Peter went with the men to meet with this Gentile. God may have been using this situation to condition Peter's heart so that he would be supportive of Paul's soon to be revealed ministry to the Gentiles *(Acts 15:7-12)*. Peter was beginning to realize that God's plan was changing drastically. The disciples were no longer to go to the *Jew only (Matthew 10:5)*. Yet, some of the other disciples continued to go to the Jew *only* until Paul showed them that God's message was to go to the Gentiles as well *(Acts 11:19)*.

Although Peter effectively reached the Jews with God's message, he was *not* God's primary spokesman to reach the Gentiles en masse. Paul was God's chosen vessel *(Acts 9:15)* to take this gospel to the despised Gentiles.

Ephesians chapter 3 also clearly reflects that God revealed the mystery directly to the Apostle Paul. Notice how clearly the passage states this truth. Paul says that the "dispensation of the grace of God" was given to him. Why do you suppose so many fail to grasp this truth? God led Paul to make this claim so that we can understand his knowledge in the mystery.

> *Ephesians 3:1 For this cause I Paul, the prisoner of Jesus Christ for you Gentiles, 2 If ye have heard of the dispensation of the grace of God which is **given me** to you-ward: 3 How that **by revelation** he made known unto me the mystery; (as I wrote afore in few words, 4 Whereby, **when ye read**, ye may understand my knowledge in the mystery of Christ)*

Our apostle tells us to read so that we may understand his knowledge in the mystery of Christ. This *complete* revelation of the mystery was not given to anyone else prior to Paul's writings. We should have no problem realizing how Paul received the knowledge of the mystery. The Lord Jesus Christ revealed the mystery directly to him. Today, men receive this understanding and knowledge by revelation also; however, this understanding now comes by reading something that was not completely revealed prior to the writings of the Apostle Paul.

Our revelation comes from the scriptures and from individuals exhorting us through the scriptures to reveal the truth to us. During the first century, God revealed the truth through the Holy Spirit directly to him (and the other apostles), without the use of the New Testament. Remember, Paul wrote the majority of the New Testament books so it was obviously inaccessible until written.

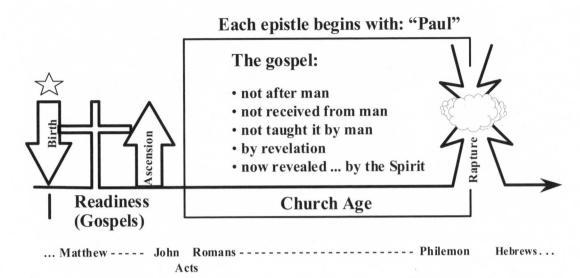

Chart 7.1 - The Gospel

*Ephesians 3:5 Which in other ages was not made known unto the sons of men, as it is **now revealed** unto his holy apostles and prophets **by the Spirit**;*

All truth must be revealed to someone initially. God chose the apostles to be the recipients of this revelation, with Paul being the primary recipient. Paul, in turn, recorded the revelation that we might gain the understanding of it when the Holy Spirit uses the scriptures to reveal this truth to us. Prior to Paul's conversion (Acts chapter 9), the complete mystery was not revealed to anyone. Paul says it is *now* being revealed. Here is the mystery:

*Ephesians 3:6 That the Gentiles should be fellowheirs, and of the same body, and partakers of his promise in Christ by the gospel: 7 Whereof I was made a minister, according to the gift of the grace of God **given unto me** by the effectual working of his power. 8 Unto me, who am less than the least of all saints, is this grace given, that I should **preach among the Gentiles** the unsearchable riches of Christ; 9 **And to make all men see** what is the **fellowship of the mystery**, which from the beginning of the world hath been hid in God, who created all things by Jesus Christ:*

Paul's calling involved making all men see the mystery. This mystery was hidden in God from the beginning of the world. A person cannot search the Old Testament scriptures and understand this truth without the knowledge of the revelation of the New Testament. In other words, only when one reads the Old Testament in light of what he knows from the New Testament will he be able to understand the pictures and types contained in the Old Testament. The Bible says that there is a veil *(II Corinthians 3:14-16)* in the reading of the Old Testament which is only done away in Christ. Such understanding is now possible only because one can look back on the Old Testament using the knowledge provided primarily in Paul's epistles.

As earlier demonstrated, Peter is a good example of someone unable to foresee the necessity of the cross. He could not understand it. He could not accept it. When the Lord said He was going to the cross, Peter rebuked Him. We have a hard time understanding why Peter would attempt to stop the Lord in light of what we know about the cross today. Without the cross, we have no hope. **However, Peter was *not* looking forward to the cross. He did not want the Lord to leave him.** He fought to stop the soldiers from taking the Lord *(John 18:10)*. When Peter went to the sepulcher, he still did not understand the resurrection *(Luke 24:12)*. Since he did not understand the cross or resurrection prior to the final chapter of Luke, there is no way he would have understood it in the first twenty-three chapters of Luke either. He could *not* have been looking forward to the cross. Later chapters in this book provide the scriptural proof to make this truth even clearer.

Peter and the Lord's other apostles are not the only ones that did not understand the death, burial and resurrection. The Old Testament saints did not completely understand the resurrection either. In retrospect, we understand that David, Joseph and Isaac are pictures and types of Christ. We understand these truths because we have the revelation of the mystery. The same cannot be said about those "looking forward." If the apostles were *not* looking forward, it should be easy to understand that the Old Testament saints also did not understand the death, burial or resurrection of our Lord and Saviour.

Paul spoke to the Gentiles and revealed the words that God had given to him. With all of the confusion in the world, is it any wonder that the primary focus of attention is usually directed toward Peter, rather than Paul? The devil instigated this confusion. Since we are to follow Paul *(I Corinthians 11:1)* you can imagine how pleased the devil is when he gets people to follow someone other than the example they are commanded to follow. When they use the Bible to justify their position, he is overwhelmed with joy. When millions of followers are deceived, one has to give all the "credit" to the devil. God gives us the key to understand within the scriptures.

As you read the next section, try to figure out how anyone before the mystery was revealed to the Apostle Paul could have been looking forward to the cross. If everyone had been looking forward, there would have been no betrayal, no cross and no Saviour of the world.

The mystery

Paul informs us that God revealed the mystery to him directly. He says it was the *hidden* wisdom prior to his writings.

*I Corinthians 2:7 But we speak the wisdom of God in a mystery, even the **hidden wisdom**, which God ordained before the world unto our glory:*

God ordained that the age in which we live would occur; however, this mystery was not revealed to man until the time that God was revealing it to the Apostle Paul. No one had the complete revelation prior to the Apostle Paul, and he is the only one that wrote with this complete understanding. Peter even admits that he had a difficult time understanding Paul's writings *(II Peter 3:15-16)*, although Peter's two epistles have many similarities to Paul's writings.

God wanted to show the Church *(Colossians 1:24)* His will, His way and His plan. He used Paul to do this. The next verse reveals exactly why God chose to wait and reveal the mystery to a man saved *after* the cross. Had Satan understood the cross prior to its fulfillment, he would not have entered into Judas Iscariot and instigated the betrayal of the Lord Jesus Christ. Since Satan is *the prince of the power of the air (Ephesians 2:2)*, none of the princes of this world could understand the mystery prior to the cross either.

I Corinthians 2:8 Which none of the princes of this world knew: for had they known it, they would not have crucified the Lord of glory.

Although the Lord Jesus Christ told the apostles about the gospel of the death, burial and resurrection *(Matthew 16:21, 17:23, 20:19)*, the true extent of God's plan had to remain a mystery. The *revelation* of this mystery could not even begin until after the cross. The revealed truth was limited until Paul penned his thirteen epistles that contain his name as the first word (Romans through Philemon).

The gospel in trust

As already seen, the Apostle Paul received the mystery. God gave him the opportunity and responsibility to reveal this mystery to the world. Furthermore, he laid the foundation because God put the gospel in his trust. Today, we hold things in trust at a bank. This is much the same concept. God gave (revealed) the gospel to him and en**trust**ed him with the responsibility to reveal it to the world. Thank God for obedient servants like the Apostle Paul.

*I Thessalonians 2:4 But as **we were allowed of God to be put in trust with the gospel**, even so we speak; not as pleasing men, but God, which trieth our hearts.*

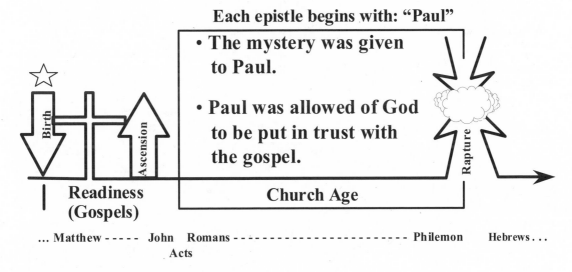

Chart 7.2 - Paul: Apostle, Ordained, Appointed

Paul clearly laid the foundation (the Lord Jesus Christ) in the thirteen epistles that bear his name as the first word. Without question, the timing of this revelation followed the resurrection of our Lord. Paul was the first to have a full understanding of the work on the cross; no one understood the mystery like Paul prior to this time.

Due to the revelation of the mystery given to Paul, he *declares* the gospel components. The Gospel of the Grace of God is not simply the "good news" as some purport it to be. The three distinct elements of the gospel should always be emphasized when the gospel is presented to others.

The Gospel Declared

*I Corinthians 15:1 Moreover, brethren, **I declare unto you the gospel** which I preached unto you, which also ye have received, and wherein ye stand; 2 By which also ye are saved, if ye keep in memory what **I preached** unto you, unless ye have* *believed in vain. 3 For I delivered unto you first of all that which I also received,* **how that Christ died for our sins according to the scriptures; 4 And that he was buried, and that he rose again the third day** *according to the scriptures:*

The three distinct elements of the gospel as follows:

- How that the Lord Jesus Christ died for our sins
- That He was buried
- That He arose on the third day

A person cannot be saved without a simple heart belief in the gospel *(Romans 10:9-10)*, believing that it is the only means of salvation. Nothing else can save a soul from hell. The *works of the law* cannot save a person *(Galatians 2:16)*. Works of righteousness cannot save an individual *(Titus 3:5)*. Apart from a repentant belief on the Lord Jesus Christ, there is no salvation *(Acts 16:31)*. These truths are learned by studying Paul's epistles; or, in the case of the Philippian jailer in Acts chapter 16, by studying Paul's presentation of the gospel to a lost man. There is no other way to learn these truths in their entirety.

> *"If Moses is the central figure amid the witnesses for God in the Old Testament, Paul is the central figure amid the witnesses for Christ in the New Testament. …Moses enfranchised a nation. Paul liberates a soul. Moses stamps the name of Jew on the world, Paul stamps the name of Christian on the world. Moses reveals God as Lawgiver, Paul reveals God as Grace-giver. Moses points to the kingdom, Paul points to the church. …Peter may represent the Christian in the flesh, James the Christian under the Law, John the Christian walking in love, but Paul represents the Christian as risen and seated at the Right Hand of God."*
>
> I.M. Haldeman, *How to Study the Bible - The Second Coming and Other Expositions* (NY: Charles C. Cook, 1904), p. 543

The word committed to Paul

Many local churches are establishing the functions of the church based upon their interpretation of the book of Acts *(II Peter 1:20)*. However, God did not give the book of Acts for this purpose. God did not give the book of Acts to show how to establish the local church or its functions. Acts is a *historical* book and is not to be treated in the same way as the books of church doctrine. The church should not base its existence or functions upon the book of Acts any more than upon a history book of the Soviet Union *(Acts 4:32)*.

The following points appear quite obvious, but must nevertheless be addressed. Why would anyone base the foundation of their church on Acts chapter 2 when **Peter** is preaching to the **Jews** on a **Jewish Feast Day** (Pentecost)? Nevertheless, there are entire organizations using this book (and chapter) as justification for their existence and for their rationale for separating from others that do not agree with them. God does not leave these issues open to the whims and wishes of man. Paul reveals that God is manifesting His word during the Church Age predominantly through the preaching of the Apostle Paul, not the Apostle Peter's preaching in the book of Acts!

*Titus 1:1 Paul, a servant of God, and an apostle of Jesus Christ, according to the faith of God's elect, and the acknowledging of the truth which is after godliness; 2 In hope of eternal life, which God, that cannot lie, promised before the world began; 3 But hath in due times **manifested his word through preaching**, which is **committed unto me** according to the commandment of God our Saviour;*

Paul exalted preaching because he knew that preaching was the method God chose to give man the truth *(I Corinthians 1:18, 21)*. God chose Paul to manifest His word through preaching. A person will never know God's will without attending the preaching of God's word. It is God's way or no way.

Paul fulfills God's word

The reader might still assume that all of this attention on the Apostle Paul serves to overemphasize his individual importance. Surely those before the flood thought that Noah took a lot upon himself too. What did it take to convince them? They were not persuaded until the rains started, and not completely convinced until they found themselves in hell. Korah and two hundred fifty *"princes of the assembly, famous in the congregation, men of renown"* gathered themselves against Moses and Aaron. They said, *"Ye take too much upon you . . . wherefore then lift ye up yourselves above the congregation of the Lord?"* These two hundred fifty were the religious leaders of the day—the sons of Levi *(Numbers 16:1-3)*. They were wrong to doubt God's spokesman and God proved it *(Numbers 16:35)*. Since God's word emphasizes Paul's ministry, so should every obedient Church Age Christian. God used Paul to fulfill His word.

> *"To Paul is committed the doctrine of the church, from Paul come the epistles to the church…"*
>
> **I.M. Haldeman, How to Study the Bible - The Second Coming and Other Expositions (NY: Charles C. Cook, 1904), p. 544.**

*Colossians 1:25 Whereof I am made a minister, according to the dispensation of God which is given to me for you, to **fulfil the word of God**;*

Each epistle begins with: "Paul"

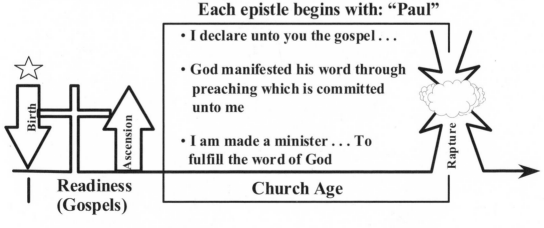

* I declare unto you the gospel . . .

* God manifested his word through preaching which is committed unto me

* I am made a minister . . . To fulfill the word of God

Birth | Ascension | Rapture

Readiness (Gospels)   **Church Age**

... Matthew - - - - - John   Romans - Philemon   Hebrews . . .
Acts

Chart7.3 - The Gospel Declared

Surely every dedicated Christian would like this to be said about them: that they fulfilled the word of God. But God only gives one man this recognition—the Apostle Paul. His ministry to the Church (thirteen epistles long) fulfilled God's word. All Christians had better take heed to what Paul says and to what this means to them. Even church traditions revolve around the things that Paul addresses in his epistles to the Church.

The traditions

Just as Paul defines the most important subject (the gospel) in his epistles, he also explains some items of lesser importance. For instance, Paul defines the church traditions. In the next passage, Paul states that we are called by the gospel he preached. Therefore, he instructs us concerning the traditions taught in his Church Age epistles.

> *II Thessalonians 2:14 Whereunto he called you by **our gospel**, to the obtaining of the glory of our Lord Jesus Christ. 15 Therefore, brethren, stand fast, and **hold the traditions which ye have been taught**, whether by word, or our epistle.*

Paul's claims are clear and unmistakable. He insures that the Christian is informed that it is **his** gospel that saves today. His presentation differs from Peter's and the other apostles' preaching during the early part of their respective ministries. The importance of this truth cannot be overstated. The whole Bible must be studied keeping in mind those things God instructs through Paul's epistles to the Church.

In churches today, more error results from *not* obeying God's clear command to follow Paul than from any other cause *(I Corinthians 11:1)*. Any person that seriously considers the errors and schisms propagated by many of the cults, denominations and churches will find that these groups generally ignore (or minimize) the writings of the Apostle Paul. Instead of considering Paul, these groups *use* the Bible to "prove" their pet doctrines. Thus, they ignore God's method of Bible study and interpretation. This greatly displeases God. Since God used the Apostle Paul to fulfill His word, the believer can be *established* only by considering Paul's writings!

Establish the believer

Paul's epistles reveal our foundation (the presentation of the Lord Jesus Christ). The Christian learns how to walk from Paul's example, and grows by following Paul as he followed the Lord Jesus Christ. Do you get the picture? A person during this Church Age can only be *established* because the Apostle Paul was obedient to the Lord, and because Paul's epistles reveal God's plan for the establishment of the individual believer.

> *Romans 16:25 Now to him that is of power to **stablish you according to my gospel, and the preaching of Jesus Christ, according to the revelation of the mystery**, which was kept secret since the world began,*

God uses *the gospel* revealed to Paul and his preaching of the Lord Jesus Christ to establish the believer. God also uses Paul's revelation of *the mystery* and his preaching of the Lord Jesus Christ to establish the believer. The Gospel of the Kingdom will *not* and cannot efficiently establish the believer today. As a matter of fact, misapplication of the Kingdom gospel to the Church today will misdirect the priorities of the believer and condemn the lost *(Matthew 10:22)*.

The purpose of the Body of Christ has absolutely nothing to do with hastening the Lord's return by bringing in the Kingdom. Our efforts will *not* somehow make this world worthy of the Lord's return. It would be great if it were possible for the actions of the Church to bring in the

Kingdom. However, the Bible clearly points out that the Rapture (prior to the Tribulation period and Kingdom) will take all believers out of a world in the midst of perilous times *(II Timothy 3:1)*. Verse 13 of this same chapter in Timothy points out that *"evil men and seducers shall wax worse and worse, deceiving, and being deceived."* The Bible plainly teaches that there is not much chance of a worldwide revival coming to pass prior to the Rapture, Tribulation and Millennium. Today, we seem to be located in the time when Christians are *not* willing to "endure sound doctrine," but instead want to hear something soothing (and untrue) *(II Timothy 4:2-4)*.

One of the main reasons Christians fail to fully mature is their ignorance concerning how to be established in the faith. Paul's writings establish the believer, and serve as the standard by which he learns *to walk*. A newborn Christian is a baby *(Hebrews 5:13)*. Every baby has to learn how to walk.

Any good parent desires to place the right influences in his child's life. Few things are more discouraging to a parent than discovering that his child has departed from his upbringing. For someone to intentionally hinder your child's development and maturity seems unthinkable. The same principle holds true of the Christian walk. God wants every baby Christian to have the right influences in his life. These influences make their greatest impressions between the time one begins drinking the milk through the time he learns to walk.

How to walk

The Christian first settles his foundation upon salvation. Next, his "walk" becomes important. *"Why* do you do what you do, and *what* are you to do?" These two critical questions and their answers reveal a great deal about a person's walk with the Lord. Any person desiring to know what to do should read Paul's epistles *first* because Paul is our apostle and spokesman. Similarly, a person under the law would read the writings of Moses to learn of God's expectations. Do you really want to know how you should walk? The Apostle Paul tells us.

> *I Thessalonians 4:1 Furthermore then we beseech you, brethren, and exhort you by the Lord Jesus, that as **ye have received of us how ye ought to walk** and to please God, so ye would abound more and more.*

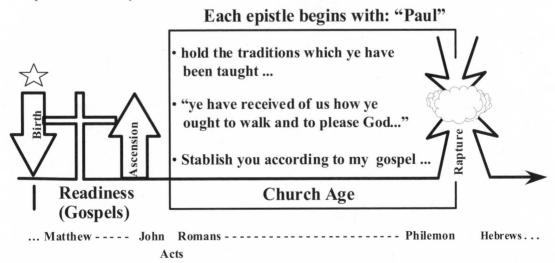

Each epistle begins with: "Paul"

- **hold the traditions which ye have been taught ...**
- **"ye have received of us how ye ought to walk and to please God..."**
- **Stablish you according to my gospel ...**

Birth | Ascension | Rapture

Readiness (Gospels) | **Church Age**

... Matthew - - - - - John   Romans - Philemon   Hebrews...

Acts

Chart 7.4 - Hold the Traditions

Paul states that an individual must read *his epistles* to find out how to walk. After one discovers how to walk with God, he will know how to please God. ***A Christian cannot please God without having an understanding of what God expects***. Paul reveals to us the expectations of God. Since Paul reveals so much to the Church, God will judge man according to the standard set in these epistles.

Judge the secrets of men

What are we, as Christians, to be doing? We are to be busy telling people about the death, burial, and resurrection of the Lord Jesus Christ. We must evangelize a lost, sin-sick world according to the gospel given to us by our apostle. Imagine a church today choosing to follow someone other than Paul. Then read the following scripture.

*Romans 2:16 In the day when God shall **judge the secrets of men** by Jesus Christ **according to my gospel**.*

God leads the Apostle Paul to be very specific in his writing. God's judgment will clearly be issued according to the gospel that Paul preached and clearly delineated in his thirteen Church Age epistles. Paul does not simply write "**the** gospel" in the previous verse, but uses the personal possessive pronoun to distinguish his gospel from any other gospel. He does this on two other occasions as well *(Romans 16:25, II Timothy 2:8)*. The book of Galatians acknowledges two gospels along with the individuals to whom each was committed. *"But contrariwise, when they saw that **the gospel of the uncircumcision** was committed unto me, as **the gospel of the circumcision** was unto Peter" (Galatians 2:7)*.

Concerning the two gospels mentioned in Galatians, there can be no question that Peter was sent to the Jews *(Matthew 15:24, John 20:21)*. The gospel *committed* to him initially was the gospel of the circumcision

> **"The Church, doctrinally, was alone fully revealed to Paul."** [Haldeman quotes Ephesians 3:1-8] **"The Church is a mystery hidden from the beginning of the world in God, and known only to God."** [Haldeman quotes Ephesians 3:9]
>
> I.M. Haldeman, *How to Study the Bible - The Second Coming and Other Expositions* (NY: Charles C. Cook, 1904), p. 391.

which he and the other apostles preached to the Jews only. The Bible also refers to it as the Gospel of the Kingdom *(Matthew 4:23, 9:35, and 23:14)*. This was Peter's initial message until he came to understand and accept the gospel of the death, burial and resurrection shortly after the cross. Even after the good news proclaimed by Peter changed, his primary ministry of proclaiming the Gospel of the Grace of God to the circumcision continued unabated *(Galatians 2:9)*.

There can be no question that by the time Paul met with Peter in Jerusalem, both were preaching the exact same gospel; otherwise Peter would have been accursed for preaching "another gospel" at that time *(Galatians 1:8)*. Although Peter came to preach the same gospel as Paul, part of Peter's problem revealed in Galatians was his hypocrisy *(Galatians 2:11-14)* which certainly limited his spiritual growth and his effectiveness toward the Gentiles. In his second epistle he even admits that he had an insufficient understanding of Paul's writings.

*II Peter 3:15 And account that the longsuffering of our Lord is salvation; even as our beloved brother **Paul** also according to the wisdom given unto him hath written unto you; 16 As also **in all his epistles, speaking in them of these things; in which are some things hard to be understood,** which they that are unlearned and unstable wrest, as they do also the other scriptures, unto their own destruction.*

We find out by reading Second Peter that Peter is preaching much the same message as Paul and ministering to the same group when he writes this epistle *(II Peter 3:15).*

"The Epistles of the Apostle Paul have a very distinctive character. All Scripture, up to the Gospel accounts of the crucifixion, looks forward to the cross, and has primarily in view Israel, and the blessing of the earth through the Messianic kingdom. But "hid in God" Eph 3:9 was an unrevealed fact—the interval of time between the crucifixion and resurrection of Christ and His return in glory; and an unrevealed purpose— the outcalling of the ecclesia, the church which is Christ's body. In Mat. 16, our Lord announced that purpose, but wholly without explanation as to how, when, or of what materials, that church should be built, or what should be its position, relationships, privileges, or duties.

All this constitutes precisely the scope of the Epistles of Paul. They develop the doctrine of the church. In his letters to seven Gentile churches (in Rome, Corinth, Galatia, Ephesus, Philippi, Colosse, and Thessalonica), the church, the "mystery which from the beginning of the world hath been hid in God" (Eph 3:9), is fully revealed, and fully instructed as to her unique place in the counsels and purposes of God.

Through Paul alone we know that the church is not an organization, but an organism, the body of Christ; instinct with His life, and heavenly in calling, promise, and destiny. Through him alone we know the nature, purpose, and form of organization of local churches, and the right conduct of such gatherings. Through him alone do we know that "we shall not all sleep," that "the dead in Christ shall rise first," and that living saints shall be "changed" and caught up to meet the Lord in the air at His return.

But to Paul was also committed the unfolding of the doctrines of grace which were latent in the teachings of Jesus Christ. Paul originates nothing, but unfolds everything, concerning the nature and purpose of the law; the ground and means of the believer's justification, sanctification, and glory; the meanings of the death of Christ, and the position, walk, expectation, and service of the Christian."

Scofield Reference Bible, Introduction to Paul's epistles, p 1189

Present the Church to the Lord Jesus Christ

One can scarcely imagine the heavenly rewards awaiting the Apostle Paul. Given the position that he held, he will certainly be greatly rewarded. The Bible tells us that the twelve apostles will sit on twelve thrones judging the twelve tribes of Israel.

Matthew 19:28 And Jesus said unto them, Verily I say unto you, That ye which have followed me, in the regeneration when the Son of man shall sit in the throne of his glory, ***ye also shall sit upon twelve thrones, judging the twelve tribes of Israel.***

With such a prestigious position given to the twelve apostles should it be surprising that the apostle who wrote so much of the New Testament will be rewarded for his endeavors too? One reward for fulfilling his duties as the apostle during the Church Age is that the Apostle Paul will present the Church to the Lord Jesus Christ. God will reward Paul's faithfulness *(II Timothy 4:7)*.

II Corinthians 11:2 For I am jealous over you with godly jealousy: for I have espoused you to one husband, ***that I may present you as a chaste virgin to Christ.***

Since he laid the foundation *(I Corinthians 3:10)*, he is the spiritual father of us all. *As a proud father he will be given the opportunity to present us (the Church) as a bride to Christ.* It is important to listen to and learn *(Philippians 4:9)* from our earthly father, our heavenly Father and also our "spiritual father."

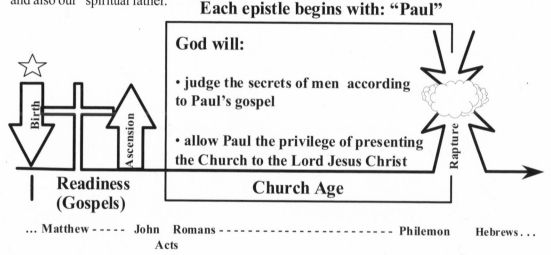

Chart 7.5 - Paul: How ye ought to walk

CAUTION: Although the Bible does refer to more than one gospel, the following point cannot be minimized. ***No one, from Adam throughout the Millennium, gets to heaven apart from the shed blood of the Lord Jesus Christ.*** Even those that died prior to the cross awaited the sacrifice of the Lord Jesus Christ *(Luke 16:26, 23:43)*. Although it is incorrect to teach that they all "looked forward to the cross," they still did *not* go to heaven without the blood of the Lord Jesus Christ being shed for them either. ***The fact that the Bible refers to more than one gospel in no way diminishes the importance of the precious blood of the Lord Jesus Christ.*** Rather it *magnifies* the blood by limiting man's attainment of heaven to his acceptance of Christ's shed blood (of course, applied after the cross).

8
Following Paul
(What we are to do)

Since some scriptural evidence has yet to be provided, the skeptic may still allege that this teaching simply exalts a man (Paul) unscripturally. This response generally emanates from the approach taken in most seminaries on how to teach the Bible. Frequently, seminaries have emphasized the *spiritualized* method of Bible teaching, rather than considering the scriptures *literally* for what they say. The result of this method of Bible teaching can clearly be seen in today's churches. Over time, spiritualizing the verses has resulted in a very shallow and carnal type of Christianity. Because of this method of "teaching," it is not uncommon for a Christian to remain a spiritual baby his entire life. God never intended for seminaries to stunt Christian growth.

The Bible student considering what Paul says to the Church today is comparable to listening to Noah before the flood, Abraham after the flood, or Moses during the exodus from Egypt. When man does *not* follow God's appointed spokesman, he does so at his own risk. Clearly and repeatedly, the Bible instructs that we are to follow Paul. Just as Paul obediently followed the Lord Jesus Christ, we are to follow the doctrines, commandments, instructions, and revelations of the Lord Jesus Christ given to us by the Apostle Paul. Otherwise, the student will remain confused about *apparent* contradictions that are, in fact, different sets of instructions given during different periods of time, under different programs. Had you been alive when Peter was preaching and he told you to give up your job, leave your family behind and become a fisher of men, how would you have responded *(Matthew 4:19)*? Would you have told him that God does not work that way? Or would you have quit your job and followed him?

Would you have thought that Peter was taking too much upon himself? No? Then why not listen to Paul since God instructed him to guide us? Would you have listened to Moses when he said, "It is time to get out of Egypt and go to the Promised Land?" Yes? Then why not believe that God still has a primary spokesman today? It is the Apostle Paul. God chooses to work through man to disseminate His word to man. Everyone is going to follow someone. Be certain to follow the one God has chosen.

Follow Paul

Consider the two alternatives: either God gave Paul the authority to command us to follow him or Paul was extremely egotistical. You be the judge now; God will be the judge later. God commands us to listen to what Paul says by reading what God led him to write. The same man who teaches us *how to walk*, tells us to follow him:

*I Corinthians 11:1 Be ye followers of me, even as I also am of Christ. 2 Now I praise you, brethren, that ye **remember me in all things**, and keep the **ordinances**, as I delivered them to you.*

The second verse of the previous passage reveals the extent of Paul's authority. God instructs us to remember Paul in *every area* of our lives ("all things"). Specifically, he mentions the ordinances. He tells us that we are to keep the ordinances as *he* delivered them to us. God could not make it any clearer than that. Paul only mentions two ordinances and both of these are found in this same book. These ordinances are baptism *(I Corinthians 1:14-17)* and the Lord's Supper *(I Corinthians 11:23-34)*. Failing to realize that baptism and the Lord's Supper are the only church ordinances or eliminating them altogether damages the credibility of the church. Eliminating them also makes one a hyper-dispensationalist. A hyper-dispensationalist divides the Bible in excess or beyond God's method of dispensational Bible study, generally resulting in the elimination of applicable Church doctrines or local church ordinances. God knows man's heart; therefore, He included the instruction concerning the ordinances in the same verse as His command to follow Paul as he followed Christ.

One is a "dispensationalist" when he scripturally eliminates the Old Testament ordinances. He becomes a hyper-dispensationalist when he incorrectly eliminates the two ordinances of baptism and the Lord's Supper from the New Testament Church. Eliminating these two ordinances has no scriptural foundation. Furthermore, most preachers that eliminate these ordinances from the local church are would-be Bible correctors and not Bible believers anyway. Many of them change the *washings* of Hebrews *(Hebrews 9:9-12)* to baptism and claim that this proves that baptism was a Jewish custom and the church has no business baptizing converts.

We are to follow Paul, as his epistles explain how to follow Christ. We are not to follow Moses or the ordinances that he gave concerning things God previously required *(Colossians 2:14-16)*. We are *not* to follow the baptismal format given by John the Baptist *(Acts 19:3-5)* or the Apostle Peter *(Acts 2:38)*. Paul even re-baptized John's converts who had been baptized with the "baptism of repentance." One should consider why Paul would re-baptize John's converts if everything remained the same *(Acts 19:1-7)*.

How does one stay straight concerning the ordinances? Follow Paul. No scriptural basis exists for adding to or taking away from these two ordinances for the Church today. If these two are not the ordinances to which Paul referred, then what are they *(Colossians 2:20-23)*?

God knows our hearts. He realizes that our natural man *(I Corinthians 2:14)* does not desire the truth. Yet, knowing which spokesman to follow is crucial. Therefore, God leads Paul to give the same command twice. Earlier in First Corinthians he wrote for us to be followers of him:

*I Corinthians 4:16 Wherefore I beseech you, **be ye followers of me**.*

Consider whether Paul was led by inspiration of God to write these things. Did God appoint him to this position? Was Paul chosen to give the truth to the Church? If you do not get your guidance from reading Paul's epistles, where do you get it? Some claim that you should place yourself *under the law* again *(Romans 6:14)*. Some say that you should follow the book of Acts. Which part of Acts are they referring to . . . building a commune *(Acts 2:44, 4:32)*, speaking in tongues *(Acts 2:4, 10:46, 19:6)* or having someone drop dead for lying *(Acts 5:5)*, etc., etc., etc?

Are you really using a history book (Acts) to determine the pattern of your church or are you just pretending to do so because you cannot explain the things you read? You must rightly divide your Bible and . . .

Listen to Paul

As demonstrated from scripture, Paul tells us how we ought to walk, but the blessings do not end there. Once we learn the truth, our obligations do not end either. We are told to hold onto the sound words that we have heard from our apostle. In other words, the words of Paul are not to go "in one ear and out the other." You are to let them *sink down into your ears (Luke 9:44)*.

II Timothy 1:13 Hold fast the form of sound words, which thou hast heard of me, in faith and love which is in Christ Jesus.

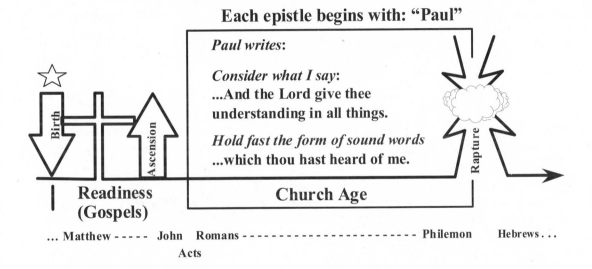

Chart 8.1 - Paul: Consider What I Say

Evidently, Paul's ministry (through his writings) remains with us today. Some may continue to have difficulty accepting this truth because of the prevailing mode of teaching. Yet, rather than *spiritualizing* these verses, just read them for what they say and consider for yourself. If you refuse to *accept the truth*, what excuse are you going to give for ignoring the evidence?

Consider Paul's sayings

The blessings of understanding Paul's ministry abound. We are told to consider what Paul says. We are also told the results of our obedience. The Lord promises to give us understanding in *all* things.

*II Timothy 2:7 Consider what I say; and the Lord give thee **understanding in all things**.*

You cannot consider what Paul has said unless you study his thirteen Church Age epistles. In other words, once we understand what Paul says to us during this Church Age, the other periods (and portions) of the Bible will be easier to understand too. The seemingly contradictory verses will be easily reconciled. One will then understand which portions of the Bible are to be applied spiritually and doctrinally. The key is to make sure that the guidance does not seem to contradict Paul's clear guidance.

Consider what Paul says first when attempting to determine what to do today. He is the apostle to the Gentiles and we are to follow him and the revelation given to him. When a person considers what Paul says first, the Lord will give him understanding of things otherwise impossible to understand and reconcile.

Do what is learned, received, heard and seen

When confronted with a question concerning baptism, the Lord's Supper, holy days, Sabbath days, special meats, how to live, how to be saved . . . consider what Paul says first. Do not go to the books of the law first. Do not go to the book of Acts or the Readiness/Tribulation books *first*. Failing to follow Paul will only result in confusion *(I Corinthians 14:33)*. Our obedience in this matter extends into every area of life. For instance, consider all the areas covered in the next verse. What are you commanded to **do**?

> *Philippians 4:9 Those things, which ye have both **learned**, and **received**, and **heard**, and **seen** in me, **do**: and the God of peace shall be with you.*

Since God led Paul inspirationally in the writing of his thirteen epistles, God also ordained that he serve as our pattern to follow. He allowed and inspired Paul to write verses such as *Philippians 4:9*. One may still feel that Paul is being lifted up . . . by whom or what? By the scriptures! This book places no greater importance on Paul's ministry than does the Bible. A person who does not recognize this fact must bear in mind the one with whom he is wrestling *(Ephesians 6:12)*.

Each epistle begins with: "Paul"

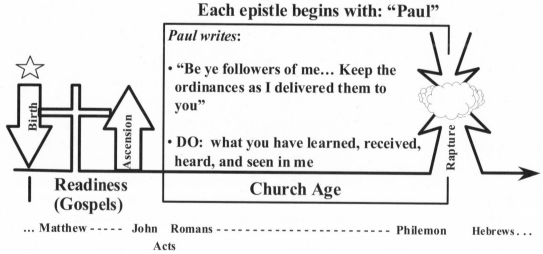

Paul writes:

• "Be ye followers of me... Keep the ordinances as I delivered them to you"

• DO: what you have learned, received, heard, and seen in me

Birth | Ascension | Rapture

Readiness (Gospels) | **Church Age**

... Matthew ----- John   Romans ----------------------- Philemon   Hebrews...
                    Acts

Chart 8.2 - Paul: Followers of me

If you had lived prior to the flood, God would have wanted you to listen to his spokesman during that time . . . right? During the exodus from Egypt, listening to God's spokesman would have been crucial. Does it not make sense that God would continue using a particular spokesman during this age and ages to come as well? What about today? Who would it be? Noah? Moses? Samuel? David? Peter? **Paul?** The two Witnesses? The 144,000? We are to **do** what we have learned, received, heard and seen in Paul. Hopefully, a single example will be sufficient to demonstrate the importance of considering Paul for every aspect of one's studies and conduct *(II Timothy 2:7)*.

An Application of Right Division

The following illustration, concerning the matter of giving, is merely one example of commonly misapplied scripture. The solution comes from a simple understanding of the transition period during the early part of the book of Acts. The cause of the misapplication can generally be attributed to a failure to consider the doctrinal context and application of these passages.

Granted, these verses are usually misapplied unintentionally, yet not always. Every preacher and deacon loves a good Sunday morning offering, but *misapplying* verses to convince a congregation to give more in the collection plate is wrong. Eventually this practice becomes counter-productive by destroying Holy Spirit conviction. By following Paul and rightly dividing the Bible, any person can know whether he is correctly applying the truths of scripture in context.

> *I Corinthians 16:1 Now concerning the **collection** for the saints, as I have given order to the churches of Galatia, even so do ye. 2 **Upon the first day of the week** let every one of you lay by him in store, as God hath prospered him, that there be no gatherings when I come. 3 And when I come, whomsoever ye shall approve by your letters, them will I send to bring your liberality **unto Jerusalem**.*

Some teach and preach this passage as though it applies to the Sunday offering of every local church. However, this passage has special and specific application. The special collection mentioned above was intended for those in Jerusalem. Following Paul *(I Corinthians 4:16)* and understanding his ministry makes it possible to grasp the application of this passage and many others like it.

Historically and doctrinally, the verses have nothing to do with the offering of any local church today. One can apply them *spiritually* to the local church, but applying them *doctrinally* is unethical. Historically, a special collection had to be taken for the poor saints *in Jerusalem*. The collection was taken to send *relief* to those in Jerusalem.

> *Romans 15:25 But now I go unto Jerusalem to minister unto the saints. 26 For it hath pleased them of Macedonia and Achaia **to make a certain contribution for the poor saints which are at Jerusalem**.*

Paul spearheaded the collection of a special offering. A collection had to be taken for the saints in Jerusalem that had obediently observed the early Acts program of giving. These saints sold all of their possessions and gave the money to the apostles. The apostles distributed the money according to each individual's needs. No one was to claim any private ownership of anything. Everyone gave up his possessions for the common good.

> *Acts 2:44 And all that believed were together, and **had all things common**; 45 And **sold their possessions and goods, and parted them to all men, as every man had need**.*

The followers of Christ, during the early part of the book of Acts, were instructed to sell their possessions and claim no personal ownership whatsoever. This practice is known as a part of *the apostles' doctrine (Acts 2:42)*. Verse 14 of this same chapter reveals the spokesman (Peter) and the identity of those to whom he was speaking ("Ye men of Judaea, and all ye that dwell at Jerusalem").

The *apostles' doctrine* is *not* the doctrine of the New Testament church during the Church Age. For any man to sell everything his family owns and give it to his church disregards the plain teaching of scripture *(I Timothy 5:8, II Corinthians 12:14)*. Yet, Peter's confession to the lame man in Acts chapter 3 confirms that Peter had no money. Peter, like all faithful Christians in the first century, obediently gave up all of his belongings. Peter literally meant that he had no money.

> *Acts 3:6 Then Peter said,* **Silver and gold have I none***; but such as I have give I thee: In the name of Jesus Christ of Nazareth rise up and walk.*

Many try to pretend that Peter's comments do not mean exactly what they say. Considering the context of the verses and applying them literally will help an individual to believe them faithfully. Peter did not own anything! Neither did the other faithful followers of the Lord Jesus Christ *at that time*.

> *Acts 4:32 And* **the multitude of them that believed** *were of one heart and of one soul: neither said any of them that ought of the things which he possessed was his own; but they* **had all things common***. 33 And with great power gave the apostles witness of the resurrection of the Lord Jesus: and great grace was upon them all. 34 Neither was there any among them that lacked: for as many as were* **possessors of lands or houses sold them***, and brought the prices of the things that were sold, 35 And laid them down at the apostles' feet: and* **distribution was made unto every man according as he had need***.*

During this time, the faithful sold everything and gave the money to the apostles for distribution among all of the followers, according to the needs of each. None of the believers lacked for any of the necessities. However, a person still had his own free will to do with his property as he pleased. The consequences of hypocrisy were severe. Consider the example of Ananias and Sapphira. They lied about their "faithful" service in an attempt to look spiritual.

They kept back part of the price of a possession they sold, bringing only a portion of the money to the apostles. As a result of their lying, each of them fell dead *(Acts 5:5, 10)*. They died because they claimed to have sold their land for a certain price but actually sold it for more. Unfaithful application of these verses is one way that many of the Charismatic churches collect so much money *(Revelation 3:17)*. These churches begin by applying Acts chapter 2 to the local church today, beginning with the events on the day of Pentecost. Then they move forward showing people that they need to give to their church (or televangelist) in the same fashion as the early Christians in the book of Acts. Using the Bible to prove this is not scriptural.

This is another poignant example of how dangerous it is for people *not* to know their Bibles. The Bible can be used to convince people that communism (having all things owned collectively) is God-ordained by applying these verses to their followers today. In fact, many of the "Bible-based" communes park right here in the book of Acts in order to deceive, control and manipulate their converts into believing just that. David Koresh (Waco, Texas) and Jim Jones of the People's Temple are two of the most widely recognized examples!

What is the answer? One may still be wondering how all of this fits together. The early believers sold all of their possessions because they were looking for the Lord Jesus Christ to return and set up His kingdom immediately. After God revealed the Age of the Church to Paul, we find that the disciples who had sold everything were poor and suffering. They had nothing left. The Bible refers to them as the poor saints at Jerusalem in **Romans 15:25** (above). The next verse says that the churches decided to send them some relief.

> **Acts 11:29** *Then the disciples, every man according to his ability,* ***determined to send relief unto the brethren which dwelt in Judaea****:*

As early as Acts chapter 11, the other churches found it necessary to send relief to those in Jerusalem and Judaea. In order to avoid error, one must first consider the doctrinal setting of the scripture. The book of Acts should not be used (or abused) to convince others to sell everything in order to be spiritual. One needs to *consider what Paul says* in order to understand the application of these *potentially* confusing passages.

There are obvious doctrinal differences between the preaching of Peter and that of Paul. These two did *not* initially preach the same message or minister to the same group of people. Peter primarily went to the Jews while the Apostle Paul was primarily sent to the Gentiles. Peter's ministry phased out of focus once Paul came on the scene. The nation of Israel was cut off and the return of the Lord would not take place until after the times of the Gentiles were fulfilled *(Luke 21:24)*. This presented some problems for those who had obediently sold all of their possessions in expectation of His imminent return to set up His kingdom *(Acts 1:6)*.

The Bible even differentiates between the gospels that these two presented. Take note of the distinction made in the next verse. Once Peter came to understand Christ's death, burial and resurrection he conformed his message to include this truth. However, Peter's name is generally associated with the Jews and his message (gospel) always has a distinctly Jewish character.

> **Galatians 2:7** *But contrariwise, when they saw that the* ***gospel of the uncircumcision*** (Gentiles) *was committed unto me, as the* ***gospel of the circumcision*** (Jews) *was unto Peter;*

Peter had one message during the early part of his ministry. Paul had another. They did not spread the exact message at that time; otherwise the scriptures would have recorded no distinction. Any Christian wanting to learn the Bible must follow God's method of instruction to the believer. Paul tells us that we are to study and rightly divide the Bible. If one does not study the Bible dispensationally, by rightly dividing it, there is no possible way to truly understand its meaning and purpose. Such a person will be a vulnerable target for those who use the Bible to teach "their doctrine." **Beware . . . the Bible can be made to say whatever a person wants to teach, simply by ignoring the correct way to study, preach and teach it.**

> **II Timothy 2:15** *Study to shew thyself approved unto God, a workman that needeth not to be ashamed,* ***rightly dividing the word of truth.***

One who divides the Bible will easily recognize that *not* all scripture is addressed to him. It is impossible to simultaneously follow everything in the book of Acts and obey the following verses. Our apostle points out that we are *not* to have all things common. For example, if a person refuses to provide *for his own household*, he is worse than an infidel.

> **I Timothy 5:8** *But if any provide not for his own, and specially for those of his own house, he hath denied the faith, and is worse than an* ***infidel****.*

Paul again instructs the Church concerning work. In the next passage, he states that not everyone has an absolute right to eat. If a man refuses to work, Paul says that neither should he eat. This is significantly different from the early Acts program of having all things distributed according to need, regardless of the amount of effort put into work.

> *II Thessalonians 3:10 For even when we were with you, this we commanded you, that **if any would not work, neither should he eat.***

Even a greater proof is contained in the next verse. Paul points out that it is the responsibility of the parents to save and provide an inheritance for their children. The early Acts program, in the first century, instructed everyone to sell everything and give the proceeds to the apostles. Paul's instructions "contradict" the apostles' doctrine. If you really are a Bible believer you will believe both truths, but be forced to study the Bible dispensationally to do so.

> *II Corinthians 12:14 Behold, the third time I am ready to come to you; and I will not be burdensome to you: for I seek not yours, but you: for the children ought not to lay up for the parents, **but the parents for the children.***

For parents to save money for their children is both a good idea and a scriptural practice. One who follows the Acts program today and surrenders ownership of all personal property is disobedient. Either the Christian follows Paul or remains confused. He cannot have it both ways. The only consistent answer to all of the doctrines and teachings within the Bible remains the same. One must rightly divide the word of truth.

Some may conclude that this study relieves them of their duty to help others or give to the church. That conclusion originates from man's propensity to do as he pleases and from his love of money. We should give of what we have to help sustain our local church, missionary ministries and other saints in genuine need of assistance. Yet, our giving must be part of a balanced, responsible stewardship of that which God has blessed us. The issue for us is not whether to own property, but what we are to do with the property we own.

We are to provide for our families (even our extended families). We are to provide for God's workmen and their ministries. We are to help others in legitimate need, and we are to spread the gospel. If a person fails to rightly divide the word of truth and then properly apply this truth to his life, he will inevitably act irresponsibly and in violation of the scripture. Today, man must follow Paul and do whatever necessary to learn from and follow him.

With the foundation established in the first eight chapters of this book, focus is now directed to fine tuning some of these biblical principles. All true Bible believers agree that missions remains the heartbeat of God, but even missionary efforts must follow the biblical principles set forth in the word of God. However, some well-meaning mission programs inadvertently distort the scriptures in order to elevate their God-called missions programs above all others. These ill-advised groups teach that giving precedence to Jewish missions, over every other missionary effort, is biblically mandated today.

God wants the Jews evangelized with the Gospel of the Grace of God! He also wants the same energy put forth to evangelize the native deep in the Amazon jungle. Missions should be primary and a most important part of every local church outreach. However, the application of **Romans 1:16** to require a *Jew first* missions requirement today has done considerable harm to otherwise worthy missionary endeavors.

9

To the Jew First?

*Romans 1:16 For I am not ashamed of **the gospel** of Christ: for it is the power of God unto salvation to every one that believeth; **to the Jew first,** and also to the Greek.*

Romans 1:16 says that the gospel is "**to the Jew first**." Have you ever really wondered about the extent of your responsibility when considering this verse? How should this verse influence your witnessing? Some preachers claim that **Romans 1:16** contains the commission for the Church. In fact, some very dedicated Christians use **Romans 1:16** to convince other evangelistically-minded Christians that God expects all others to join with them to witness to the Jew **first**. These individuals claim that going to the Jew first is the only way to be in the will of God. Entire ministries exist today with the basis that this verse gives the commission for the Church to go to the Jew first. Simply ignoring the passage is not an option. How are Christians to act in response to the content of this passage?

The only way to understand the application of this verse is by "rightly dividing" the Bible. The Bible student must now go one step further than previously discussed and divide Paul's thirteen Church Age epistles into two groups. These two groups are called his Missionary Epistles and his Prison Epistles. This chapter covers some specific applications to each group of epistles.

Missionary Epistles

Paul's Missionary Epistles are those books which contain specific application to his Acts missionary journeys. The book of Acts records Paul's three missionary journeys, beginning in Acts chapter 13 through his imprisonment in Acts chapter 28. Paul's final trip, ending in Rome, is not generally considered to be his *fourth* missionary journey since he was in chains on his way to prison at that time.

The first group of four books (Romans through Galatians) is referred to as Paul's *Missionary Epistles* because they contain doctrinal applications specific to the time covered by Paul's missionary journeys. *In some cases*, the application of particular doctrines during this time differs from the doctrines applicable after Paul goes into prison. Therefore, the application of these particular doctrines ends before the first century concludes (that is, before A.D. 100). These doctrines include the gospel presentation to the "Jew first," speaking in tongues, supernatural signs and abstaining from certain meats forbidden under the law. (Note: Application of this teaching does not apply to baptism and the Lord's Supper. When churches apply this teaching to these two subjects, they might as well apply it to the salvation taught in the book of Romans as well. God does not want us to eliminate *all* application of Paul's first four books to the Church Age, as some would have us believe. Hyper-dispensationalism finds its roots in *over*-application of this truth.)

Prison Epistles

The second group of Paul's nine letters is referred to as his *Prison Epistles*. Not all of these books were necessarily written while Paul was *physically* in prison, but most of them were. Regardless of specifically when these books were actually written (I & II Thessalonians, for instance) their doctrinal application follows this teaching. Since we are told to *rightly divide* (not rearrange) our Bibles, we need to recognize a division between the end of the Missionary Epistles (Galatians) and the book of Ephesians, with the transition taking place in Galatians. This division helps us understand some changes in God's plan as set forth within the Church Age itself.

We must recognize the importance of dividing Paul's epistles. God completely phased out some *unusual* features of Paul's early ministry around the time he went into prison in Acts chapter 28. Without a thorough understanding of this truth and its application, it will be impossible for the Christian to be "approved unto God" *(II Timothy 2:15)*. Even the book of Galatians seems to transition Paul's ministry as he points out the dangers and corrects the errors of trying to become too much like the Jews.

Each of the charts in this chapter is divided in half. The use of a **dotted line** signifies that a division falls within a major period that must be considered collectively. The dividing point has "A.D. 100" denoted beneath. This date signifies *a point in time* when all Bible scholars agree that the sixty-six books of the Bible were already complete. The date does *not* signify when the actual books listed were written, nor does it represent the date of Paul's imprisonment. The date A.D. 100 simply signifies that God's word was perfected (or completed) by this time.

Paul's Thirteen Church Age Epistles

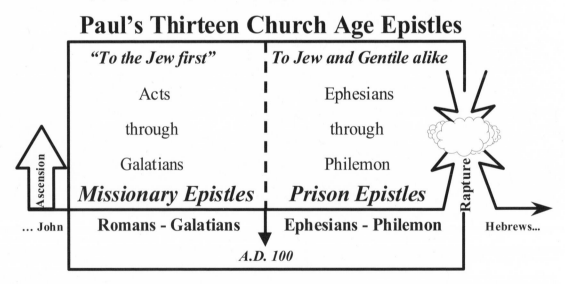

Chart 9.1 - Division of Paul's Epistles

After completing this study, the importance and necessity of dividing Paul's Church Age epistles should be evident. A thorough understanding of this chapter is necessary to understand other issues covered in later chapters. However, a warning seems appropriate at this point. While we must recognize the division between Paul's *missionary* and *prison* ministries, we must not apply it in excess of God's intended purpose. Excessive application of this division causes as much error and harm as does the failure to apply it at all. Some groups take this division to an extreme by eliminating most of the application of Paul's first four epistles to the Church today. Over-dividing the Bible becomes a very divisive issue and is to be vigilantly avoided. Those who "hyper-divide" their Bibles are called hyper-dispensationalists. We will point out the reasons for their actions and the erroneous results later.

First, we must establish some basic truths concerning the application of this division.

The Timing of Romans

Establishing the timing of the book of Romans is a good starting point. When Paul writes Romans, he states in the first chapter that he was praying about making a journey to Rome.

> **Romans 1:10** *Making request, if by any means now at length I might have a **prosperous journey** by the will of God **to come unto you.***

Since Paul travels to Rome for the first time in Acts chapter 28, the timing of the book of Romans must be during his missionary journeys and prior to Acts chapter 28 when he finally arrives in Rome. Although Paul intended to travel to Rome on several different occasions, God did not allow him to do so. God may have prevented this journey on several occasions since it would have required Paul to leave an area primarily populated by Jews and go to an area primarily populated by Gentiles. Regardless of the reason, it was not the will of God for Paul to go to Rome at this time. Paul continues in the first chapter:

> **Romans 1:13** *Now I would not have you ignorant, brethren, that oftentimes **I purposed to come unto you**, (but was let hitherto,) that I might have some fruit among you also, even as among other Gentiles.*

Paul says he purposed to visit Rome, but was directed elsewhere. Even as late as the next to last chapter of Romans, he makes mention of his desire to visit Rome and his inability to do so. Paul then expresses his plans to visit Rome while on his way to Spain.

> **Romans 15:22** *For which cause also **I have been much hindered from coming to you.** 23 But now having no more place in these parts, and having **a great desire these many years to come unto you**; 24 Whensoever I take my journey into **Spain**, I will come to you: for I trust to see you in my journey, and to be brought on my way thitherward by you, if first I be somewhat filled with your company. 25 But now I go unto Jerusalem to minister unto the saints.*

His "prosperous journey" was not what he had anticipated . . . he came to Rome bound in chains *(Acts 28:20)*. Paul, unlike many Christians today, was willing to accept the fact that God's will sometimes takes a person through the fire in order to bring about His ultimate glory.

Before we look at specific applications of the division between Paul's Missionary and Prison Epistles, we must establish that many of his latter epistles make mention of his imprisonment. We have seen that the book of Romans was written and has application during Paul's *missionary journeys. He* is still in a traveling mode. The three other books included with Romans have specific application to the same time period. These are First and Second Corinthians, and Galatians. None of these books makes mention that Paul was in bonds or chains. The first of his epistles that mentions his bonds is the book of Ephesians.

Paul in Roman Prison

God places the tools for Bible study within the Bible itself. Paul's mentioning of bonds in these books affirms the fact that he wrote them after his final journey to Rome in Acts chapter 28. Again, some of the books were written earlier, but God's placement determines their application. Some preachers teach to "rearrange" rather than "rightly divide." Leave the books in their God-given order and study them accordingly. The first of the Prison Epistles, the book of Ephesians, contains three passages which emphasize Paul's imprisonment.

*Ephesians 3:1 For this cause I Paul, the **prisoner** of Jesus Christ for you Gentiles,*

*Ephesians 4:1 I therefore, the **prisoner** of the Lord, beseech you that ye walk worthy of the vocation wherewith ye are called,*

*Ephesians 6:20 For which I am an ambassador **in bonds:** that therein I may speak boldly, as I ought to speak.*

The books of Philippians, Colossians, and First and Second Timothy also mention Paul's bonds.

*Philippians 1:7 Even as it is meet for me to think this of you all, because I have you in my heart; inasmuch as both **in my bonds**, and in the defence and confirmation of the gospel, ye all are partakers of my grace.*

*Philippians 1:13 So that my bonds in Christ are manifest in all the palace, and in all other places; 14 And many of the brethren in the Lord, waxing confident by **my bonds**, are much more bold to speak the word without fear. 15 Some indeed preach Christ even of envy and strife; and some also of good will: 16 The one preach Christ of contention, not sincerely, supposing to add affliction to my bonds:*

*Colossians 4:3 Withal praying also for us, that God would open unto us a door of utterance, to speak the mystery of Christ, for which I am also **in bonds**:*

Paul's Thirteen Church Age Epistles

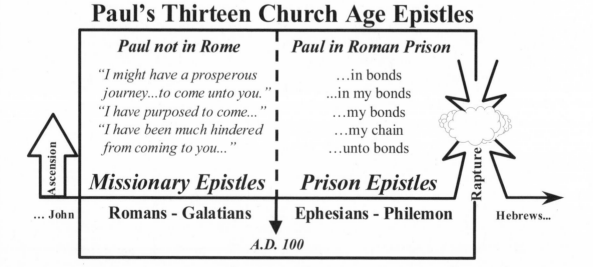

Chart 9.2 - Missionary vs Prison Epistles

Colossians 4:18 The salutation by the hand of me Paul. Remember **my bonds**. Grace be with you. Amen.

II Timothy 1:16 The Lord give mercy unto the house of Onesiphorus; for he oft refreshed me, and was not ashamed of **my chain**:

II Timothy 2:9 Wherein I suffer trouble, as an evil doer, even **unto bonds**; but the word of God is not bound.

Just as Paul's first Prison Epistle mentioned his bonds, so does his last one.

Philemon 9 Yet for love's sake I rather beseech thee, being such an one as Paul the aged, and now also a prisoner of Jesus Christ. 10 I beseech thee for my son Onesimus, whom I have begotten **in my bonds**:

Each of the preceding verses makes reference to Paul's imprisonment; all of these verses are found in Paul's last nine Church Age books, his Prison Epistles. Recognizing this division is very important. The division becomes *critical* when one attempts to answer the cults and those churches propagating false doctrine. Many Christians get involved with these groups because they never have been taught the truth. Too many preachers have quit trying to explain the truth because seminaries have not sufficiently trained their students. They have been taught the *spiritual* application of the scripture, rather than its *literal* application and *doctrinal* implications.

In turn, those in the pews unknowingly repeat the same falsehoods by spreading the doctrines they have been taught. As you study some of the various issues concerning the Church today, you might find that they do not completely agree with what you have been taught. For a moment, if the possibility exists that what you have been taught is wrong, ignore it. No matter the cost, recognizing the truth is always more important and will free you from the burden that error causes *(John 8:32)*.

Reaching the Jewish Remnant

The next issue to consider deals with the Jewish *remnant (Romans 11:5)* mentioned in the first Missionary Epistle. God commissioned Paul to present the gospel **first** to this *remnant of Jews* during his missionary journeys. For this reason, Paul goes to the Jew first *(Romans 1:16)*. God gives the Jews an opportunity to accept Him before breaking off the nation of Israel completely *(Romans 11:20)*. After Israel is broken off, during the first century, the Jewish people no longer enjoy any special standing before God. They find God in the same way as all other men, and God no longer requires them to be reached *first*. Jews must come to God the same way as does any Gentile.

When Paul traveled into a city, he would go into the synagogue and preach to the Jew first *(Acts 13:14, 14:1, 17:1, 18:4, 19:8)*. Once Paul reached the remnant of these Jews in a certain region, God started treating Jew and Gentile alike. By the time Paul ended up in prison, the remnant had been reached. Consequently, the Jew's advantage of being presented the gospel *first* has no doctrinal bearing on the Church's activities after the first century.

During the *missionary journeys*, God used signs to reach the Jews. God used signs to reach them simply because the Jews required a sign *(I Corinthians 1:22)*. The Israelites came to expect this treatment throughout much of the Old Testament because signs frequently accompanied the message from God. One sign used by God during this period was the apostles' gift of tongues *(I Corinthians 14:22)*.

The signs followed the Apostle Paul through his missionary journeys. However, the signs do not last throughout the entire Church Age. While God offered the gospel to the *Jew first* through Paul, these signs served as a confirmation of his message to them. Paul followed this plan in every place he visited in the book of Acts, by going to the synagogue first during every preaching endeavor.

Consider the implications of the gospel going to the *Jew first*. If Christians are to follow Paul in this matter *today (I Corinthians 11:1)*, then every Christian should find the synagogue in every city he visits *prior to* preaching to any Gentile. A Christian has only two other alternatives when considering the "Jew first" principle:

1. Determine that these instructions are "time-sensitive."
2. Ignore any potential application of the verse altogether and pretend that the scripture does not mean what it plainly says.

The Bible is a great book. God leaves nothing open to chance. The command of **Romans 1:16** is "time sensitive." God was transitioning from a 2,000-year period of Jewish prominence, beginning with Abram, to a time in which He would use the Gentiles to fulfill His plan and purpose. In His mercy and grace, the move from the Jews was *gradual*, rather than an abrupt cutting off of Israel. We should study God's divisions in the same fashion. The transition is gradual, thus the division is likewise gradual. *The tendency to **abruptly sever** the Bible into many segments, limiting its application to only a few epistles today, does not conform to God's method of rightly dividing the Bible.* It is very dangerous and divisive to apply the division between Paul's Missionary and Prison Epistles to more than the few areas God intended.

Although we may now recognize this transition to be gradual, it was a profound change to the Jews. For a time, God would no longer consider them His chosen people. God would instead use "Gentile dogs" *(Matthew 15:26)* to do His work. The Jews were accustomed to receiving signs and wonders for so long that God apparently gave them a "short time" to transition into this change. Otherwise, it is likely that even fewer of them would have accepted the truth. The Jews were dependent on signs, and God was merciful and gracious in providing them.

By studying Paul's actions, as recorded in the book of Acts, it is easy to see that he obeyed the command to go to the Jew **first** during each of his missionary journeys. A few references should serve to prove his obedience to this command. Acts chapter 9 records Paul's Damascus Road conversion to the Lord Jesus Christ. The same chapter records his first "preaching engagement."

> *Acts 9:20 And **straightway** he preached Christ **in the synagogues**, that he is the Son of God.*

Paul immediately preached about the Lord in the synagogues, obeying the command of **Romans 1:16**. This was the best place to find the Jews. This pattern continued throughout the book of Acts. Even Paul's testimony to King Agrippa points out that he went to the Jew **first**.

> *Acts 26:19 Whereupon, O king Agrippa, I was not disobedient unto the heavenly vision: 20 But shewed **first** unto them of Damascus, and at Jerusalem, and throughout all the coasts of Judaea, and **then to the Gentiles**, that they should repent and turn to God, and do works meet for repentance.*

Confusion can arise from reading what others were doing during the same time that Paul was ministering to the Jew *first*. Many of the apostles' converts continued to follow the commands and examples of *Matthew 10:5, Matthew 15:24* and *John 20:21* by going to the Jews **only**. God revealed something new to the Apostle Paul, and many of the others seemed not to be completely aware of this change yet.

> *Acts 11:19 Now they which were scattered abroad upon the persecution that arose about Stephen travelled as far as Phenice, and Cyprus, and Antioch, **preaching** the word to none but **unto the Jews only**.*

All of the other apostles began their ministries by going to the *Jews only*. Paul was the exception. In every city he went into *during his Acts missionary journeys*, he would try to reach the Jew *first and then* go to the Gentiles. The program of *Romans 1:16* was to be taught and followed *at this time*.

Not everyone knew of the changes being made by God; therefore, the book of Acts records instances of those still following the "old plan." For instance, those referenced in Acts chapter 11 (above) were still unaware of the change concerning the Gentiles. Even Peter was unaware of this change. As late as Acts chapter 10, the Bible records Peter's reluctance to accept God's changing plan. God even showed him this truth in a dream. The main point of the "unclean" animals *(Acts 10:13)* and his instructions to go to Cornelius—a Gentile *(Acts 10:20)* —were to clearly reveal this transition to Peter. God finally gets Peter's attention by using the sign of tongues *(Acts 10:46)* to prove that God's plan now involved the Gentiles.

Peter was *not* qualified to be the main spokesman to the Gentiles. He had previously been commanded to go to the **Jew only** *(Matthew 10:5)*. If Peter had become the main spokesman to announce God's change of direction, he would have appeared to be a confused preacher to everyone he had previously instructed. Instead, God expected Peter to support the apostle chosen to make this change—Paul. However, credibility was not Peter's only problem. Even once he saw the truth, he was *not* committed to living the consistent, unwavering testimony necessary to be effective in teaching the Jews to reach the Gentiles. The Bible records an instance in which Paul had to rebuke Peter for his inconsistent testimony concerning the Jews' treatment of the Gentiles *(Galatians 2:11-14)*.

Following the Apostle Paul through the remainder of the book of Acts, we see that he was obedient . . . going to the Jew first. However, remember that this is a time of *transition*. God knew the difficulty facing the Jews. They expected the customary signs for proof. If God had abruptly ended the signs, it would have appeared that He was just arbitrarily casting Israel aside. Paul explains that God had not just cast away his people (the elect of *Romans 11:7*).

> *Romans 11:1 I say then, **Hath God cast away his people? God forbid**. For I also am an Israelite, of the seed of Abraham, of the tribe of Benjamin.*

There was a **remnant** of Jews to be reached before God ended all of the signs, wonders, and miracles. Continuing in the same context, we read in verse 5 of the same chapter:

> *Romans 11:5 Even so then at **this present time** also there is a **remnant** according to the election of grace.*

Notice the key phrase "at this present time." This phrase indicates that the context of Romans 11 is time-sensitive, similar to the *Jew first* gospel presentation of the first chapter of

Romans. **There was a remnant of Jews during the first century that God wanted to reach before He changed directions completely and placed priority on reaching Jew and Gentile alike.** Paul absorbed himself in the work—making everyone aware of his responsibility to reach this remnant. Paul conveyed the sense of urgency, best expressed in First Corinthians. Concerning this remnant, Paul points out that the "time is short" and even calls it a "present distress."

I Corinthians 7:26 I suppose therefore that this is good for **the present distress,** *I say, that it is good for a man so to be.*

During this short time, even marriage took a back seat to reaching the Jewish remnant before the signs ended. God gave signs and wonders (including tongues and healing) to enable the Jews to accept the preaching of the Gospel of the Grace of God. God knew that the signs and wonders would allow more of the Jews to accept this change. Paul characterized the time as a "present distress" because time was running out. He knew the signs were waning and would soon be eliminated. How much harder it would be for the Jews to accept the Lord without the supernatural signs. Time was short!

I Corinthians 7:29 But this I say, brethren, **the time is short***: it remaineth, that both they that have wives be as though they had none;*

Paul warned the believers that time was short. During this period of time (Paul's Acts missionary journeys), God allowed those witnessing to do certain things for the benefit of the Jews. Two chapters later, Paul points out that he adapted himself according to the group to whom he was ministering. Notice how peculiar this next verse reads.

I Corinthians 9:20 And **unto the Jews I became as a Jew,** *that I might gain the Jews; to them that are under the law, as under the law, that I might gain them that are under the law;*

Paul was a Jew! Yet, the verse says that Paul *became* a Jew. Why would Paul need to become "as a Jew?" The answer is very simple. Once a person is saved, he becomes a Christian and his "religious" background means nothing. This is especially true concerning the Jews. In the Body of Christ, being a Jew means nothing. Paul considered himself a Christian, not simply a Jew.

Galatians 3:28 **There is neither Jew nor Greek***, there is neither bond nor free, there is neither male nor female: for* **ye are all one in Christ Jesus***.*

Once Paul was converted, his Jewish ancestry did not matter to God *(Philippians 3:4-8).* However, God did not just cast His people (the Jews) away; therefore, *during Paul's missionary journeys* God allowed the message to be delivered with signs and wonders. God wanted the Jews to remain in a place of prominence for a short time by receiving the message *first*. During this time, God permitted Paul to use his Jewish ancestry to aid him in reaching his "brethren in the flesh." God also allowed Paul to perform some other actions in order to reach the Jews. For instance, Paul's circumcision of Timothy in Acts chapter 16 had no spiritual benefit to Timothy. The sole purpose of this action was to aid in Timothy's reaching the Jews with the Gospel of the Grace of God.

Paul's Thirteen Church Age Epistles

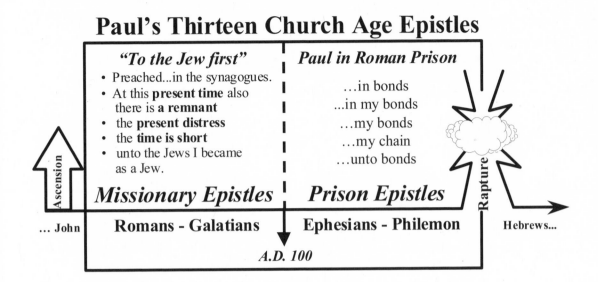

"To the Jew first"
- Preached...in the synagogues.
- At this **present time** also there is **a remnant**
- the **present distress**
- the **time is short**
- unto the Jews I became as a Jew.

Missionary Epistles

Romans - Galatians

Paul in Roman Prison

...in bonds
...in my bonds
...my bonds
...my chain
...unto bonds

Prison Epistles

Ephesians - Philemon

Ascension

... John

Rapture

Hebrews...

A.D. 100

Chart 9.3 - The Remnant

Circumcision

It is important to consider further the example of Timothy's circumcision. Paul was preparing to take Timothy with him on his preaching trips. Timothy's uncircumcised state was a problem since Paul preached in the synagogues. The Jews would reject Paul's preaching if he brought someone uncircumcised into the synagogue.

> *Acts 16:1 Then came he to Derbe and Lystra: and, behold, a certain disciple was there, named **Timotheus**, the son of a certain woman, which was a Jewess, and believed; but his **father was a Greek**: 2 Which was **well reported** of by the brethren that were at Lystra and Iconium. 3 Him would Paul have to go forth with him; and took and **circumcised him because of the Jews** which were in those quarters: for they knew all that his father was a Greek.*

Paul circumcised Timothy. The Bible says that Timothy was circumcised "because of the Jews." Timothy's circumcision had absolutely nothing to do with obedience to the law. Neither did it have any bearing on his spiritual walk with Christ. God wanted the remnant to be reached. Paul would not allow the matter of circumcision to be a stumblingblock to those Jews who would otherwise refuse to listen. God had conditioned them (the Jews) and He would allow a short time for them to be reconditioned to the new way of thinking.

Paul circumcised Timothy in order to reach the Jews with the gospel. The issue was different in Galatians when Titus accompanied Paul. In that instance, false brethren were trying to convince the believers that they had to be circumcised to be right with God. When salvation or fellowship with God were connected with circumcision, Paul refused to be a part of the practice. For example, consider the account of the false brethren trying to convince Paul that Titus should be circumcised.

> *Galatians 2:1 Then fourteen years after I went up again to Jerusalem with Barnabas, and **took Titus with me also**. 2 And I went up by revelation, and communicated unto*

*them that gospel which I preach among the Gentiles, but privately to them which were of reputation, lest by any means I should run, or had run, in vain. 3 **But neither Titus**, who was with me, being a Greek, **was compelled to be circumcised**: 4 And that because of **false brethren** unawares brought in, who came in privily to spy out our **liberty** which we have in Christ Jesus, that they might bring us into **bondage**:*

Even during his missionary journeys, Paul placed limits on what he would do "as a Jew" in his dealings with the Jews. Timothy's circumcision was voluntary for the effectiveness of his testimony and ministry. On the other hand, Titus' circumcision would have brought him under bondage. Circumcision was the same act physically for Timothy as for Titus. However, Paul circumcised the former but not the latter because of the motivation behind the act.

Paul would not circumcise Titus because the issue in Galatians had nothing to do with reaching the remnant of Jews. However, Timothy's uncircumcised state (in Acts) was not allowed to hinder *the remnant* from hearing the gospel delivered to Paul. In Galatians, "false brethren" were attempting to confuse the gospel by adding circumcision to it. God is not the author of confusion *(I Corinthians 14:33)*. Salvation is completely dependent on the shed blood of the Lord Jesus Christ. Circumcision has no place in the Body of Christ.

*Galatians 5:6 For in Jesus Christ neither **circumcision** availeth any thing, nor uncircumcision; but faith which worketh by love.*

*Galatians 6:15 For in Christ Jesus neither **circumcision** availeth any thing, nor uncircumcision, but a new creature.*

The Bible clearly points out that a person's circumcision status is irrelevant. Yet, circumcision was a requirement at one time. Once again, we should readily recognize that God's plan for man changes, and it is man's responsibility to adapt to and recognize the change.

Special Meats

For the Jews *under the law*, no options existed concerning *circumcision (Leviticus 12:3)*. The same expectations applied to the Jewish dietary laws. These dietary standards were just as stringent and unwavering as the rules for circumcision. God's specific commands concerning the eating and abstaining from certain kinds of meats were plainly given by Moses.

Under the law, certain meats were allowed and certain meats were not permitted. Do the same rules apply today? The next passage clearly shows that God's rules changed concerning special meats.

*I Timothy 4:1 Now the Spirit speaketh expressly, that in the latter times some shall depart from the faith, **giving heed to seducing spirits, and doctrines of devils**; 2 Speaking lies in hypocrisy; having their conscience seared with a hot iron; 3 Forbidding to marry, **and commanding to abstain from meats**, which God hath created to be received with thanksgiving of them which believe and know the truth. 4 For every creature of God is good, and nothing to be refused, if it be received with thanksgiving: 5 For it is sanctified by the word of God and prayer.*

The scripture plainly teaches a four-fold *condemnation* of the command to abstain from eating certain meats. Remember that these included foods that were forbidden *under the law*.

The Bible says commanding to abstain from meats is:

1. Departing from the faith

2. Giving heed to seducing spirits and doctrines of devils

3. Speaking lies in hypocrisy

4. Having the conscience seared with a hot iron

A *religious requirement* forbidding a person to get married has the equivalent condemnation attached to it. Both of these actions, concerning meats and marriage, are doctrines of a devil! God demands that the Christian handle these matters according to His Church Age requirements. God could not be more emphatic. He says that to do otherwise is satanically inspired. This hardly sounds like the rules given under the law.

> *Leviticus 11:46 **This is the law of the beasts,** and of the fowl, and of every living creature that moveth in the waters, and of every creature that creepeth upon the earth: 47 **To make a difference between the unclean and the clean, and between the beast that may be eaten and the beast that may not be eaten.***

The Jewish reaction to these changes is understandable. Peter's reaction to the unclean meats recorded in Acts chapter 10 is typical *(Acts 10:14)*. The standard reaction from any orthodox Jew would mirror Peter's refusal to eat the "unclean" animals. God knew how the Jews would respond. In His mercy, God allowed some transition time (during Paul's missionary journeys) for the Jews to adjust and accept this newly revealed truth.

God uses the book of Timothy to draw the line. Yet, the next few passages reveal a completely different picture. These passages are applicable during the time of transition (the Missionary Epistles). Paul tells those in Rome that they are not to take an absolute, dogmatic stand on the issue of meats:

> *Romans 14:1 Him that is weak in the faith receive ye, but not to doubtful disputations. 2 For **one believeth that he may eat all things: another, who is weak, eateth herbs**. 3 Let not him that eateth despise him that eateth not; **and let not him which eateth not judge him that eateth**: for God hath received him. 4 Who art thou that judgest another man's servant? to his own master he standeth or falleth. Yea, he shall be holden up: for God is able to make him stand. 5 **One man esteemeth one day above another: another esteemeth every day alike**. Let every man be fully persuaded in his own mind.*

The previous passage deals with two important transitional issues—special days and meats. To be spiritually right with God, the *weak* brother believes that you should eat only herbs and no meats. Furthermore, Paul points out that every person must be persuaded in his own mind about holy days, meats, etc. In contrast, the Paul of First Timothy chapter 4 issued a blanket condemnation to those that would follow the Levitical Law and command others to do so. This issue (of the condemnation) was not even raised until after the remnant had been reached because reaching the remnant had the highest priority.

Later in the same chapter of Romans, Paul elaborates even further. The change from the Levitical Law is pronounced. Verse 14 says there is *nothing* unclean . . . what a change from the law.

*Romans 14:14 I know, and am persuaded by the Lord Jesus, that there is **nothing unclean** of itself: but **to him that esteemeth any thing to be unclean, to him it is unclean**. 15 But if thy brother be grieved with thy meat, now walkest thou not charitably. Destroy not him with thy meat, for whom Christ died. 16 Let not then your good be evil spoken of: 17 For the kingdom of God is not meat and drink; but righteousness, and peace, and joy in the Holy Ghost. 18 For he that in these things serveth Christ is acceptable to God, and approved of men. 19 Let us therefore follow after the things which make for peace, and things wherewith one may edify another. 20 **For meat destroy not the work of God**. All things indeed are pure; but it is evil for that man who eateth with offence. 21 **It is good neither to eat flesh, nor to drink wine, nor any thing whereby thy brother stumbleth, or is offended, or is made weak**. 22 Hast thou faith? have it to thyself before God. Happy is he that condemneth not himself in that thing which he alloweth. 23 And he that doubteth is damned if he eat, because he eateth not of faith: for whatsoever is not of faith is sin.*

It must have been a startling revelation for those Jews to read Paul's epistle. There is nothing unclean?! It is only unclean to the person that believes it to be unclean?! We cannot overstate the significance of abstaining from certain meats under the law. Certain meats that were deemed unclean by God under the law were no longer an issue. God's plan was changing. Anyone that heard and received the truth would understand that there is nothing innately unclean. Yet, if someone still considered certain meats unclean, during this time of transition, it was unclean to him. It was important not to cause a weak individual to spiritually stumble.

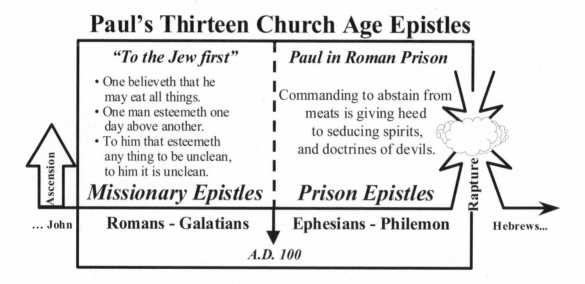

Paul's Thirteen Church Age Epistles

"To the Jew first"	Paul in Roman Prison
• One believeth that he may eat all things. • One man esteemeth one day above another. • To him that esteemeth any thing to be unclean, to him it is unclean.	Commanding to abstain from meats is giving heed to seducing spirits, and doctrines of devils.
Missionary Epistles	*Prison Epistles*
Romans - Galatians	**Ephesians - Philemon**

Ascension ... John   A.D. 100   Rapture   Hebrews...

Chart 9.4 Meats and Days

God was transitioning the Jews from the Gospel of the Kingdom and the circumcision to the gospel of the uncircumcision. The Jews were a people accustomed to walking by sight and had very little experience walking by faith alone *(II Corinthians 5:7)*. This change would require of the Jews the same expectations placed on the Gentiles. However, it was much easier for the Gentiles to accept things by faith because they had not become accustomed to the signs, as had the Jewish nation. For thousands of years, God gave signs to the Jews. The Old Testament abounds with examples.

During Paul's missionary journeys, God was allowing the Jews to have some time before He expected them to walk by faith alone without signs, wonders, or miracles. Everyone today has the same requirement. The Bible points out that our Jewish or Gentile background lacks relevance. God demands that we all come to salvation exactly the same way.

During the transition, if a "Jewish Christian" regarded something as unclean, to him it was unclean. It was a sin for him to ignore his conscience concerning these matters. If he thought something he was doing was inappropriate because of the Levitical Law, it was a sin for him to go ahead and do it anyway. The Jews were given a liberty not afforded them under the law. But the Gentile or Jewish Christian's responsibility was different during this time too. The Christian was not to exercise his liberty in Christ Jesus if doing so would cause a weak Jewish Christian to fall or stumble.

*I Corinthians 8:8 But meat commendeth us not to God: for neither, if we eat, are we the better; neither, if we eat not, are we the worse. 9 But take heed lest by any means this **liberty** of yours become a stumblingblock to them that are **weak**.*

Paul told the believers that they should *not* allow their liberty to eat any meat to be a stumblingblock to someone that was weak (in the faith). They were to abstain from certain things *for testimony's sake*. God wanted to reach these Jews and did not want man's selfishness to stand in the way.

*I Corinthians 8:10 For if any man see thee which hast knowledge sit at meat in the idol's temple, shall not the conscience of him which is weak be emboldened to eat those things which are offered to idols; 11 And through thy knowledge shall the weak brother perish, for whom Christ died? 12 But when ye sin so against the brethren, and wound their weak conscience, ye sin against Christ. 13 **Wherefore, if meat make my brother to offend, I will eat no flesh while the world standeth, lest I make my brother to offend**.*

Every Christian has liberty to eat any meat he so desires because the Old Testament commandments concerning meats are no longer applicable today. Yet, during the transition, God led Paul to deal with this subject differently. Paul emphasized that this liberty was not to be a stumblingblock to weak Jews still unsure of all the changes taking place.

A word of caution again: God does not necessarily limit Himself dispensationally. In verse 13, Paul says he would eat no flesh **while the world is standing**! This responsibility of a *Christian's testimony* to a brother transcends all time periods. The more important issue, as far as Paul (and God) was concerned, was to avoid doing anything that would offend your brother and make it impossible to be an effective witness. **Some people who learn their Bible become very dangerous with the little bit of knowledge God gives them. They take that knowledge and the Bible and hit people upside the head with it.**

This newfound freedom (or liberty) is used to destroy those that do not have the same knowledge or faith. These individuals are more interested in flaunting their "rights" than with being concerned with the life and walk of other fellow Christians or the lost. They use this knowledge in a way that not only destroys the baby in Christ, but also eliminates their effectiveness in reaching the lost for the Lord Jesus Christ. This should not be the case!

Paul would refrain from meats altogether if it would enable him to reach the Jews. He put ministering to others above his own personal "rights" and liberties. We need to do the same. Jeremiah tells us that God loves Israel with an everlasting love *(Jeremiah 31:3)*. Should we display anything less? Churches have neglected Jewish evangelism for far too long! We must become more Christ-like by supporting evangelistic efforts to reach the Jews with Christ.

In the next passage, Paul deals with idolatry. He says that if you are invited to a lost person's feast, eat whatever is set before you and do not ask if it was offered to idols. But if the host volunteers this information to you, do not eat *for his sake*. Your liberty is to be limited based on the spiritual condition of others.

> *I Corinthians 10:27 If any of them that **believe not** bid you to a feast, and ye be disposed to go; whatsoever is set before you, eat, asking no question for conscience sake. 28 But if any man say unto you, This is offered in sacrifice unto idols, **eat not for his sake** that shewed it, and for conscience sake: for the earth is the Lord's, and the fulness thereof:*

One should see that Paul and the others had liberty to eat, but self-imposed limitations to this liberty existed. If eating meats would destroy a young Christian or hinder reaching the lost for the Lord Jesus Christ, the liberty to eat was not to be exercised. Paul emphasized that an individual's opportunity to evangelize is much more important than his exercising the God-given right to eat whatever he wishes. The change taking place is evident. Can you imagine the difficulty that the Jews would have listening to some pork-eating "Jewish-Christian?" God foreknew and He allowed Paul to give some instruction on how to reach the Jewish remnant. (Peter knew the truth too—see *Galatians 2:11-14* again).

The point God wants us to recognize is the change in emphasis. During Paul's missionary journeys the emphasis concerning the meats and holy days was on recognizing the transition and allowing the Jews some time to adjust to the changes. Once Paul's missionary journeys ended, the emphasis switched to dealing very dogmatically with those who influenced others to abstain from certain meats and observe holy days. Our responsibility to love others remains the same, but the point of Paul's emphasis changes because God's plan transitions.

The Weak and Beggarly Elements

Even during Paul's missionary journey letters, God does not allow any confusion about the danger of Christians trying to submit themselves to the Old Testament ordinances. In Galatians (a Missionary Epistle), God rebukes any Christian that tries to apply the ordinances under the law to the Church. Here, God has given the Jews a period of time to accept and learn what He expects of them. Once again, Galatians seems to be a transition book to Paul's Prison Epistles.

> *Galatians 4:9 But now, after that ye have known God, or rather are known of God, how turn ye again to **the weak and beggarly elements**, whereunto ye desire again to be in **bondage**?* What are these things that he is referring to? Read the next verse and see: *10 Ye observe days, and months, and times, and years.*

Observing days, months, times and years is not to be done today. However, these special days and seasons were certainly to be observed *under the law*. Have you ever considered the implications of these verses on our observance of Easter and Christmas? One proof of the *un*holiness of these days comes from taking note of how the world handles these days. If these two days are in fact Christian holidays (or holy days), why do the Christ-rejecting United States government and the American public school systems still recognize them? Think about that! These groups have vehemently refused to allow any semblance of Christianity in the schools. Yet, they still allow the recognition of these two "holy" days. There is more to this issue than meets the eye.

The only time Easter is mentioned in your King James Bible is in *Acts 12:4* when an *unbelieving* Herod wants to wait until after *he* celebrates Easter to put Peter to death. A lost man in the Bible wanted to celebrate Easter and then kill a Christian! Easter was a Babylonian feast to the sun goddess Ashtor and a celebration of fertility. Have you ever wondered why two prominent symbols of fertility surround our celebration of Easter? Consider the Easter bunny and eggs? Did you know that rabbits do not lay eggs? Easter began as a celebration of fertility and has nothing to do with the resurrection of the Lord Jesus Christ. Holy days sicken God today. Fortunately, those that are wise will nevertheless use these holidays as occasions for family gatherings and appropriate godly celebration, but the truth remains the truth.

Once again, God gives us some additional straightforward information in Paul's Prison Epistles. Ordinances such as those of special meats were nailed to the cross with the Lord Jesus Christ. We should have no doubt concerning the position that God takes. He expects us to take the same position.

> *Colossians 2:13 And you, being dead in your sins and the uncircumcision of your flesh, hath he quickened together with him* (Jesus)*, having forgiven you all trespasses; 14* ***Blotting out the handwriting of ordinances that was against us, which was contrary to us, and took it out of the way, nailing it to his cross****; 15 And having spoiled principalities and powers, he made a shew of them openly, triumphing over them in it. 16 Let no man therefore judge you in* **meat**, *or in* **drink**, *or in respect of an* **holyday**, *or of the* **new moon**, *or of the* **sabbath days***: 17 Which are a shadow of things to come; but the body is of Christ.*

The Mosaic Law explicitly spelled out what one could and could not eat, specifically prescribed a host of holydays, established guidelines for Sabbath days, etc. The law was very rigid and unchanging until the Lord came *(Matthew 5:39)*. All of the holy days, special meats, etc. ended by being nailed to the cross by the death of the Lord Jesus Christ. The Bible says He nailed them to His cross and took them out of the way. Although He nailed these ordinances to the cross, the application of these principles was not revealed until the revelation given to the Apostle Paul. These aspects remained a mystery.

Later in the same chapter of Colossians, God gives us further instruction concerning these matters. The Bible says Christians are dead with Christ; therefore, why should they subject themselves to all of these ordinances . . . touch not, taste not, etc.? These things have been eliminated by the application and understanding of the cross.

> *Colossians 2:20 Wherefore if ye be dead with Christ from the rudiments of the world, why, as though living in the world, are ye subject to ordinances, 21 (Touch*

not; taste not; handle not; 22 Which all are to perish with the using;) after the commandments and doctrines of men? 23 Which things have indeed a shew of wisdom in will worship, and humility, and neglecting of the body; not in any honour to the satisfying of the flesh.

Christians notoriously are known for ignoring the plain teachings of the scriptures. They constantly try to put themselves back under the law in various ways. Paul says these keepers of the law "look good." They look spiritual, but obedience requires that Christians not allow themselves to get caught up in anything that has an *outward appearance* of spirituality with no inward effect. Keeping the Levitical ordinances does not help the Christian be more spiritually right with God.

Paul's Thirteen Church Age Epistles

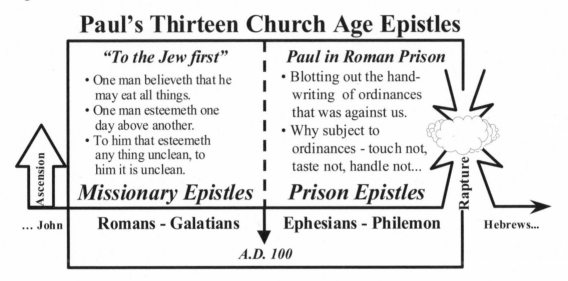

Chart 9.5 Ordinances

Not only was the transition "time-sensitive," as we stated earlier, but it was also "location sensitive" as the transition progressed. As you study these areas concerning the remnant, the *Jew first*, holy days, special meats, etc., you must determine when the transition was complete in that particular geographic region. At what point in the first century did the Jews no longer have an advantage?

The Transition Record/The Remnant Reached

The book of Acts has the answer to this question. A definite pattern emerges. By reading and studying Paul's missionary journeys in the book of Acts, one can see the pattern. The purpose of each of the three journeys, including the trip to Rome, was to reach the remnant of Jews before the signs and wonders ceased. Once the remnant was reached, God *turned* Paul's primary focus to the Gentiles in each particular area.

Acts chapter 13 contains the first of these *turning* points. Acts chapters 18 and 28 contain the other two turning points. Each time, Paul points out the *necessity* of God's word being presented to the Jews *first* and the writer of Acts points out their rejection and blasphemy *(Mark 3:29)*. Acts chapter 13 contains the turning point in Asia Minor.

*Acts 13:44 And the next **sabbath day** came almost the whole city together to hear the word of God. 45 But when the **Jews** saw the multitudes, they were filled with envy, and spake against those things which were spoken by Paul, contradicting and **blaspheming**. 46 Then Paul and Barnabas waxed bold, and said, It was necessary that the word of God should **first** have been spoken to you: but seeing ye put it from you, and judge yourselves unworthy of everlasting life, lo, **we turn to the Gentiles**.*

Five chapters later the same pattern repeats itself. Paul presents the gospel to the *Jews first*; they blaspheme; and Paul informs them of his changing direction—to the Gentiles (in Europe).

*Acts 18:5 And when Silas and Timotheus were come from Macedonia, Paul was pressed in the spirit, and testified to the Jews that Jesus was Christ. 6 And when they opposed themselves, and **blasphemed**, he shook his raiment, and said unto them, Your blood be upon your own heads; I am clean: **from henceforth I will go unto the Gentiles***

The concluding chapter of the book of Acts records the final turning point throughout the world. Paul was finishing this part of his course. The remnant that Paul was attempting to reach had been reached. Jews in the future times were not going to receive any advantage due to their Jewish ancestry. In verse 17, we find that Paul gathers the "chief of the Jews together" and preaches to them. They would not listen and the result is recorded as follows:

*Acts 28:26 Saying, **Go unto this people**, and say, Hearing ye shall hear, and shall not understand; and seeing ye shall see, and not perceive: 27 For the heart of **this people** is waxed gross, and their ears are dull of hearing, and their eyes have they closed; lest they should see with their eyes, and hear with their ears, and understand with their heart, and should be converted, and I should heal them. 28 Be it known therefore unto you, that the **salvation of God is sent unto the Gentiles**, and that they will hear it.*

Paul's Thirteen Church Age Epistles

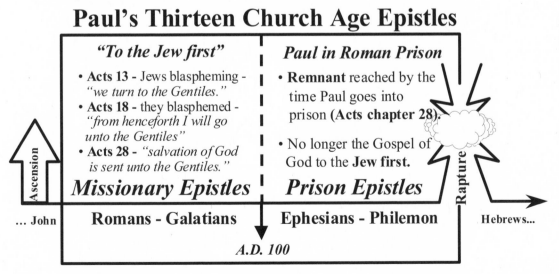

Chart 9.6 - Turn to the Gentiles

God always gives us the information we need to understand His word and its context. Consequently, in this final chapter of Acts, the Bible calls attention to Paul's imprisonment (*Acts 28:20 . . . for the hope of Israel I am bound with this **chain**)*. Thus, the Bible seems to make a connection between Acts chapter 28 and *Paul's Prison Epistles*. The importance of this link with his Prison Epistles must be recognized. We have already established the significance of recognizing the distinction between the two groups of epistles.

No longer the Gospel of God to the Jew First

Man's natural inclination frequently leads contrary to the dictates of God. Consider man's fascination with astrology, the zodiac and psychic readers. The devil controls these areas and the people that become enamored of them. Heed the warning of the word of God. In the last days, increased emphasis will be placed on these satanic devices. The world will see an increased fascination with the astrological predictions of men like Nostradamus. However, God wants man to view each day as an opportunity to serve and worship Him. He does not want man to become superstitious about anything. Either God leads a person or some other force will take His rightful place.

As we have seen, the special meats and times are not the only areas that have changed. Another area of change concerns God's use of tongues. God used tongues as a sign to convince the unbeliever to believe God's message. See chapters 11 and 12 in this book for further information concerning Signs and Wonders. Also take note that any preacher or teacher attempting to use this division of Paul's epistles to convince you that baptism and the Lord's Supper are to be treated just like the special meats and holy days is a false teacher *(II Timothy 4:3)*. The verse they most often use to "prove" their position is *I Corinthians 1:17*.

> *"We must recognize that the Bible is written to, or about distinct classes. According to the general view everything from Genesis to Revelation is written to, or about the church and Christians. No greater mistake could be made. The truth is, the church and Christians occupy a very restrained area of the Bible. If all is said directly about the church and Christians was printed by itself it would make a very small book. Not even all of the New Testament is directly written to, or about the church."*
>
> *I.M. Haldeman, How to Study the Bible - The Second Coming and Other Expositions (NY: Charles C. Cook, 1904), p. 2*

> *I Corinthians 1:17 For **Christ sent me not to baptize**, but to preach the gospel: not with wisdom of words, lest the cross of Christ should be made of none effect.*

However, these same individuals fail to point out that **none** of us is sent to baptize. We are all sent to evangelize. Use right division of the Bible as a tool to understand the Bible. Do not use it as a tool to confuse or eliminate the Christian's responsibility to be gracious, godly and separated. People tend to get puffed up as they learn the facts of their Bible *(Colossians 2:8)*. Studying and learning the Bible is to give us hope *(Romans 15:4)*. However, take heed: the sodomites are not the only ones changing the truth of God into a lie *(Romans 1:25, I Timothy 6:20)*.

10

The Gospel – Rightly Divided

I Corinthians 11:1 Be ye followers of me, even as I also am of Christ. 2 Now I praise you, brethren, that ye remember me in all things, and keep the ordinances, as I delivered them to you.

God commands the Church to follow Paul as he follows the Lord Jesus Christ. One specific area directly addressed in the previous passage concerns the church ordinances. They are to be Pauline. Paul tells us to remember *him* and keep the ordinances *as he* delivered them. The **only** church ordinances mentioned in Paul's epistles are baptism and the Lord's Supper. Following Paul is simply a matter of obedience. Failing to obey this mandate causes confusion, error and sometimes even heresy.

The Apostle Paul's writings clarify many other issues as well as that of the church ordinances. However, *the most critical issue* clarified by Paul concerns the Gospel of the Grace of God *(Acts 20:24)*. Failing to follow Paul concerning the gospel could lead to mass confusion for yourself and all others you influence. There is no understanding more important than an understanding of the gospel. This entire chapter deals with this one subject. Paul clearly defines the gospel in First Corinthians chapter 15 as the death, burial and resurrection of the Lord Jesus Christ.

*I Corinthians 15:1 Moreover, brethren, I declare unto you **the gospel** which I preached unto you, which also ye have received, and wherein ye stand; 2 By which also ye are saved, if ye keep in memory what I preached unto you, unless ye have believed in vain. 3 For I delivered unto you first of all that which I also received, **how that Christ died for our sins according to the scriptures**;* (Notice the word "how." *How* did he die? The most important thing about his death is the shedding of His blood for our sins. The gospel continues . . .) *4 **And that he was buried, and that he rose again the third day according to the scriptures:***

Paul refers to this gospel as **the** gospel which he preached because there were other gospels too *(Matthew 24:14)*. All other "gospels" today are either counterfeit *(Galatians 1:6-7)* or have been replaced *(Matthew 9:35)* by the one Paul declared. Every Christian must testify **this** gospel and no other. The revelation of this gospel was given to our apostle—the Apostle Paul *(Galatians 1:11-12)*! Therefore, we are to preach that a person must trust in the death, burial, and resurrection of the Lord Jesus Christ in order to be saved. Does the Bible teach that this is the only gospel that ever existed? Before jumping to a conclusion based upon your personal prejudices, read *Matthew 4:23* and see if the Bible mentions any other gospel.

Before considering fully the question about *multiple* gospels in the Bible, it is important to mention how Paul received the gospel. Did the Apostle Peter teach it to him? Was it taught to him by one of the other apostles? Did he read about it somewhere else? The answer to each of these questions is a resounding "no!"

Where did Paul receive the gospel message that he gives to us in Romans, Ephesians, etc.? As the next passage clearly reveals, Paul received the gospel he preached directly from the Lord Jesus Christ. No man taught it to him.

> **Galatians 1:11** *But I certify you, brethren, that **the gospel** which was preached of me is **not after man**. 12 For I **neither received** it of man, **neither** was I **taught** it, but by the revelation of Jesus Christ.*

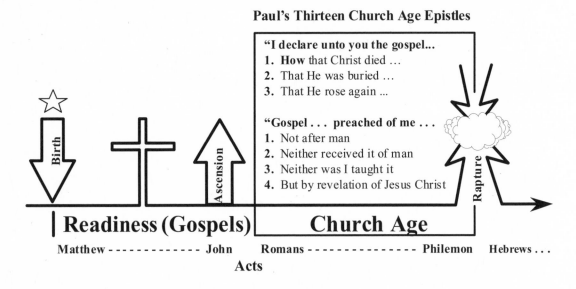

Chart 10.1 - Paul's Gospel

Paul says he did not receive the gospel from any man. Instead, he received it directly from the Lord Jesus Christ *by revelation*. Yet, Peter and the other apostles were still alive when Paul was saved. It should seem unusual to the reader that God would use this method to reveal the gospel to Paul. Here are some important questions to ponder when considering these issues:

1. Why didn't Paul receive the gospel from some other man?
2. Why didn't the other apostles teach Paul the gospel?
3. Why did God find it necessary to reveal the gospel directly to a new apostle?
4. Had something changed?
5. Why would the Lord find it necessary to give the gospel directly to Paul for the Church?
6. Was this gospel something different, something new, something that the other apostles did not yet understand?

The Lord Jesus Christ foretold His death, burial and resurrection to the apostles. However, these apostles did not believe, or understand these things until sometime *after* the resurrection. Paul records the account of his visit to the apostles at Jerusalem to communicate to them the gospel he was preaching among the Gentiles.

*Galatians 2:1 Then fourteen years after I went up again to **Jerusalem** with Barnabas, and took Titus with me also. 2 And I went up by revelation, and **communicated unto them that gospel which I preach among the Gentiles**, but privately to them which were of **reputation**, lest by any means I should run, or had run, in vain.*

Paul said he had to communicate the gospel that he preached to them who "were of reputation." His concern was that he had run in vain or would run in vain in the future. His concern was about the gospel he was preaching. Why would Paul find it necessary to *privately* communicate to the other apostles the gospel that he preached? The apostles of the Lord were still having some adjustment problems understanding the changes that God was implementing. However, Paul did find out that the Holy Spirit had revealed these same truths to the others also *(**Ephesians 3:5**)*. Galatians clearly distinguishes between the gospel that Peter initially preached and the one that Paul preached.

*Galatians 2:6 But of these who seemed to be somewhat, (whatsoever they were, it maketh no matter to me: God accepteth no man's person:) for they who seemed to be somewhat in conference added nothing to me: 7 But contrariwise, when they saw that **the gospel of the uncircumcision** was committed unto me, as **the gospel of the circumcision** was unto Peter; 8 (For he that wrought effectually in **Peter** to the **apostleship of the circumcision**, the same was mighty in me toward the Gentiles:)*

The last verse of this passage points out that Peter was an apostle to the circumcision (Jews). When these leaders of the church in Jerusalem saw that Paul's gospel to the "uncircumcision" was blessed of God, they extended to him the right hand of fellowship *(verse 9)*. They accepted Paul's teaching as the truth. Yet, verse 7 unmistakably recognizes the distinction in ministries . . . the one to the circumcision and the other to the uncircumcision.

The gospel defined

This truth is *not* hard to accept if one considers the definition of *gospel*. By comparing *Isaiah 61:1* (the good tidings) with the replaced words of *Luke 4:18* (the gospel), we find that the definition of gospel is simply "good tidings." Once we accept this Bible definition, it is easy to see that the *good tidings* presented by Paul differed from the *good tidings* initially presented by Peter to the circumcision. This passage may reflect that both men may have presented the death, burial, and resurrection, but the gospel message was not identical. Otherwise no distinction would be made.

Peter's gospel (good tidings) included a Jewish flavoring. The events recorded at the church in Jerusalem reveal the apostles' propensity to mix their heritage with their presentation of the message to the Gentiles. Peter was a major player in this church *(verse 7)*. Paul visits with the apostles in Jerusalem to discuss some issues that he was battling out with some of the other Jewish brethren. The leaders come to some conclusions with the agreement of the whole church *(verse 22)* and send an epistle *(verse 30)* for the Gentiles. They tell the Gentiles *the necessary things*.

*Acts 15:28 For it seemed good to the Holy Ghost, and to us, to lay upon you no greater burden than **these necessary things**; 29 That ye **abstain from meats offered to idols, and from blood, and from things strangled, and from fornication**: from which if ye keep yourselves, ye shall do well. Fare ye well.*

This message (glad tidings/gospel) differs from the one that we preach and from the gospel (glad tidings) revealed by the Apostle Paul. Peter was consenting to this communication to the Gentiles. Of course, Paul was the one that delivered their message *(verse 30)*.

Peter had difficulty accepting the transition at the time. He went from preaching the Gospel of the Kingdom or gospel of the circumcision (in the Gospels) to the same gospel that Paul preached. Peter was very effective in reaching these Jews because he used enough of the Jewish "buzz" words to keep their attention and not turn them away from the truth.

Peter's Message of the Kingdom

> *"...there is no hint of a possible position in Christ in any teaching of the law or of the kingdom."*
>
> Lewis Sperry Chafer, *Systematic Theology*, p. 98.

How do we know that Peter's original message (gospel) differed from what the Apostle Paul reveals to us? First and foremost, we know this because the results of the crucifixion were not revealed until after the cross. Peter had been preaching "the gospel" for several years by then, but it was the Gospel of the Kingdom that he preached. We will cover this topic in more detail in later chapters. Most of what we read about Peter's preaching covers a time *before* the cross in the four Gospel books.

The Gospel of the Grace of God was revealed in its entirety to the Apostle Paul. His thirteen Church Age epistles contain the details of that revelation. They all bear Paul's name as the very first word in each book. The importance of following the right leader (spokesman) cannot be overemphasized. God insured that everyone could easily recognize which epistles Paul wrote for the Church to follow. How else would God insure that we would know how to follow Paul *(I Corinthians 11:1)* and obey Him in the process? God did not instruct us to follow a man (as this man follows Christ) and then keep us guessing about how to accomplish this task. Paul revealed the full purpose and effect of the cross—something which had remained a mystery prior to his revelation.

> *Ephesians 3:2 If ye have heard of the **dispensation of the grace of God** which is given me to you-ward: 3 How that **by revelation he made known unto me the mystery;** (as I wrote afore in few words,*

Thank God for Paul's faithfulness and obedience. The Lord Jesus Christ told others of His death, burial and resurrection prior to the cross, but He waited to open their understanding until *after* the resurrection. The truth was hidden from them. If God had opened the apostles' understanding prior to the cross, Satan would have understood the truth also.

Had Satan understood the significance and impact of the cross, he would never have instigated Christ's crucifixion. He never would have convinced Judas Iscariot to betray the Lord *(John 6:70)*. Satan would not have convinced Pilate to wash his hands of the whole matter *(Matthew 27:24)*. Instead, Satan was convinced that he was defeating God by supporting and encouraging the Jews' rejection of the Lord and their killing of the Messiah.

The Book of Luke

Those prior to the cross did not fully understand its significance. Yet, some would correctly point out that the Bible records instances of the gospel being preached prior to the cross. But what gospel? In Luke chapter 9, the Lord sends out the twelve disciples and commands them to preach.

*Luke 9:1 Then he called **his twelve disciples** together, and gave them power and authority over all devils, and to cure diseases. 2 And he **sent them to preach the kingdom of God**, and to heal the sick.*

Verse 2 says the twelve were sent to preach the Kingdom of God. Verse 6 further specifies exactly what the apostles preached. It was "the gospel" (or "glad tidings") for them in that day. Obviously, these apostles could not have been preaching the death, burial and resurrection prior to the time of the crucifixion recorded in Luke chapter 23. A few verses later we are told that they went through the towns "preaching the gospel."

*Luke 9:6 And they departed, and went through the towns, **preaching the gospel**, and healing every where.*

They went preaching the gospel. Which gospel? The context of this gospel is found in verse 2—it is the Gospel of the Kingdom *(Mark 1:14)*. It includes the miracles of healing. Was it the gospel of the death, burial and resurrection? No!

Paul's Thirteen Church Age Epistles

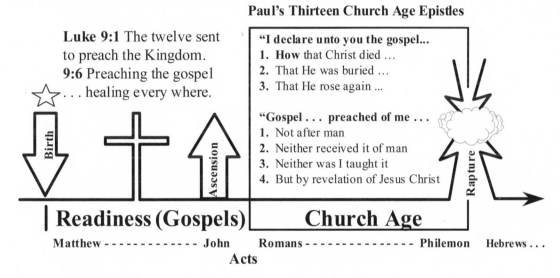

Luke 9:1 The twelve sent to preach the Kingdom. **9:6** Preaching the gospel ... healing every where.

"I declare unto you the gospel...
1. **How** that Christ died ...
2. That He was buried ...
3. That He rose again ...

"Gospel ... preached of me ...
1. Not after man
2. Neither received it of man
3. Neither was I taught it
4. But by revelation of Jesus Christ

Birth

Ascension

Rapture

| **Readiness (Gospels)** | **Church Age** |

Matthew - - - - - - - - - - - - John   Romans - - - - - - - - - - - - - Philemon   Hebrews . . .

Acts

Chart 10.2 - Kingdom Gospel

In Luke chapter 18, nine chapters after the Lord sends the disciples out to preach "the gospel," we find Him explaining to them once again what we now know as the gospel today. Was the gospel that they preached different from the gospel that we preach? Had the apostles preached the same gospel that we preach today *(I Corinthians 15:1-4)*, their response to Christ's message to them would have surely been much different.

*Luke 18:31 Then he took unto him the **twelve**, and said unto them, Behold, we go up to Jerusalem, and **all things that are written by the prophets concerning the Son of man shall be accomplished.** 32 For he shall be delivered unto the Gentiles, and shall be mocked, and spitefully entreated, and spitted on: 33 And they shall scourge him, and **put him to death: and the third day he shall rise again**.*

The Lord tells the apostles in verse 33 about the death, burial and resurrection (our gospel). Then the Bible records something very interesting. **The next verse, verse 34, states that they did not understand what the Lord was talking about!** In fact, it was hidden from them.

*Luke 18:34 And they **understood none** of these things: and this saying was **hid** from them, **neither knew** they the things which were spoken.*

The apostles did not understand the gospel of the death, burial and resurrection. Yet, they preached "the gospel" (of the Kingdom). God hid the gospel we preach today from the apostles, yet they were all saved with the exception of Judas Iscariot *(John 17:12)*. A person would be lost today if this same gospel were hidden from him *(I Corinthians 4:3-4)*.

Consider the magnitude of this truth. Nine chapters after the apostles go forth to preach *the gospel* (Luke 9), we are told they do not understand *the gospel* which a person must trust in order to be saved today. Verse 33 is the gospel as we know it. Verse 34 clearly states that the apostles did not understand our gospel. God actually **hid** if from them. Be sure to grasp this truth. Rejecting this truth because it is a foreign concept or because it is difficult to believe places a person in danger of being unable to receive any further light from God.

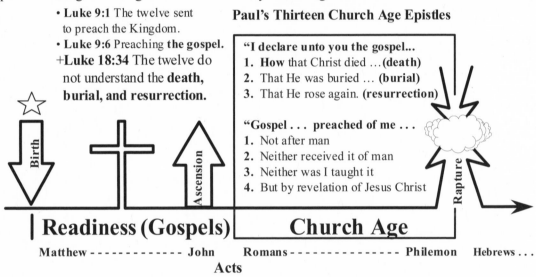

- **Luke 9:1** The twelve sent to preach the Kingdom.
- **Luke 9:6** Preaching **the gospel.**
+**Luke 18:34** The twelve do not understand the **death, burial, and resurrection.**

Paul's Thirteen Church Age Epistles

"I declare unto you the gospel...
1. **How** that Christ died ...**(death)**
2. That He was buried ... **(burial)**
3. That He rose again. **(resurrection)**

"Gospel ... preached of me ...
1. Not after man
2. Neither received it of man
3. Neither was I taught it
4. But by revelation of Jesus Christ

Birth   Ascension   Rapture

Readiness (Gospels)   **Church Age**

Matthew - - - - - - - - - - - - John   Romans - - - - - - - - - - - - - Philemon   Hebrews . . .

Acts

Chart 10.3 - Kingdom Gospel II

Satan's problems have nothing to do with not hearing the truth. He perverts and twists the truth when he hears it. However, Satan could not comprehend the purpose of the gospel prior to its fulfillment. Had Satan understood the Gospel of God's Grace prior to its fulfillment, he would never have caused the Lord to be crucified. This gospel had to remain a mystery to him and everyone else. The scripture reveals this truth.

*I Corinthians 2:7 But we speak the wisdom of God in a mystery, even the hidden wisdom, which God ordained before the world unto our glory: 8 **Which none of the princes of this world knew: for had they known it, they would not have crucified the Lord of glory**.*

Satan and his pawns would not have crucified the Lord had they understood the mystery prior to its fulfillment. Satan learned the truth too late. The outcome of the cross was not apparent until after the resurrection. By then, it was too late! Satan is powerful, but he cannot undo that which is already done. Even his knowledge is sometimes limited. For instance, the Bible says he learns many truths from the Church (See *Ephesians 3:9-10*).

Satan would never have played a part in the crucifixion had he realized the full conse-quences of his actions. The Lord laid down His life *(John 10:17-18)*; Satan became the tool to fulfill prophecy, resulting in God's greatest victory. Consequently, the Lord could tell the apostles about the death, burial and resurrection, but had to wait to open their understanding. Even the apostles' misunderstanding of the empty tomb becomes more apparent to us when we consider this truth.

Luke chapter 24 records the account of the resurrection and the empty tomb. The women were on their way to the tomb to anoint the body of the Lord and instead find an empty tomb. The Bible conveys the women's bewilderment. The two men by the sepulcher after the resur-rection repeat the words of the Lord concerning the crucifixion and resurrection.

> *Luke 24:6 He is not here, but is risen: remember how he spake unto you when he was yet in Galilee, 7 Saying, The Son of man must be delivered into the hands of sinful men, and be crucified, and the third day rise again. 8 **And they remembered his words,***

Verse 7 contains the gospel of the death, burial and resurrection. The women remember His words, but still do not grasp the full significance of what has happened. They return from the sepulcher and tell the good news of the resurrection to the eleven remaining apostles.

> *Luke 24:9 And returned from the sepulchre, and told all these things unto the eleven, and to all the rest. 10 It was Mary Magdalene and Joanna, and Mary the mother of James, and other women that were with them, which told these things unto the apostles. 11 **And their words seemed to them as idle tales, and they be-lieved them not**.*

Did you catch that? To the apostles, the resurrection seemed an "idle tale." As recorded in the final chapter of Luke, they still do not understand the gospel of the death, burial, and resur-rection! Not until later in this chapter is their understanding of the Gospel of God's Grace opened. **Can you imagine believing and teaching that these apostles preached the same gospel back in chapter 9 that we preach today?**

The scripture records that even Peter wondered about the resurrection *(verse 12)*. There can be no doubt that he and the others did not **understand** our gospel prior to the cross, nor did they understand it shortly following the resurrection. They did not understand it until it was revealed to them directly by the Lord when He opened their understanding.

> *Luke 24:12 Then arose **Peter**, and ran unto the sepulchre; and stooping down, he beheld the linen clothes laid by themselves, and departed, **wondering in himself at that which was come to pass**.*

Although the apostles were greatly used by God, they were not His chosen vessels to reveal this gospel to the world. God chose someone else to be the spokesman to the Gentile world concerning the gospel of the death, burial and resurrection—the Apostle Paul.

In the final verses of the concluding chapter of Luke, the apostles finally come to understand the death, burial and resurrection. The Lord takes this opportunity to open the scriptures to the apostles, the disciples and the world. The apostles finally understand the victory *to some extent*; Satan, on the other hand, understands the defeat quite clearly.

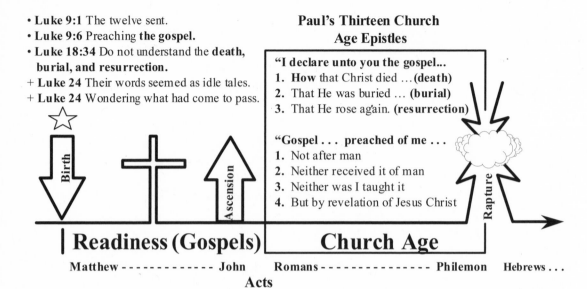

- **Luke 9:1** The twelve sent.
- **Luke 9:6** Preaching **the gospel.**
- **Luke 18:34** Do not understand the **death, burial, and resurrection.**
- + **Luke 24** Their words seemed as idle tales.
- + **Luke 24** Wondering what had come to pass.

Paul's Thirteen Church Age Epistles

"I declare unto you the gospel...
1. **How** that Christ died ...**(death)**
2. That He was buried ... **(burial)**
3. That He rose again. **(resurrection)**

"Gospel . . . preached of me . . .
1. Not after man
2. Neither received it of man
3. Neither was I taught it
4. But by revelation of Jesus Christ

Readiness (Gospels)   **Church Age**

Matthew - - - - - - - - - - - - John   Romans - - - - - - - - - - - - - - Philemon   Hebrews . . .
                          Acts

Chart 10.4 - Kingdom Gospel III

*Luke 24:44 And he said unto them, These are the words which I spake unto you, while I was yet with you, that all things must be fulfilled, which were written in the law of Moses, and in the prophets, and in the psalms, concerning me. 45 **Then opened he their understanding, that they might understand the scriptures**, 46 And said unto them, Thus it is written, and thus it behoved Christ to suffer, and to rise from the dead the third day:*

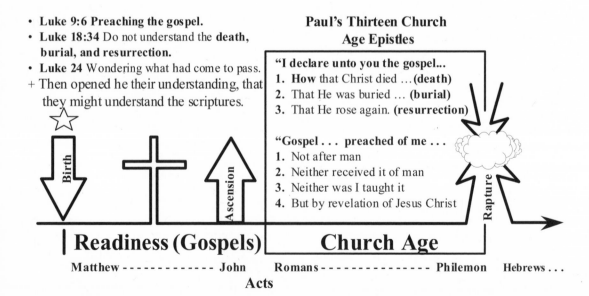

- **Luke 9:6** Preaching **the gospel.**
- **Luke 18:34** Do not understand the **death, burial, and resurrection.**
- **Luke 24** Wondering what had come to pass.
- + Then opened he their understanding, that they might understand the scriptures.

Paul's Thirteen Church Age Epistles

"I declare unto you the gospel...
1. **How** that Christ died ...**(death)**
2. That He was buried ... **(burial)**
3. That He rose again. **(resurrection)**

"Gospel . . . preached of me . . .
1. Not after man
2. Neither received it of man
3. Neither was I taught it
4. But by revelation of Jesus Christ

Readiness (Gospels)   **Church Age**

Matthew - - - - - - - - - - - - John   Romans - - - - - - - - - - - - - - Philemon   Hebrews . . .
                          Acts

Chart 10.5 - Kingdom Gospel IV

The right-hand side of the previous chart (in the box) clearly reveals the gospel we preach found in Paul's thirteen Church Age epistles. The left-hand side of the chart reveals that the Lord sent forth the twelve in Luke chapter 9 and they preached "the gospel." Yet, in chapter 18 they did not understand the death, burial and resurrection (our gospel). Chapter 24 says they wondered what had come to pass when the body of the Lord turned up "missing." Finally, we see that the Lord opened their understanding so that they could comprehend the death, burial, and resurrection (our gospel). It is reasonable to assume, that those who died before the cross were not looking *forward* to the cross any more than these apostles were looking forward to it.

> *"There is a dangerous and entirely baseless sentiment abroad which assumes that every teaching of Christ must be binding during this age simply because Christ said it. The fact is forgotten that Christ, while living under, keeping, and applying the Law of Moses, also taught the principles of His future kingdom, and, at the end of His ministry and in relation to His cross, He also anticipated the teachings of grace. If this threefold division of the teachings of Christ is not recognized, there can be nothing but confusion of mind and consequent contradiction of truth."*
>
> Lewis Sperry Chafer, *Systematic Theology*, Volume 4, (TX: Dallas Seminary Press, 1947) p. 224.

The Book of Mark

The other three Gospel books reveal the same truth. Since this teaching may be somewhat foreign to the understanding of many of the readers, we will consider how the book of Mark presents this same truth. Mark chapter 9 gives us another plain example of the apostles' lack of understanding of the death, burial and resurrection prior to its occurrence. The Lord told them about the resurrection so they would believe it when He opened their understanding.

Mark 9:9 And as they came down from the mountain, he charged them that they should tell no man what things they had seen, till the Son of man were risen from the dead. 10 And they kept that saying with themselves, questioning one with another what the rising from the dead should mean.

Can you imagine a preacher today not understanding what the "rising from the dead" means? A person today without this *basic* knowledge is not qualified to preach. Without reservation, it seems probable that *most* of us would agree with this fact.

The Book of John

John 2:18 Then answered the Jews and said unto him, What sign shewest thou unto us, seeing that thou doest these things? 19 Jesus answered and said unto them, Destroy this temple, and in three days I will raise it up. 20 Then said the Jews, Forty and six years was this temple in building, and wilt thou rear it up in three days? 21 But he spake of the temple of his body. 22 When therefore he was risen from the dead, his disciples remembered that he had said this unto them; and they believed the scripture, and the word which Jesus had said.

As early as the second chapter of John, the Bible points out that the apostles would not understand the gospel of the death, burial and resurrection *until after the Lord was risen from the dead.* God *spoke* a truth to them, but did not *reveal* the truth until there was a need for them to know. We should always remember not to get ahead of God. God will reveal the truth He wants us to know in His time. We must only be faithful to accept the truth when He reveals it. For example, God could use this particular book in your life to do the same thing—reveal the truth. The time for this message may be now. No doubt God wants *you* to see this truth or **He** would not have revealed it to *you* thus far.

John chapter 14 shows God's purpose for revealing something of the crucifixion to the apostles prior to its occurrence. Generally, the Lord planted the seed so that they would believe after the event came to pass.

> **John 14:28** *Ye have heard how I said unto you, I go away, and come again unto you. . . . 29 And now **I have told you before it come to pass,** that, when it is come to pass, ye might believe.*

The purpose for the apostles' hearing the truth is evident. Christ foretold the future (prophesied) of what would take place here on this earth. For instance, John chapter 20 confirms what He said in chapter 2.

> **John 20:8** *Then went in also that other disciple, which came first to the sepulchre, and he saw, and believed. 9 **For as yet they knew not the scripture, that he must rise again from the dead.***

Even after the betrayal, trial and crucifixion, the apostles do not understand the empty sepulcher. Therefore, they did not understand the resurrection (or our gospel). The point about their preaching a different gospel during the earthly ministry of the Lord seems too obvious to belabor. Yet, there is one more Gospel book that we have not yet considered—the book of Matthew. This book clearly reveals the truth as well. Peter's reaction to the presentation of the death, burial and resurrection provides clear evidence of the apostles' lack of understanding.

The Book of Matthew

> **Matthew 16:21** *From that time forth began Jesus to shew unto his disciples, how that he must go unto Jerusalem, and suffer many things of the elders and chief priests and scribes, and be **killed,** and be **raised again the third day.** 22 Then **Peter** took him, and **began to rebuke him,** saying, Be it far from thee, Lord: this shall not be unto thee.*

Peter (the leader of the twelve) obviously did not understand the death, burial and resurrection! In fact, he rebuked the Lord when He foretold these things. How could anyone justify following Peter as an example to emulate during this period in his ministry when he did not as yet understand the basics concerning Christ's death? Peter's ministry does not change until after the resurrection. Following the resurrection, the truth of the gospel revealed in Paul's epistles had also been revealed to Peter *(Ephesians 3:5)*.

Summary

All four Gospel books agree; all four present a gospel message different from the one we preach today. Each book definitely reveals that the *Gospel of the Kingdom* preached by the apostles and the Lord differed from the gospel preached today. This example offers another proof of how critical right division of the scripture has become in today's confusing world. There is no lack of religion, but there is a famine of truth *(Amos 8:11).*

As is evident from studying the Bible, misinterpretation of the scripture runs rampant. Listen to any *scripture-quoting* cultist and one can easily recognize the grave danger in not knowing how to rightly divide the word of truth. A cultist is a cultist because he does not recognize or simply refuses to accept God's method of Bible study. By going to just any part of the Bible and ripping verses out of their context, the application of the truth becomes perverted. We must always consider the individuals to whom the scripture is addressed. The Bible clearly instructs the student of God's word. Whether you heed the instruction or ignore it is a matter of truth or error; of obedience or disobedience. Paul wrote:

> *II Timothy 2:7 Consider what I say; and the Lord give thee understanding in all things.*

God sometimes makes Bible study very easy. Verse 15 *of the same book* explains **how** to consider what Paul says:

> *II Timothy 2:15 Study to shew thyself approved unto God, a workman that needeth not to be ashamed, **rightly dividing the word of truth**.*

Whenever reading the Bible, consider what Paul says (by rightly dividing it) and the Lord will give you all the understanding necessary. If some verses seem to teach contradictory things, consider what Paul says. If some Bible truth seems to contradict what the Apostle Paul writes for us, give the Apostle Paul's words precedence.

Some might wonder exactly how to *rightly* divide the Bible. If the Gospel books (Matthew through John) reveal the preaching of a different gospel from the one revealed in Paul's thirteen Church Age epistles, would that not seem like a natural division? Sure it would, and it is! The book of Acts located between John and Romans, transitions from one presentation to the next and makes a natural division (and a smooth transition) from the Jews' Apostle (Peter) to the Gentiles' Apostle (Paul).

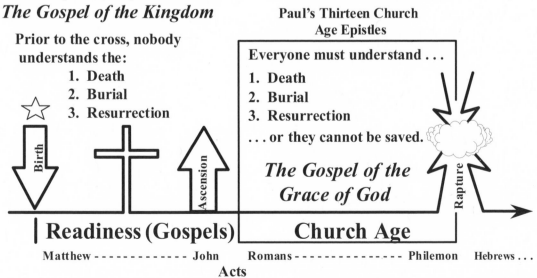

Chart 10.6 - More than One Gospel

> *"...salvation of whatever specific character is always the work of God in behalf of man and never a work of man in behalf of God. This is to assert that God never saved any one person or group of persons on any other grounds than the righteous freedom to do so which the Cross of Christ secured. There is, therefore, but one way to be saved and that is by the power of God made possible through the sacrifice of Christ.*
>
> *Thus it is disclosed that the salvation of an Israelite, who lived in the Mosaic age, which age will be completed in the coming Tribulation, was guaranteed by covenant; yet the individual could, by failing to do God's revealed will as contained in the Mosaic Law, sacrifice his place in the coming Kingdom and be cut off from his people (cf. Luke 10:25-28; 18:18-21; Matt.8:11, 12; 24:50, 51; 25:29, 30). Jehovah's salvation of Israel will be on the ground of Christ's death. The human terms, because of the covenant promise regarding their salvation, are not the same as that required by Abraham or an individual in this age, whether Jew or Gentile."*
>
> Lewis Sperry Chafer, "Inventing Heretics Through Misunderstanding," Bibliotheca Sacra, volume 102, number 405 (Jan. – March, 1945), 1, 4-5.

Will people be agreeable with this method of rightly dividing your Bible and following what Paul says? Not all of them! Others may hold the same opinion **of you** as the Apostle Paul's peers did of him.

*Acts 24:14 But this I confess unto thee, that after the way which **they call heresy**, so worship I the God of my fathers, believing all things which are written in the law and in the prophets:*

Any **Bible-believer** that is called a heretic should not be ashamed. God revealed the truth directly to the Apostle Paul and the religious world called it (the truth!) heresy. The truth is what really matters, not the titles men bestow upon those with whom they disagree. The Bible clearly points out that it is better to suffer for doing right than to suffer for compromising the truth *(I Peter 3:17)*. Paul will be rewarded for the title "heretic" that he wore in his day; not because he asked for it, but because he stood for the truth no matter the cost. What will your title be?

As we travel through the "last days" of the Church Age, *perilous times* shall come upon those willing to take an uncompromising stand for the truth *(II Timothy 3:1)*. Truth and error shall meet head to head. A major point of contention will revolve around whether the traditional church model has lost its ability to provide spiritual sustenance.

The church's effectiveness has diminished in direct proportion to the spiritual compromise of the pulpit. In fact, the current generation has witnessed the emergence of a whole new kind of church. Today's church has been transformed from an emphasis of soul winning and flock feeding to simply trying to improve society. The next few chapters explore how to battle this modern church phenomenon by identifying its root causes.

11

Signs & Wonders
Historical Background

Old Testament Signs and Wonders

The next few chapters build upon the foundational principles already presented. A person *cannot* fully comprehend the subject at hand without first having a thorough understanding of the earlier chapters. The reader is cautioned not to study this chapter without first grasping the preceding material.

The basic components of the chart have already been presented. This chapter presents some chart modifications. The three chart modifications are as follows:

1. **"The Jews Require a Sign"**—This span of time covers a period beginning in Exodus through the time when God gives His completed word to man (prior to A.D. 100). During this time, God deals predominantly with the Jews using many signs and wonders and treats them differently from all other nations. For example, *Romans 1:16* says the gospel is to the "Jew first." The followers of the Lord were to go to the Jews and then to the Gentiles until the point in time when God would cut off the nation of Israel *(Romans 11:17)*.

2. **The line dividing Paul's epistles**—The line signifies the time when the Jews were no longer given an advantage. The presentation of the gospel was no longer to the "Jew first." Thus, the Jews receive no further signs from God during the Church Age. The line signifies and emphasizes that this division occurs within a major period (the Church Age), and has an application much more limited than a division between ages.

3. The "**signs**" designation within Paul's epistles indicates how the signs tapered off until they stopped completely prior to A.D. 100. Although the Apostle Paul is imprisoned prior to A.D. 65, man does not receive God's completed word until many years later. The A.D. 100 date signifies a point in time when we know all sixty-six books were completed. Thus, the word of God is perfected (completed) by that time. Once Paul had reached the remnant of Jews (Acts chapter 28), the signs ceased *for him*. Therefore, he does not mention any of the signs or wonders in his prison epistles, except one time negatively *(II Thessalonians 2:9)*.

The purpose of this chapter is to consider what the Bible says about signs, wonders, tongues and miracles. By studying the Bible, rightly divided, we can determine how the "signs, wonders, tongues and miracles" apply to the various time periods. Since Christians are told to "walk by *faith*" the importance of determining the role that signs and wonders might have in our lives today is crucial.

II Corinthians 5:7 (For we walk by faith, not by sight:)

The Jews require a sign

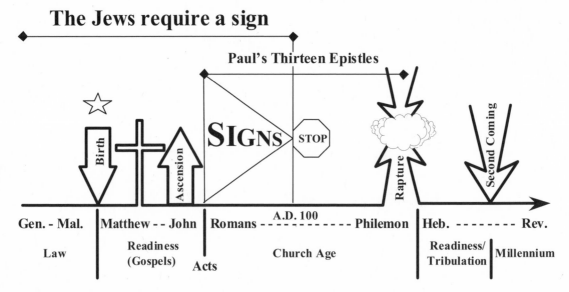

Chart 11.1 - Signs and Wonders

The life of every Christian should exemplify a walk of faith, but what is faith? Contrasting the believer's faith and supernatural signs from God is a good starting point. **Personal faith** and the **expectation of signs** are at opposite ends of the spectrum. The more signs one experiences (or expects), the less faith he will exercise and have perfected in his life. In other words, the greater a person's faith, the less he or she will seek or need signs from God. Personal faith *decreases* in direct proportion to the amount of evidence (signs) given. **Hebrews 11:1** offers the proof text: *"Now **faith** is the substance of things hoped for, the **evidence of things not seen**."* Faith eliminates the need for signs. If a person has evidence from signs, their personal walk of faith will be adversely affected!

Faith = evidence of things *not* seen

Signs = evidence by sight

Few Christians actually want to depend on faith to live. This is a by-product of man's natural tendency to sin and his desire to sense and feel God. Israel's 4,000-year history repeatedly proves this truth. A dependency on signs has extremely negative long-term effects on personal faith. However, many preachers attempt to prove that signs are a benefit to us in this age by using **Mark 16:14-20**. Before considering supernatural signs in depth, we must examine the application of this passage.

Establishing the scriptural **context** of the verses remains a good starting point. A clear understanding of the context of the entire passage shows up in verse 19. It records the time *following the resurrection* and *just prior to the Lord's ascension* into heaven. The Lord Jesus Christ finishes his preaching to his apostles.

> **Mark 16:19** So then after the Lord had spoken unto them, **he was received up into heaven**, and sat on the right hand of God.

Obviously, the events of the passage occur just prior to the ascension. Therefore, the Lord Jesus Christ has died on the cross, gone into the lower parts of the earth *(Ephesians 4:9, Acts 2:27, 31)* having tasted death for every man *(Hebrews 2:9)*, met the thief in paradise *(Luke 23:43)* and on the third day, He was reunited with His body in the tomb *(Mark 16:6)*. To further identify the context, we must take note of the individuals to whom the Lord was speaking. The beginning of the passage points out that the Lord was speaking to the *eleven* (apostles).

*Mark 16:14 Afterward he appeared unto **the eleven** as they sat at meat, and upbraided them with their unbelief and hardness of heart, because they believed not them which had seen him after he was risen.*

These two verses clearly reveal the context of Mark chapter 16. We see *when* and *to whom* the Lord was speaking. Therefore, the message we are about to consider was given to the apostles, just prior to the ascension. The next verse tells *these apostles* what to preach and to whom they are to preach the message. The Lord then explains the responses to that preaching and the consequences of those responses.

*Mark 16:15 And he said unto them, Go ye into all the world, and **preach the gospel to every creature.** 16 He that believeth and is baptized shall be saved; but he that believeth not shall be damned.*

They (the apostles) are to preach this particular message. The transition should be obvious—they are now to go into all the world, rather than simply limiting their preaching to one single locale.

Once God gives the message, He points out that certain signs will "follow them that believe." These signs are titled the ***signs of an apostle (II Corinthians 12:12)*** and are listed beginning in verse 17 of Mark chapter 16. The apostles were given the power to perform these signs. They are clearly listed in the next verses.

*Mark 16:17 And **these signs shall follow them** that believe; In my name shall they **cast out devils**; they shall speak with new **tongues**; 18 They shall **take up serpents**; and if they **drink any deadly thing**, it shall not hurt them; they shall **lay hands on the sick**, and they shall recover.*

The signs are as follows:

- Casting out devils
- Speaking with new tongues
- Taking up serpents
- Immunity to poison
- Healing

After the Lord reveals these signs to the apostles, He is received up into glory. The apostles obediently follow His commission, preaching everywhere (confirming the word with signs).

*Mark 16:19 So then after the Lord had spoken unto them, he was received up into heaven, and sat on the right hand of God. 20 And they went forth, and preached every where, the Lord working with them, and **confirming the word with signs** following. Amen.*

The time-frame of Mark chapter 16 has been established as the ascension. By determining the timing of Mark chapter 16, the context of the first chapter of Acts can also be established. *Acts 1:9* mentions the ascension. Thus, the events of Acts chapter 1 occur in the same time-frame as do the events of Mark chapter 16.

> *Acts 1:9 And when he had spoken these things, while they beheld, **he was taken up**; and a cloud received him out of their sight.*

This next chart illustrates that the signs were manifested before the cross, after the cross and for a short period of time following the ascension. The vertical line signifies the period of time when the perfect (or completed) word of God was given to man (prior to A.D. 100). This line also signifies the point in time when these signs were completely phased out by God. The reasoning behind this conclusion will be covered in subsequent discussions.

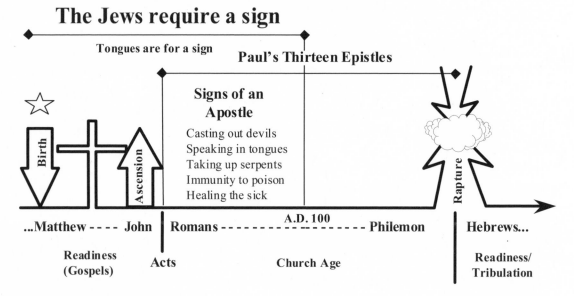

Chart 11.2 - Signs of an Apostle

The eleven (apostles) of Mark chapter 16 obediently went forth preaching. As they preached, they were to baptize their converts and to use signs to prove their message. These *signs of an apostle* included casting out devils, speaking in tongues, taking up serpents, having immunity to poison and performing acts of healing. The **Apostle** Paul *(I Corinthians 9:1)* clearly gives the title of these signs, calling them the **SIGNS OF AN APOSTLE.**

> *II Corinthians 12:11 I am become a fool in glorying; ye have compelled me: for I ought to have been commended of you: for in nothing am I behind the very chiefest **apostles**, though I be nothing. 12 Truly **the signs of an apostle** were wrought among you in all patience, in signs, and wonders, and mighty deeds.*

If the five supernatural things mentioned by the Lord and listed in Mark chapter 16 are not the "signs of an apostle," then what constitutes these signs? *Mark 16:19* says these **apostles** went forth "confirming the word **with signs**." What are the signs of an apostle if they are not the signs *given to the apostles* as listed in Mark chapter 16? The Bible clearly defines the most sought after of these—tongues—as a sign from God. Regardless of what one was taught, thought, thinks or does, he must believe that tongues are a sign or else reject the plain truth of the scripture.

*I Corinthians 14:22 Wherefore **tongues are for a sign**, not to them that believe, but to them that believe not: but prophesying serveth not for them that believe not, but for them which believe.*

This verse gives the purpose of tongues. *Tongues are for a sign*. This point *cannot* be overemphasized and there can be no disputing it. God used the gift of tongues as a sign. The signs, including tongues, are irreconcilable with a Christian walking by faith today. God never gave the Gentile or the Christian today any promise of signs. God used tongues to prove **to the Jew** that He was performing a miracle, thus confirming the identity of His messenger. (See chapter 13 of this book for a discussion of apostles, prophets, evangelists and teachers.)

The Bible records instances of God's performing a miracle on someone other than a Jew. However, the purpose of the miracle (sign) was to confirm to the *Jewish* messenger that he was acting correctly in going to the Gentiles *(Acts 10:45-46)*. The Jew had to have this proof (sign). God's dealings with the Jewish people historically conditioned them to expect God to confirm His work through signs. During this period, God's contacts with the Jews were no different. They *required* a sign from God.

*I Corinthians 1:22 **For the Jews require a sign**, and the Greeks seek after wisdom:*

The Old Testament and early New Testament historical records reveal sign after sign given to the Jews in order to convince them to believe and follow God. Consider the manna, the water from the rock, the parting of the Red Sea, Peter's walking on the water, the raising of the dead, the healings, etc. If God's purpose were simply to heal disease (without the act being as a sign), He certainly could have healed everyone, everywhere. However, God's purpose for the healings was to give the Jews a sign from Himself. "Tongues" were utilized for the same purpose. God's method of dealing with the Jews was to give them signs.

The Bible leaves no room for dispute. God used tongues to prove to the Jews that He was the Author of the miracle being witnessed. Thus the Jews received supernatural confirmation of their actions. Many churches today misapply these scriptures. When these churches base a large part of their ministry on tongues and healing, they have no scriptural basis. Furthermore, they are completely ignoring the context of the passage and its application. Proving this premise in these next two chapters using the right division approach will convince any sincere student of the scriptures.

Satan uses signs and wonders, such as tongues, for another purpose. He uses them to convince people that they are receiving something extraordinary from God, when they are not. Once Satan convinces a person that this "gift" originates from God, he can give them any message he wishes in the future because they have opened themselves up to satanic delusion. Eventually, he completely erodes their willingness to live by faith. Gentiles are to seek out the wisdom and knowledge of God from the Bible, not from some "signs." I have personally heard people say that they did not care what the Bible says, they knew what they had experienced and that was enough for them. They chose to rely on what they had experienced. These people were trusting in "signs," regardless of the scriptural mandate to *try the spirits* to determine if they were of God or not.

*1 John 4:1 Beloved, believe not every spirit, but **try the spirits whether they are of God***: *because many false prophets are gone out into the world.*

History of the Signs

Studying the history of the signs will aid a person's understanding of right division and the word of God. One must consider where the signs began in order to determine where they are headed and why they ever existed. For example, *I Corinthians 14:22* states that tongues are a sign "to them that believe not." The tongues (and signs in general) began because of *unbelief*. The unbelief of Moses was evident and profound as he spoke to the burning bush! Had Moses only believed God, God probably would not have resorted to the use of signs in order to prove His faithfulness. Our unbelief, like that of Moses, will cause us more problems than almost any other factor in our life. Our unbelief destroys the work of God and limits what God can do *(Psalm 78:41)*. Moses' unbelief is the beginning of what we see today in a wicked and adulterous sign-seeking generation *(Matthew 16:4)*.

The signs and wonders of Mark chapter 16 have their roots in the book of Exodus. God tells Moses in *Exodus 3:14*, I AM THAT I AM. God then tells Moses that He is going to smite Egypt with all His wonders and Pharaoh **will** let His people go.

*Exodus 3:20 And I will stretch out my hand, and smite Egypt with all my wonders which I will do in the midst thereof: and after that **he will let you go***.

Scripture plainly states that God was going to smite Egypt with His wonders so that the Pharaoh *would* let His people go. No word of signs is yet mentioned. However, Moses did not believe God. The first verse of the next chapter reveals his heart condition in this matter . . . one of unbelief. God says they will believe and Moses replies *to God*: "No, they won't, Lord."

*Exodus 4:1 And Moses answered and said, But, behold, **they will not believe me,** nor hearken unto my voice: for they will say, The Lord hath not appeared unto thee.*

Moses disagreed with God. He told God that the people would *not* believe him. Yet, the underlying motive seemed to spring from Moses' unwillingness to personally believe God. He wanted proof through a sign that this was truly the voice of God. Because of Moses' unbelieving heart and his fear of trusting God, he required signs to prove that God was speaking to him. Take note of the first sign. It is one of those listed in Mark chapter 16. It deals with snake handling.

*Exodus 4:2 And the LORD said unto him, What is that in thine hand? And he said, A rod. 3 And he said, Cast it on the ground. And he cast it on the ground, and it became a **serpent**; and Moses fled from before it.*

God performed a miracle (or a sign) for Moses by changing his rod into a serpent. Obviously, this sign did not prove anything to the Jews in Egypt. God knew what Moses really wanted. He wanted proof for himself. Remember the serpents mentioned in Mark chapter 16? The next verse tells us the purpose of this sign. The purpose of the sign will be for Israel to *see (II Corinthians 5:7)*. Maybe Moses' lack of conviction would cause the Jews to disbelieve, much like our lack of faith in God's promises impedes the work of God.

Exodus 4:5 That they (the Jews) *may believe that the LORD God of **their fathers** . . . hath appeared unto thee.*

The signs were not performed to convince the Pharaoh of anything. The signs were for the Jews, *unbelieving* Jews. This particular sign would be used to prove **to the Jews** that God had appeared to Moses. Had Moses believed God, he may have gone into Egypt trusting God, without need of these signs either before or after arriving in Egypt. But this was not the case; so Pharaoh's magicians were given the opportunity to change their rods into snakes too. *The Lord originates and Satan imitates!* The Lord performed and gave signs never before seen to confirm the messenger and to validate the truth of an important message to His people, the Jews. Satan imitated the miracles **just as he does today**.

God decided that the next sign would be the sign of healing. Healing is another of the *signs of an apostle* mentioned in Mark chapter 16! These signs all originate with Moses because of his unbelief. The Jews would need signs, too, due to Moses' unbelief. Maybe his unbelief changed his manner of delivery. He was unable to convince others without signs because he himself was not convinced without them. God created a situation (disease), so that He could be glorified.

> **Exodus 4:6** *And the LORD said furthermore unto him, Put now thine hand into thy bosom. And he put his hand into his bosom: and when he took it out, behold,* ***his hand was leprous as snow***.

In verse 7, the first sign of healing is recorded in the Bible. Why did God perform this sign? Need it be repeated? This sign happened because of the unbelief of Moses. Moses refused to live by faith. God gave him a sign of healing to get him to believe (and go). He was like many churches today who want to see, feel and touch God. Their unwillingness to live by faith, and faith alone, causes them to be dependent upon some signs no matter where these signs originate. God clearly defines the snake handling and healing—they are signs!

> **Exodus 4:8** *And it shall come to pass, if they will* ***not believe*** *thee, neither hearken to the voice of the* ***first sign***, *that they will believe the voice of the* ***latter sign***.

In verse 9, God tells Moses what will happen if the Jews do not believe the first **two signs**. Another sign would be given. God would turn the water into blood. Mark chapter 16 mentions a similar sign from God—the protection from drinking any deadly thing. Poisonous substances could not hurt the apostles. Here we witness a drink (water) being turned into blood. No one can live by drinking blood in place of water. Yet, drinking something poisonous would not have adversely affected the apostles because they were protected according to Mark chapter 16.

> **Exodus 4:9** *And it shall come to pass, if they will not believe also these* ***two signs***, *neither hearken unto thy voice, that thou shalt take of the* ***water*** *of the river, and pour it upon the dry land: and the water which thou takest out of the river* ***shall become blood*** *upon the dry land.*

Mark chapter 16 clearly parallels Exodus chapter 4, sign for sign. So far we have seen snake handling, healing and poisonous water. Now comes the big one for Moses! Moses raises the issue of his inability to speak. Inability to speak is no problem for God to overcome. Here comes the sign of tongues . . . Mark chapter 16 again!

> **Exodus 4:10** *And Moses said unto the LORD, O my Lord,* ***I am not eloquent***, *neither heretofore, nor since thou hast spoken unto thy servant: but I am slow of speech, and of a slow* ***tongue***.

Moses asks for another sign and receives the "gift of tongues." His tongues will come in a different manner than those referred to in Mark chapter 16 and displayed in the book of Acts. Aaron became the mouth of Moses. Aaron literally spoke for him. The next chart depicts the signs given to Moses (and Israel) in Exodus and the signs given in Mark chapter 16. We see that the signs of Mark chapter 16 last so long as there were apostles. Once the apostles died, so did the signs. All of this culminated about the time that God provided His perfect (completed) word to man.

The Jews require a sign

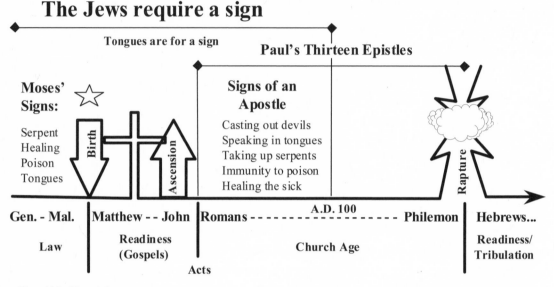

Chart 11.3 - Moses' signs

Four of the Mark chapter 16 signs match the signs found in Exodus, given because of Moses' unbelief. Moses and Israel were given signs to help them believe. Once dependence on signs was established, Israel never recovered. From then on, the people **required** signs in order to believe. Israel learned to walk by sight and **not** by faith. Anyone who receives signs walks by sight and does not exercise faith. (Gideon is a great biblical example of this phenomenon—see *Judges 6:37-40*.)

The Lord concludes His meeting with Moses by telling him the means by which the signs would be accomplished:

*Exodus 4:17 And thou shalt take this rod in thine hand, wherewith **thou shalt do signs**.*

As already demonstrated, God provided all of these signs to Moses for one reason—his unbelief. The unbelief of Israel, in turn, came about as a result of the insecurity and unbelief of Moses. Be sure to keep in mind that none of these signs was manifested for the benefit of Pharaoh or for anyone besides the Jews. The performance of the signs in Egypt was for the benefit of the Jews only. God knew Pharaoh's heart; He foreknew Pharaoh's reactions and behavior. Pharaoh hardened his own heart *(Exodus 5:2)*. Therefore, God hardened his heart so that he would not let the Jews go until God was ready for it to happen. It would have been nonsensical for God to give Pharaoh signs in order to convince him to release the Jews, if the signs were not for them.

Six chapters later in Exodus, God instructs the children of Israel to tell their children about the **signs** done in Egypt. The effect would be twofold. Their descendents would appreciate where they came from and they would also learn to *require signs* on their own behalf in the future *(I Corinthians 1:22)*.

> *Exodus 10:1 And the LORD said unto Moses, Go in unto Pharaoh: for I have hardened his heart, and the heart of his servants, **that I might shew these my signs before him**: 2 **And that thou mayest tell in the ears of thy son**, and of thy son's son, what things I have wrought in Egypt, and **my signs** which I have done among them; that ye may know how that I am the LORD.*

Thus, Pharaoh became God's pawn. God hardened Pharaoh's heart in order to have the time to show His signs to Israel. God used the signs to confirm His message and His messenger. Israel was not to doubt that God was performing these signs in their sight. The end result is the same. The Israelites learned to walk by sight, and *not* by faith. Faith is the substance of things not seen *(Hebrews 11:1)*. Signs *are* things seen. If a person does not *see* a sign, it does him no good. The book of Exodus reveals why the Jews came to expect signs from God. Once a person has received signs, he becomes dependent on them in the future. Once Israel received the signs, they became conditioned to *expect* them. Paul reveals that Israel came to *require* signs *(I Corinthians 1:22)*.

God commands the fathers to tell their children of the signs that He had performed in times past. Future generations of Israelites were to be taught about the serpents, the healing, the tongues, etc. During His earthly ministry, the Lord Jesus Christ performed many of the same miracles for the Jews so that they would believe that He was God manifest in the flesh *(I Timothy 3:16)*. The apostles were told that they would have the same power. God used these signs in the early ministry of the Apostle Paul—when he was going to the **Jew first**—in order to *confirm* his ministry to the people of Israel *(Mark 16:20, Acts 15:25, 32)*.

> *"The coming of the Holy Spirit at Pentecost was not altogether a new thing; the coming of the Comforter, as promised, was something entirely new: this promise was that the Holy Spirit should be a permanent abiding presence, in the bodies of men. Such an indwelling of the Spirit had never taken place. The Holy Spirit never dwelt as an abiding presence in any man, not in Adam, or Abraham, or Moses, or John the Baptist. He had moved men; He had filled them, filled them from their birth, but He had never stayed in men continuously. David could pray, "Take not Thy Holy Spirit from me." No man who has the Spirit of God can offer that prayer to-day without being guilty of excuseless ignorance, because the Holy Spirit, as an abiding presence in any man, is there as a seal, "sealing him unto the day of redemption.*
>
> *Men could ask the Father, in the days of Christ, to send them the Holy Spirit. In this day no child of God can offer that prayer without confessing ignorance of the Word of God, because when the Spirit comes to take up His abode in the body, that body becomes the temple of the Holy Spirit, which Spirit, saith an apostle, "is in you, which ye have of God."*
>
> I.M. Haldeman, *How to Study the Bible* (NY: Charles C. Cook, 1904) p. 94-95.

"On the day of Pentecost He (the Holy Spirit) opened the Kingdom of Heaven to the Jew, but, according to the seventh chapter of the Book of Acts, the Jews rose up and shut the door in the Spirit's face, martyred Stephen, and piled the stones above him as a witness that they rejected a risen Lord, even as they had crucified a seeking King. At once the Spirit postponed the kingdom in Israel, turned to the Gentiles, opened to them the kingdom spiritually, set aside Peter, called Paul, through him revealed the doctrine of the church; and from henceforth began to work, not to extend the kingdom in the world, but to withdraw men from the world into the kingdom; to build up the Church of Christ, not as a kingdom, but as a temple of God for a coming kingdom."

I.M. Haldeman, *How to Study the Bible - The Second Coming and Other Expositions* (NY: Charles C. Cook, 1904) p. 101.

12

Signs & Wonders
To Whom/For What?

New Testament Signs and Wonders

In the previous chapter, we studied the *historical record* of God's signs to the Jews. This chapter primarily looks at a few New Testament examples of God's use of supernatural signs. The application of these signs demonstrates their God-intended purpose: to convince the *Jews* to believe His message and/or His messenger.

The first sign considered involves the Apostle Peter in Acts chapter 5. Peter's power to perform miracles was not limited only to those with whom he came into direct contact. Miraculously, Peter's shadow passing over a person had the power to heal the sick or possessed. Try to imagine the impact these miracles had on the churches during the first century. God's program was changing. God used these miracles to prove that the apostles were His servants and that they were doing the will of God.

> **Acts 5:15** *Insomuch that they brought forth the sick into the streets, and laid them on beds and couches, that at the least **the shadow of Peter** passing by might overshadow some of them. 16 There came also a multitude out of the cities round about unto Jerusalem, bringing sick folks, and them which were vexed with unclean spirits: and they were **healed every one**.*

Peter, the spokesman to the Jews, had the power of healing. Take note that *every single sick or possessed* person contacting Peter's shadow was healed. God's power through His apostle was not limited by the faith of the sick person (as some claim to be the reason that they fail to heal everyone on television today).

To help avoid any misconceptions, the point must be made that God can still heal today. However, His purpose for healing today differs drastically from what it was during the first century. God no longer uses healing to cause someone to believe in Him. Yet, He still heals for His glory *(John 11:4)*. God commands us to live by faith today. His healing is not manifested through the methods perpetrated by the televangelists upon the public. In other words, the person healed today will generally be able to point to another plausible explanation for the divine healing. Attributing the healing to God can only be done through *faith*.

In the next passage, some Gentiles receive the Holy Ghost. However, these Gentiles did not speak in tongues for their own benefit. The purpose of their speaking in tongues was to serve as a sign to Peter and the other Jews with him. God used this sign to show that He was beginning to pour out His Spirit on the Gentiles too.

*Acts 10:44 While Peter yet spake these words, **the Holy Ghost fell on all them which heard the word.** 45 And they of the **circumcision** (the Jews) **which believed were astonished**, as many as came with Peter, because that on the Gentiles also was poured out the gift of the Holy Ghost. 46 For they heard them speak with **tongues**, and magnify God. Then answered Peter, 47 Can any man forbid water, that these should not be baptized, which have received the Holy Ghost as well as we? 48 And he commanded them to be baptized in the name of the Lord. Then prayed they him to tarry certain days.*

During the first century, the Jews had a difficult time believing that God's program was changing. These saved Jews that accompanied Peter were *unbelieving* concerning God's blessing directly on the Gentiles. Their reaction to the Gentiles' receiving the Holy Ghost was one of astonishment. Because of the sign (tongues), the Jews understood and believed that God was now pouring out His Spirit on the Gentiles. The sign served to prove the truth—they heard the Gentiles speak with tongues and magnify God.

Take note that the Jews definitely understood what these Gentiles were saying "in tongues" because they recognized that they were magnifying God. It was *not* just gibberish! These Gentiles spoke in a tongue that could be understood by the Jews *(Acts 2:6)*. Thus, we have additional evidence that God performed this sign for the Jews. The sign was *not* intended for the benefit of the Gentile that spoke in tongues, but for the Jews that heard them speak. In Acts chapter 14, Paul has signs and wonders being **granted** too.

*Acts 14:3 Long time therefore abode they speaking boldly in the Lord, which gave testimony unto the word of his grace, and **granted signs and wonders** to be done by their hands.*

These are only a few of the many instances recorded in this one book relating the ***events of the first century***. Throughout the book of Acts, God grants signs and wonders. The final chapter of Acts records the last of these signs during this period involving the Apostle Paul. The signs and wonders continued the whole time Paul was attempting to reach the *remnant* of Jews while on his missionary journeys. God gave him signs to reach the Jews when he was to go to the Jew first *(Romans 1:16)*. After the Jews rejected the gospel, he was commanded to turn to the Gentiles in each region of the world. That is exactly what he did.

Scripture records that Paul went into prison in Acts chapter 28. The signs and wonders were winding down at this time. Before he reached Rome, Paul was shipwrecked on an island. A poisonous snake on the island bit Paul, yet the bite had no effect on him. The barbarians (non-Jews) witnessed the snakebite and saw that it caused him no harm. Since these barbarians were not Jews, one might think that this occurrence would contradict the "signs for the Jews" position. However, we are to believe every word of God. This event does not contradict the truth at all.

*Acts 28:4 And when **the barbarians saw the venomous beast** hang on his hand, they said among themselves, No doubt this man is a murderer, whom, though he hath escaped the sea, yet vengeance suffereth not to live. 5 And he shook off the beast into the fire, and **felt no harm**.*

The promise of Mark chapter 16 says "they shall take up serpents." Paul had the signs of the apostles. Yet, why did this event occur at this particular time since the barbarians (non-Jews) were the only ones mentioned as witnessing this event? It is possible that the supernatural intervention occurred for Paul's sake. God wanted to show Paul that he was still protected even though he was going to lose his personal liberties. The sign was certainly not intended for the benefit of the barbarians (Gentiles) as the next passage proves!

*Acts 28:6 Howbeit they looked when he should have swollen, or fallen down dead suddenly: but after they had looked a great while, and saw no harm come to him, they changed their minds, and **said that he was a god.***

God would never use a sign to cause someone to think Paul was a god! These Gentiles reached that conclusion because they could not understand how someone could live after being bitten by this poisonous creature. People draw their own conclusions and many times they are incorrect. The same can be said of all of these "signs and wonders" preachers on the television. They are causing people to look at them as though they are gods and God has nothing whatsoever to do with it.

After Paul's missionary journeys have ended, God no longer gives the Jew an advantage. Jew and Gentile are treated alike. God no longer uses signs and wonders to confirm His message and messenger. By this time, the signs and wonders are phasing out over the entire world. By the end of the first century (A.D. 100), the signs are completely phased out.

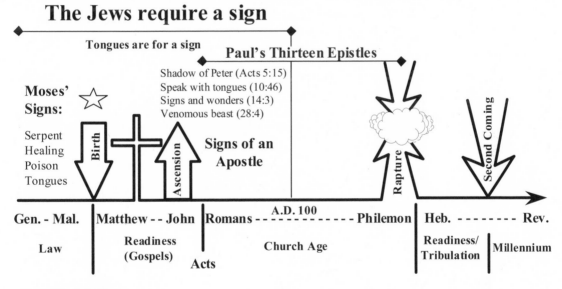

Chart 12.1 - Acts' Signs

God granted signs and wonders to give testimony of His grace to the Jews. God's program was changing. The Jews always had supernatural signs as proof that God was doing a work. However, God's changing program included the new expectation that Christians (Jew and Gentile alike) should live by faith. God was phasing out the signs. The primary question to be answered regards when the signs ended. The sign of *healing* provides a good basis for study. The best indication that God was *phasing out* healing as a sign can be found by studying First and Second Timothy along with the book of Acts. Paul obviously had the gift/sign of healing. Yet, the advice Paul gives Timothy surely indicates otherwise. Timothy is told to use some wine for medicinal purposes in order to recover from his sickness.

*I Timothy 5:23 Drink no longer water, but **use a little wine** for thy stomach's sake and thine **often infirmities**.*

Why would Paul advise Timothy to use something medicinally to regain his health? Since God was no longer using healing as a sign, Timothy would need to depend on medicine. Do not construe this to mean that God can no longer heal someone miraculously. He can and He does. However, He will heal a person today in such a way that the individual generally must wonder if God healed him or something just occurred naturally. Today, a person must claim His healing power **by faith and not by sight!** Forget what you see on television; God has nothing to do with that foolishness.

Paul writes Timothy another letter. This time Paul informs Timothy that he had to leave Trophimus in Miletum *because he was sick*! The signs were completely phasing out and Paul's healing powers were not the same any longer.

*II Timothy 4:20 Erastus abode at Corinth: but **Trophimus have I left at Miletum sick**.*

Acts chapter 20 records Paul and Trophimus together in Miletum. He mentions Trophimus in the fourth verse. In verse 15, he informs us that they arrive at Miletus (Miletum). However, the most interesting point is made in the next verse concerning Asia. Paul did not want to spend time in Asia.

*Acts 20:16 For Paul had determined to sail by Ephesus, **because he would not spend the time in Asia**: for he hasted, if it were possible for him, to be at Jerusalem the day of Pentecost.*

God had already reached the remnant of Jews and turned to the Gentiles in this part of the world (Asia Minor). Paul was no longer able to perform the signs (including supernatural healing) because of the Jews' rejection of the gospel and blasphemy of the Holy Ghost *(Acts 13:45-46)*. *Acts 13:14* says that this was in Antioch of Pisidia (Asia Minor). The relationship between the two events is easily identifiable. God turns to the Gentiles in Asia Minor in Acts chapter 13; when Paul and his company come through Asia Minor seven chapters later, he can no longer perform the miracles in that area. Consequently, Paul has to leave Trophimus behind sick. (Note: *Acts 21:29* makes mention of Trophimus. This verse references Trophimus as being with Paul on a previous occasion. The verse does not say that they presently saw Trophimus with Paul, but "had seen.")

Why would Paul leave Trophimus behind sick? The reason is very simple. The signs had stopped in that particular region. Paul no longer had the power to heal anyone *in Asia Minor*. This is the case throughout the book of Acts concerning Asia. Acts chapter 16 records that the Holy Ghost forbade Paul even to preach in that area. The remnant there had been reached and God wanted Paul elsewhere.

*Acts 16:6 Now when they had gone throughout Phrygia and the region of Galatia, and were **forbidden of the Holy Ghost to preach the word in Asia**,*

Traditionally, it has been taught that the signs, tongues and wonders *abruptly* ended when Paul went into prison in Acts chapter 28. However, part of Paul's commission included finding the Jewish remnant in each region. Once he reached that remnant by going to the Jew first, then the signs, tongues and wonders ceased in that particular region. Prophecy, on the other hand, ceases "when that which is perfect is come" *(I Corinthians 13:10)*. This phrase refers to the time when the word of God was **completed** on this earth (all sixty-six books). An in-depth discussion on this topic will follow later. By the time Paul was imprisoned, he had written only a few of his books. We know that John still had yet to pen the book of Revelation at this time. Therefore, it is conceivable that others were still able to perform the signs and wonders after Paul went into prison so long as they were going to the "Jew first" in an attempt to reach the Jewish remnant.

Once God reached the remnant in any particular area, the signs of Mark chapter 16 ceased in that region. Paul's responsibility to go to the areas where the remnant had not been reached is evident. For instance, Paul writes that he desired to go to Rome to see the converts there, but God expected him to go where the gospel had not been preached (and the remnant, of course, had not been reached).

> ***Romans 15:20*** *Yea, so have I strived to preach the gospel, **not where Christ was named**, lest I should build upon another man's foundation: 21 But as it is written, To whom he was not spoken of, they shall see: and they that have not heard shall understand. 22 For which cause also I have been much hindered from coming to you. 23 **But now having no more place in these parts**, and having a great desire these many years to come unto you;*

Paul explains to those in Rome that he had no place more in "these parts" to preach. Everyone in that area had heard. Since the remnant had been reached, he would soon be able to go to Rome. Little did Paul know how all of this would transpire! Paul also points out to the Corinthian church that he was going to the regions beyond them where no one else had gone. He knew that his time to reach the remnant was short and that there were areas he and the others had not yet reached.

> ***II Corinthians 10:16*** *To preach the gospel **in the regions beyond you**, and not to boast in another man's line of things made ready to our hand.*

By studying the turning points in the book of Acts, the student can easily pinpoint three different regions where God reaches the Jewish remnant and subsequently turns to the Gentiles. In each instance, Paul announces that God is changing his direction in a particular region. Although the record is given of these three turning points in the book of Acts, the signs do not completely cease precisely at the point when Paul goes into prison. The signs continue until God's preachers reach the remnant and God's perfected word is given to man. We know this occurred sometime prior to A.D. 100. Once John writes the book of the Revelation, the signs have all ceased.

Ceasing of all the Signs

First Corinthians chapter 13 clearly defines that point in time at which all the signs ceased. They stopped when something perfect replaced them. The word "perfect" in the scriptures has a meaning different from the context to which we are accustomed. The word perfect in the next verse refers to the word of God being perfected (or completed). The Bible defines *perfect* as *complete* in *II Chronicles 8:16, II Timothy 3:17* and *Ephesians 4:12-13,* and other passages. The student of God's word should always allow the Bible to define the words it contains.

*I Corinthians 13:8 Charity never faileth: but whether there be **prophecies, they shall fail**; whether there be **tongues, they shall cease**; whether there be **knowledge, it shall vanish away**. 9 For we know in part, and we prophesy in part. 10 **But when that which is perfect is come**, then that which is **in part** shall be done away.*

This passage says charity never fails. Yet, prophecies shall fail, tongues shall cease, and knowledge shall vanish away. The context of the passage clearly indicates the time at which these things will end. Paul says, at this time "we know and prophesy *in part*." Without the *completed* word of God this was true; men did know and prophesy in part. Only *part* of the revelation was available in written form by the time Paul penned First Corinthians. The full revelation of God remained *in part* until all sixty-six books were completed. When Paul wrote First Corinthians, man had only a partial revelation. Without the written word of God, man was dependent upon *prophesies* to know what to do and what would happen.

When *that which is perfect* is come (God's word), then prophecies and supernatural knowledge would end. God gave each of these to impart His revelation in a supernatural way. Without the completed word of God, only a partial prophecy of the things of God existed. Once God's perfect word came down to man, man would no longer need these things. With the completed word of God, no additional revelation or signs were necessary. The Bible contains everything man needs to know. However, prior to its completion (during the first century) God did provide additional tools to man.

A Christian today can look into the Bible to find out exactly what God wants him to know because he has the *completed* revelation. Today, we have all that God wants us to have. When did this happen? All sixty-six books were given to man before A.D. 100.

Prophecies, tongues and knowledge ended with the *completion* of the word of God and the end of the apostolic era. With the completed word of God, there was no further need for prophecy. Prophecy is only necessary in the absence of the written revelation. Without the *completed* word, one is totally dependent upon God for a direct revelation through prophecy. We have that direct revelation through God's word today *(II Peter 1:16-19)*. Finishing out the chapter, we read:

*I Corinthians 13:11 When I was a child, I spake as a child, I understood as a child, I thought as a child: but when I became a man, I put away childish things. 12 For now we see through a glass, darkly; but then face to face: **now I know in part**; but then shall I know even as also I am known. 13 And **now abideth faith**, hope, charity, these three; but the greatest of these is charity.*

This passage expresses the fact that God's word is a living book. When it speaks *(Romans 9:17, Galatians 3:8)*, this is equivalent to God speaking the words directly to our face ("face to face") *(II John 12)*. When the pages of God's word are opened, it is like looking into the Saviour's face *(Hebrews 4:12)*.

Paul says in verse 12 that "now I know in part." When did the Church stop knowing "in part?" They stopped when the word of God was *completed*. Verse 13 says that the three that abide (or remain) are faith, hope and charity, thus emphasizing the fact that we are to live by these three. We are not to live by some signs that were given to the Jews that have served their purpose and have now ceased. This truth becomes very important when one considers the future of those that continue to be deceived into believing that signs (such as tongues) are still in existence.

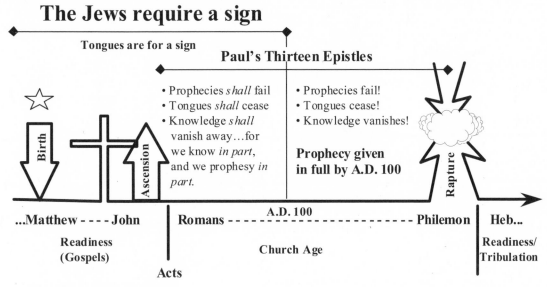

The Jews require a sign

Tongues are for a sign

Paul's Thirteen Epistles

• Prophecies *shall* fail
• Tongues *shall* cease
• Knowledge *shall* vanish away…for we know *in part*, and we prophesy *in part*.

• Prophecies fail!
• Tongues cease!
• Knowledge vanishes!

Prophecy given in full by A.D. 100

Birth

Ascension

Rapture

...Matthew - - - - John   Romans - - - - - - - - - - - - - - - - - - Philemon | Heb...

A.D. 100

Readiness (Gospels)

Church Age

Readiness/ Tribulation

Acts

Chart 12.2 - Paul's Epistles Division

Some Christians will reject this teaching because the list of those things that ended includes *knowledge*. Some will say that it is ridiculous to claim that knowledge has vanished. This claim results from an ignorance of the scriptures. The knowledge that vanished was the supernatural type of knowledge like that which allowed Peter to know that Ananias and Sapphira were lying *(Acts 5:3)*.

In this example, the apostles needed no physical proof to find these two guilty. They had a special knowledge that had nothing to do with their intelligence or learning. This special gift of knowledge vanished away too because God's newly completed word was now present to give wisdom to the believer *(II Timothy 2:7)*, thus enabling the Christian to spiritually function in the world. With the word of God completed, the indwelling of the Holy Spirit, and the purpose of the gift of knowledge fulfilled, God discontinued these special gifts. Prophecy had been necessary because it was the only way the New Testament Christian (prior to completion of the scriptures) knew what God expected or was doing. These early Christians received a *direct* revelation that we now receive *indirectly* from the reading the completed scriptures.

With the word of God *completed*, a person no longer needed prophecy. A prophecy from God is equivalent to the written word of God itself. If a person truly had a prophecy from God, that person should write it down and place it in the Bible. The two forms of communication from God are equal. They are both the word of God. However, when the word of God was *completed*, God determined He would no longer use these means (signs) to give the same revelation that was now available from His written word.

False Signs and Wonders

Everyone had better heed the warning that Satan is the great imitator. Since God has stopped using the signs, Satan uses them more frequently to deceive. He would use the signs and wonders to **his** advantage and for his purpose. Satan will easily influence those who place a heavy emphasis on what they see and feel. I have had people that are deeply involved with the tongues and healing movement tell me that they do not care what the Bible says, they know what they have experienced. They choose, instead, to rely on what they have experienced. Satan has them exactly where he wants them . . . trusting in sight and not in the truth of God's word.

> *II Thessalonians 2:8 And then shall **that Wicked** (Anti-Christ) be revealed, whom the Lord shall consume with the spirit of his mouth, and shall destroy with the brightness of his coming: 9 Even him, whose coming is **after the working of Satan with all power and signs and lying wonders**,*

Satan works "with all power and signs and lying wonders." One should easily see the danger of believing experience alone over the clear teachings of the scriptures. Many Christians are being taught or led to believe that **only** God can heal. This is simply not the truth! The Great Liar is setting them up. Satan can heal! For instance, the Beast in Revelation chapter 13 will receive a deadly wound and be healed *(Revelation 13:12)*. The world will follow him because of this and many other miracles, including the use of tongues. Those on this earth during the Tribulation will follow experience over the written word of God and the leadership of the Holy Spirit. Unfortunately, people today are making the same mistake and ushering in the time when Satan will have free reign to deceive *(II Thessalonians 2:7)*.

The Jews require a sign

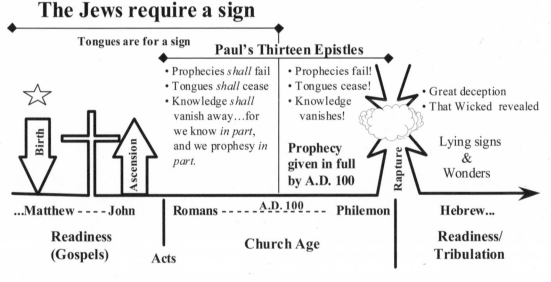

Chart 12.3 - Tribulation Signs

Satan is setting the world up for the Anti-Christ. During the Tribulation, Satan will heal the Beast's deadly wound! If Satan will do that in the future, do you not think that he will use signs to deceive a Christian today? Study, read, believe and live your Bible—**not your experience**.

The Bible clearly points out where this confusion is heading. One might wonder why Satan would desire to convince the world that all of these signs and wonders today are from God. The answer to these thoughts comes from studying some passages found in Matthew chapter 24. First, the context:

*Matthew 24:21 For then shall be **great tribulation**, such as was not since the be-ginning of the world to this time, no, nor ever shall be.*

Obviously, Matthew chapter 24 refers to the great Tribulation (following the Rapture of the Church). Earlier in the same chapter, the Lord Jesus Christ warns that in the Tribulation (and leading up to it) there will be many deceivers.

*Matthew 24:3 And as he sat upon the mount of Olives, the disciples came unto him privately, saying, Tell us, when shall these things be? and what shall be **the sign of thy coming**, and of the end of the world? 4. And Jesus answered and said unto them, **Take heed that no man deceive you**.*

There will be many false prophets. These false prophets will deceive many of those on the earth at that time.

*Matthew 24:11 **And many false prophets shall rise, and shall deceive many**. 12 And because iniquity shall abound, the love of many shall wax cold. 13 But **he that shall endure unto the end, the same shall be saved**. 14 And this **gospel of the kingdom** shall be preached in all the world for a witness unto all nations; and then shall the end come.*

During the Tribulation, there will be many false prophets who are going to deceive many. They are going to use signs and wonders and healing to deceive. People are going to fall for the lie because of the errors being taught in many churches and on many religious television pro-grams today. The false teaching that only God can heal is exactly what Satan wants a person to believe. However, this teaching is simply **not** correct.

*Revelation 13:3 And I saw one of his heads as it were wounded to death; and his **deadly wound was healed**: and all the world wondered after **the beast**.*

Satan heals the Beast in the Tribulation of a deadly wound. God is not the only healer. The Beast will also have power over all tongues. Revelation clearly describes the result of following experience over the truth. The whole world will be deceived.

*Revelation 13:7 And it was given unto him to make war with the saints, and to over-come them: and power was given him over all kindreds, and **tongues**, and nations.*

The world will witness the healing of the Beast. He will have power over every language *and tongue*. Satan has been preparing the world for this time by using the churches that place their "experience" ahead of the teachings of the word of God. This is Satan's set up. Consider the opportunity for Satan to deceive. Most charismatics go to Acts chapter 2 which cites "tongues *like as* of fire" (verse 3) and use this as one of their symbols. When the Beast brings actual fire down from heaven, what do you think will be the outcome?

*Revelation 13:13 And he doeth great wonders, so that he **maketh fire come down from heaven** on the earth in the sight of men, 14 **And deceiveth them that dwell on the earth by the means of those miracles** which he had power to do in the sight of the beast; saying to them that dwell on the earth, that they should make an image to the beast, which had the wound by a sword, and did live.*

These poor souls in "tongues-speaking" churches have been taught that *their heritage* included these kinds of signs. They will be the easiest to deceive. They will fall for the lie without batting an eye. Not all church members are saved. Those that are not saved will be on this earth during the Tribulation, and the devil will use these individuals the most to influence people to believe the lies of the Anti-Christ. The churches will be one medium used by Satan to deceive the world! He is setting it up right now *(II Thessalonians 2:7)*!

Failing to realize God's timetables can damn a person's soul if he is not saved. If he is saved, failing to realize God's timetables puts him at risk for not being right with God. Failing to be right with God opens a person up to the deception of the devil. A Christian can easily be deceived if he departs from or ignores the truth of God's word. Satan can then use such a person to mislead others . . . others who may be unsaved. These may remain unsaved because of the deception that has been amplified and given credibility.

The division of Paul's epistles has been added on *chart 12.4*. For Paul (and his writings), the signs stopped when he had reached the remnant. This corresponds to the time that he went into prison in Rome and penned his remaining epistles. Therefore, his last nine books contain no reference to the Jew having an advantage. The requirement to go to the Jew first had ended. He no longer makes reference to tongues, knowledge, healings, signs and wonders. Others may still have performed the signs up until the completion of the word of God around A.D. 100.

The Jews require a sign

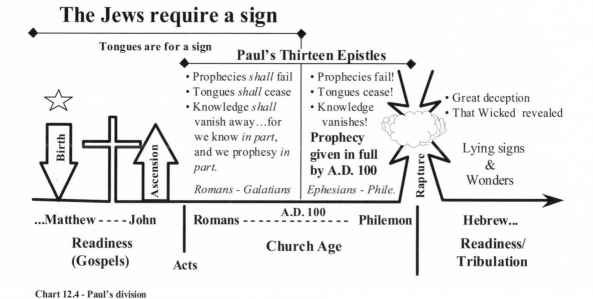

Chart 12.4 - Paul's division

The only way to know the truth is to obey *II Timothy 2:15* and to rightly divide the Bible. Once a person has rightly divided the Bible, the evidence of God's changing dealings with man becomes very clear. God is not stagnant. If God dealt with Adam, Noah, Moses and Israel differently, why should it surprise us that He deals with us differently today? God has a reason for everything that He does. When He reveals His purpose and plan, we have a responsibility and duty to find out what it is and how it affects us.

Obey God! Read the Book! Study it! Rightly divide it! See Appendix C for additional scriptural proof on reasons for sickness. God can and will heal a person through prayer, but it is a private matter between God and man. It is certainly not the show you see on television.

13
Apostles and Prophets

The Bible mentions only two offices *of the New Testament Church*. These two offices are those of bishop and deacon. Both offices are essential for the effective, biblical administration of any New Testament church.

The office of a bishop and deacon:

> *I Timothy 3:1 This is a true saying, If a man desire **the office of a bishop**, he desireth a good work.*

> *I Timothy 3:10 And let these also first be proved; then let them use **the office of a deacon**, being found blameless.*

The offices of bishop and deacon are to be filled by *men* who are members of the local New Testament church. While the Church Age epistles mention Paul's office—the Apostle of the Gentiles *(Romans 11:13)*—the New Testament church structure does not include his office as part of the local church organization. After Paul dies, the Bible gives no record of any one replacing him. Matthias was the only replacement to fill the twelfth seat vacated by Judas Iscariot.

In addition to the two offices specifically mentioned in the local church, the Bible reveals that other groups also minister to the Body of Christ. These include the apostles, prophets, evangelists, and pastors and teachers. Each group has a particular role to play in either the establishment or ongoing function of the church.

> *Ephesians 4:11 And he gave some, **apostles**; and some, **prophets**; and some, **evangelists**; and some, **pastors and teachers**; 12 For the perfecting of the saints, for the work of the ministry, for the edifying of the body of Christ:*

Verse 11 cites the four groups involved in the establishment and functioning of the local church. Pastors and teachers together make up the fourth group. Verse 12 gives the overall purpose of the groups listed in verse 11. Although each group has its own unique purpose, they all share certain similarities of purpose. God gave all four groups for the perfecting of the saints, the work of the ministry and the edifying of *the Body of Christ*. God did not give all four groups to everyone throughout time. This is why the Bible says that God gave *some* (but not *all*). In other words, all four groups were not meant to minister *together* throughout time. Once the individual purpose of the early founders (apostles and prophets) was complete, they died and were not replaced.

The book of Acts specifically records the first three groups (apostles, prophets and evangelists) as being active during the early first century churches. The purpose of this study is to determine the impact each of these groups might have in the church today. God gave each group a particular assignment; therefore, these offices differ based on their particular functions.

*Romans 12:4 For as we have many members in one body, and **all members have not the same office**:*

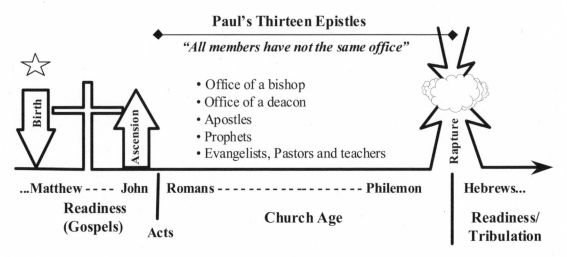

Chart 13.1 - Different Offices

The previous chart illustrates the various offices and titles given to the different groups of ministers. It is obvious that not everyone held the same office. Since not all of the groups would remain in effect throughout the Church Age, they were given different designations. Each of these groups will be studied individually, beginning with the apostles.

Apostles

Even those with limited knowledge of the Bible agree that the apostles were present during the Lord's earthly ministry. The Lord Jesus Christ initially called out twelve men to occupy this position. However, these were not the only apostles to be called throughout the entire Bible record. The Bible records the names of other apostles as well. For instance, Paul and Barnabas were also apostles, but were not a part of the twelve *(Acts 14:14)*.

The Bible gives specific qualifications necessary to be an apostle. These qualifications will be studied later. We will first examine the indicators of apostleship. The greatest indicator that a person was an apostle was the signs that were to follow him.

*II Corinthians 12:12 Truly the **signs of an apostle** were wrought among you in all patience, in signs, and wonders, and mighty deeds.*

These signs *of an apostle* are clearly given to the twelve in Mark chapter 16 (at the time, only the eleven without Judas Iscariot). The only scripture indicating what the signs of an apostle could be are listed in Mark chapter 16 (below). Casting out devils, speaking with new tongues, taking up serpents, immunity to poison and laying hands on the sick to recover were the signs that would follow the apostles. The account of the Lord Jesus Christ's giving the *signs to the apostles* follows:

*Mark 16:14 Afterward he appeared unto **the eleven** as they sat at meat, and up-braided them with their unbelief and hardness of heart, because they believed not them which had seen him after he was risen. 15 And he said unto them, Go ye into all the world, and preach the gospel to every creature. 16 He that believeth and is baptized shall be saved; but he that believeth not shall be damned. 17 And **these signs** shall follow them that believe; In my name shall they **cast out devils**; they shall speak with new **tongues**; 18 They shall **take up serpents**; and if they **drink any deadly thing**, it shall not hurt them; they shall **lay hands on the sick**, and they shall recover.*

After the Lord gave the signs to the apostles, He ascended back into heaven. The apostles went forth preaching everywhere, with the *signs* confirming the word that they preached.

*Mark 16:19 So then after the Lord had spoken unto them, he was received up into heaven, and sat on the right hand of God. 20 And they went forth, and preached every where, the Lord working with them, and **confirming the word with signs following**. Amen.*

Although many preachers, teachers and churches are confused about these signs in Mark chapter 16, these are definitely the signs of an apostle as referenced in *II Corinthians 12:12*. The scriptures also give the qualifications for one to be an apostle. The record of the method used to replace Judas Iscariot gives us the blueprint for an apostle's qualifications. The potential apostle was to be a man that had been a disciple of the Lord since the baptism of John (since John the Baptist baptized the Lord).

*Acts 1:20 For it is written in the book of Psalms, Let his habitation be desolate, and let no man dwell therein: and his bishoprick let another take. 21 Wherefore of these men which have companied with us all the time that the Lord Jesus went in and out among us, 22 **Beginning from the baptism of John**, unto that same day that he was taken up from us, **must one be ordained to be a witness with us of his resurrection**.*

Although Judas' replacement had to be a disciple from the baptism of John forward, the main qualification to become an apostle was to be a witness of the resurrection. Every apostle was a witness of the resurrection. The Bible gives record of Christ's appearing to the eleven. Matthias also witnessed the resurrection according to the record given here. The Apostle Paul had this same qualification. He was a witness of the resurrection when the Lord Jesus Christ appeared to him on the road to Damascus *(Acts 9:17)*. The next passage gives Paul's testimony of his witnessing the resurrection.

*I Corinthians 9:1 Am I not an apostle? am I not free? **have I not seen Jesus Christ our Lord?** are not ye my work in the Lord? 2 If I be not an apostle unto others, yet doubtless I am to you: for the seal of mine apostleship are ye in the Lord.*

In fact, the Corinthian church questioned Paul's apostleship. This church had serious problems with carnality *(I Corinthians 3:1)* and found it difficult to believe almost any truth presented. The Apostle Paul felt it necessary to give them proof that he was an apostle. After he asks them if he is an apostle, he puts the qualification in the form of a question, too. Paul then appeals to the fact that the Corinthians, of all people, should recognize his apostleship.

In chapter 15 of First Corinthians, Paul gives the record of the order of the Lord's appearances and points out that he was **the last** one to see the resurrected Lord. This served as proof of his qualification for the office of Apostle to the Gentiles. It also serves as notice that the appearances of the Lord to a God-called apostle ended with Paul. Anyone that has not literally seen the Lord Jesus Christ following the resurrection is not an apostle of God! Paul proves his apostleship in the next passage.

> *I Corinthians 15:5 And that he was seen of Cephas, then of the twelve: 6 After that, he was seen of above five hundred brethren at once; of whom the greater part remain unto this present, but some are fallen asleep. 7 After that, he was seen of James; then of all the apostles. 8 **And last of all he was seen of me also,** as of one born out of due time. 9 For I am the least of the apostles, that am not meet to be called an apostle, because I persecuted the church of God.*

The Bible can keep a person from error. Yet, an individual must recognize and accept the truth in order for the scriptures to impact his life. Since one of the main qualifications to be an apostle was that the person must be a witness of the resurrection, there are **no** apostles today. Paul was *the last* person to be an eyewitness of the resurrection. This means that no matter the claim, all "apostles" today fall into the next category:

> *II Corinthians 11:13 For such are **false apostles**, deceitful workers, transforming themselves into the apostles of Christ. 14 And no marvel; for Satan himself is transformed into an angel of light. 15 Therefore it is no great thing if his ministers also be transformed as the ministers of righteousness; whose end shall be according to their works.*

The scripture leaves no room for private interpretation. If the person has *not* been a witness of the resurrection (that is, has not personally seen the Lord), he **(or she)** is not an apostle. If that individual continues to claim to hold the office of apostle, regardless of God's word, he **(or she)** is a false apostle deserving of God's judgment. Those claiming that the resurrected Lord has appeared to them can be answered with the following two passages:

> *II Corinthians 5:7 (For we walk by faith, not by sight:)*

> *II Corinthians 11:14 And no marvel; for **Satan** himself is **transformed into an angel of light.***

Satan would like nothing more than to get a Christian to walk by sight. Regretfully, some of the most well known televangelists claimed that Jesus appeared and audibly spoken to them. One of them boldly claimed that a nine-hundred foot tall Jesus appeared to him. This "Jesus" told him that he would speak to his ministry partners to give more money so that he could complete his *City of Faith*. This same charismatic preacher later claimed that God appeared to him and had given him twelve months to raise eight million dollars or he was going to die.

Satan has also been known to appear as an angel of light, like the angel "Moroni" supposedly did to Joseph Smith. Joseph Smith was the founder of the Mormons (or the Church of Jesus Christ of Latter Day Saints). If Satan sees the opportunity to deceive someone, he will go so far as to imitate an appearance of the Lord in order to do so.

The next chart clearly reflects that there were no new apostles after the first century. An apostle had to be a witness of the resurrection and the Apostle Paul was the last one. Anyone claiming to hold the title or position of any apostle is a false apostle.

The Jews require a sign

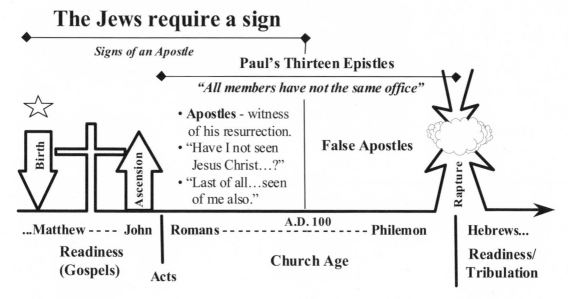

Chart 13.2 - Apostles

The Bible clearly presents the parameters of God-called apostles. The qualifications of the prophets are not left to chance or private interpretation. God's word delineates these qualifications as well. Yet, the error surrounding prophets is just as prevalent in many churches today.

Prophets

The Old Testament records the work and calling of *prophets* beginning with Abraham *(Genesis 20:7)*. A large portion of the Old Testament is designated as the "Law and the Prophets." (See *Matthew 5:17, Matthew 7:12, Matthew 11:13, and Matthew 22:36.*) Obviously, revealing prophecy was the primary purpose of being a prophet.

The four books of Matthew, Mark, Luke and John include many references to prophets, as does the book of Acts. Acts records the actions of the early church prophets. Acts chapters 11, 12, 13 and 15 give specific instances of prophets by name. For instance, Agabus is mentioned in Acts chapter 11:

*Acts 11:27 And **in these days came prophets** from Jerusalem unto Antioch. 28 And there stood up one of them named **Agabus**, and signified by the Spirit that there should be great dearth throughout all the world: which came to pass in the days of Claudius Caesar.*

Others prophets mentioned by name were Barnabas, Simeon, Lucius, and Manaen in Acts chapter 13.

*Acts 13:1 Now there were in the church that was at Antioch certain **prophets and teachers; as Barnabas, and Simeon** that was called Niger, and Lucius of Cyrene, and Manaen, which had been brought up with Herod the tetrarch, and Saul.*

Acts chapter 15 also mentions two other prophets named Judas and Silas.

*Acts 15:32 And **Judas and Silas, being prophets** also themselves, exhorted the brethren with many words, and confirmed them.*

All of these Bible references to specific prophets take place prior to the end of the first century. The book of Acts records the events following the ascension (A.D. 33) up until the Apostle Paul is imprisoned in Rome (about A.D. 63). By considering the time-frame of Acts (A.D. 33-63), we can easily determine that the word of God had not yet been completed. Paul had not penned most of his epistles, nor had John penned the book of the Revelation, among others.

Now that we have determined when the true prophets were in office, we can focus our attention on the rules for a prophet in the early church. The scriptures give at least four specific guidelines that every New Testament prophet was to follow in the church. Any prophet that did not abide by these parameters was out of the will of God and not of God.

> *I Corinthians 14:29 Let the **prophets** speak two or three, and let the other judge. 30 If any thing be revealed to another that sitteth by, let the first hold his peace. 31 For ye may all prophesy one by one, that all may learn, and all may be comforted. 32 And the spirits of the prophets are subject to the prophets. 33 For God is not the author of confusion, but of peace, as in all churches of the saints.*

Four Biblical rules for a prophet:

1. Only two, or at most three, prophets were to speak in the church service. *(verse 29)*

2. The other prophets were to judge whether the prophet speaking was of God. *(verse 29)* The scriptural principle applied is clearly given: *"Beloved, believe not every spirit, but **try the spirits** whether they are of God: because many **false prophets** are gone out into the world." (I John 4:1).*

3. The prophets were only to speak one at a time and were to allow the next prophet to speak when he was ready. *(verses 30-31)*

4. The spirits of the prophets were subject to them (e.g. under their own control). The claim today that God causes a person to lose control of his **(or her)** spirit is not scriptural. For instance, God has nothing to do with the so-called "laughing revival" where people claim to be losing control. It is simply a satanic delusion *(verse 32)*. They have another spirit *(II Corinthians 11:4)*. These other spirits can and do work miracles, but are the spirits of devils *(Revelation 16:4)*.

If these people are in fact losing control of themselves, it is not "of God." The first century church needed to have prophets because the word of God was not yet given to man in completed form. The word of God would shortly be completed, and God's prophecy would continue until that time. When God gave man His completed word, He revealed to us all the prophetic events that He desires for us to know.

Although the book of Acts records many instances of prophets, we are told in First Corinthians that prophecy would fail in the future. Since we are told **prophecy will fail**, every student of the word should endeavor to determine when this will occur *or if it has already occurred*. Again, a simple truth must be stated: the need for prophets ceases to exist when prophecy ceases. No prophecy means no need for prophets.

> *I Corinthians 13:8 Charity never faileth: but whether there be **prophecies, they shall fail**; whether there be tongues, they shall cease; whether there be knowl-*

*edge, it shall vanish away. 9 For we know in part, and we **prophesy in part**. 10 But when that which is **perfect** is come, then that which is **in part shall be done away**.*

At the time when Paul pens First Corinthians, he states that "we prophesy in part." He points out that prophecies shall fail when that which is perfect (complete) is come, because man will no longer know *in part* or prophesy *in part*. Think about it from another perspective. When mankind receives the completed prophecy (the sixty-six books of the Bible) he will no longer have only *part* of the prophecy. When man receives the *completed* prophecy, the need for further prophecy will cease.

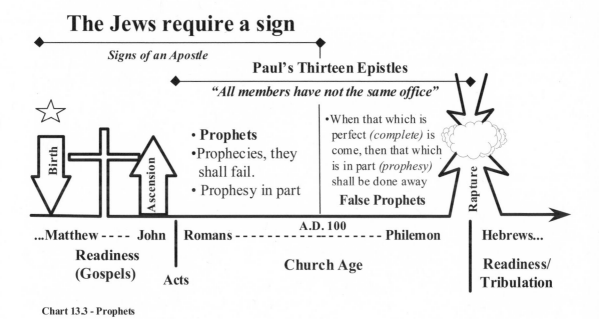

Chart 13.3 - Prophets

Conclusion concerning apostles and prophets:

By studying the scriptures concerning apostles and prophets, one learns that neither group should be found in the churches following the end of the first century. An *apostle* had to be an eye witness of the resurrection. Paul was the last apostle to see the resurrected Lord. Prophesy, and thus *prophets,* ceased once the *perfected* word of God was given to man. The two remaining groups, listed in **Ephesians 4:11**, are the evangelist, and the pastor and teacher. Pastor and teacher are two titles within the same office; thus they are a compound name of a single office. The Bible does not tell us that either of these two groups ceased to exist in the same fashion as did the apostles and prophets. We will now examine the office of evangelist, and then that of pastor and teacher.

Evangelist

The Old Testament makes no mention of any evangelists. The New Testament references the evangelist only three times. The word *evangelist* is found once in Ephesians (quoted at the beginning of this discussion). We find another mention of an evangelist in **Acts 21:8,** referring to Philip, *the evangelist*. Philip is the only person mentioned by name in the scriptures as being an evangelist. The fact that there are so few references to evangelists would probably indicate that this position is not as widely held as the others.

The final usage of the word is found in Second Timothy when Paul commands Timothy to do the work of an evangelist *(II Timothy 4:5)*. We are not given details about what an evangelist does, but should assume that his primary priority and purpose is to evangelize the lost. Unlike apostles and prophets, the Bible gives no indication that evangelists ceased to exist after the first century. This fact is logical considering the work assigned to each group. The work of the apostles and prophets (laying the foundation) has been completed, whereas the work of the evangelist and pastor never seems to end and remains unfinished.

Pastor and Teacher

Two books of the Bible contain all of the references to the title *pastor*. The only Old Testament references are found in the book of Jeremiah (mentioned eight times). Ephesians contains the one New Testament reference. Generally, churches teach that the pastor holds the office of the bishop of the church. Therefore, the qualifications for the pastor are found under those dealing with the office of the bishop.

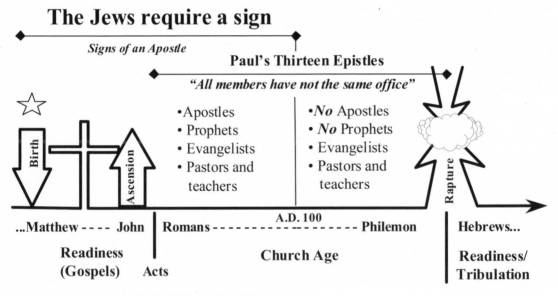

Chart 13.4 - Apostles and Prophets

God never lacks purpose in anything that He does. The revelation given directly to the apostles and prophets was *not* given directly to the evangelists and pastors. For this reason, the priorities of service differ for each. Too many preachers fail to make any distinction between the offices and their respective duties, but God does make this distinction. For instance, the apostles and prophets had the mystery revealed to them.

> ***Ephesians 3:4*** *Whereby, when ye read, ye may understand my knowledge in the mystery of Christ) 5 Which in other ages was not made known unto the sons of men, as it is **now revealed unto his holy apostles and prophets by the Spirit;***

God initially used the apostles and prophets to spread His word around the world. He did not use the evangelists and pastors for this purpose. The word of God was directly revealed to the apostles and prophets. They, in turn, penned the scriptures for the evangelists and pastors to spread around the world. Thus, the *apostles and prophets* laid the foundation with the revelation given to them.

> *Ephesians 2:20 And are **built upon the foundation of the apostles and prophets**, Jesus Christ himself being the chief corner stone;*

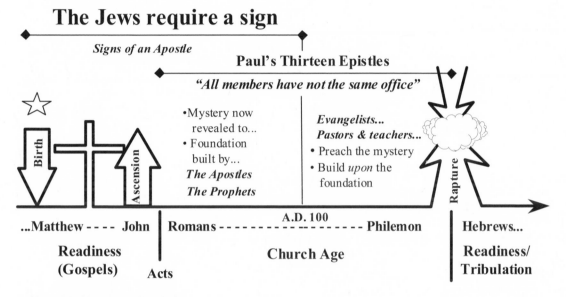

Chart 13.5 - Mystery and Foundation

Preachers and teachers, on the other hand, build upon this foundation. They preach and teach the scriptures penned by the apostles and prophets. Obviously, once the foundation was completed, there was no further need for the offices of apostle or prophet. The word of God recognizes the office of the writer in many passages to emphasize this truth.

The next four passages reveal that God does make a distinction. The office of each individual is very important. It was the apostles and prophets that gave us God's word. Since we now have the word of God in completed form, no further need exists for these two offices.

1. The Apostle Peter references the words and commandments by the prophets and apostles:

    > *II Peter 3:1 This second epistle, beloved, I now write unto you; in both which I stir up your pure minds by way of remembrance: 2 That ye may be mindful of **the words which were spoken before by the holy prophets**, and of **the commandment of us the apostles** of the Lord and Saviour:*

2. The book of Acts refers to the reading of the law and the prophets:

    > *Acts 13:15 And after **the reading of the law and the prophets** the rulers of the synagogue sent unto them, saying, Ye men and brethren, if ye have any word of exhortation for the people, say on.*

3. Paul refers to the Old Testament as the voices of the prophets:

    Acts 13:27 *For they that dwell at Jerusalem, and their rulers, because they knew him not, nor yet* **the voices of the prophets which are read** *every sabbath day, they have fulfilled them in condemning him.*

4. Paul again refers to the scriptures of the prophets:

    Romans 16:26 *But now is made manifest, and by* **the scriptures of the prophets**, *according to the commandment of the everlasting God, made known to all nations for the obedience of faith:*

Priest

The Bible references the office of priest throughout the Old Testament, continuing through the four Gospel books and into the book of Acts. Paul's thirteen Church Age epistles never mention this position even a single time. However, the book of Hebrews again mentions the office of priest in ten of its thirteen chapters. The majority of the references in Hebrews are to Christ as our High Priest and not the reestablishment of an earthly priesthood.

The location of the priestly references in the word of God proves that the priesthood was directly associated with the nation of Israel and not with the Gentile *nations*. The only other books that mention the *priesthood* are First Peter and Revelation. First Peter mentions the priesthood of the believers twice. The book of Revelation refers to the priesthood of the believer in the same context as First Peter three more times. However, the primary Church Age epistles (Romans through Philemon) never make any reference to the office of priest.

The main duty of the priest was the offering of sacrifices. Under the Old Testament, God permitted the priest to perform the required sacrifices under the law. Although the Levitical priesthood was important, their sacrifices could never take away sins. Only Christ's sacrifice on Calvary can take away sins. The duty of the priest was to offer the sacrifices under the law which temporarily restored fellowship between God and His people.

Nowhere in the scriptures is this position re-established in the New Testament for the Church Age. The sacrifice of the Lord on the cross eliminated the need for priestly functions. When the Lord became the final sacrifice for sin on the cross of Calvary, the duties of the priest transferred to Christ. He became the High Priest by offering His own blood on our behalf.

Ephesians 5:2 *And walk in love, as Christ also hath loved us, and* **hath given himself for us an offering and a sacrifice** *to God for a sweetsmelling savour.*

The Lord performed the office of priest by offering Himself as the sacrifice on the cross. His sacrifice is the *one* and *only* sacrifice capable of saving all who call upon Him from the penalty of sin.

Hebrews 10:11 *And every priest standeth daily ministering and offering oftentimes the same sacrifices, which can never take away sins: 12 But* **this man**, *after he had* **offered one sacrifice for sins for ever**, *sat down on the right hand of God;*

The scripture says that His sacrifice was offered for sins *once*—not annually, weekly or daily. The only priest that can save everyone that comes to Him is the Lord Jesus Christ. He lives to make intercession for us.

Hebrews 7:24 But this man (Jesus Christ), *because he continueth ever, hath an unchangeable priesthood. 25 Wherefore **he is able also to save them to the uttermost that come unto God by him, seeing he ever liveth to make intercession for them.** 26 For such an high priest became us, who is holy, harmless, undefiled, separate from sinners, and made higher than the heavens; 27 Who needeth not daily, as those high priests, to offer up sacrifice, first for his own sins, and then for the people's: **for this he** (Jesus) **did once, when he offered up himself.***

The Old Testament high priest had to offer up a sacrifice for his own sins and then for the sins of the people. Jesus was without sin! He offered no sacrifice FOR Himself, but offered up Himself one time for the sins of the whole world. It is the Christian's responsibility and blessing to proclaim this great truth to others. Everyone desperately needs to be told about the payment made by Christ on his behalf *(I Corinthians 6:20, 7:23).*

For this reason, the Bible appoints Christians as Christ's *ambassadors*. We are to represent Christ on this earth. We are to tell the world about His wonderful sacrifice made on their behalf so that they too can be reconciled with their Creator.

*II Corinthians 5:20 Now then **we are ambassadors** for Christ, as though God did beseech you by us: we pray you in Christ's stead, be ye reconciled to God. 21 **For he hath made him to be sin for us**, who knew no sin; that we might be made the righteousness of God in him.*

Christ paid the penalty for our sin by offering Himself. Man's capacity to comprehend this great love is severely limited. God became a man, lived a sinless life and was made sin for us so that He could suffer and die in our place. An individual will only appropriate for himself Christ's payment when he realizes Christ's sacrifice and the dire consequences that await him. This is why the Bible compels every sinner with the following words: *"Be ye reconciled to God."*

Reverend

Another of the favorite titles of the "clergy" is that of reverend. The adjective *reverend* is only used one time in the word of God. Psalm 111 uses it to describe the name of God. The Bible says that His name is holy and reverend.

*Psalm 111:9 He sent redemption unto his people: he hath commanded his covenant for ever: **holy and reverend is his name.***

The term is never biblically used outside this association with God. The dictionary defines reverend as worthy to be revered; entitled to reverence. Another definition says that to be reverend is to be worthy of adoration. It is quite obvious to see why man would want to apply this description to himself. Because of man's natural disposition, he has a desire to be revered and adored by others. However, an ambassador is not to bring attention to himself, but to point others to the One he represents.

It is dangerous for any preacher to appropriate a description that belongs exclusively to God. The title *reverend* is no more scriptural than any modern day prophet or apostle. All of these titles are scripturally incorrect today and have caused great confusion and harm. They have become even more destructive when an artificial barrier is placed between the so-called "clergy" and "laity." The Bible makes no such distinction. In fact, such emphasis sounds similar to the

Pharisees during the Lord's earthly ministry. The religious leaders of Jesus' day wanted to be addressed by their brethren as Rabbi and father. God rebukes those who behave in such a fashion.

> *Matthew 23:6 And love the uppermost rooms at feasts, and the chief seats in the synagogues 7 And greetings in the markets, and to be called of men, Rabbi, Rabbi. 8 But be not ye called Rabbi: for one is your Master, even Christ; and all ye are brethren. 9 And call no man your father upon the earth: for one is your Father, which is in heaven.*

The Pharisees loved the best seats and to be greeted with pompous titles. However, they are not the only ones guilty of such sinful pride! Man is notorious for wanting to be recognized and considered superior to his fellow man. This is why the distinction between "clergy" and "laity" originated. It is a false distinction that causes an artificial distinction, elevating the "clergy" above those they serve.

Preachers should do everything within their power to break down these man-made barriers. Preachers are just sinners . . . some saved, some not. Preachers are to serve and cherish their heavenly Father in a spirit of abject humility *(Philippians 2:8)*. This is why Jesus refers to the Father as the "Holy Father." He is the only one that is to be elevated and set apart from all others.

> *John 17:11 And now I am no more in the world, but these are in the world, and I come to thee. Holy Father, keep through thine own name those whom thou hast given me, that they may be one, as we are.*

The man-made clergy/laity barriers cause division and tend to artificially elevate one individual above another. We should be more like Paul who wrote: *"...by the grace of God I am what I am."* Paul's humble spirit did not allow him to be lifted up with pride.

> *I Corinthians 15:9 For I am the least of the apostles, that am not meet to be called an apostle, because I persecuted the church of God. 10 But by the grace of God I am what I am: and his grace which was bestowed upon me was not in vain; but I laboured more abundantly than they all: yet not I, but the grace of God which was with me.*

If you lift yourself up, or allow someone to place you upon a pedestal, God will knock the legs out from under you. We are to give God the glory and let Him reward us in His due time *(Matthew 6:5)*. The book of Proverbs warns of the destructive nature of pride and haughtiness.

> *Proverbs 16:18 Pride goeth before destruction, and an haughty spirit before a fall.*

> *Proverbs 18:12 Before destruction the heart of man is haughty, and before honour is humility.*

Preachers could use some lessons from the book of Proverbs. It would certainly be wise to heed the warning rather than suffer the anguish that certainly follows a prideful heart. The next chapter addresses a very real problem among those who become haughty concerning their understanding of God's word. These individuals have a tendency to overemphasize the divisions of the Bible. In doing so, they tend to reject scriptural application outside of Paul's epistles. This is a dangerous tendency.

14

Hyper-Dispensationalism

Although God commands us to **divide** the Bible according to *II Timothy 2:15, all* of the books of the Bible still fit together like the pieces of a puzzle. No book within the sixty-six books should be treated as if it were inapplicable or irrelevant to the Church today. The scriptures clearly dismiss any method of applying the teaching of right division to the extreme. *Eliminating* personal application of any part of the Bible is utilizing the principles of right division to an extreme degree.

> *II Timothy 3:16 All scripture* is given by inspiration of God, and *is profitable* for *doctrine, for reproof, for correction, for instruction in righteousness.*

All scripture is profitable! Man is to study *all scripture* even though *II Timothy 2:15* commands that he should rightly divide the Bible. A person does not need to limit himself to studying only Paul's epistles (or a portion of his epistles), to the exclusion of all other portions of the scriptures. God requires the Church to consider what Paul's epistles say **first** *(II Timothy 2:7)*. However, this emphasis on Paul's epistles should *not* prompt the student of the Bible to exclude any of the other epistles. To **exclude** any part of the Bible from study and application is to "hyper-divide" it. This practice is called hyper-dispensationalism or **ultra-dispensationalism**.

> *"No matter what may be the equipment of the Christian, no matter what intellectual, moral, or spiritual endowment he may have, unless he understands dispensational truth he will never fully lay hold of Bible doctrine..."*
>
> I.M. Haldeman, *How to Study the Bible - The Second Coming and Other Expositions* (NY: Charles C. Cook, 1904), p.7.

What exactly does it mean to be hyper/ultra-dispensational? First, "dispensationalism" must be defined. Dispensationalism is the dividing of the Bible as commanded in *II Timothy 2:15*. **It is the only theologically systematic way to study the Bible.** Those that do not incorporate its precepts into their Bible study must incorrectly spiritualize many passages.

Hyper-dispensationalism defined

"Hyper-dispensationalism" is any false division of the Bible. It is a practice involving over-division of the Bible such that the majority of the scriptures are reduced to a position of little or no application to the Christian today. Generally, a person engages in hyper-dispensationalism in order to incorrectly force some portion of the Bible to apply *only* to individuals living in another time period. This type of "Bible study" produces a false sense of having relieved the individual of some of his responsibilities. One of the most frequently hyper-divided areas of the Bible pertains to the issues of grace and law, bondage and liberty. A thorough review of these areas will help the student to avoid this type of grave theological error.

The hyper-dispensationalist will generally overemphasize the period in which we now live, calling it the "Age of Grace." (However, not everyone that uses this designation is a hyper-dispensationalist.) Such individuals use this terminology to suggest that the modern era is the only period of time in which God has dealt with man through grace. To deny the role of God's grace in other periods of time is to assign these periods a status of relative inferiority and insignificance. Nothing could be further from the truth or more misunderstood. The life of the Lord Jesus Christ was the epitome of grace (and truth) *(John 1:17)*. The exercise of God's wonderful grace began with Adam and Eve in the Garden *(Genesis 3:21)*, although the word *grace* itself is first used in reference to Noah.

*Genesis 6:8 But **Noah found grace** in the eyes of the LORD.*

This passage concerning Noah clearly reveals that God administered grace to those living long before the Church Age. Although it may seem an elementary point—grace did *not* somehow *originate* with Paul's epistles. Other Old Testament books also make reference to grace. The book of Ezra, for example, makes reference to grace and mercy and fittingly defines both.

GRACE: *Ezra 9:8 And now for a little space **grace** hath been shewed from the LORD our God, to leave us a remnant to escape, and to give us a nail in his holy place, that our God may lighten our eyes, and give us a little reviving in our bondage.*

> **"In the study of Scripture, it is most important to understand that scriptural revelation falls into well defined periods. These are clearly separated, and the recognition of these divisions and their divine purposes constitute one of the most important factors in true interpretation of the Scriptures. These divisions are termed "dispensations," and in successive periods of time different dispensations may be observed . . .It is probable that the recognition of the dispensations sheds more light on the whole message of the Bible than any other aspect of Biblical study."**
>
> Lewis Sperry Chafer, *Major Bible Themes,* Revised by John F. Walvoord, (MI: Zondervan, 1974) p. 126.

MERCY: *Ezra 9:13 And after all that is come upon us for our evil deeds, and for our great trespass, seeing that thou our **God hast punished us less than our iniquities deserve, and hast given us such deliverance as this**.*

Grace cannot be administered without mercy; these two elements are inseparable. *Mercy* is dispensed when one is punished less than he deserves; *grace* becomes the means by which that mercy is extended. This study includes many Old Testament examples which prove that grace and mercy are *not* limited to the New Testament.

The book of Ezra shows that God was merciful and dispensed grace to the Jews. David is another prime example of someone "under the law" that received God's mercy and grace. Most students are very familiar with the story of David and his sin with Bathsheba. David sinned with

Bathsheba and was guilty of *a sin unto death (I John 5:16-17)*, yet he did not die. God was merciful and gracious to him and to Bathsheba.

> ***II Samuel 12:13*** *And David said unto Nathan, I have sinned against the LORD. And Nathan said unto David,* ***The LORD also hath put away thy sin****; thou shalt* ***not*** *die*.

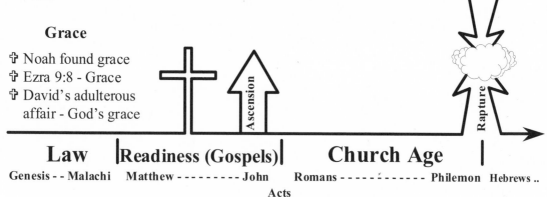

Grace

✝ Noah found grace
✝ Ezra 9:8 - Grace
✝ David's adulterous
   affair - God's grace

Law |Readiness (Gospels)| **Church Age**

Genesis - - Malachi   Matthew - - - - - - - - - John   Romans - - - - - - - - - - - Philemon   Hebrews ..

Acts

Chart 14.1 -Old Testament Grace

David fully expected to die because of God's pronouncements against his sin given in the law. Adultery was a capital offense under the law. Why did David escape? God extended mercy and grace to him. Compare the outcome of David's sin with the punishment for adultery prescribed under the law.

> ***Leviticus 20:10*** *And* ***the man that committeth adultery with another man's wife****, even he that committeth adultery with his neighbor's wife, the adulterer and the adulteress* ***shall surely be put to death.***

David did not die because he found grace in the eyes of the LORD. He and Bathsheba deserved to die according to the law. He was guilty of adultery **and** murder and there existed no adequate animal sacrifice to cover over these two sins.

All three references—from Genesis, Ezra, and Second Samuel—reveal that Noah, the nation of Israel and David all found grace in the Old Testament. Thus, the Bible clearly indicates that God's grace not only existed *under the law* but also predated the law. The theme of grace runs throughout the Bible, from Genesis to Revelation. **Not a single soul could or ever will enter heaven except by the grace of God.** There are absolutely no exceptions to this rule from Adam throughout the end of time.

The law of Moses spans most of the Old Testament books. The significance of the law in our lives confuses many believers and nonbelievers alike. The first group (the believers) claims that the law ended with the death of Christ; many in the second group (the nonbelievers) claim that the law contains the very keys to heaven. Both groups are dead wrong!

Establishing the law

This chapter deals primarily with inaccuracies promulgated by *teachers who should know better*, rather than with the ignorance of *unbelievers or misled believers*. The author realizes that many people have never studied this subject matter. Individuals who are unfamiliar with this subject are encouraged to search the scriptures to find the truth. Pray and ask God for the wisdom necessary to discern the truth. All Bible students should be as the Bereans who spent time daily in the word of God.

> ***Acts 17:10*** *And the brethren immediately sent away Paul and Silas by night unto **Berea**: who coming thither went into the synagogue of the Jews. 11 These were more noble than those in Thessalonica, in that they received the word with all readiness of mind, and **searched the scriptures daily**, whether those things were so.*

Since the law was given to the children of Israel, many people believe it has very little or no application to the Body of Christ today. They incorrectly conclude that grace and law are *completely* incompatible. Thus the Old Testament's usefulness becomes severely limited today. As a result of this philosophy, much clear-cut guidance from God's word is ignored, and many of His examples are allowed to go by the wayside. This thinking creates a problem for those with a thorough understanding of the scriptures. If God ended the law, would it not also be **void**? However, to consider the law void would contradict Paul's writing in ***Romans 3:31***.

> ***Romans 3:31*** *Do we then make **void the law** through faith? God forbid: yea, **we establish the law***.

Paul says **we establish the law**. By definition, **to establish** means to make firm; to confirm; to ratify that which has been previously set or made. Since we are to establish the law, why do so many Christians ignore its personal application? Christians ignore the law because they have been taught that the Lord Jesus Christ (or the "Age of Grace") made the law void. To be **Void** means to have no legal or binding force.

With these two definitions in mind, reconsider the preceding verse. The Body of Christ establishes the law! However, hyper-dispensationalists want no law established; desire no rules for living; and oppose any attempt to present the truth concerning application of the law to a Christian's daily walk with God. These individuals consider the law to be outdated and obsolete. The hyper-dispensationalists' reaction to the law seems more rooted in their hidden agenda, than in a sincere search for the truth. They desire to avoid the law's explicit guidance and convicting properties.

When a person teaches that the law is inapplicable today (as does the hyper-dispensationalist), he is forced to ignore, change or spiritualize many of Paul's clear statements concerning the law. Consider, for instance, ***I Timothy 1:8***: *"But we know that the law is good, if a man use it lawfully."* A hyper-dispensationalist, instead of believing the entire Book, conveniently passes over verses like these. Man today does not need preaching which ignores the law, but rather preaching that reveals how *to use* the law according to our Apostle Paul—**lawfully**.

Preaching and teaching which circumvents God's directions by making the Old Testament apply *only* to somebody else, *only* during some other time period is wicked. Backslidden Christians and the lost alike have been twisting the scriptures for centuries. The law is firm and restrictive. However, man has proven throughout the ages that, when left to rule himself, he will do that which is right in his own eyes ***(Judges 21:25)*** rather than that which is pleasing to a holy and just God.

Two major reasons for many Christians' lack of resolve to live a godly lifestyle emerge from perverted use of the law. Frequently, one of two **extremes** dominates in most Bible-believing churches. There is either the lack of preaching and teaching of the law altogether—resulting in carnality. Or there is the *unlawful* application of the law by those who preach and enforce parts of it—resulting in legalism. The first teaching can create a very carnal Christian. The second teaching generally produces a very weak Christian, one dependent upon the teacher to be the "Holy Spirit" for him. The first group is never taught fully what God says; the second lives depending upon a man to tell him where to go, what to look at, what to wear, etc.

The end results are very clear. The first group tends to over-emphasize the flesh (constantly quoting passages from Romans chapter 7). It becomes increasingly easier for these believers to justify the sins of the flesh. A member of the second group "falls away" from God once *the man* usurping the function of the Holy Spirit no longer influences him. It is unfortunate how both groups point to the shortcomings of the other, yet neither group seems to realize where God wants it to be.

Christianity needs to find the dividing point between the complete rejection of the law and spiritual legalism. The purpose of this study of the scriptures is to point out that balance as revealed in the word of God.

As a starting point for this study, one needs to consider **Romans 3:31** again. Paul states that the law still has binding force (it is not **void**) and that we confirm (**establish**) that which was previously set. To those who ignore the law, this verse should present some difficulties. Some preachers claim that one is taking away a person's liberty and putting him in spiritual bondage by considering any application of the law to the Church. Scripture from Galatians is inappropriately applied to justify this errant position.

*Galatians 5:18. But if ye be led of the Spirit, **ye are not under the law**.*

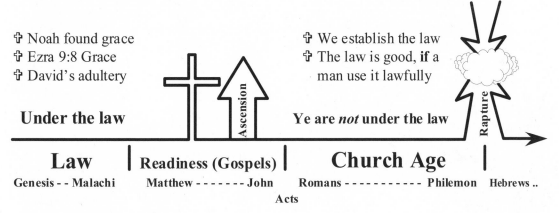

Chart 14.2 -Law and Grace

The Church establishes the law

The Bible does not contain any contradictions. Yet, what could Paul mean by writing that we **establish** the law when he also writes that we are *not* **under** the law? Obviously, the *purpose* of the law for the Christian has changed. Christians are certainly not *under the law* **(Romans 6:14-15, Galatians 3:23, 4:21, 5:18)** in the same sense that Israel was under the law. Since the purpose of the law for the Christian has changed, determining its new purpose is essential.

Prior to the cross, if a man fulfilled the requirements under the law, he would be temporarily *righteous* **(I Kings 8:32, II Chronicles 6:23, Psalm 1:5-6, Ezekiel 18:24)**. However, if he sinned and did not fulfill the necessary sacrifices, he could *die in his sins* **(Ezekiel 18:21, 24)**. Paul refers to this righteousness WHICH IS OF THE LAW as one's "own righteousness."

> **Philippians 3:9** *And be found in him, not having* **mine own righteousness, which is of the law,** *but that which is through the faith of Christ, the righteousness which is of God by faith:*

Nobody could keep the law in its entirety; therefore, the required course of action for sin was also clearly defined. "Under the law," a person's *temporal* righteousness could have been established by keeping the statues of the law by providing the necessary sacrifices when he failed in any particular area. However, the Bible criticized Israel because they sought *the law of righteousness* through works without faith.

> **Romans 9:31** *But* **Israel,** *which followed after the law of righteousness,* **hath not attained to the law of righteousness.** *32 Wherefore?* **Because they sought it not by faith, but as it were by the works of the law.** *For they stumbled at that stumblingstone;*

The best way to describe righteousness under the law is for the author to use the analogy of how things work in his professional occupation. Along with being a preacher, I am also a CPA (Certified Public Accountant). As a CPA, if I filed a Federal income tax form incorrectly, I broke the law. If I did this intentionally and did not file the corrected forms, I would be guilty of breaking the law and could be punished accordingly. However, a timely amended return would bring me back into conformity with the law.

God's law worked much the same way. The sacrifices worked like the amended return functions for the CPA. A *righteous* person under the law was not an individual who had never broken the law. Rather a *righteous* person was the individual who offered the required sacrifices to cover over his sin after breaking the law. Those who fulfilled the law were *not* the ones who never broke it (which is impossible anyway), but were those who offered the required sacrifices in repentance for indiscretions.

However, it must again be noted that the individual's righteousness was never sufficient to get the person to heaven. Only the blood of Jesus Christ could sufficiently atone for sin in such a way as to make the individual heaven-bound. Christ died for our sin. If anyone could be perfectly righteous by keeping the law then Christ died in vain. Paul tells us:

> *"Dispensationalism avoids confusion and contradiction and at the same time unites all the parts into the whole...The basic scheme involving the different dispensations remains the most helpful tool of consistent, noncontradictory interpretation of Scripture."*
>
> Charles C. Ryrie, *Dispensationalism*, p. 37, 11-12

> **Galatians 2:21** *I do not frustrate the grace of God: for* **if righteousness come by the law, then Christ is dead in vain.**

Anyone seeking to establish his or her own righteousness by fulfilling the law is lost and will remain lost forever. To be saved, one must receive the righteousness of the Lord Jesus Christ on his behalf **(II Corinthians 5:21)**. When anyone receives **Christ's righteousness**, he becomes righteous *in God's eyes*, having all sins forgiven. Even if a person could keep the entire law (and no one can), works play no part in his salvation. Paul says we are not justified by the law and that no flesh will be justified by it.

> *Galatians 2:16 Knowing that a man is **not justified by the works of the law,** but by the faith **of** Jesus Christ, even we have believed in Jesus Christ, that we might be justified by the faith of Christ, and not by the works of the law: for **by the works of the law shall no flesh be justified.***

Paul clearly and repeatedly teaches that a person cannot become righteous by keeping the law. The law simply cannot justify. Consequently, some preachers have concluded that the law lacks significance in the lives of Christians today. Because there will be no Christians in hell, they conclude that there is no need to be concerned about the law any longer.

The effect of the cross on the law

Considering the effect of Christ's death on the law will help Christians better understand the function of the law in their lives today. Romans chapter 10 clearly reveals how the application of the law changed by the death of the Lord Jesus Christ. He ended the law. However the scripture does not simply stop at that point. To what extent did Christ end the law? The answer is very simple. He ended the law **for righteousness**.

> *Romans 10:4 For Christ is the **end of the law for righteousness** to every one that believeth.*

Many preachers incorrectly determine that the scriptures say that the Lord Jesus Christ simply *ended the law*. Read **Romans 10:4** again, without ignoring any part of the verse. Does the verse say that the Christ simply ended the law? No! The verse says that Christ is the end of the law **for righteousness**. The Lord eliminates all misunderstanding—no one can become righteous by keeping the precepts of the law. The law has absolutely nothing to do with a personal righteousness during the Church Age. That is why Paul never refers to the individual as righteous, but writes, *"There is none righteous, no, not one"* **(Romans 3:10)**.

If one attempts to keep the law and the sacrifices, he will be damned to hell. This is true no matter how religiously the individual attempts to keep the law. Reading the previous verse **(Romans 10:4)** in its complete context will give a fuller understanding. The three verses that immediately precede verse 4 are as follows:

> *Romans 10:1 Brethren, my heart's desire and prayer to God for **Israel** is, that they might be saved. 2 For I bear them record that **they have a zeal of God, but not according to knowledge**. 3 For they being ignorant of God's righteousness, and **going about to establish their own righteousness**, have not submitted themselves unto the righteousness of God. 4 For Christ is **the end of the law for righteousness to every one that believeth**.*

Following the death of the Lord Jesus Christ, the Jews continued trying to establish their own righteousness through the law. Paul plainly indicates that neither they (Israel) nor anyone else can establish his own righteousness by keeping the statutes of the law. Righteousness, in the sight of God, *only* comes through the Lord Jesus Christ and this is *the righteousness of God* **(II Corinthians 5:21)**. The Lord Jesus Christ ended the law **for righteousness**. Attempting to keep the works and sacrifices of the law in order to be righteous and acceptable to God does **nothing** for a person. **Absolutely nothing!**

Christ's faithfulness counts, not ours; His work matters, not ours. The Christian's faithfulness and work only become important *following* salvation. Many verses, including *Ephesians 2:10* and *Titus 3:8,* clearly proclaim that the Christian should do good works *following* salvation. However, any lost person seeking to establish his own righteousness will end up in hell.

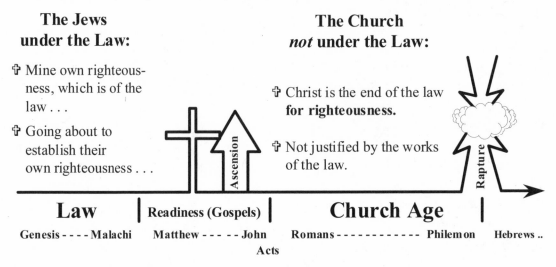

Chart 14.3 -Law and Righteousness

The law and our walk with God

The first part of this study was devoted to proving that the law has no part in salvation, except to make us conscious of our sinful condition *(Galatians 3:24-25)*. As a Christian, everyone needs to determine how the law *should* affect his walk with God. Once a person's relationship with the Lord is settled at salvation, his desire should be to tell others about the Saviour. Too many times, Christians tend to lose sight of this calling and instead spend most of their time arguing over their "pet doctrines."

In their zeal for truth, Christians tend to forget that God called each and every one of us to be servants to others. The souls, the lives and the characters of those the Christian influences are the important elements of any *ministry* (or of any *life,* for that matter). All of this probably sounds admirable, but how many Christians really put it into practice?

Here is a practical application of these principles. When considering any action, ask yourself the following questions:

1. Are my motives of God? . . . or of Satan?

2. Will my actions please my Saviour? . . . or my flesh?

3. Will my testimony be enhanced? . . . or be diminished?

Each of these questions, either directly or indirectly, deals with how easily the Christian puts others before himself. Simply put, an individual's answers to these questions indicate how obediently he loves others, as scripturally commanded. This "love" does not simply refer to the sentimental "love" of the televangelists and Christian psychiatrists and psychologists; it refers to *the love of the Bible—which is the fulfillment of the law.*

> ***Galatians 5:13*** *For, brethren, ye have been called unto liberty; only use not liberty for an occasion to the flesh, **but by love serve one another**. 14 For all **the law is fulfilled** in one word, even in this; Thou shalt **love** thy neighbour as thyself.*

God uses Paul to directly link the law with loving one's neighbor. The way this works is rather simple. The manner in which a person lives his life directly affects the lives of others. On account of their love for one another, people should do certain things and refrain from doing certain others. Few things are more regrettable than a bad testimony that results in others' stumbling in their walk with the Lord. Nothing is worse than a poor testimony that causes others to reject the Saviour.

A Christian's unconcern for others will be reflected in his walk and testimony. Since a person's walk best demonstrates his love for others, his testimony serves as the best evidence of his love. Be sure to grasp these two interconnected truths. The key to the law is to love your neighbor. The key to *fulfilling* the law is to avoid walking after the flesh.

> ***Romans 8:4*** *That the righteousness of the law might be fulfilled in us, who walk not after the flesh, **but after the Spirit**.*

Only those Christians walking after the Spirit and not after the flesh can fulfill the righteousness of the law. This is true because Christians walking *after the flesh* cannot love their neighbor as the law requires. Walking *after the flesh* adversely affects so many areas of life. For instance, a Christian walking after the flesh will not witness as he should; he will not submit to God's authority; and his overall testimony before others will be negative. One cannot simultaneously serve his flesh and serve others. **During the Church Age, men are to keep the law out of love one for another.**

The purpose of the law

The *purpose* of the law has changed. Under the Old Testament, the main purpose of the law was to affect the Jews' relationship with God. During the Church Age, the main purpose of the law is to directly impact our relationship *with others*, rather than our relationship with God. Paul clearly points out that a person's submission to God's laws displays his obedience to the duty of loving others.

Romans 13:8 begins by stating that men are to owe others one thing . . . to love one another. Verse 9 explains *how* to fulfill verse 8.

> ***Romans 13:8*** *Owe no man any thing, but to love one another: for he that loveth another hath fulfilled the law. 9 **For this**, Thou shalt not commit adultery, Thou shalt not kill, Thou shalt not steal, Thou shalt not bear false witness, Thou shalt not covet; and if there be any other commandment, it is briefly comprehended in this saying, namely, **Thou shalt love thy neighbour as thyself**. 10 Love worketh no ill to his neighbour: therefore love is the fulfilling of the law.*

Since the Apostle Paul quotes directly from the law, it should be evident that one cannot simply ignore the law. To find out whether you are a hyper-dispensationalist or not, re-read the previous passage and decide whether God expects the law to affect how you live your life. If you decide that the law has no place in your life because it only applied to Israel, you have a name for your sin: hyper-dispensationalism. Paul repeatedly states that loving others as much as we love ourselves is the way we fulfill the law *today*. Because of our desire to love one another and fulfill the law, we are to do the actions of verses 9 and 10. Paul says, **"for this"** *reason* (because we love others) we are to keep the commandments of the law (i.e. the **"thou shalt not's"**). The truth is not difficult to understand. It might be difficult to accept, but God makes the truth easy to comprehend.

Please understand that the *purpose* of considering any application of the law to the Church is *not* in order to become righteous. It is *not* for fear of hell or punishment, but **entirely** out of the love we are to have for one another. The law should impact a person's relationship with others. Those who absolutely reject any application of the law generally have problems treating others according to the teachings of scripture. Simply speaking, we are to keep the law for our neighbor's sake—displaying a good testimony to a lost, hell-bound, dying world. We are also to keep the law as testimony to a saved, backslidden Body of Christ.

Those people familiar with the law might wonder how to keep the law during this Church Age, especially since portions of the law are contrary to God's instructions to the Church. Yet, God never leaves us without explanation. The most important point to remember when considering Church Age application of the law is the following concept: **thou shalt love thy neighbor as thyself.**

However, God gives further guidance in First Timothy to help solidify our understanding. We are to *use* the law *only* as it lines up with the epistles Paul has written to the Church. The clearest explanation comes from the following passage.

> *I Timothy 1:8 But we know that the law is good, if a man use it lawfully; 9 Knowing this, that the law is not made for a righteous man, but for the lawless and disobedient, for the ungodly and for sinners, for unholy and profane, for murderers of fathers and murderers of mothers, for manslayers, 10 For whoremongers, for them that defile themselves with mankind, for menstealers, for liars, for perjured persons, and if there be any other thing that is contrary to sound doctrine; 11 **According to the glorious gospel of the blessed God, which was committed to my trust.***

The middle verses (verses 9 and 10) list the persons for whom God made the law. Those who have a problem keeping their flesh in check do not like being included in the cast of characters in these verses. Yet, secular historians even agree with the truth expressed in these two verses. As societies have become more lawless, this lawlessness necessitates the creation of more laws. The truth especially applies to God's laws. These laws are written because sinful man needs specific instructions on how to overcome his propensity to sin.

Verses 9 and 10 list those for whom God made the laws. Yet, these verses (9 and 10) are a parenthetical thought, occurring between the two portions of the main thought of the passage. The main theme of the passage is communicated in verses 8 and 11. To more clearly understand the concept God is conveying, the reader needs to skip over the parenthetical thought (verses 9 and 10) and read verses 8 and 11 together. When reading these verses together, while skipping over the intervening parenthetical thought, one reads that . . . **the law is good, if a man uses it lawfully . . . according to the gospel committed to Paul** (the author of First Timothy). Verse 11 completes the thought begun in verse 8.

Paul: "... the law is good, if a man use it lawfully ... according to the glorious gospel of the blessed God, which was committed to my trust."

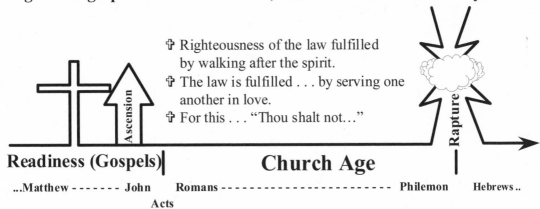

✝ Righteousness of the law fulfilled by walking after the spirit.
✝ The law is fulfilled ... by serving one another in love.
✝ For this ... "Thou shalt not..."

Ascension

Rapture

Readiness (Gospels)   **Church Age**

...Matthew - - - - - - John   Romans - Philemon   Hebrews ..
                        Acts

Chart 14.4 -The Law and Paul

What about the ordinances under the law?

The thirteen Church Age epistles that bear Paul's name as the first word (Romans through Philemon) must be considered first, in order to know what God expects from us concerning the law. Keeping this in mind, let us examine a few of Paul's instructions concerning the law.

> ***Ephesians 2:13** But **now in Christ Jesus** ye who sometimes were far off are made nigh by the blood of Christ. 14 For he is our peace, who hath made both one, and hath broken down the middle wall of partition between us; 15 **Having abolished** in his flesh the enmity, even **the law of commandments contained in ordinances**; for to make in himself of twain one new man, so making peace;*

Paul says the Lord abolished something. What is it that the Lord abolished? The law? Read the passage again. Paul says Christ abolished **the law of commandments** *contained in ordinances.* The verse does not say that He abolished the law itself. No matter how hard one searches, he will *not* find a single place where Paul tells the Church that *the law*, all-inclusive, has been abolished or ended. God does say *the ordinances* are gone. These ordinances would include Sabbath days, holy days, special meats, drinks, circumcision, etc. Yet, concerning the law, Paul says that *we establish it* and *we are to use it lawfully*. Keeping the law cannot and will **not** save a person; however, nowhere does Paul say we can ignore the law or that it has been abolished.

Some will liken this principle to the Seventh Day Adventist teaching of a moral and ceremonial law. The author can only affirm that many try to change the subject, instead of the error of their ways. The scriptures teach that the law has *not* been abolished, but that the ordinances (or ceremonial portion of the law) have ended. An individual must not reject this truth simply because it resembles the teaching of a group with which he disagrees on many other doctrinal issues. When considering any such religious group, a Christian should try to discern and reject the error they promote, while accepting the truths that they teach. Nobody is 100% wrong and nobody is 100% right. Colossians gives further instruction concerning ordinances. This passage clearly points out the effect that the crucifixion had upon the law.

*Colossians 2:14 **Blotting out** the handwriting of **ordinances** that was against us, which was contrary to us, and took it out of the way, **nailing it to his cross;** 15 And having spoiled principalities and powers, he made a shew of them openly, triumphing over them in it. 16 Let no man therefore judge you in **meat**, or in **drink**, or in respect of an **holyday**, or of the **new moon**, or of the **sabbath days**:*

The Old Testament **ordinances** "died" with the Lord; therefore, God no longer allows anyone to judge another person for eating pork or catfish, or for not observing Sabbath or holy days. Anyone who tries to put a person under the ordinances of the law is a hypocrite and is giving heed to seducing spirits and doctrines of devils. These doctrines of devils include not only ordinances concerning meats, but also forbidding marriage *for religious purposes*. The effects of these false teachings are not usually attributed to the errors that produce them.

*I Timothy 4:1 Now the Spirit speaketh expressly, that in the latter times some shall depart from the faith, **giving heed to seducing spirits**, and **doctrines of devils;** 2 **Speaking lies in hypocrisy;** having their conscience seared with a hot iron; 3 **Forbidding to marry, and commanding to abstain from meats**, which God hath created to be received with thanksgiving of them which believe and know the truth.*

Although many "religious" organizations ignore this passage, God says it is a doctrine of a devil for someone to forbid marriage or to command to abstain from meats for religious purposes. These groups are giving heed to seducing spirits. The book of First Corinthians clarifies Paul's God-given position for determining the ordinances of the Church. God leads Paul to give us the following instruction about the ordinances.

*I Corinthians 11:1 **Be ye followers of me**, even as I also am of Christ. 2 Now I praise you, brethren, that ye remember me in all things, and **keep the ordinances, as I delivered them to you**.*

In First Corinthians, the same book in which Paul tells us to follow him concerning the ordinances, he points out the two ordinances of the church. The ordinances Paul gives **us** are

---

Bullinger had two dispensations between Pentecost and the end of the church age. He placed the Gospels and the book of Acts under the Law and commenced the dispensation of the Church with the ministry of Paul after Acts 28:28. The prison epistles, therefore—Ephesians, Philippians, and Colossians—set forth the fullness of the revelation of the mystery of this church age. He also denied that water baptism and the Lord's supper are for this age.

Virtually All ultradispensationalists, of whatever school, agree that it (the church) did not begin at Pentecost. All dispensationalists agree that it did. Therefore, ultradispensationalism may be defined, or certainly characterized rather definitively, as the school of interpretation that places more than one dispensation between Pentecost and the end of the church age.

Charles C. Ryrie, *Dispensationalism* (Chicago, IL: Moody Press, 1995), p. 198, 200.

water baptism and the Lord's Supper. These are found in First Corinthians chapter 1 and chapter 11. *If* the ordinances given to us by Paul are not the Lord's Supper and baptism, what else could they be? We are to keep the ordinances that Paul delivered to us, and there are no others listed anywhere in any of his other epistles.

As we have seen, special meats, Sabbath days and holy days were all nailed to the cross. *The list found in Colossians does not include baptism or the Lord's Supper.* Yet, religious organizations claim that these two ordinances were Old Testament in nature, too. Baptism and the Lord's Supper were not taught in the Old Testament and Paul mentions both as being part of the New Testament church. These two cannot be equated with the Old Testament ordinances that were nailed to the cross. Some preachers even use the Greek language to change instances of "washings" to "baptism" in an attempt to place baptism into the Old Testament, and thereby justify abolishing it *(Hebrews 9:10)*. One group even associates water baptism with the Davidic Covenant, although the scriptures make no reference to this fairy tale association. This is simply infidelity to the scriptures.

Paul: ... **"keep the ordinances, as I have delivered them to you."**

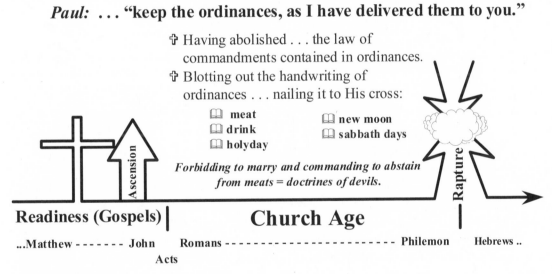

Chart 14.5 - Ordinances

What is bondage?

Only a Bible-rejecter ignores the plain facts of the scriptures. Paul makes known which ordinances are to be observed by the church, explaining that the ordinances under the law were "nailed to the cross." Paul also offers instruction concerning the law and its application. We have been *called unto liberty; only use not liberty for an occasion to the flesh, but by love serve one another (Galatians 5:13)*. Some teach that our liberty in Christ Jesus makes us free from the law. This teaching is unscriptural and counterproductive. Christians still have a responsibility to live right in the eyes of God, regardless of their newfound liberty in the Body of Christ. Churches and preachers who teach that Christians should not drink, smoke or be overcome with television or the internet are not robbing their congregations of their liberties and putting them under bondage. They are sounding a much needed alarm which Christians should hear and heed.

Christians must *willingly* submit to the law out of their love one for another. By willingly submitting to the Spirit of God and following what Paul says, Christians can easily understand which parts of the law are applicable and which are not. Individuals who remain confused about the application of the law to their lives sometimes conclude that Paul defines bondage as being placed in submission to the law. In contrast, Paul uses the concept of bondage in reference to being placed in submission to the ***ordinances*** under the law. The book of Galatians gives us further insight into this truth.

> ***Galatians 2:4*** *And that because of false brethren unawares brought in, who came in privily to spy out our* ***liberty*** *which we have in Christ Jesus, that they* ***might bring us into bondage****:*

The false brethren mentioned in the preceding verse were attempting to bring believers into submission to their ordinances under the law. Galatians chapter 4 provides further insight into this situation.

> ***Galatians 4:9*** *But now, after that ye have known God, or rather are known of God, how turn ye again to the weak and beggarly elements, whereunto* ***ye desire again to be in bondage****?* (The definition of bondage is found in the next verse.) *10 Ye* ***observe days, and months, and times, and years.*** (ordinances under the law.)

Observing days (holy days, Sabbath days, etc.) places a person under the bondage of the law. In this age, holy days are an abomination to God. A practical application of this truth would be to consider the manner in which Christmas and Easter are celebrated. Often, several months are required for a person to recover from the financial bondage caused by "celebrating" Christmas. The world makes a tremendous amount of money during these "hol(y)days." Many Christians find themselves caught in the middle of all of this confusion. They become overwhelmed by the bondage of the world. This is a practical example of observing days, months, times and years.

Still not absolutely clear? God knows that our flesh would rather reject the truth. Therefore, God in His mercy sometimes indulges us with another example . . . but only to make our ungodliness more evident, and to prove how much we really long to reject the truth. Our rejection usually stems from the fact that we believe our ideas are more important than the truths that God sets forth. Changed minds are a sign of spirituality; attempting to change the scriptures is a sign of the flesh and the devil.

> ***Galatians 5:1*** *Stand fast therefore in the* ***liberty*** *wherewith Christ hath made us free, and* ***be not entangled again with the yoke of bondage****.* (Once again someone is trying to be in bondage. We can understand bondage by allowing Paul to explain what it is in the next verse.) *2 Behold, I Paul say unto you, that if ye be* ***circumcised****, Christ shall profit you nothing. 3 For I testify again to every man that is circumcised, that he is a debtor to do the whole law. 4 Christ is become of no effect unto you, whosoever of you are* ***justified by the law****; ye are fallen from grace.*

Paul tells these individuals to stand fast in their liberty (remain firm in their conviction). In this instance, someone had attempted to entangle people in bondage by claiming that circumcision was a practice necessary for salvation.

When Paul writes the preceding passage, he addresses those who have never been saved (justified). The reasoning behind this conclusion is very simple. The people referred to in this passage were attempting to be justified by the law **(verse 4)**. Circumcision was one of the ordinances of the law they were attempting to follow in order to be justified. However, Paul explains that keeping the Old Testament ordinance of circumcision makes a person **a debtor to do the whole law (verse 3).** Anyone that tries to use the law in order to bolster his relationship with God must keep the law with its sacrifices. For those that choose this route. Christ has no affect on their lives. Yet, most people would rather trust in their own ability to keep the law, rather than in the One Who fulfilled it for us—the Lord Jesus Christ. There is no temporal and certainly no eternal justification for a sinner who attempts to keep the law *(Romans 5:1)*. The law does not affect our relationship with God—only Christ affects this relationship.

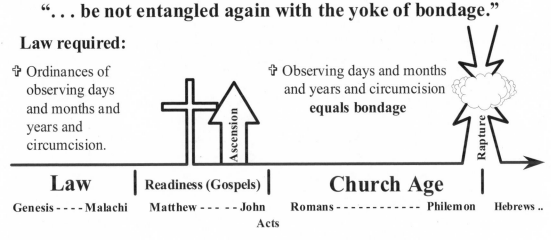

"... be not entangled again with the yoke of bondage."

Law required:

✝ Ordinances of observing days and months and years and circumcision.

✝ Observing days and months and years and circumcision **equals bondage**

Ascension

Rapture

Law | Readiness (Gospels) | **Church Age** |

Genesis - - - - Malachi   Matthew - - - - - John   Romans - - - - - - - - - - - Philemon   Hebrews ..

Acts

Chart 14.6 - Bondage

What is liberty?

The topic most closely related to bondage is liberty. We have already considered bondage. Now our attention focuses on the doctrinal application of **liberty** during the Church Age. In *Galatians 2:4* and *5:1* (earlier), bondage was closely connected with liberty. The purpose of using bondage and liberty together is quite simple. *Bondage* refers to the attempt to place someone under the Old Testament ordinances. *Liberty* is the freedom from these ordinances.

Liberty can be defined as freedom from restraint. Yet, biblical liberty does *not* imply a license to sin. Human flesh desires that liberty include complete freedom from the entire law; however, the Bible does not define liberty in this manner. The flesh hates any application of restraint placed upon it, especially by something as restrictive as God's law. First Corinthians chapter 10 also clarifies that our liberty is a freedom *from ordinances* and not from the law itself. This passage deals with a person called to a feast. A person invited to a feast is at **liberty** to eat whatever is set before him, except in one case:

> *I Corinthians 10:28 But if any man say unto you, This is offered in sacrifice unto idols, **eat not for his sake** that shewed it, and for conscience sake: for the earth is the Lord's, and the fulness thereof: 29 Conscience, I say, not thine own, but of the other: **for why is my liberty judged of another man's conscience**? 30 For if I by grace be a partaker, why am I evil spoken of for that for which I give thanks?*

Paul explains that a person should not exercise his liberty to eat whatever he receives with thanksgiving *(I Timothy 4:4)* if eating will have the effect of destroying the weak conscience of another brother. Paul frequently emphasizes the importance of loving one another. Loving one another is more important than exercising our liberty to eat anything we please. Moreover, Paul does not simply explain how we are to live; Paul also *lived* the example for us to follow. His example . . . put others first. (This also shows another example of Paul's use of liberty).

"... use not liberty for an occasion to the flesh."

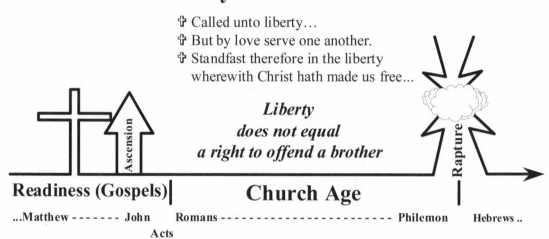

✝ Called unto liberty…
✝ But by love serve one another.
✝ Standfast therefore in the liberty wherewith Christ hath made us free…

Liberty does not equal a right to offend a brother

Ascension

Rapture

Readiness (Gospels)   **Church Age**

…Matthew - - - - - - - John   Romans - Philemon   Hebrews ..
                Acts

Chart 14.7 - Liberty

*I Corinthians 8:8 But meat commendeth us not to God: for neither, if we eat, are we the better; neither, if we eat not, are we the worse. 9 But take heed lest by any means this **liberty** of yours become a stumblingblock to them that are weak. 10 For if any man see thee which hast knowledge sit at meat in the idol's temple, shall not the conscience of him which is weak be emboldened to eat those things which are offered to idols; 11 And through thy knowledge shall the weak brother perish, for whom Christ died? 12 But when ye sin so against the brethren, and wound their weak conscience, ye sin against Christ. 13 **Wherefore, if meat make my brother to offend, I will eat no flesh while the world standeth, lest I make my brother to offend**.*

Paul instructs us how to live, and lives the example of "practicing what he preaches." First Corinthians falls within Paul's *Acts ministry* epistles. During this period, God is still giving the Jew an advantage. According to Paul, exercising your right to eat pales in comparison to your responsibility to love your brother. Paul makes this point by promising that he would eat no meat so long as the world was standing if doing so would cause his brother to stumble *(verse 13)*. Therefore, Paul felt his responsibility to his brother did not end at the point in time when God stopped giving an advantage to the Jew. One who is a true hyper-dispensationalist will spiritualize, dispensationalize and pervert this truth in order to make it apply to someone else in some other time, and not to himself today. Too many Christians that come to understand their "rights" fail to understand their corresponding responsibilities *(I Corinthians 6:7)*.

A person must recognize the division between Paul's Acts ministry and his prison epistles, a division which is located between the books of Galatians and Ephesians. However, this division is often excessively applied. It is extreme to believe that only *nine* books of the Bible are applicable and relevant to the Church today. Too many people desire as little instruction as possible, and hyper-dispensationalism is their modus operandi.

When Paul says to consider what he says, he means to consider it *all (II Timothy 2:7)*. God never led Paul to eliminate all need for the other scriptures. As proof, consider these general statements by Paul concerning the Old Testament:

> ***Romans 15:4*** *For whatsoever things were **written aforetime** were written **for our learning**, that we through patience and comfort of the scriptures might have hope.*

> ***I Corinthians 10:6*** *Now these things were **our examples**, to the intent we should not lust after evil things, as they also lusted.* (Verse 1—the fathers; verse 2—Moses.)

> ***I Corinthians 10:11*** *Now all these things happened unto them **for ensamples**: and they are written **for our admonition**, upon whom the ends of the world are come.*

Hyper-dispensationalists eliminate too much of the Bible. Generally they will eliminate much of the Old Testament, the Gospels, Acts, part of Paul's Church Age epistles, and Hebrews through Revelation. However, the infidelity of the hyper-dispensationalists frequently does not stop there. These individuals also have real problems accepting Paul's first four epistles. As has been demonstrated, a distinction is to be made between Paul's Missionary Epistles and his Prison Epistles (i.e. the application of ***Romans 1:16*** and the signs of an Apostle), but not to the extent of eliminating all application of the former. *All scripture is given . . . for doctrine, for reproof, for correction, for instruction in righteousness **(II Timothy 3:16)***.

Although the Old Testament was written for the Church Age saint's *learning*, giving us *examples* and *ensamples* to consider, some aggressive Bible students still fail to heed these scriptural admonitions. Even with these truths now staring them in the face they will refuse to acknowledge that the entire Bible has some type of application to the Church today. The following are two more passages that reinforce this point.

The Apostle Paul writes in the last chapter of Romans that the *"revelation of the mystery... now is made manifest, and **by the scriptures of the prophets**...made known to all nations for the obedience of faith" **(Romans 16:25-26)***. As the Holy Spirit does His work, those *scriptures of the prophets* help manifest the revelation of the mystery which was *kept secret since the world began*. That which remained a mystery to those under the law is the revelation to the Church.

The Apostle Paul also points out in his second letter to Timothy that the holy scriptures known by Timothy since childhood were *"able to make thee wise unto salvation" **(II Timothy 3:15)***. This truth reinforces the fact that the law found in the Old Testament is our *schoolmaster **(Galatians 3:24)*** to bring us unto Christ. The law cannot bring salvation, but as the schoolmaster, it brings to light the unregenerate state of a man without Christ. The schoolmaster (the righteous law) points out the utter hopelessness of man to attain salvation by works. Then the Gospel of the Grace of God comes to the rescue pointing the sinner to Christ and His saving grace. Thank the Lord for His law that convicts of sin and for the Saviour Who forgives all those that come to Him.

When did the Church begin?

The is perhaps the question most frequently asked of the author! Did the Church, which is Christ's Body *(Colossians 1:18, 24),* begin prior to or following Paul's conversion to Christianity? The answer to this question is easily obtained and grasped with just a basic understanding of the scriptures Given the biblical indications to the contrary, it is inconceivable how anyone with even a superficial grasp of the Bible could claim that the Church began after Paul's conversion. In fact, Paul repeatedly wrote that he persecuted the (already existing) Church.

*Philippians 3:6 Concerning zeal, **persecuting the church**; touching the righteousness which is in the law, blameless.*

*I Corinthians 15:9 For I am the least of the apostles, that am not meet to be called an apostle, because **I persecuted the church of God.***

> **"Dispensationalism and ultradispensationalism are related in some ways, but there are some basic differences between the two schools of thought. The primary one is the difference over when the church, the Body of Christ, began historically. Dispensationalists say that the church began at Pentecost, while ultradispensationalists believe it began with Paul sometime later."**
>
> Charles C. Ryrie, *Dispensationalism* (Chicago, IL: Moody

*Galatians 1:13 For ye have heard of my conversation in time past **in the Jews' religion**, how that beyond measure **I persecuted the church of God,** and wasted it:*

If the Church began with Paul, how could he have persecuted an entity not yet in existence? Paul not only admitted to persecuting the Church, but also knew that he began preaching the very faith that he once persecuted.

*Galatians 1:23 But they had heard only, That **he which persecuted us in times past now preacheth the faith which once he destroyed.***

Paul persecuted the Church and preached the faith he once ambitiously worked to eradicate. If the Body of Christ/the Church began with Paul, why would he write that there were others *in Christ (Romans 12:5, I Corinthians 15:22, etc.)* before him?

*Romans 16:7 Salute Andronicus and Junia, my kinsmen, and my fellowprisoners, who are of note among the apostles, who also were **in Christ before me.***

A person *in Christ* is a member of the Body of Christ—a saved child of God. Many of the hyper- or ultra-dispensationalists never comprehend that *the mystery* of the Gospel of the Grace of God involves Gentiles joining their Jewish brethren **already in the Body**! Redeemed Gentiles become fellow-heirs with the Jews, not the other way around.

*Ephesians 3:4 Whereby, when ye read, ye may understand **my knowledge in the mystery** of Christ) 5 Which in other ages was not made known unto the sons of men, as it is now revealed unto his holy apostles and prophets by the Spirit; 6 That* *the Gentiles should be fellowheirs, and of the same body*, *and partakers of his promise in Christ by the gospel:*

Praise God that the Gentiles can now become heirs with the Jews in the same Body simply by trusting in Christ. This is the mystery that had been kept secret since the world began. In fact, the Bible refers to the Gentiles as having been grafted in among the Jews who were already in that Body.

Romans 11:13 *For I speak to you Gentiles, inasmuch as I am the apostle of the* *Gentiles*, *I magnify mine office:...17 And if some of the branches be broken off, and* *thou, being a wild olive tree, wert graffed in among them*, *and with them partakest of the root and fatness of the olive tree;*

Romans chapter 11 clearly depicts how the Jews as a nation were broken off and how the Gentiles were "surgically" brought into a place of blessing. In Ephesians chapter 2, Paul develops the truth further by articulating the utter hopelessness of Gentiles. Their only hope comes from realizing that the wall separating them from God is broken down by Jesus who makes one new man with Jew and Gentile together.

Ephesians 2:13 *But now in Christ Jesus ye who sometimes were far off are made nigh by the blood of Christ. 14 For he is our peace, who hath made both one, and hath* *broken down the middle wall of partition between us;* *15 Having abolished in his flesh the enmity, even the law of commandments contained in ordinances;* *for to make in himself of twain one new man*, *so making peace; 16 And that he might* *reconcile both unto God in one body by the cross,* *having slain the enmity thereby: 17 And came and preached peace to you which were afar off, and to them that were nigh. 18 For through him* *we both have access* *by one Spirit unto the Father.*

Christ made one new Body through the cross. Now, both Jew and Gentile have direct access to God! Paul continues the thought later in the same chapter by emphasizing out that the Gentiles are no longer strangers and foreigners.

Ephesians 2:19 *Now therefore ye are no more strangers and foreigners, but* *fellowcitizens with the saints, and of the household of God;* *20 And are* *built upon the foundation of the apostles and prophets*, *Jesus Christ himself being the chief corner stone;*

These scripture references should convince the most ardent skeptic that the Body of Christ must have existed before the Apostle to the Gentiles was even saved. Only those who elevate Paul's position to an inappropriate degree would teach that the Body of Christ began with him. The evidence of scripture clearly and repeatedly proves otherwise.

The hyper-dispensationalist is not the only one who should be on guard. Beware of allowing your knowledge of the correct way to study the Bible to cause you to become a fool. God wants you to study, preach, teach and love your Bible from the first page of Genesis to the last page of the book of the Revelation. God bless you as you seek Him in the pages of His book. Follow Paul, but study it all *(I Corinthians 11:1)*.

Gospel. The great theme may be summarized as follows:

I. In itself the word Gospel means good news.

II. Four forms of the Gospel are to be distinguished:

(1) The Gospel of the kingdom. This is the good news that God purposes to set up on the earth, in fulfillment of the Davidic Covenant (2 Sam. 7.16, and refs.), a kingdom, political spiritual, Israelitish, universal, over which God's Son, David's heir, shall be King, and which shall be, for one thousand years, the manifestation of the righteousness of God in human affairs. See Mt. 3.2, note.

Two preachings of this Gospel are mentioned, one past, beginning with the ministry of John the Baptist, continued by our Lord and His disciples, and ending with the Jews rejection of the King. The other is yet future (Mt. 24.14), during the great tribulation, and immediately preceding the coming of the King in glory.

(2) The Gospel of the grace of God. This is the good news that Jesus Christ, the rejected King, has died on the cross for the sins of the world, that He was raised from the dead for our justification, and that by Him all that believe are justified from all things…

(3) The everlasting Gospel (Rev. 14.6). This is to be preached to the earth-dwellers at the very end of the great tribulation and immediately preceding the judgment of the nations (Mt 25.31, refs). It is neither the Gospel of the kingdom, nor of grace. Though its burden is judgment, not salvation, it is good news to Israel and to those who, during the tribulation, have been saved...

(4) That which Paul calls, "my Gospel" (Rom. 2.16, refs.). This is the Gospel of the grace of God in its fullest development, but includes the revelation of the result of that Gospel in the outcalling of the church, her relationships, position, privileges, and responsibility. It is the distinctive truth of Ephesians and Colossians, but interpenetrates all of Paul's writings.

III. There is "another Gospel" (Gal. 1.6; 2 Cor. 11.4) "which is not another," but a perversion of the Gospel of the grace of God, against which we are warned. It has had many seductive forms, but the test is one—it invariably denies the sufficiency of grace alone to save, keep, and perfect, and mingles with grace some kind of human merit. In Galatia it was law, in Colosse fanaticism (Col. 2. 18, etc.). In any form its teachers lie under the awful anathema of God.

Scofield Reference Bible, Revelation 14:6 footnote, p 1343.

15
Dispensational Ages (Old Testament)

Throughout the span of human existence (past, present, *and future*), God deals with mankind in a variety of ways. The Bible gives us a clear record of these variations. As this book has already demonstrated, *rightly dividing the word of truth* primarily means properly dividing the Bible into the various periods of God's dealings with man. Bible believers commonly refer to these periods as dispensations *(I Corinthians 9:17, Ephesians 1:10, 3:2, Colossians 1:25)*. The next chart provides an overview of the dispensations or ages *(Ephesians 2:7, 3:5, 3:21; Colossians 1:26)* of the Old Testament.

Dispensational Overview - Old Testament

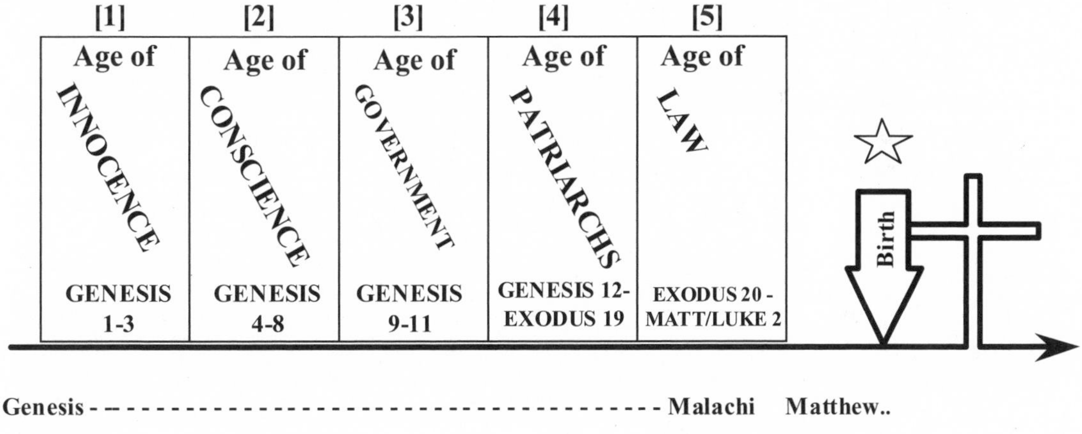

[1]	[2]	[3]	[4]	[5]
Age of INNOCENCE	Age of CONSCIENCE	Age of GOVERNMENT	Age of PATRIARCHS	Age of LAW
GENESIS 1-3	GENESIS 4-8	GENESIS 9-11	GENESIS 12- EXODUS 19	EXODUS 20 - MATT/LUKE 2

Genesis - Malachi   Matthew..

Chart 15.1 -Old Testament Dispensations

Although dispensational study emphasizes the differences across various time periods, there are many constants throughout all ages of time. For example, while God changes in His *actions* with mankind *(John 13:34)*, He is eternally unchanging in His *attributes (Malachi 3:6, Hebrews 13:8, James 1:17)*. (To accept and acknowledge God's changing actions in no way contradicts His unchanging attributes.) Another constant throughout all ages is that every man is a hopeless sinner *(Psalm 14:1-3; Romans 3:10, 23, 5:12)* until redeemed by the shed blood of the Lord Jesus Christ *(Hebrews 9:22-28)*.

The fact that God would provide a means of salvation from the wages of man's sin is an evidence of His mercy and grace. (Mercy is *not* giving what *is* deserved—in this case, eternal death; grace *is* giving what is *not* deserved—in this case, eternal life.) One can find references to God's grace and mercy throughout both the Old and New Testaments. God's mercy and grace are not limited to the New Testament. For example, God's will is that mankind be saved from their sin in all ages *(I Timothy 2:4, II Peter 3:9)*, *ultimately* by having the shed blood of the Lord Jesus Christ applied on their behalf. However, the blood could not be applied to the sinner *prior* to the cross, thus the necessity of Paradise being located in the heart of the earth until then. (Compare the location of Paradise in *Luke 16:26* and *23:43* prior to the resurrection and its location in *II Corinthians 12:4* following the resurrection.)

It is important to note that no one living prior to the cross "looked forward to the cross" in order to be saved. Yet, **God** knew about the future redemptive work of the cross at this time; and He saved people by *His* **looking forward to the cross for them** as they believed what He told them. In the meantime, He put them in Abraham's Bosom (presumably, even before there was an Abraham) until the Lord Jesus Christ completed His work.

Throughout man's sinful existence on earth, God repeatedly expresses His will to dispense mercy and grace to save man from the wages of sin. This expression occurs in each time period. However, in each period **God articulates His plan to be believed in order to fulfill His consistent will to save.**

The Bible clearly reveals God's expectations for man. It also reveals that, *for the most part*, His commands and instructions get more detailed and complex as human history progresses from age to age. Perhaps this is God's way of showing mankind's sinful shortcomings. The further man gets from God, the more God must write down for him and the greater the detail He must use in order to hold man's attention. Whether the instructions are general or specific, simple or complex, mankind as a race perpetually fails, dooming itself to eternal damnation. Thank God, His mercy and grace prevail in every age, providing the means for an *individual* to have his sinful soul saved.

Every age includes this basic set of components:

1. God issues His commands through His spokesman or spokesmen.

2. By faith, man repents, believes and obeys—or else persists in unrepentance, disbelief and disobedience. (Thus, in every age, salvation comes *by faith through grace*. The **content** of that faith changes according to what God commands man to believe and obey in any given time period.) Repentance, belief and obedience are more pronounced in some ages than others. This will be evident as we study through the various ages. For example, in the Age of the Church, when a man believes on the Lord Jesus Christ he is saved as he repents of believing in anything else for salvation and *obeys the gospel (II Thessalonians 1:8).* While the heart of every member of mankind is deceitful and desperately wicked on its own, God looks on the heart of every person in search of repentance, belief and obedience *(I Samuel 16:7, Jeremiah 17:9-10)*.

3. God redeems those who repent, believe and obey.

4. God judges those who fail to repent, believe and obey *(I Peter 4:17)*.

Several factors can hinder a person's understanding about dispensational truth. First, man's finite mind has trouble differentiating the *actions* of God from His *attributes*. Another hindering factor is the tendency to view "things" in terms of definite start and stop times. Some dispensational ages *do* begin and/or end with definite events at definite times. For example, the Church Age ends at the Rapture of the Church. However, in other cases, God extends the initial dispensing of His commands beyond a single particular event and time.

A third hindrance to understanding dispensational truth is man's tendency to look to and long for "what used to be." Because of this, as will be shown, man attempts to apply the commands of the preceding dispensational age to the current one. This phenomenon could be related to man's resistance to change—along with his inclination to rebel against God's will. (As a result, most of this book deals with rightly dividing this present Church Age from the two previous ages.)

Another factor complicating man's understanding is the urge to play "what if" throughout the Bible. "What if Adam hadn't sinned?" and "What if the Jews had accepted Christ as the Messiah?" are two examples. These might make for interesting "parlor talk," but will not result in very profitable Bible studies. One should stick to the facts of what *did* happen and refrain from playing "what if" over what did not occur.

Nevertheless, diligent dispensational study can overcome these hindrances to discovering the truth. A survey of the different dispensational ages will again emphasize the necessity of rightly dividing the word of truth. Of course, the first dispensation appears in the first few chapters of Genesis.

I. Age of Innocence (Genesis 1-3)

God created man in a state of innocence of good and evil. He placed him in a perfect environment and gave him rule over the earth. He also gave him a commandment of *what to do* and put him in the Garden.

> *Genesis 1:28 And God blessed them, and God said unto them, **Be fruitful, and multiply, and replenish the earth, and subdue it: and have dominion** over the fish of the sea, and over the fowl of the air, and over every living thing that moveth upon the earth.*

> *Genesis 2:15 And the LORD God took the man, and **put him into the garden** of Eden **to dress it and to keep it**.*

In this state of innocence, man was to be fruitful and multiply to replenish the earth and dress and keep the Garden of Eden. God gave only one commandment of *what **not** to do*. It concerned the tree designated by God that would give the knowledge of good and evil. Man had no need to have the knowledge of good *and evil*, but God—in His plan for humanity—had to let man make this choice. In God's logic, true love is demonstrated by free will, under a test.

> *Genesis 2:16 And the LORD God commanded the man, saying, Of every tree of the garden thou mayest freely eat: 17 **But of the tree of the knowledge of good and evil, thou shalt not eat of it:** for in the day that thou eatest thereof thou shalt surely die.*

Remember that up until this point, Adam and Eve only knew good. Had they obeyed God's **one** command not to eat of the tree, presumably they would never have suffered *the wages of sin (Romans 6:23)* and would have remained in a perpetual state of innocence.

Age of Innocence

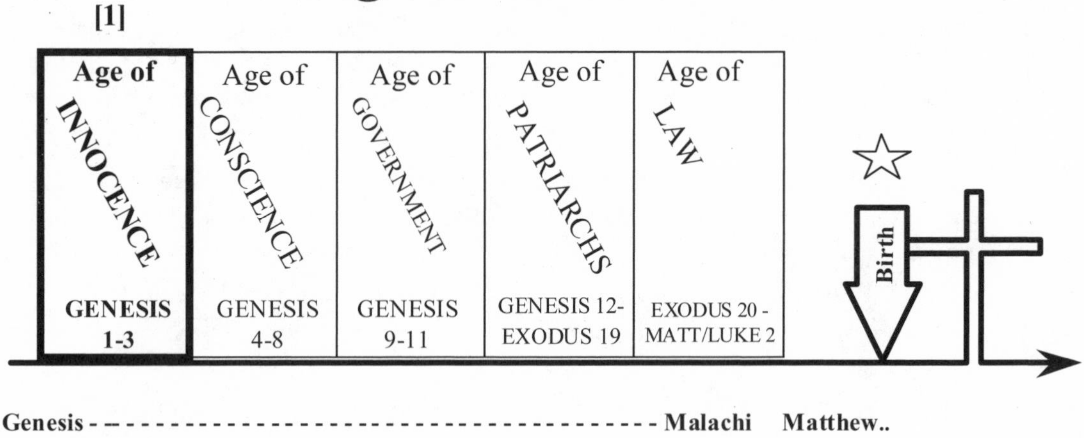

[1]

Age of INNOCENCE	Age of CONSCIENCE	Age of GOVERNMENT	Age of PATRIARCHS	Age of LAW		
GENESIS 1-3	GENESIS 4-8	GENESIS 9-11	GENESIS 12- EXODUS 19	EXODUS 20 - MATT/LUKE 2	Birth	

Genesis - — - Malachi   Matthew..

Chart 15.2 - Age of Innocence

We do know for certain that Adam and Eve disobeyed God's command. Thus, sin ended the Age of Innocence and doomed the race of man until a way of *eternal redemption (Hebrews 9:12)* would be provided through the shed blood of the Lord Jesus Christ *(Romans 3:24)*. Adam and Eve's disobedience made them sinners.

> *Genesis 3:6 And when the woman saw that the tree was good for food, and that it was pleasant to the eyes, and a tree to be desired to make one wise, she took of the fruit thereof, and did eat, and gave also unto her husband with her; and he did eat. 7 **And the eyes of them both were opened**, and they knew that they were naked; and they sewed fig leaves together, and made themselves aprons.*

Adam and Eve ate of the forbidden fruit and immediately became conscious of their sinful condition. Thus began man's feeble and futile attempt to *cover* sin, but to no avail. Man died not only spiritually, but also brought God's judgment on his physical life *(Genesis 3:16-19).* He traded life for death and a glorious covering for fig leaves and skins of lambs.

In the course of time, Adam and Eve repented of their disobedience and submitted to God's authority again. Perhaps it was in their fear and nakedness or maybe in their acceptance of the garments of skin provided by God that they received redemption. The point is clear. God provided redemption by killing the animals and providing a blood covering for Adam and Eve's sin and nakedness. Their acceptance of the garments reflects acknowledgment of their repentance and acceptance of the redemption provided *(Psalm 130:7).*

> *Genesis 3:21 Unto Adam also and to his wife did the LORD God make coats of skins, and clothed them.*

God expelled Adam and Eve from the Garden of Eden *(Genesis 3:22-24)*, thus making their physical death an eventual certainty and formally closing the Age of Innocence. **The very first dispensational age unquestionably proves that innocence of evil and a perfect environment will *not* preclude man from his propensity to sin and disobey God.** Innocence lost will never again be regained until eternity future. The knowledge of evil and man's expulsion from Eden brings us to the next dispensation known as the Age of Conscience.

II. Age of Conscience (Genesis 4-7)

The knowledge of good and evil awakened man's conscience. He was now subject to the "sorrow" pronounced upon him by God in *Genesis 3:16 and 17*. Based on that God-given sorrow, man was to do all known good and to refrain from all known sin. He was now to live by the following rule.

Genesis 4:7a If thou doest well, shalt thou not be accepted? and if thou doest not well, sin lieth at the door. . .

God accepted man based on what he did. However, God always provides a means of acceptance after failure. In the event of sin, God respected the blood sacrifice of the *sorrowful*, repentant person. For instance, consider the case of Abel.

Genesis 4:4 And Abel, he also brought of the firstlings of his flock and of the fat thereof. And the LORD had respect unto Abel and to his offering:

God accepted Abel's blood sacrifice. Yet, most of humanity does not want to submit to the expectations of God and generally chooses to do it their own way. Cain is a good example of this rebellious humanistic philosophy. God did not accept his sacrifice because Cain reverted to the Age of Innocence and its "garden economy" *(Genesis 2:15)*. He brought an offering of the fruit of the ground. He began his own self-righteous religion, expecting God to adapt *(Romans 10:3)*.

Genesis 4:3 And in process of time it came to pass, that Cain brought of the fruit of the ground an offering unto the LORD.

God required blood as an offering for sin. Cain's offering did not work anymore than Adam and Eve's fig leaves because God had changed His commands and His manner of dealing with man. This is the first recorded change, but not the last. God expected man to abide by His dispensational commands and would not accept anything less *(Genesis 4:5a)*.

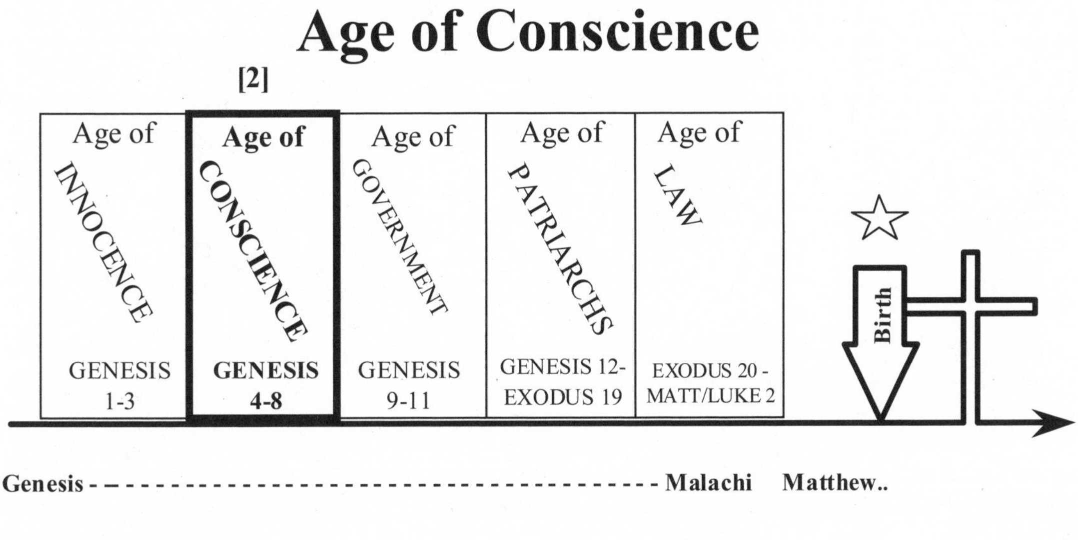

Age of Conscience

Chart 15.3 - Age of Conscience

Soon there seemed to be many more "Cain's" than "Abel's." The *Cain's* wanted to be accepted by God on their own terms. Inevitably, man's sin far exceeded his sorrowful repentance and God's judgment would shortly come to pass.

*Genesis 6:5 And GOD saw that the wickedness of man was great in the earth, and that **every imagination of the thoughts of his heart was only evil continually**.*

Man in every dispensation seems to want to "stretch the limit." The Age of Conscience was no exception. Therefore, God executed a universal physical judgment upon mankind.

*Genesis 6:7 And the LORD said, **I will destroy man** whom I have created from the face of the earth; both man, and beast, and the creeping thing, and the fowls of the air; for it repenteth me that I have made them.*

*Genesis 7:23a And **every living substance was destroyed** which was upon the face of the ground, both man, and cattle, and the creeping things, and the fowl of the heaven; and they were destroyed from the earth . . .*

Thankfully, God patiently waited until He found one man that found grace in His eyes *(Genesis 6:8)*. This man and his family saved the human race from extinction. His name was Noah, and Noah was a "preacher of righteousness" *(II Peter 2:5)*.

Noah was a welcomed exception to the corruption and violence that had otherwise engulfed the human race. Rather than being overcome by the wicked ways of his fellow man, Noah believed God's commandment for the age in which he lived *(Genesis 4:7)* and obediently followed God. He also taught his family to do the same. In spite of the innately sinful hearts of these people, God saw repentance, belief and obedience and graciously imparted righteousness to them.

*Genesis 6:8 But **Noah found grace in the eyes of the LORD**. 9 These are the generations of Noah: **Noah was a just man** and perfect in his generations, and **Noah walked with God**.*

*Genesis 7:1 And the LORD said unto Noah, **Come thou and all thy house** into the ark; for **thee have I seen righteous** before me in this generation.*

Noah's righteousness covered his whole family. No one else accepted God through the witness of Noah; therefore, no one else was accepted of God. The flood and God's judgment were worldwide. However, God provided redemption for Noah and his family through the building of an ark and thereby created a covenant with Noah and his family. Noah and his family accepted this covenant.

*Genesis 6:18 But **with thee will I establish my covenant**; and thou shalt come into the ark, thou, and thy sons, and thy wife, and thy sons' wives with thee.*

Noah obeyed God's commands given to him. Obedience to the commands of God is paramount in every age.

*Genesis 6:22 Thus did Noah; **according to all that God commanded him, so did he**.*

As in all ages, God insured that man was "without excuse" *(Romans 1:20)*. God provided a spokesman with His message. In this case, it was Noah.

II Peter 2:5 *And spared not the old world, but saved* **Noah** *the eighth person,* **a** **preacher of righteousness***, bringing in the flood upon the world of the ungodly;*

Noah warned the world through preaching. He built and boarded the ark in faithful obedience to God's commandment. He did not exit the land of the living until God commanded him to do so *(Genesis 8:15)*.

Even in all the relief and excitement of stepping out onto dry ground, Noah wasted no time in continuing his faithful obedience and worship of God. He built an altar and offered burnt sacrifices, just as Adam had taught his sons before him.

Genesis 8:20 *And* **Noah builded an altar** *unto the LORD; and took of every clean beast, and of every clean fowl, and* **offered burnt offerings on the altar***.*

Every human being alive at that time witnessed this sacrifice. Their sacrifice pointed to the coming Deliverer—*(Genesis 3:15)*. With the closing of Genesis chapter 8, God closes the Age of Conscience. Because of man's sin nature, his conscience had not guided him well. It was now time for God to change His method of interaction with man once again.

III. Age of Government (Genesis 9-11)

God gave the survivors of the flood some *new* commands and reiterated some commands from the past. God also told these individuals to replenish and rule over the entire earth, just as He had told Adam in *Genesis 1:28*.

Genesis 9:1 *And God blessed Noah and his sons, and said unto them, Be fruitful, and multiply, and* **replenish** *the earth. 2 And the fear of you and the dread of you shall be upon every beast of the earth, and upon every fowl of the air, upon all that moveth upon the earth, and upon all the fishes of the sea;* **into your hand are** **they delivered.**

One of God's *new* commands concerned the eating of animal flesh.

Genesis 9:3 **Every moving thing that liveth shall be meat for you***; even as the green herb have I given you all things.*

God would allow men in this new age to eat the animals, but specified that man must cook the flesh and not eat it raw with the blood *(Genesis 9:4)*. Man was now to govern himself and the animal world by exercising *judgment and justice* for any shedding of man's blood, whether by animal or fellow man.

Genesis 9:5 *And surely your blood of your lives will I require; at the hand of every beast will I require it, and at the hand of man; at the hand of every man's brother* **will I require the life of man***. 6 Whoso sheddeth man's blood,* **by man shall his** **blood be shed***: for in the image of God made he man.*

Man was now responsible for the governing of other men. No longer was government simply an individual responsibility as given in the Age of Conscience *(Genesis 4:7)*. God no longer "set a mark" on murderers *(Genesis 4:15)*, but now required capital punishment at the "hand of man." Henceforth, God exhorted man to order his own government upon the foundational concepts of *judgment and justice (Proverbs 21:3)*. There was to be *judgment* of actions and *justice* imposed for wrongdoings in order to establish and maintain order. God the Son will one day take this responsibility upon Himself *(Isaiah 9:6-7)*, but until then mankind is responsible for administering true justice in this world.

Age of Government
[3]

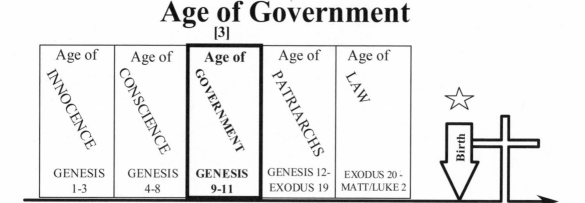

Age of	Age of	Age of	Age of	Age of
INNOCENCE	CONSCIENCE	GOVERNMENT	PATRIARCHS	LAW
GENESIS 1-3	GENESIS 4-8	**GENESIS 9-11**	GENESIS 12- EXODUS 19	EXODUS 20 - MATT/LUKE 2

Genesis - — - Malachi   Matthew..

Chart 15.4 - Age of Government

God's plan was for Noah to establish a godly order, to replenish the earth and to wait for the Promised Deliverer.

Of course, as is his nature, man wasted little time in resuming his sinful ways. He did this not only through individual sins *(Genesis 9:21-22)*, but also through societal sins. Man collectively rebelled against God's command to *replenish* the entire earth. Instead of scattering over the earth, man stayed together and devised a plan.

*Genesis 11:4 And they said, Go to, **let us build us a city and a tower**, whose top may reach unto heaven; and let us make us a name, **lest we be scattered** abroad upon the face of the whole earth.*

Once again, man tried to reach God his own way without regard to His commandments. For this, mankind incurred the judgment of God again. This time, it was a social judgment resulting in the beginning of languages and the scattering of the people over the face of the earth.

*Genesis 11:6 And the LORD said, Behold, the people is one, and they have all one language; and this they begin to do: and now nothing will be restrained from them, which they have imagined to do. 7 Go to, let us go down, and there **confound their language**, that they may not understand one another's speech. 8 **So the LORD scattered them** abroad from thence upon the face of all the earth: and they left off to build the city. 9 Therefore is the name of it called **Babel**; because the LORD did there **confound the language of all the earth**: and from thence did the LORD scatter them abroad upon the face of all the earth.*

It is interesting to note that God not only scattered mankind by dividing him into language groups, but He also reinforced that scattering by dividing the earth's dry land mass. This judgment presumably explains how the continents came into existence or at least how God divided the nationalities.

*Genesis 10:25 And unto Eber were born two sons: the name of one was Peleg; **for in his days was the earth divided**; and his brother's name was Joktan.*

The progressive imposition of judgments by God is interesting. God progressively imposed judgments on all three components of man's being—his spirit, body and soul *(I Thessalonians 5:23)*.

- During the Age of Innocence, God pronounced judgment on man's *spirit*.

- During the Age of Conscience, God pronounced judgment on his *body* (first with the flood and then with the ongoing command in the Age of Government to execute killers.)

- During the Age of Government: God judges the *soul* (the mental intellect of man) by imposing a variety of languages and thus restraining man's collective imagination.

Man has made such a mess of himself that only God can straighten him out—first, by a new birth, but eventually with a new earth *(Revelation 21:1)*. Once again, man irrefutably failed God's commands in the Age of Government. Therefore, God closed this age in Genesis chapter 11 and again changed His dealings with man.

IV. Age of Patriarchs/Promise (Genesis 12-Exodus 19)

Once again, the world was degenerating into an idolatrous mess. God therefore called out and redeemed Abram, a man who was willing to obey the commands of the previous Age of Government. He then used him to initiate the next age—the Age of Patriarchs (or the Age of Promise). Abram was willing to come out from his family and obedient to go wherever God would have him go.

Genesis 12:1 Now the LORD had said unto Abram, **Get thee out of thy country, and from thy kindred, and from thy father's house, unto a land that I will shew thee:**

Age of Patriarchs

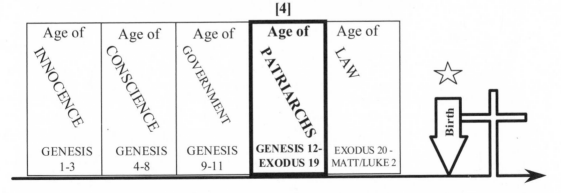

Chart 15.5 - Age of Patriarchs

Abram obeyed God! God promised blessings *to* Abram and a blessing *through* him. The blessings *to* Abram were conditional, based on his obedience to God's command to get out of his father's house and country. The blessing *through* Abram was also conditional, based on how others treated him and the nation that was to come forth from him.

*Genesis 12:2 **And I will make of thee a great nation, and I will bless thee,** and make thy name great; and thou shalt be a blessing: 3 And **I will bless them that bless thee, and curse him that curseth thee**: and in thee shall all families of the earth be blessed.*

As the spokesman for this age, Abraham (changed from Abram by God in **Genesis 17:5**) continued in faithful obedience to and worship of God as set down by his godly forefathers. Abram built an altar unto the LORD everywhere he traveled.

*Genesis 12:7 And the LORD appeared unto Abram, and said, Unto thy seed will I give this land: and **there builded he an altar unto the LORD,** who appeared unto him. 8 And **he removed from thence unto a mountain on the east of Bethel,** and pitched his tent, having Bethel on the west, and Hai on the east: and **there he builded an altar unto the LORD, and called upon the name of the LORD.***

Abraham also believed and obeyed additional commands as God revealed them to him. When God reminded Abraham of His promise and used the stars as a sign of the certainty of His promise, Abraham believed God and *his belief was counted unto him for righteousness.*

*Genesis 15:5 And he (God) brought him (Abram) forth abroad, and said, Look now toward heaven, and tell the stars, if thou be able to number them: and he said unto him, So shall thy seed be. **And he believed in the LORD; and he counted it to him for righteousness.***

Genesis chapter 15 is a turning point in Abram's life. Later, in Genesis chapter 22, God tested Abraham's faith with a command that would cut to the core of any loving father's heart. Would Abraham obey God at all costs and love Him above all others; or would Abraham place the love of his son over obedience to the Father?

*Genesis 22:1 And it came to pass after these things, that God did tempt Abraham, and said unto him, Abraham: and he said, Behold, here I am. 2 And he said, **Take now thy son**, thine only son **Isaac**, whom thou lovest, and get thee into the land of Moriah; **and offer him** there for a burnt offering upon one of the mountains which I will tell thee of.*

Could Abraham obey God and put Him first and foremost in his life? With no recorded indication of hesitation or a faith that faltered, Abraham obeyed God. He passed the test by promptly attempting to obey this extraordinary command—until halted by God.

*Genesis 22:11 And the angel of the LORD called unto him out of heaven, and said, Abraham, Abraham: and he said, Here am I. 12 And he said, **Lay not thine hand upon the lad**, neither do thou any thing unto him: **for now I know that thou fearest God**, seeing thou hast not withheld thy son, thine only son from me.*

Some would think God unrighteous for asking such a thing. How foolish to doubt the infinite wisdom of God *(Psalm 147:5)*! The tests of life are not for an omniscient God, but so that we may come to learn who and what we really are. Abraham learned that there was nothing between him and his God, not even that which he treasured most on this earth.

After this test, God used this opportunity to confirm His commitment to fulfill His promise to Abraham based on Abraham's act of obedience.

*Genesis 22:15 And the angel of the LORD called unto Abraham out of heaven the second time, 16 And said, By myself have I sworn, saith the LORD, for because thou hast done this thing, and hast not withheld thy son, thine only son: 17 That in blessing **I will bless thee**, and in multiplying **I will multiply thy seed as the stars of the heaven**, and as the sand which is upon the sea shore; and thy seed shall possess the gate of his enemies; 18 And in thy seed shall all the nations of the earth be blessed; **because thou hast obeyed my voice**.*

Abraham believed and obeyed God. This combination of belief and obedience pleased God to the fulfillment of His covenant with Abraham. Centuries later, under the inspiration of the Holy Ghost, Paul and James both cite Abraham as support for the doctrine they advance in their respective, and different, dispensational ages.

Paul writes to the Gentiles:

*Romans 4:1 What shall we say then that Abraham our father, as pertaining to the flesh, hath found? 2 For if Abraham were justified by works, he hath whereof to glory; but not before God. 3 For what saith the scripture? **Abraham believed God, and it was counted unto him for righteousness.***

James writes to the Jews:

*James 2:20 But wilt thou know, O vain man, that faith without works is dead? 21 **Was not Abraham our father justified by works**, when he had offered Isaac his son upon the altar? 22 Seest thou how faith wrought with his works, **and by works was faith made perfect**? 23 And the scripture was fulfilled which saith, Abraham believed God, and it was imputed unto him for righteousness: and he was called the Friend of God. 24 **Ye see then how that by works a man is justified, and not by faith only.***

These citations by Paul and James appear contradictory. They each address a different aspect of Abraham's responses to God's commands. Clearly, there is no contradiction in the mind of God. When God inspired Paul to write the passage in Romans chapter 4, God knew **James 2:20-24** had been or would be written. Therefore, God had a particular purpose for each of these two passages of inspired scripture.

In Romans chapter 4, God wants Paul to emphasize Abraham's simple faith as expressed in **Genesis chapter 15**. God led Paul to point out that Abraham was *not* saved by his works. On the other hand, James emphasizes Abraham's works to point out that the testing of his faith in **Genesis chapter 22** enabled the perfection (or completion) of his faith *by his works*.

Until tested, Abraham's simple belief in what God had said was sufficient for God to impute righteousness, forgive his iniquities and cover his sins. Abraham's heart was right with God, and God always looks at the heart condition first *(I Samuel 16:7)*.

Abraham had to fulfill his faith in God. God "tried the reigns" of Abraham's heart *(Jeremiah 17:10)* and found his ways and doings pleasing. Abraham not only *talked the talk*, but he also *walked the walk.* As a result, God counted Abraham perfect (complete) before Him and blessed him with fruitfulness on earth.

> **Genesis 17:1** *And when Abram was ninety years old and nine, the LORD appeared to Abram, and said unto him, I am the Almighty God;* **walk before me, and be thou perfect.** *2 And I will make my covenant between me and thee, and will multiply thee exceedingly.*

Although these were conditional blessings, God made an everlasting *covenant* with Abraham and his seed. He would always be their God.

> **Genesis 17:7** *And I will establish* **my covenant** *between me and thee and thy seed after thee in their generations for an everlasting covenant,* **to be a God unto thee, and to thy seed after thee.**

God gave Abraham a literal and personal sign for all to know of His covenant, and He would give us our own seal (the Holy Spirit) in time. It was literally a personal, private token known as circumcision. Paul calls it "the sign of circumcision, a seal of the righteousness of the faith which *he had yet* being uncircumcised" *(Romans 4:11)*. Believers in the Church Age also receive a seal, but one that is far more effectual in attesting to and preserving *our* righteousness—which is in fact, God's righteousness *(II Corinthians 5:21)*. Our seal is the Holy Spirit *(II Corinthians 1:22, Ephesians 1:13 and 4:30)*; this seal is given on the basis of our trusting in the Lord Jesus Christ and His finished work on the cross of Calvary.

This seal of the Holy Spirit will be intact all the way to the day of our completed redemption *(Romans 8:23)*. The permanence of this seal is in no way contingent upon *our works* of faith. Our soul and spirit are redeemed at salvation, and our bodies are redeemed at the Rapture of the Church. We look for the Lord's return Who *shall change our vile body* into one like the glorious body of our Saviour.

> **Philippians 3:20** *For our conversation is in heaven; from whence also we look for the Saviour, the Lord Jesus Christ: 21* **Who shall change our vile body, that it may be fashioned like unto his glorious body,** *according to the working whereby he is able even to subdue all things unto himself.*

Back to Abraham: Although God knows all, Abraham's acting out what was truly in him caused God to say that He now knew that Abraham feared Him. Abraham trusted God so completely that he knew that God would be true to His word.

> **Genesis 22:12** *And he said, Lay not thine hand upon the lad, neither do thou any thing unto him:* **for now I know that thou fearest God,** *seeing thou hast not withheld thy son, thine only son from me.*

God even named the place of comfort, located next to hell in the heart of the earth, after Abraham. Abraham's Bosom served as the location of all saints who died prior to our Lord's sacrifice of Himself for sin.

> **Luke 16:22** *And it came to pass, that the beggar died, and was carried by the angels into* **Abraham's bosom**: *the rich man also died, and was buried; 23 And in hell he lift up his eyes, being in torments, and seeth Abraham afar off, and Lazarus in his bosom.*

As God's spokesman for the Age, Abraham set the stage for godly obedience to God's commands in the Age of Patriarchs/Promise. He obeyed God and God blessed him and his descendents who followed his example of obedience. Furthermore, God bestowed His blessings upon people who blessed Abraham and his descendents, and cursed those who did not. The account of Abimelech in Genesis chapter 20 is a good case in point.

Another example is the instance of the Pharaoh of Egypt. So long as the Egyptians were good to Joseph and his extended family, God was good to Pharaoh and Egypt. God established a tremendous precedent that would continue through this and **all** succeeding ages—"salvation is of the Jews" *(John 4:22)* . . . the Lord Jesus Christ Himself being of the seed of Abraham (a Jew). Yet, true to form, man failed again.

To begin with, trouble arose from outside *the nation* of Abraham's descendents. A new king of Egypt arose that did not know Joseph *(Exodus 1:8)*. He was concerned with the number of the children of Israel and perceived a threat upon his people. He was concerned that because of their numbers and might the Israelites would side with Egypt's enemies should a war begin.

> *Exodus 1:11 Therefore they **did set over them taskmasters to afflict them with their burdens**. And they built for Pharaoh treasure cities, Pithom and Raamses. 12 But the more they afflicted them, the more they multiplied and grew. And they were grieved because of the children of Israel. 13 **And the Egyptians made the children of Israel to serve with rigour: 14 And they made their lives bitter with hard bondage**, in morter, and in brick, and in all manner of service in the field: all their service, wherein they made them serve, was with rigour.*

Notice that the more the Egyptians afflicted the children of Israel, the more they grew. The Egyptians were hard yet the Lord did not forsake His people. God heard the cries of His people and remembered His covenant with them by raising up a deliverer.

> *Exodus 2:24 And God heard their groaning, **and God remembered his covenant with Abraham**, with Isaac, and with Jacob. 25 And God looked upon the children of Israel, and God had respect unto them.*

God heard His people and He raised up another spokesman, Moses, to communicate His message to man. Although they had some misgivings about how God was using Moses to lead them *(Exodus 5:21, 6:9, and 14:11-12),* the Jews still cried out to their God *(Exodus 14:10)*. So, despite these misgivings, God miraculously redeemed the children of Israel from Egyptian bondage, and from the death and destruction He brought upon the Egyptians.

God also began giving the Jews what would become part of His new set of commands for them in the next age. He instituted the Passover feast and the redemption of the firstborn as signs, tokens and memorials of His delivering them from bondage in Egypt. *Initially*, the children of Israel believed and obeyed God.

> *Exodus 4:31 And **the people believed**: and when they heard that the LORD had visited the children of Israel, and that he had looked upon their affliction, then **they bowed their heads and worshipped**.*

> *Exodus 12:26 And it shall come to pass, when your children shall say unto you, What mean ye by this service? 27 That ye shall say, It is the sacrifice of **the LORD'S***

*passover, who passed over the houses of the children of Israel in Egypt, when he smote the Egyptians, and delivered our houses. **And the people bowed the head and worshipped.** 28 And the children of Israel went away, and did as the LORD had commanded Moses and Aaron, so did they.*

Unfortunately, it was not long before Israel also began rebelling against *the Patriarchs and the Promises* given them. They stopped crying out to God, and instead murmured against His spokesman. Like all other ages, this one would end in abject failure.

*Exodus 15:24 And the people **murmured against Moses**, saying, What shall we drink?*

*Exodus 16:2 And the whole congregation of the children of Israel **murmured** against Moses and Aaron in the wilderness:*

Their murmuring directed towards God's spokesman was in effect directly against God Himself! The people expressed their displeasure with Moses, but the Bible says that that murmuring was really against God Himself.

*Exodus 16:7 And in the morning, then ye shall see the glory of the LORD; for that he heareth your **murmurings against the LORD**: and what are we, that ye murmur against us? 8 And Moses said, This shall be, when the LORD shall give you in the evening flesh to eat, and in the morning bread to the full; for that **the LORD heareth your murmurings which ye murmur against him**: and what are we? your murmurings are not against us, but against the LORD.*

In His mercy and grace, God spared the rebellious and ungrateful children of Israel. In fact, He did so repeatedly as they repeatedly **repented, believed and obeyed**. God even continued blessing those Gentiles who recognized and worshipped "the LORD." For instance, consider the case of Jethro, Moses' Midianite father-in-law *(Exodus 18:8-12).*

However, God began to give more and more commands as He prepared to proceed into the next age. He laid out His "new deal" to the people of Israel in Exodus chapter 19.

*Exodus 19:3 And Moses went up unto God, and the LORD called unto him out of the mountain, saying, Thus shalt thou say to the house of Jacob, and tell the children of Israel; 4 Ye have seen what I did unto the Egyptians, and how I bare you on eagles' wings, and brought you unto myself. 5 Now therefore, **if ye will obey my voice** indeed, and keep my covenant, **then ye shall be a peculiar treasure unto me above all people**: for all the earth is mine: 6 And ye shall be unto me **a kingdom of priests, and an holy nation**. These are the words which thou shalt speak unto the children of Israel.*

The Lord makes an unprecedented offer to the nation of Israel. If they obeyed His voice and kept His covenant, they would be a peculiar treasure above all people. In fact, they would be a holy nation. Moses leaves the mount and presents the offer to the people.

*Exodus 19:7 And Moses came and called for the elders of the people, and laid before their faces all these words which the LORD commanded him. 8 And all the people answered together, and said, **All that the LORD hath spoken we will do**. And Moses returned the words of the people unto the LORD.*

The people wholeheartedly accept God's conditions. From Mount Sinai in Exodus chapter 19, God closes the Age of Patriarchs/Promise and ushers in the Age of the Law.

V. Age of the Law (Exodus 20 - Matthew 2/Luke 2)

God spelled out His commands under the law in great detail. He also detailed a variety of punitive and corrective actions to be taken when any of the law was violated. In His mercy and grace, God also provided an elaborate system of sacrifices and offerings. Both individually and collectively, God provided a means for an *atonement (Exodus 29:33-37)* and *forgiveness (Leviticus 4:20, 26, 31, 35; 5:6, 10, 13, 16, 18; 6:7)* in the temporary *purifying of the flesh Hebrews 9:13).*

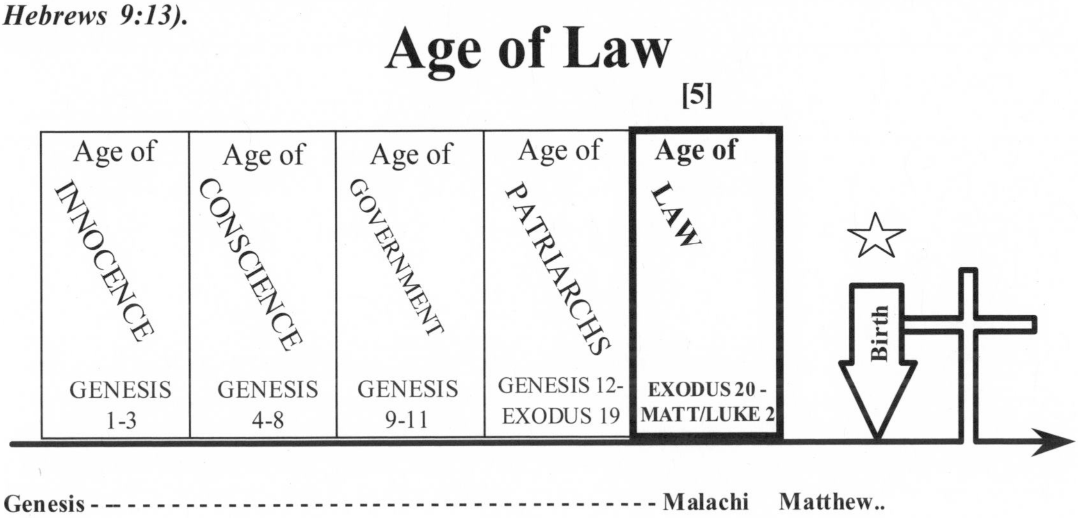

Age of Law
[5]

Chart 15.6 - Age of Law

In itself, the law could never save anybody *(Galatians 2:16, 3:21; Hebrews 7:19)*. God articulated the law to demonstrate the sinfulness of man *(Galatians 3:19, I Timothy 1:9)*. The law served as a schoolmaster to bring man to a point of recognizing his sinful condition and his inability to overcome this condition on his own *(Galatians 3:24)*. Faith in God's word and obedience to it by taking the steps to demonstrate that faith established and maintained a man's state of *personal righteousness* with God *(Number 23:10)*.

We are told under the law that "the just shall live by **his** faith" *(Habakkuk 2:4)*, referring to the faith of the individual (rather than to the faith of the Lord Jesus Christ as in the Age of the Church—see *Philippians 3:8-9)*. Long life was still conditional and dependent on maintaining the right heart and actions under the law *(Ezekiel 18:24-32).* If the righteous man sinned without repentance, he died in his sin.

However, if he repented with a "new heart and a new spirit," he would be forgiven and would live *(Ezekiel 18:31).* Under the law, God the Holy Spirit did not permanently indwell and seal the believer as He does today. For instance, when King Saul remained unrepentant in his sins, the Spirit left him to his sins *(I Samuel 16:14; 18:12)*. King David, on the other hand, did not want this to happen to him. Thus, David repented from his sins and implored God to give him a new heart and spirit, and asked God not take His Spirit from him *(Psalm 51:10-11)*. David knew that all the sacrifices in the world would do no good unless they stemmed from *a right heart*. Only sacrifices offered from a broken and a contrite heart contained the means of pleasing God under the law.

The problem for man was that he forgot the source of his blessings. Even those who were religious mistakenly put their faith in their *works* rather than in the God that gave them all blessings. The scribes and Pharisees were meticulous in keeping the letter of the law, but neglected the spirit of it *(Matthew 23:23)*. Rather than having a broken and contrite heart, they took pride in their piety *(Matthew 23:1-6)*. Yet, through their tragic rebellion against God's will, a remnant of the Jewish people repented and remained righteous until the time of God's redemption. A certain priest named Zacharias and his wife Elisabeth were part of that remnant.

> *Luke 1:5 There was in the days of Herod, the king of Judaea, a certain priest named Zacharias, of the course of Abia: and his wife was of the daughters of Aaron, and her name was Elisabeth. 6 And **they were both righteous before God, walking in all the commandments and ordinances of the Lord blameless.***

As God prepared to close the Age of the Law, God had the angel Gabriel announce to Zacharias and Elisabeth the birth of their son John.

> *Luke 1:13 But the angel said unto him, Fear not, Zacharias: for thy prayer is heard; and thy wife **Elisabeth shall bear thee a son,** and thou shalt call his name John. 14 And thou shalt have joy and gladness; and many shall rejoice at his birth. 15 For he shall be great in the sight of the Lord, and shall drink neither wine nor strong drink; and he shall be filled with the Holy Ghost, even from his mother's womb. 16 **And many of the children of Israel shall he turn to the Lord their God.** 17 And he shall go before him in the spirit and power of Elias, to turn the hearts of the fathers to the children, and the disobedient to the wisdom of the just; **to make ready a people prepared for the Lord.***

Did you know...

Isaac Watts (1674-1748), best known as a hymn writer, was also a theologian...whose writings fill six large volumes. In a forty-page essay entitled "The Harmony of all the Religions which God ever Prescribed to Men and all his Dispensations towards them," he defined his concept of dispensations and presented his system.

Except for the exclusion of the Millennium (he did not consider it a dispensation), (his) outline is exactly like that in the Scofield Reference Bible. ...If Scofield parroted anybody's scheme it was Watt's...

Charles C. Ryrie, *Dispensationalism,* **p. 66, 67, 69.**

"The Scofield Reference Bible is the best reference Bible in the world..."

John R. Rice, *Prayer—Asking and Receiving* **(Murfreesboro: Sword of the Lord Publishers, 1942, 1970) p. 96.**

16

Dispensational Ages
(New Testament)

The previous chapter dealt with the first five dispensations, all found in the Old Testament. The New Testament contains four additional distinct dispensations or ages.

Dispensational Overview - New Testament

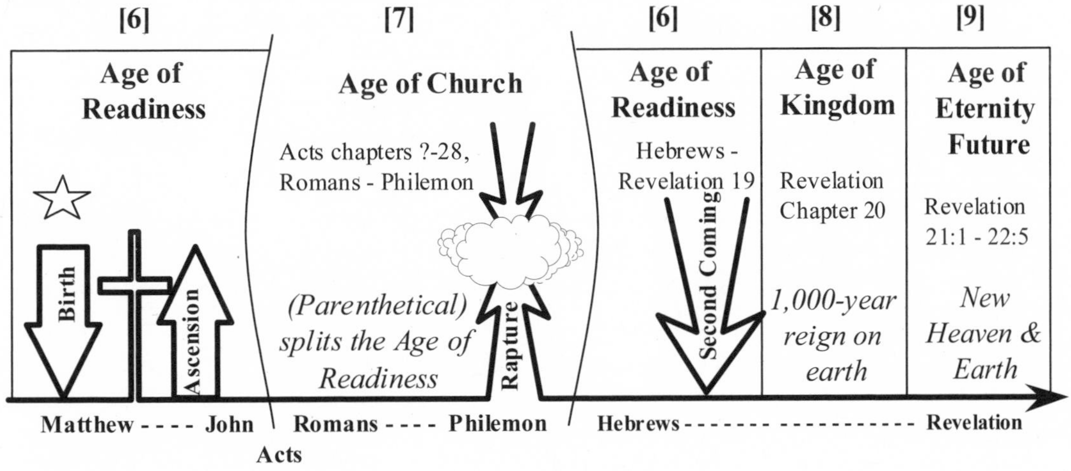

[6]	[7]	[6]	[8]	[9]
Age of Readiness	**Age of Church**	**Age of Readiness**	**Age of Kingdom**	**Age of Eternity Future**

Chart 16.1 -New Testament Dispensations

The first of these New Testament Dispensations is the Age of Readiness. This age begins with John the Baptist.

VI. Age of Readiness (Matthew 3/Mark 1/Luke 3/John 1 - Acts) and (Hebrews - Revelation 19)

The vast majority of mankind has either under-emphasized or over-emphasized the law, while ignoring the Lawgiver. With the onset of the New Testament, this truth becomes even clearer and more pronounced when considering the actions of the Pharisees, Sadducees and religious leaders. Thus, God once again altered His dealings with man. To do this, He chose to use John the Baptist. Luke chapter 16 clearly expresses the transitioning from the law and the prophets.

Luke 16:16 The law and the prophets were until John: since that time the kingdom of God is preached, and every man presseth into it.

The primary purpose of John's ministry was to *ready* a people for the kingdom, thus the name of the Age is *Readiness (Matthew 24:44)*. God had John the Baptist herald the coming of the Son of God to fulfill the law, take vengeance on those who scorned it, and establish His kingdom. Thus we find that the ministry of the Lord Jesus Christ did not terminate the law, but renewed and expanded its emphasis. Christ's ministry also fulfilled the law.

*Matthew 5:17 **Think not that I am come to destroy the law**, or the prophets: **I am not come to destroy, but to fulfil**. 18 For verily I say unto you, Till heaven and earth pass, one jot or one tittle shall in no wise pass from the law, till all be fulfilled. 19 Whosoever therefore shall break one of these least commandments, and shall teach men so, he shall be called the least in the kingdom of heaven: but whosoever shall do and teach them, the same shall be called great in the kingdom of heaven. 20 **For I say unto you**, That except your righteousness shall exceed the righteousness of the scribes and Pharisees, ye shall in no case enter into the kingdom of heaven.*

It is easy to recognize the dual purpose of many of the Lord's statements. Repeatedly, the Lord Jesus Christ declared: "Ye have heard…" and then proceeded to state some element of the law and the prophets. He would then declare: ". . . but I say unto you . . ." and next provide an additional or expanded insight into the law. The Lord fulfilled even these additions to the law. For instance, consider His submission to the baptism of repentance. Though the Lord Jesus Christ certainly did not need this baptism for Himself, John baptized Him in order to fulfill all righteousness on behalf of all mankind.

*Matthew 3:13 **Then cometh Jesus** from Galilee to Jordan unto John**, to be baptized of him.** 14 But John forbad him, saying, I have need to be baptized of thee, and comest thou to me? 15 And Jesus answering said unto him, Suffer it to be so now**: for thus it becometh us to fulfil all righteousness.***

After His baptism, the Lord Jesus Christ began His public ministry. Both John and the Lord Jesus Christ preached and taught about the coming Kingdom. The exhortation was for others to be *ready*.

Consider the preaching of John the Baptist:

*Matthew 3:1 In those days came **John the Baptist**, preaching in the wilderness of Judaea, 2 And saying, Repent ye: for **the kingdom of heaven is at hand**.*

Consider the preaching of the Lord Jesus Christ:

*Matthew 4:17 From that time **Jesus** began to preach, and to say, Repent: for **the kingdom of heaven is at hand**.*

Both John the Baptist and the Lord Jesus Christ preached that the Kingdom was "at hand" or within reach. The Lord and His disciples also preached the Kingdom Gospel. Gospel means "good tidings." (Gospel is defined by comparing the replacement of *good tidings* in *Isaiah 61:1* with the word *gospel* in *Luke 4:18*.) As demonstrated in previous chapters, this Gospel of the Kingdom differs from the Gospel of the Grace of God preached during the Church Age.

Age of Readiness

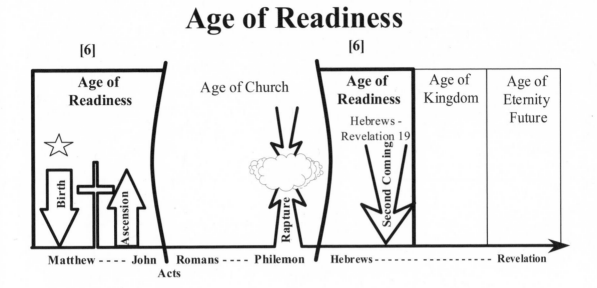

Chart 16.2 - Age of Readiness

Matthew 4:23 And Jesus went about all Galilee, teaching in their synagogues, and preaching the gospel of the kingdom, and healing all manner of sickness and all manner of disease among the people.

This Gospel (of the Kingdom) included supernatural healing. Furthermore, the Lord foretells that this Kingdom Gospel will be preached (during the Tribulation) throughout the entire world prior to the end of time *(Matthew 24:14)*. The disciples of the Lord were also God's instruments to preach about the Kingdom during His earthly ministry.

Luke 9:1 Then he called his twelve disciples together, and gave them power and authority over all devils, and to cure diseases. 2 And he sent them to preach the kingdom of God, and to heal the sick.

A few verses later in the same chapter, we are told that this preaching of the disciples included *the gospel*. As we have already seen, this gospel (prior to the cross) did not include the death, burial and resurrection of the Lord Jesus Christ.

Luke 9:6 And they departed, and went through the towns, preaching the gospel, and healing every where.

The Gospel of the Kingdom during this period of time (the earthly ministry of the Lord) involved **seeking** the Kingdom rather than actually living in the Kingdom. The Lord instructed His followers after this manner:

Matthew 6:33 But seek ye first the kingdom of God, and his righteousness; and all these things shall be added unto you.

Luke 12:31 But rather seek ye the kingdom of God; and all these things shall be added unto you.

Although the kingdom was at hand, the Lord was not offering the kingdom during the time that He was in ministry on this earth. In fact, He avoided being made king because His time had not yet come.

> **John 6:15** *When Jesus therefore perceived that they would come and take him by force, to* **make him a king**, *he departed again into a mountain himself alone.*

Although the Lord Jesus Christ avoided the people's attempts to make Him a king, the Kingdom was indeed at hand. Therefore, the main emphasis of this age was getting ready and staying **ready** for the **Kingdom yet to come**.

> **Matthew 24:44** *Therefore* **be ye also ready***: for in such an hour as ye think not the Son of man cometh.*

> **Matthew 25:10** *And while they went to buy, the bridegroom came;* **and they that were ready** *went in with him to the marriage: and the door was shut.*

The readiness period receives its name from the requirements to seek the Kingdom and to be ready whenever it might come. "Readiness" consists of three distinct components: repentance from sin, acceptance of Christ's fulfillment and endurance. For a discussion of the distinctive features of the Age of Readiness, see Appendix D at the end of the book.

The feature that makes the Age of Readiness quite unique is that it has another age, the Age of the Church, parenthetically inserted within it. The Age of Readiness *tapers* off in effect as the Age of the Church comes into effect. However, following the Rapture of the Church, the Age of the Church will end and the Age of Readiness will resume and continue throughout the Tribulation period.

The twelve apostles continued readiness preaching into the Acts time period and during the advent of the Age of the Church. God did not include Paul as one of twelve, nor did Paul's doctrine include Age of Readiness doctrine. (See *Acts 1:26, 2:14, and 6:2* which prove Paul was not one of the twelve apostles.)

Although the books of Hebrews through Revelation are written during the first century and are consistent in doctrine with the Age of Readiness, they also contain *prophetic* application following the Rapture of the Church.

This brings us to our present dispensational age—the Age of the Church.

VII. Age of the Church (Romans - Philemon)

In the middle of the Age of Readiness and its commands to be ready for the coming Kingdom, God gives man his greatest opportunity ever!

In the Age of the Church, God reduces the complexity level of His commands back to a level comparable to that in effect during the Age of Innocence. However, the arrangement is better than ever this time! During the Age of the Church, as in the Age of Innocence, God prescribes only one commandment that man must obey in order to be saved. In Acts chapter 16, the Apostle Paul succinctly relates this single commandment in answer to a question from the Philippian jailer.

> **Acts 16:29** *Then he called for a light, and sprang in, and came trembling, and fell down before Paul and Silas,* 30 *And brought them out, and said, Sirs,* **what must I do to**

be saved? 31 *And they said,* **Believe on the Lord Jesus Christ**, *and thou shalt be saved, and thy house.*

When a man living in the Age of the Church believes on the Lord Jesus Christ, he is accepting application of the faith of the Lord Jesus Christ to his account. During this age, instead of reading that "the just shall live by **his** faith" *(Habakkuk 2:4)*, we read simply that "the just shall live by faith" *(Romans 1:17)*. The faith spoken of here in Romans is the faith of Jesus Christ! (See Chapter 5, pages 59-60 for further study on the faith of Jesus Christ.)

Age of Church

[7]

Age of Readiness	Age of Church	Age of Readiness	Age of Kingdom	Age of Eternity Future

Birth Ascension

Acts chapters ?-28, Romans - Philemon

(Parenthetical) splits the Age of Readiness

Rapture

Hebrews - Revelation 19

Second Coming

Matthew ---- John Romans ---- Philemon Hebrews ------ --------- Revelation
Acts

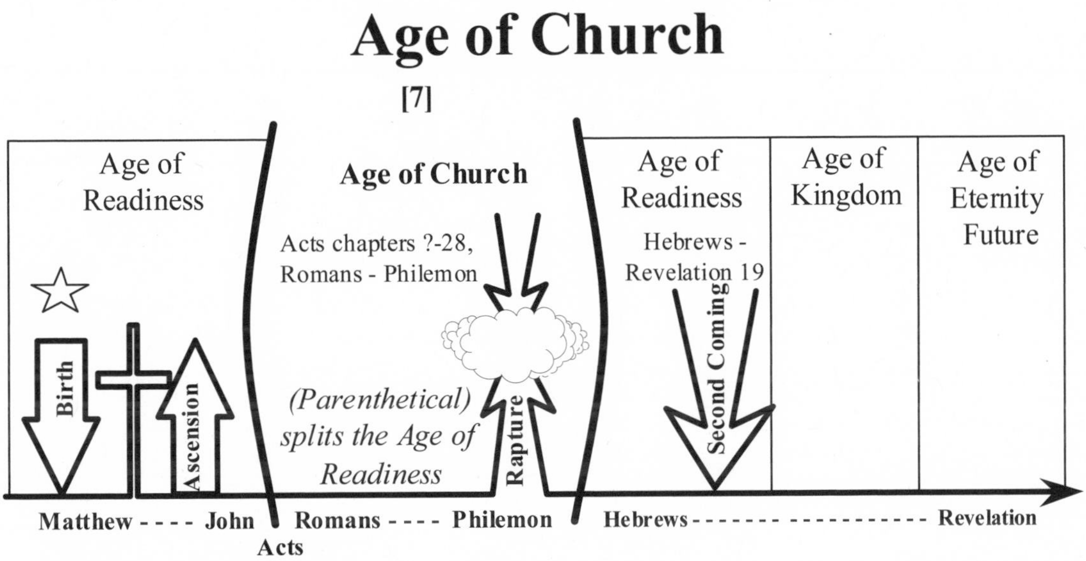

Chart 16.3 Age of Church

A person receives the righteousness of God by the faith of Jesus Christ. It is *unto all*, but only *upon all* them that **believe**.

> **Romans 3:21** *But now the righteousness of God without the law is manifested, being witnessed by the law and the prophets; 22 Even **the righteousness of God which is by faith of Jesus Christ** unto all and upon all them that believe: for there is no difference:*

The faith of Jesus Christ is the thing that justifies the believer. Nothing can be equated to this faith:

> **Galatians 2:16** *Knowing that a man is not justified by the works of the law, but by the **faith of Jesus Christ**, even we have believed in Jesus Christ, that we might be **justified** by the **faith of Christ**, and not by the works of the law: for by the works of the law shall no flesh be justified.*

Having that single command to obey in order to receive the faith of Jesus Christ is reason enough for us to rejoice, but there is even more! In this age, when a man obeys that single command and believes on the Lord Jesus Christ, he gets salvation *and* God's guarantee that he will never lose that salvation. Here is basically how it works:

This present age is called the Age of the Church because during this time the Holy Spirit indwells and baptizes every believer into the Church, the Body of Christ *(I Corinthians 12:13)*. The believers then assemble themselves into local bodies, also called churches. Note: There are other churches mentioned in the Bible, such as the Jewish Old Testament "church in the wilderness" *(Acts 7:38)* and the churches of the pagans *(Acts 19:37)*. However, these have no bearing on the Church Age.

Nevertheless, the Age of the Church is named in reference to the Church "which is His Body." Not every member of the local church is saved. Every member of the Church—which is the Body of Christ—*does* have the Spirit of God dwelling in him. These members of the Church are the only individuals who have experienced true salvation.

> *Romans 8:11 But if the Spirit of him that raised up Jesus from the dead dwell in you, he that raised up Christ from the dead shall also quicken your mortal bodies by **his Spirit that dwelleth in you**.*

Although many Christians may not be aware of this truth, the fact remains the same. For instance, Paul stressed this point with the Corinthian Church. Paul rebuked these believers because they did not know that they had the Spirit of God indwelling them. Every blood-bought child of God should learn this truth soon after salvation.

> *I Corinthians 3:16 Know ye not that ye are the temple of God, and that **the Spirit of God dwelleth in you**?*

The next passage reveals the means by which God places the believer into His Church. The Holy Spirit (without water) baptizes one into the Body of Christ.

> *I Corinthians 12:12 For as the body is one, and hath many members, and all the members of that one body, being many, are one body: so also is Christ. 13 For **by one Spirit are we all baptized into one body**, whether we be Jews or Gentiles, whether we be bond or free; and have been all made to drink into one Spirit.*

The Holy Spirit baptizes us into "one body." The next passage makes the connection between the Body of Christ and the Church.

> *Ephesians 1:22 And hath put all things under his feet, and gave him to be the head over all things to **the church**, 23 **Which is his body**, the fulness of him that filleth all in all.*

We (Christians) are the *Body* of Christ and the Lord Jesus Christ is the head of this Body. Neither the Body, nor the Head is complete without the other part.

> *Colossians 1:18 And **he is the head of the body, the church**: who is the beginning, the firstborn from the dead; that in all things he might have the preeminence.*

Be sure to grasp the following distinction between this age (the Age of the Church) and the previous one (the Age of Readiness). During the Age of Readiness, believers were said to be *in* Christ's hand *(John 10:28).* In contrast, during this Age of the Church, believers now *are* Christ's hand! Christians in this age are literally *members* (parts) of the Body of Christ, and He is the Head of the Body. Furthermore, in this age, when a man believes on the Lord Jesus Christ, God forever forgives **all** of his sins—past, present and future!

*Colossians 2:13 And you, being dead in your sins and the uncircumcision of your flesh, hath he quickened together with him, **having forgiven you all trespasses**;*

*Titus 2:13 Looking for that blessed hope, and the glorious appearing of the great God and our Saviour Jesus Christ; 14 **Who gave himself for us, that he might redeem us from all iniquity**, and purify unto himself a peculiar people, zealous of good works.*

The believer has all sins forgiven, even those yet to be committed in the future. At the same time the Holy Spirit baptizes the believer into the Church "which is His body"; the Holy Spirit *seals* the believer into the Body of Christ.

*II Corinthians 1:21 Now he which stablisheth us with you in Christ, and hath anointed us, is God; 22 Who hath also **sealed us**, and given the earnest of the Spirit in our hearts.*

*Ephesians 1:13 In whom ye also trusted, after that ye heard the word of truth, the gospel of your salvation: in whom also after that ye believed, **ye were sealed with that holy Spirit** of promise,*

*Ephesians 4:30 And grieve not **the holy Spirit of God, whereby ye are sealed** unto the day of redemption.*

To summarize: believers in the Age of the Church are forever forgiven, permanently indwelt by the Holy Spirit, baptized into the Body of Christ and sealed there until the day of the redemption of their mortal bodies! Because of these facts, many practical day-to-day practices are different for saints living in this age than they were for those living in other ages. For example, the indwelling and sealing of the Holy Spirit affects:

- How we deal with our sins and their practical consequences of them
- How and why we forgive the sins of others
- How and what we pray for
- How, when and where we worship and serve God

All of these things make the gospel we preach today *(I Corinthians 15:1-6)* different from all other gospels. (Look at *Luke 18:31-34*. Here, we read that the disciples who had been out preaching the Gospel of the Kingdom did not even understand the gospel as we know it and preach it.) Remarkably, this amazing gospel of the Church Age was not fully known by any man until God revealed it to the Apostle Paul and had him preach and write about it!

*Galatians 1:11 But I certify you, brethren, that **the gospel which was preached of me is not after man.** 12 For I neither received it of man, neither was I taught it, but by the revelation of Jesus Christ.*

*Ephesians 3:1 For this cause I Paul, the prisoner of Jesus Christ for you Gentiles, 2 If ye have heard of the dispensation of the grace of God which is given me to you-ward: 3 How that **by revelation he made known unto me the mystery**; (as I wrote afore in few words, 4 Whereby, when ye read, ye may understand my knowledge in the mystery of Christ) 5 Which in other ages was not made known unto the sons of men, as it is now revealed unto his holy apostles and prophets by the Spirit;*

God offers the Church Age saint the most glorious of all opportunities—that of presenting His truth to the world. Of course, even with such a good deal as the Age of the Church provides, man still fails. The world's population continues to grow, with sadly disproportionate growth in the size of the Church. With all our technological advancements and innovations to spread the gospel, there are millions of people who still have never even heard the Gospel of the Grace of God. Paul says he speaks this to our shame *(I Corinthians 15:34)*.

As "ambassadors for Christ" *(II Corinthians 5:20)*, we are not representing His interests "unto the ends of the earth" *(Acts 13:47)* as He told us to do. The "remnant" of believers continually shrinks in proportion to the vast population on the broad way "that leadeth to destruction" *(Matthew 7:13)*.

At some point in time, known only to God, the Age of the Church will abruptly end with the Rapture as described in **I Thessalonians 4** and **II Thessalonians 2**. It seems as though God will at last tire of our feeble and weakening attempts to spread the Gospel of God's Grace, and will literally yank us (the Church) up out of the way. Christians, indwelt and sealed with the Holy Spirit, will leave this world and *the Age of Readiness will resume*. (See second half of **Chart 16.2** emphasis.)

Soon after the Rapture of the Church, the earth and its inhabitants will go through the seven-year Tribulation. During this time, instead of using the Church to preach His word, God will use angels in the seven churches *(Revelation 2:1, 2:8, 2:12, 2:18, 3:1, 3:7, 3:14)* and in the midst of heaven *(Revelation 14:6)*. He will also use 144,000 male virgin Jews *(Revelation 7:4 and 14:3-4)* and the two Witnesses *(Revelation 11:3)* to preach the *everlasting gospel* "unto them that dwell on the earth" *(Revelation 14:6)*.

The Lord Jesus Christ will then return to earth to end the Tribulation and the Age of Readiness. He will cast the Beast and the false prophet into the lake of fire *(Revelation 19:20)*. Likewise, He will slay those who fought against Him *(Revelation 19:21)*. He will judge the survivors on the basis of whether they aligned themselves with the Jews during the Tribulation *(Matthew 25:31-46)*. The Lord will then cast Satan into the bottomless pit *(Revelation 20:1-3)*. Finally, He will establish His kingdom as promised *(Revelation 20:4)*, thus ending the Age of Readiness. There will then be no more getting ready for the Kingdom—it will have come!

VIII. Age of the Kingdom (Revelation 20)

God reveals very little about the Age of the Kingdom *in the book of Revelation*. During this time period, the Lord Jesus Christ rules and reigns on the earth with "a rod of iron" for a thousand years. He calls all the shots and man obeys!

At this time, Satan will be in the pit and out of the picture, unable to deceive man for the first time since the Garden of Eden. During this thousand year period, the inhabitants who survived the Tribulation and the judgment will presumably be having children and replenishing the earth. Then Satan will be loosed. He will go about to deceive the inhabitants of the earth after God releases him from his prison for "a little season." For one last time, after living for a thousand years under the direct and perfect rule of the Lord Jesus Christ, man will fail again! Only those who remain loyal to King Jesus will survive God's judgment.

Unfortunately, multitudes—"the number of whom is as the sand of the sea" *(Revelation 20:8)*—will succumb to Satan's deception and rebel against God. God will devour these all with fire, cast the devil into the lake of fire forever and so end the Age of the Kingdom with the Great White Throne judgment.

Age of Kingdom

[8]

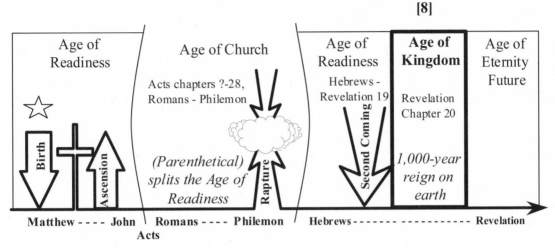

Chart 16.4 - Age of Kingdom

IX. Age of Eternity Future (Revelation 21:1 - 22:5)

Following the Millennial reign of the Lord Jesus Christ, God creates a new heaven and a new earth with a New Jerusalem, the holy city. Finally, man is pure, free from sin and able to worship and serve God perfectly.

> ***Revelation 21:22*** *And I saw no temple therein: for the Lord God Almighty and the Lamb are the temple of it. 23 And* **the city** *had no need of the sun, neither of the moon, to shine in it: for the glory of God did lighten it, and the Lamb is the light thereof. 24 And the nations of them which are saved shall walk in the light of it: and the kings of the earth do bring their glory and honour into it. 25 And the gates of it shall not be shut at all by day: for there shall be no night there. 26 And they shall bring the glory and honour of the nations into it. 27* **And there shall in no wise enter into it any thing that defileth***, neither whatsoever worketh abomination, or maketh a lie: but they which are written in the Lamb's book of life.*

> ***Revelation 22:3*** *And there shall be* **no more curse***: but the throne of God and of the Lamb shall be in it; and his servants shall serve him: 4 And they shall see his face; and his name shall be in their foreheads. 5 And there shall be no night there; and they need no candle, neither light of the sun; for the Lord God giveth them light: and they shall reign for ever and ever.*

In the Age of Eternity Future there will be no more sin, wickedness or influence of Satan. The curse placed upon man and the earth will be lifted. Man will dwell with God and God will dwell with man. God will have servants that are not mere robots, but instead were created with a freewill to choose whether to accept or reject their Saviour God.

Eternity

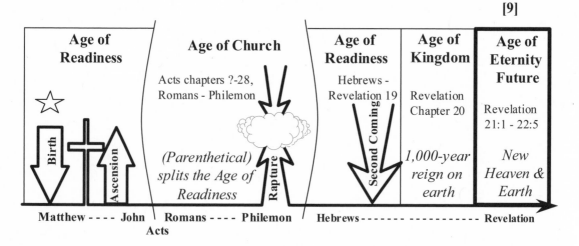

Chart 16.5 - Eternity

The two previous chapters present the Bible from cover to cover. God, in His infinite plan, has designed His dealings with man to show man his sinfulness and his complete inability to function without God being in control. The more God controls things and the less man is involved, the better off mankind finds himself. Ultimately, God's rule in eternity will involve Himself alone. "Even so, come, Lord Jesus." *(Revelation 22:20)*

"As a messenger of the covenant Christ comes only to the lost sheep of the house of Israel, characteristically refuses to listen to the Gentile woman when she appeals to Him on Jewish ground, and bids His disciples not to go into the way of, nor to preach the good news of the Messiah to any of the Gentiles."

I.M. Haldeman, *How to Study the Bible - The Second Coming and Other Expositions* (NY: Charles C. Cook, 1904), p. 12.

"I say in small and arbitrary matters, God had dispensations in His dealings with men. The Holy Spirit once was with Christians and now dwells in Christians (John 14:17). The change came when Jesus was glorified at His resurrection (John 7:37-39; John 20:22). I say there are such dispensational changes in some matters; but in the great fundamentals that are a part of the very nature of God there are no dispensations. God Himself cannot change. He never did; He never will."

John R. Rice, *Prayer – Asking and Receiving* (Murfreesboro: Sword of the Lord Publishers, 1942, 1970) p. 21.

17
Questions and Answers

The study of the Bible "rightly divided" can answer many of the questions that arise from study. However, the same study can and will raise many questions. The focus of this chapter is to answer some questions posed by both students and critics.

1. Kingdom

Q1—The Church Age emphasizes grace, rather than the Kingdom. Didn't Paul preach the Kingdom too?

A1—There are four references in the book of Acts stating that Paul preached the "Kingdom of God." For example, consider the following:

> **Acts 20:25** *And now, behold, I know that ye all, among whom I have gone **preaching the kingdom of God,** shall see my face no more.*

Some may claim that such preaching was done only during Paul's Acts missionary journeys. However, this simply is not the case. The final chapter of Acts finds Paul in bonds as he continues to preach the Kingdom of God.

> **Acts 28:30** *And Paul dwelt two whole years in his own hired house, and received all that came in unto him,* 31 **Preaching the kingdom of God,** *and teaching those things which concern the Lord Jesus Christ, with all confidence, no man forbidding him.*

2. Kingdom of God

Q2—Since Paul preached the "kingdom of God," does this contradict his preaching concerning the grace of God?

A2—Allowing the scripture to define the meaning of the "kingdom of God" provides the best answer. The best definition of the Kingdom of God is found in the next two verses.

> **Romans 14:17** *For **the kingdom of God** is not meat and drink; but **righteousness,** and **peace,** and **joy** in the Holy Ghost.*

> **I Corinthians 4:20** *For the **kingdom of God** is not in word, but in **power.***

The scriptures tell us that the **Kingdom of God** is *not* meat and drink (physical properties). It is righteousness, peace, joy, and power (spiritual properties). The spiritual properties are the distinguishing features of the Kingdom of God.

Paul preached the Kingdom of God, but did not preach the Kingdom of heaven. Recognizing the distinguishing features between these two concepts is very important. The Kingdom of God differs greatly from the *Kingdom of heaven*. However, both kingdoms were *at hand* during the Lord's earthly ministry.

The **Kingdom of heaven** is a literal, physical, visible kingdom. This kingdom will be in existence on the earth when the Lord sets up His millennial kingdom. The Kingdom of heaven will be a literal, physical, visible kingdom. In this kingdom, the will of God will be done on earth all the time.

> **Matthew 6:10** *Thy **kingdom** come. Thy will be done in earth, as it is in **heaven.***

This kingdom will exist as foretold in Daniel:

> **Daniel 2:44** *And in the days of these kings **shall the God of heaven set up a kingdom,** which shall never be destroyed: and **the kingdom shall not be left to other people,** but it shall break in pieces and consume all these kingdoms, and it shall stand for ever.*

However, the **Kingdom of God** is a spiritual, righteous, and moral kingdom. The new birth places the believer into this kingdom by grace upon salvation during the Church Age. The Kingdom of God is the only kingdom in existence on earth today. The **Kingdom of heaven** indicates a time when the "heavens" will rule over the earth in the future. Both kingdoms will be in existence here on earth during the Millennium when the Lord sets up a *literal*, *physical*, *visible* kingdom that is also a *spiritual*, *righteous,* and *moral* kingdom.

Although the Apostle Paul did preach the Kingdom of God, he did not preach the same message concerning the Kingdom as did the apostles in the four Gospels. These apostles preached about a future time when the Lord would set up a physical, literal, earthly kingdom. Thus the disciples asked the Lord about the restoration of His Kingdom just prior to His ascension.

> **Acts 1:6** *When they therefore were come together, they asked of him, saying, Lord, wilt thou at this time **restore again the kingdom** to Israel?*

The disciples were asking the Lord Jesus Christ about a literal, physical, visible setting up of God's kingdom on earth (*the Kingdom of Heaven*). Paul's preaching on the subject of the *Kingdom of God* has nothing to do with the establishing of such an earthly kingdom. The references to Paul's preaching the Kingdom of God do not contradict the grace of God since they do not refer to an earthly, visible kingdom. The Church will not bring in the Kingdom, but will be raptured out of the world instead.

3. Church Patterned After Acts

Q3—Many churches claim to pattern their operations around the historical record found in the book of Acts. What scripture can be cited to demonstrate whether this practice is good or bad?

A3—Churches should pattern themselves by following a book of doctrine, rather than a book that is predominantly historical in nature. The danger of patterning a church entirely after the book of Acts has already been demonstrated. However, studying one additional area may help to convince the skeptic. The book of Acts gives four different accounts of how a person received the Holy Ghost. These differing accounts should emphasize why Acts is not a "how to" book on organizing a local New Testament church. First, consider the preaching of Philip:

> **Acts 8:12** *But when **they believed** Philip preaching the things concerning the kingdom of God, and the name of Jesus Christ, **they were baptized**, both men and*

*women. 13 Then Simon himself believed also: and when he was baptized, he continued with Philip, and wondered, beholding the miracles and signs which were done. 14 Now when the apostles which were at Jerusalem heard that Samaria had received the word of God, they sent unto them **Peter and John**: 15 Who, when they were come down, **prayed for them,** that they might receive the Holy Ghost: 16 (For as yet he was fallen upon none of them: only they were baptized in the name of the Lord Jesus.) 17 **Then laid they their hands on them,** and **they received the Holy Ghost.***

The sequence of events in Acts chapter 8 is as follows:

- They believed *(verse 12)*
- They were baptized *(verse 12)*
- Peter and John prayed for them to receive the Holy Ghost *(verse 15)*
- Peter and John laid hands on them *(verse 17)*
- They received the Holy Ghost *(verse 17)*

The student should take note that they believed and were baptized *(verse 12)*, but did not receive the Holy Ghost *(verse 16)* until after Peter and John arrived from Jerusalem. The apostles in Jerusalem heard that those in Samaria had "received the word of God" and yet had not received the Holy Ghost. For this reason, many charismatic churches teach that one must pray to receive the Holy Ghost; however, this practice is clearly contrary to the pattern for the Church during this age. If Acts chapter 8 gives the pattern for the New Testament Church today, when were these people saved? Since they were baptized before they received the Holy Ghost, were they lost when they were baptized *(Romans 8:9)*?

The sequence of events in Acts chapter 8 should create a problem for any local New Testament church trying to pattern itself after the book of Acts. The next chapter records Saul's experience:

*Acts 9:17 And **Ananias** went his way, and entered into the house; and **putting his hands on him** said, Brother Saul, the Lord, even Jesus, that appeared unto thee in the way as thou camest, hath sent me, that thou mightest receive thy sight, and be **filled with the Holy Ghost.** 18 And immediately there fell from his eyes as it had been scales: and he **received sight** forthwith, and arose, **and was baptized.***

After Saul meets the Lord Jesus Christ on the road to Damascus, the Bible records the following series of events concerning his receiving the Holy Ghost and his baptism:

- Ananias laid hands on Saul *(verses 17, 12)*
- Saul was filled with the Holy Ghost *(verse 17)*
- Saul was healed of blindness *(verses 17, 18)*
- Ananias baptized Saul *(verse 18)*

If the local church is to pattern itself after the book of Acts, which of these two sequences should it follow? One might point out that Saul (later, Paul) was saved earlier in the chapter. However, he did not receive the Holy Ghost until much later. Is this the pattern for the salvation of a soul today? Some make this claim, but Paul clearly reveals otherwise in his Church Age epistles!

To further complicate matters, read and consider Acts chapter 22. Here, Paul retells his conversion experience. Paul quotes Ananias as follows:

*Acts 22:16 And now why tarriest thou? arise, **and be baptized, and wash away thy sins**, calling on the name of the Lord.*

Does this verse confuse you about the purpose of baptism? The book of Acts is a transitional book. One chapter after Paul's conversion, we read still another sequence of events. God's Church Age pattern does not stabilize until after the transition is complete.

*Acts 10:44 While Peter yet spake these words, the **Holy Ghost fell on all them which heard the word.** 45 And they of the circumcision which believed were astonished, as many as came with Peter, because that on the Gentiles also was poured out the gift of the Holy Ghost. 46 For **they heard them speak with tongues**, and magnify God. Then answered Peter, 47 Can any man forbid water, that these should not be baptized, which have received the Holy Ghost as well as we? 48 And **he commanded them to be baptized in the name of the Lord.** Then prayed they him to tarry certain days.*

- They heard *(verse 44)*
- The Holy Ghost fell on them *(verse 44)*
- They spoke with tongues *(verse 46)*
- They were baptized *(verse 48)*

Unlike the sequences provided in the first two examples, no one laid hands on these people in order for them to receive the Holy Ghost. In fact, while Peter was **still speaking** the Holy Ghost fell on them. Presumably, the Holy Ghost interrupted Peter's preaching before he could tell the people to repent and be baptized *(Acts 2:38)*. These examples should convince the Bible student that all of the patterns contained in Acts could not possibly be intended for the New Testament Church. One more example from the same book should help drive home this truth.

*Acts 19:3 And he said unto them, Unto what then were ye **baptized**? And they said, **Unto John's baptism.** 4 Then said Paul, John verily baptized with the baptism of repentance, saying unto the people, that they should believe on him which should come after him, that is, on Christ Jesus. 5 When they heard this, they were **baptized in the name of the Lord Jesus.** 6 And when Paul had **laid his hands upon them**, the **Holy Ghost came on them;** and they **spake with tongues, and prophesied**.*

- They were baptized (John's baptism) *(verse 3)*
- **They were baptized again (in Jesus' name) *(verse 5)***
- Paul laid hands on them *(verse 6)*
- They received the Holy Ghost *(verse 6)*
- They spoke with tongues *(verse 6)*
- They prophesied *(verse 6)*

This time, the individuals spoken of are baptized twice! After the dual baptisms, Paul laid hands on them and they received the Holy Ghost. At this point, they not only spoke in tongues but also prophesied. Any church claiming to pattern itself after the book of Acts should question the method by which it is to choose one pattern over the other. *These are only a few of the examples provided in the book of Acts. Which one of these or other patterns is the church to claim as its own? What justification does the church have for accepting one pattern and rejecting the others? One who rightly divides the Bible will not have a problem understanding what to do. Such a person will understand that the book of Acts is predominantly a history book which, as its title clearly indicates, contains the acts (actions) of the apostles.*

4. Other Unusual Patterns

Q4—Are there any other unusual patterns (besides those presented in Q3) included in the book of Acts?

A4—Yes. Acts chapter 8 records the conversion of the Ethiopian eunuch. This conversion most closely resembles the pattern that will span the majority of the Church Age. The man is first convicted of his need; then we read:

> ***Acts 8:35*** *Then Philip opened his mouth, and began at the same scripture, and **preached unto him Jesus.** 36 And as they went on their way, they came unto a certain water: and the eunuch said, See, here is water; what doth hinder me to be baptized? 37 And Philip said, If thou believest with all thine heart, thou mayest. And he answered and said, I **believe** that **Jesus Christ is the Son of God**. 38 And he commanded the chariot to stand still: and they went down both into the water, both Philip and the eunuch; and he **baptized** him.*

- The eunuch heard the preaching of God's word *(verse 35)*
- The eunuch believed with his heart *(verse 37)*
- The eunuch confessed with his mouth *(verse 37)*
- Philip baptized the eunuch *(verse 38)*

Notice that the emphasis of this account is *not* on the Holy Ghost, tongues or prophesying. It contains the least dramatic account of any of the examples given. One can only imagine why the devil would want a person to miss this account in the midst of all of the other patterns presented in the book of Acts.

5. Missing Verse

Q5—The version of the Bible I am using does not contain Acts chapter 8, verse 37. Why not?

A5—Modern critics of God's word claim that this verse is not found in the "oldest and best manuscripts." These individuals will usually footnote the verse. You be the judge concerning whether it should, in fact, be included in the chapter. Should the man get saved before he is baptized? Of course he should! Don't allow the devil to rip even one verse of the word of God out of your hands. Many other verses are also missing in the modern versions. (See *One Book Stands Alone* by the author for an extensive study on the changes made in the modern versions.)

6. Baptisms

Q6—Why do there seem to be so many "contradictions" in the Bible about how and when to be baptized?

A6—This question can best be answered by considering the application of two more baptism passages—Mark chapter 16 and Acts chapter 2. The Lord tells the apostles in *Mark 16* to preach the gospel (of the Kingdom). Many groups who teach baptismal regeneration misapply this passage by saying that an individual must believe *and* be baptized in order to be saved. Another of their favorites is Peter speaking to the nation of Israel in *Acts 2:38* telling them to repent and be baptized "in the name of Jesus" for the remission of sins. *Then* they would receive the gift of the Holy Ghost. Both of these baptisms are directly associated with the nation of Israel, and not with the Church. The Bible records at least seven types of baptisms.

7. Pattern for Receiving the Holy Spirit Today

Q7—What is our pattern for receiving the Holy Spirit today?

A7—The book of Ephesians clearly and distinctly gives the Church its pattern for receiving the Holy Spirit.

> **Ephesians 1:13** *In whom ye also **trusted**, after that ye **heard** the word of truth, the gospel of your salvation: in whom also after that ye **believed**, ye were **sealed with that holy Spirit of promise**,*

- We are to hear (the word of truth—the gospel)
- We are to trust in that gospel
- We are to believe in that gospel
- We are sealed with the Holy Spirit

This is the Church Age pattern for the believer today. The first four examples from the book of Acts do *not* depict the pattern for the Church today. According to our spokesman, the Apostle Paul, a person is *not* saved unless the Spirit of God dwells in him.

> **Romans 8:9** *But ye are not in the flesh, but in the Spirit, if so be that the Spirit of God dwell in you. **Now if any man have not the Spirit of Christ, he is none of his**.*

Furthermore, the Bible states that the Holy Spirit within each believer reveals to him that he is saved. In other words, many people make a profession without any possession. Many churches are guilty of getting someone to make a decision "to accept Christ" without any conviction or repentance on the part of the individual. This effort of "get a decision at all costs" has filled the pews, without truly converting the sinner. Doubts arise because there is no Holy Spirit witness.

> **Romans 8:16** *The Spirit itself beareth witness with our spirit, that we are the children of God:*

Once saved, the Holy Spirit dwelling in the believer confirms to him that he is a child of God. However, many churches today claim that someone must lay hands on *a saved person* in order for him to receive the Holy Spirit and the gifts of the Spirit. Supposed justification for this teaching comes from taking the account of Acts chapter 19 and misapplying it to the Church *(Acts 19:6)*. The pattern for the Church cannot be found in *Acts 19:6* anymore than it can be in *Leviticus 19:6*.

8. Paul's Baptism of a Convert

Q8—Since the church today is to follow the example of Paul, where in scripture is there an account of his baptizing a convert?

A8—The Bible records at least two such examples, although neither case provides much detail. Clearly, these passages indicate that the individuals believed on the Lord Jesus Christ, confessed Him with their mouths and were saved prior to baptism. Since baptism so closely followed conversion in these instances, we can assume that Paul evidently dealt with believers about the matter of baptism immediately following their conversion. Baptism was unquestionably a matter of service, rather than a matter of salvation, in each case.

> *Acts 18:8 And Crispus, the chief ruler of the synagogue, **believed on the Lord** with all his house; and many of the Corinthians hearing believed, **and were baptized.***

This passage places its emphasis upon the belief of Crispus and the others. Thus, the issue of baptism is here addressed. The instance of the Philippian jailer is another clear example of Paul's baptism of converts. Paul and Silas instructed the jailer to believe and be saved.

> *Acts 16:30 And brought them out, and said, Sirs, what must I do to be saved? 31 And they said, Believe on the Lord Jesus Christ, and thou shalt be saved, **and thy house**. 32 And they spake unto him the word of the Lord, and **to all that were in his house**. 33 And he took them the same hour of the night, and washed their stripes; and was **baptized, he and all his, straightway.***

The Bible records the baptism of the jailer along with all those in his house. These baptisms took place only after each person in the household had believed on the Lord. Some use the fact that the jailer's household was baptized as justification for infant baptism. However, the next verse ends by telling us that all those that were baptized were: *"believing in God with all his house" (Acts 16:34)*.

9. Was Paul against Baptism?

Q9—Some teach that Paul was opposed to baptism because of his comments to the Corinthian church in *I Corinthians 1:17*. *"For Christ sent me not to baptize, but to preach the gospel: not with wisdom of words, lest the cross of Christ should be made of none effect."* Why did Paul make this statement?

A9—The context of Paul's statement clearly shows that he was not against baptism. Members of this carnal (Corinthian) church were using baptism as a means of self-glorification by bragging about which man baptized them. Paul rebuked the church. He gives the reason for his comments concerning baptism in verses 14 and 15.

> *I Corinthians 1:14 I thank God that I baptized none of you, but Crispus and Gaius; 15 **Lest any should say that I had baptized in mine own name.** 16 And I baptized also the household of Stephanas: besides, I know not whether I baptized any other. 17 **For Christ sent me not to baptize,** but to preach the gospel: not with wisdom of words, lest the cross of Christ should be made of none effect.*

Paul felt guilty by association. Because of the carnality of these individuals, Paul was relieved that his association with their error concerning baptism was minimal. These Corinthians used baptism as a status symbol and allowed it to become a very divisive issue. Paul wanted no part in such things. The same standard can be applied to any matter that is dealt with in a carnal fashion. A person can have the wrong heart when it comes to giving to the church. Taking part in a competition to see who can give the most is about as spiritual as pridefully publicizing who baptized you.

10. Sent Not to Baptize?

Q10—But why would Paul write that *Christ sent me not to baptize?*

A10—Our commission is to preach the word *(II Timothy 4:2).* Unlike the disciples' commission in Mark chapter 16, our commission today does *not* include baptism. However, this fact must not be construed to mean that baptism is not a very important step in a new convert's life. Yet, souls are going to hell in multitudes because the Church remains unfocused, and the gospel is not being preached. The part of verse 17 that should be emphasized is the second phrase: *17 For Christ sent me not to baptize, but to preach the gospel . . .*

Our focus should be on this one thing . . . disseminating the gospel. A church focused on spreading the gospel does *not* have to completely eliminate any involvement in other areas. However, this additional involvement must *never* be undertaken at the expense of neglecting the primary purpose of the Church—to communicate the gospel to lost souls. Consider a practical application of this principle: *Christ sent me not to have **a building program,** but to preach the gospel.* Can a church build buildings and have a building program? Yes! However, building structures should not be accomplished to the *neglect* of spreading the gospel around the world (and in the immediate community).

11. Follow Peter?

Q11—Why does it seem that the world recognizes Peter as the primary apostle?

A11—Satan wants Paul's ministry to the Church de-emphasized. The best way to do that is to emphasize Peter's positional prominence in the Bible. However, the majority of Peter's ministry revealed by scripture reflects his preaching of the Gospel of the Kingdom to the Jews. The Church should not place an undue emphasis on the content of Peter's messages prior to the cross or shortly thereafter.

12. Baptism for the Attainment of Heaven

Q12—Why is there so much confusion concerning the biblical reason for baptism?

A12—Baptism has been one of the most divisive issues among churches and denominations throughout history. Many groups teach that a person must be baptized in order to get to heaven. The confusion concerning the issue of baptism generally arises from following the wrong spokesman and, in effect, reading someone else's mail. Many groups also baptize infants but have no scriptural basis for such a practice.

13. Basis for Teaching Baptism for Salvation

Q13—What scriptures do some churches and groups use to justify this teaching concerning baptism?

A13—As mentioned earlier, these groups use verses such as *Acts 2:38, Acts 22:16, Mark 16:15-20, I Peter 3:21,* and many others to justify their position. Each of these verses can be understood in its proper context if the reader obeys *II Timothy 2:15* and understands the full implications of *II Timothy 2:7*, along with the fact that baptismal regeneration is heresy.

14. John's Baptism

Q14—What is *"John's baptism"* in *Acts 19:3?*

A14—John's baptism is not the same as the baptism of the New Testament convert. The local New Testament church baptizes a new believer following salvation. However, John was the *forerunner* of Christ and baptized those that came to him prior to the cross. In Acts chapter 19, Paul restates John's message that accompanied his baptism saying *"...that they should believe on him which should come after him, that is, on Christ Jesus" (Acts 19:4).*

When John's disciples heard THIS—that they were to believe on the Lord Jesus Christ—presumably they acted upon this new information, believed and were re-baptized following their salvation. The next verse continues the account: *"When they heard **this**, they were baptized in the name of the Lord Jesus" (Acts 19:5).* You might picture a gap of missing information following "this" indicating that they were not simply hearers of the word, but doers also. They heard "this," trusted in the Saviour and then followed Him in believer's baptism.

15. Tongues Defined

Q15—What is tongues?

A15—The gift of tongues is generally a language, as seen in the following verses:

> ***Acts 2:6*** *Now when this was noised abroad, the multitude came together, and were confounded, because that every man **heard** them **speak in his own language.***

> ***Acts 2:8*** *And how **hear** we every man **in our own tongue,** wherein we were born?*

> ***Acts 2:11*** *Cretes and Arabians, we do **hear** them speak **in our tongues** the wonderful works of God.*

The word of God emphasizes that the tongues spoken of in Acts chapter 2 were recognized languages. Every person heard the apostles speak in his own language. Thus, God supernaturally gave each person an understanding of the words being spoken, in his own language. The miracle was the fact that the others could hear these apostles speak in their own language.

> ***Acts 10:46 For they heard*** *them speak with tongues, and magnify God. Then answered Peter,*

How did the people recognize the tongues as a gift from God? The hearers could recognize and *understand* what was being said. They knew that the words being spoken glorified God.

16. Unknown Tongues

Q16—Do *unknown* tongues, like those referred to in First Corinthians chapter 14, really exist?

A16—Yes, Corinthians refers to a language as an unknown tongue when it is a tongue unknown to the speaker, and perhaps the hearer. Paul says that a person that speaks in an unknown tongue:

- Speaks to God *(I Corinthians 14:2)*
- Does not speak to man *(I Corinthians 14:2)*
- Is understood by no man *(I Corinthians 14:2)*
- Edifies himself and not the church *(I Corinthians 14:4)*

Consider the following guidelines given by the Apostle Paul concerning unknown tongues:

- Paul said he would rather speak five words with understanding than 10,000 in an unknown tongue *(I Corinthians 14:19).*
- If a person were going to speak in an unknown tongue:

  It was to be only two or three that spoke *(I Corinthians 14:27).*

  It was to be by course—one at a time *(I Corinthians 14:27).*

  There was to be an interpreter *(I Corinthians 14:27).* [This is not a translator!]

  The women were *not* to speak in tongues in the church *(I Corinthians 14:33).*

In this instance, the term *unknown* is used to communicate that a language is not known by those who speak it *(I Corinthians 14:14)* or hear it *(I Corinthians 14:2),* except by means of supernatural interpretation *(I Corinthians 14:13)*. The fact that certain tongues were unknown cannot be incorrectly construed to mean that these languages did not exist. The hearers were merely unaware of the meaning of these languages and an interpreter was necessary.

We can more easily understand the use of the word *unknown* in this passage by considering another occurrence of the same word. The Athenians had an altar with the following inscription:

*Acts 17:23 For as I passed by, and beheld your devotions, I found an altar with this inscription, **TO THE UNKNOWN GOD.** Whom therefore ye ignorantly worship, him declare I unto you.*

The altar was built to recognize a god that was unknown to the Athenians. Paul knew Who that God was and made the Athenians aware of Him. This same concept should be applied to the issue of the unknown tongues. An interpreter was necessary because the hearers were ignorant of a particular language. The fact that the hearers failed to understand a language does not necessarily mean that the language did not exist. The interpreter interpreted the meaning.

17. Acts Named

Q17—Why was the book of Acts given its name?

A17—The book was so-named because of its content. The book contains the actions of the apostles. It is a historical book depicting *the acts of the apostles* from the ascension of the Lord Jesus Christ to Paul's imprisonment. The book of Acts details the ministry of the Apostle Peter until a time soon after the conversion of the Apostle Paul. After this point, the primary focus of the book is Paul's missionary journeys. The details concerning these journeys begin in Acts chapter 13 and follow through the end of the book (chapter 28).

18. Transition Book

Q18—What do people mean when they describe Acts as a transition book?

A18—The book of Acts clearly has many transitions. A few of these transitions are as follows:

- From Peter to Paul
- From law to grace
- From Jerusalem to Rome (a Gentile city)
- From Jew to Gentile

The term *transitional* is often applied to the book of Acts since it begins with the first and moves over (transitions) into the second. During this time of transition, **change** is the key word. New patterns replace the old ones.

19. Pentecostal Experience

Q19—Some churches make an invitation by saying that you should come to their church to experience Pentecost. Is Pentecost an experience?

A19—Pentecost is a Jewish feast day similar to Passover . . . *John 6:4 And the **passover, a feast of the Jews,** was nigh.* Pentecost has **absolutely nothing** to do with the Gentiles' hearing the word of God. The book of Acts alone covers over thirty years of *Jewish* Pentecost feast days. God probably used this special day (Pentecost in Acts chapter 2) because He knew that *the Jews* would be gathered together from every nation on this occasion *(Acts 2:5).* The feast of Pentecost was a prime opportunity for God to use the sign of tongues to reach many of the Jews with the truth. This truth was *confirmed by the signs (**Mark 16:20**).*

Acts chapter 2 records the one and only day of Pentecost anywhere in the Bible in which any supernatural experience occurred. Pentecost is simply one of the seven feast days listed in **Leviticus chapter 23**. These feast days include the following:

- Feast of the Passover *(verse 5)*
- Feast of Unleavened Bread *(verse 6)*
- Feast of the First Fruits *(verse 11)*
- Feast of Pentecost *(verse 16)*
- Feast of Trumpets *(verse 24)*
- Day of Atonement *(verse 27)*
- Feast of Tabernacles *(verse 34)*

In Acts chapter 2, God emphasizes those individuals present at this Jewish feast day of Pentecost in at least four different places. Here, the Apostle Peter speaks to these Jews and tells them that they must repent, both individually and collectively as a nation.

> *Acts 2:5 And there were **dwelling at Jerusalem Jews,** devout men, out of every nation under heaven.*

> *Acts 2:14 But Peter, standing up with the eleven, lifted up his voice, and said unto them, **Ye men of Judaea,** and all **ye that dwell at Jerusalem,** be this known unto you, and hearken to my words:*

> *Acts 2:22 **Ye men of Israel,** hear these words; Jesus of Nazareth, a man approved of God among you by miracles and wonders and signs, which God did by him in the midst of you, as ye yourselves also know:*

> *Acts 2:36 Therefore let **all the house of Israel** know assuredly, that God hath made that same Jesus, whom ye have crucified, both Lord and Christ.*

These passages clearly indicate that Peter was predominantly speaking to Jews. For Gentiles to go into the book of Acts and attempt to repeat the events of this one particular day is as logical as attempting to repeat some of the occurrences recorded in the book of Exodus. Two examples should cause the reader to ponder. Simply because the instance of Moses and the burning bush is recorded in the Bible, can we somehow repeat that experience today *(Exodus 3:2)?* What about Moses' turning the water into blood *(Exodus 7:19)?* It makes no more sense to attempt to repeat the events of Acts chapter 2 than it does to attempt to repeat the occurrences recorded in Exodus chapters 3 or 7.

20. Literal Fire in Acts Chapter 2

Q20—My question concerns the fire that came down from heaven in Acts chapter two on the day of Pentecost. Some say that it was *not* a literal fire. Was it?

A20—The fire that came down was *not* a literal fire. The Bible says it was **like** as of fire. *"And there appeared unto them cloven tongues **like as of fire,** and it sat upon each of them (**Acts 2:3).** Something that is "like" fire is *not* literal fire. Satan wants to condition people to be looking for fire from heaven. He will cause fire to come down from heaven to deceive the nations during the Tribulation.

> *Revelation 13:13* And he doeth great wonders, so **that he maketh fire come down from heaven on the earth in the sight of men, 14 And deceiveth them that dwell on the earth by the means of those miracles** which he had power to do in the sight of the beast; saying to them that dwell on the earth, that they should make an image to the beast, which had the wound by a sword, and did live.

21. Baptize with the Holy Ghost and Fire

Q21—I thought the Lord said He was going to baptize with the Holy Ghost *and fire.* Where in the Bible is this found and what does it mean?

A21—Matthew chapter 3 contains the particular scripture in question. John the Baptist told those around him that he was baptizing with water, but that the Lord Jesus Christ would not be baptizing with water. Instead, the Lord would baptize some with the Holy Ghost and baptize *others* with fire.

> *Matthew 3:11 I indeed baptize you with water unto repentance: but he that cometh after me is mightier than I, whose shoes I am not worthy to bear: he shall baptize you with the Holy Ghost, **and with fire:***

Many people miss the point of this scripture. The Lord differentiates between the saved and the lost by using the two baptisms to illustrate His point. The saved would be baptized with the *Holy Ghost.* The lost would be baptized *with fire.* The next verse (verse 12) explains the nature of the fire to which the second baptism refers:

> *Matthew 3:12 Whose fan is in his hand, and he will throughly purge his floor, and gather his wheat into the garner; but he will burn up the chaff **with unquenchable fire.***

Verse 12 defines the fire mentioned in verse 11. Anytime the Bible mentions an **unquenchable** fire, it refers to "hell fire." Therefore, the *baptism with fire* is a submerging of the lost person into the flames of hell, *never to be quenched.* Churches misapplying this verse usually connect the fire spoken of here in Matthew to the *tongues like as of fire* spoken of in Acts chapter 2. The nature of the "fire" referred to in Acts chapter 2 has already been addressed; it is not a literal fire. Because of the confusion surrounding this "fire," Satan will have no difficulty deceiving the world with his literal fire from heaven during the Tribulation.

22. Lord's Supper

Q22—Where can you find the pattern for the Lord's Supper?

A22—Churches follow the pattern of the Lord's Supper given in First Corinthians chapter 11.

23. Frequency of the Lord's Supper

Q23—How often are we to partake of the Lord's Supper?

A23—The Bible does not give a definite answer to this question. Of course, ritualism must be avoided. Our spokesman gives the guidelines concerning the frequency of the Lord's Supper. He says **"for as oft as,"** meaning that the local church should administer the Lord's Supper *as often as* they feel God leads them to do so. Therefore, churches have no scriptural basis for claiming that the Lord's Supper *must* be administered weekly, monthly or on any set schedule.

However, the administration of the Lord's Supper serves as a good time for members of the local church to reflect on their relationships with the Lord and with their fellow brethren. This ordinance of the church should *not* be taken lightly. Yet, the ordinance should not be administered in a ritualistic fashion that lessens its effectiveness to be used to convict backslidden church members.

24. Required Every Sunday?

Q24—Are the churches which require administration of the Lord's Supper every Sunday correct?

A24—Absolutely not, if they are attempting to use scripture to justify their position.

25. Why Every Sunday?

Q25—What basis do these churches use to justify partaking of Lord's Supper every Sunday?

A25—These churches misapply verses from the book of Acts by taking them out of context. Consider the following, for example:

*Acts 20:7 And **upon the first day of the week,** when the disciples came together to **break bread,** Paul preached unto them, ready to depart on the morrow; and continued his speech until midnight.*

These churches teach that one of the purposes for the church to come together "on the first day of the week" is to break bread. They define breaking of bread as the observance of the ordinance of the Lord's Supper. However, the reference to breaking of bread here has absolutely nothing to do with the Lord's Supper. In this case, the disciples simply came together to eat (fellowship) and to bid farewell to Paul.

Paul proceeds to preach. He preaches until midnight. Eutycus falls asleep and falls from the third story loft and is taken up dead. Notice what he does when Paul raises him from the dead. He breaks bread!

*Acts 20:10 And Paul went down, and fell on him, and embracing him said, Trouble not yourselves; for his life is in him. 11 When he therefore was come up again, and had **broken bread, and eaten,** and talked a long while, even till break of day, so he departed. 12 And they brought the young man alive, and were not a little comforted.*

The breaking of bread in verse 7 was no more an observance of the Lord's Supper than were Eutycus' actions in verse 11 following his resurrection from the dead.

26. Apostles Breaking Bread

Q26—Doesn't the Bible refer to the apostles breaking bread?

A26—Yes. See *Acts 2:42 And they continued stedfastly in the apostles' doctrine and fellowship, and in **breaking of bread,** and in prayers.*

In Acts chapter 2, the apostles were breaking bread; however, they were not observing the Lord's Supper as some teach. Four verses later, the reader finds that by taking the incorrect position on verse 42, one could "prove" that a person must participate in the Lord's Supper daily. To apply one verse and ignore the other is scriptural infidelity.

*Acts 2:46 And they, continuing **daily** with one accord in the temple, and **breaking bread** from house to house, did eat their meat with gladness and singleness of heart,*

The reader should take note that the apostles were breaking bread *daily*. Furthermore, the breaking of bread occurred from house to house. There is no mention of any Sunday morning church service. Another consideration is that the name of the ordinance is the Lord's *Supper*. Supper is the evening meal; thus, the Lord's Supper should be administered in the evening service!

27. Other References

Q27—Are there other verses that prove that "breaking bread" is *not* a reference to the Lord's Supper, but simply mention of a meal?

A27—Yes. Consider the following examples:

*Luke 24:35 And they told what things were done in the way, and how he was known of them in **breaking of bread.***

A few verses earlier, we find a very clear record of exactly what occurred.

*Luke 24:29 But they constrained him, saying, Abide with us: for it is toward evening, and the day is far spent. And he went in to tarry with them. 30 And it came to pass, as he sat at meat with them, **he took bread,** and blessed it, **and brake,** and gave to them.*

Read *Acts 27:33-35* for another account of breaking bread apart from any observance of the Lord's Supper. The Lord's Supper is one of the two ordinances of the local church *(I Corinthians 11:1-2).* Churches should administer this ordinance in accordance with the guidelines given in First Corinthians chapter 11. Those that claim that it must be observed every week are unscriptural.

28. Division of the Church Age Epistles

Q28—Some teach that the Church Age continues through *Revelation 4:1.* How should one deal with this matter?

A28—Addressing this issue is simply a matter of approach. If the teacher of the word of God includes Hebrews through Revelation chapter 4 in the Church Age, certain books or passages must be *excluded* as Tribulational. If the split is made between Philemon and Hebrews, then allowances must be made for any Church Age application within the books of Hebrews through Revelation. The general rule to keep in mind is that doctrine within the books of Hebrews through Revelation *can* have Church Age application as long as it does not contradict the doctrine prescribed by the Apostle Paul to the Gentiles.

29. Application within this Book

Q29—Why does this book choose to take the Church Age through Philemon?

A29—The author believes that the greater danger lies in the potential misapplication to the Church Age of the explicit Tribulational passages found in Hebrews and James to the Church Age. Therefore, the division is made after Philemon in order to emphasize that the books following Philemon contain doctrine with application during the Tribulation period. We are commanded to *rightly* divide because of the inherent danger of such misapplication.

30. Paul out of God's Will?

Q30—Was Paul out of the will of God for going to Jerusalem after being warned not to go?

A30—Some claim that Paul was out of the will of God as a result of this action. Your guess is as good as mine.

1. He spent two years in silence because of it *(Acts 24:27)*.

2. Paul purposed to go to Jerusalem *(Acts 19:21)* and then on to Rome. The scriptures point out Paul's desire to go to both places. However, God's timing remains critical.

    Why would God *not* want Paul to go to Jerusalem and then to Rome at this time? Claudius had commanded all Jews to depart from Rome *(Acts 18:1)*. At this time, Paul was still attempting to reach the Jew. God did not want Paul to go to Rome until he had completed reaching the Jewish remnant. The remnant at this time consisted of the Jews that would be saved before the nation was broken off *(Romans 11:20)*.

3. Paul was warned of God, through man, not to go.

    a. The disciples tell Paul (through the Spirit) that he should not go to Jerusalem *(Acts 21:4)*.

    b. The *Prophet* Agabus warns Paul not to go to Jerusalem *(Acts 21:10-13)*. *Thus saith the Holy Ghost . . .both we, and they of that place, besought him not to go up to Jerusalem.*

4. Paul goes to Jerusalem. There, James (the leader in the Jerusalem church) instructs Paul to go through some Jewish rituals and show that he is walking orderly and keeping the law *(Acts 21:18-26)*. This is critical.

    Do we find Paul out of the will of God in Jerusalem? He did not finish his purification (7 days) *(Acts 21:27)* and my guess is that we see that Paul is as human as we are.

31. Paul's Citizenship

Q31—Was Paul a Roman citizen?

A31—Yes, Paul says he was a Jew, a Roman, and a Pharisee.

1. Paul says in *Acts 21:39*   "I am a Jew"

2. Paul says in *Acts 22:27*   "I am a Roman"

3. Paul says in *Acts 23:6*   "I am a Pharisee"

Paul used each of his various positions to attempt to bring about the glory of God *(I Corinthians 9:22)*.

32. Paul Only?

Q32—Are we to consider *only* what Paul says?

A32—No. Any person attempting to follow solely the Apostle Paul will miss many important doctrines and Bible truths. For instance, the virgin birth and hell—among many other critical doctrines—are not mentioned in Paul's epistles. However, Paul does allude to hell without mentioning it by name in *II Thessalonians 1:6-9*.

33. Most Important Scripture

Q33—It seems that *II Timothy 2:15* might be the most important verse in the Bible about studying the scriptures. Why doesn't the version of the Bible I am using include the words "rightly divide" or "study" in this passage?

A33—The *only* version of the Bible that contains **both** commands—to study and to rightly divide—is the King James AV 1611 Bible. This is the *only* verse in the Bible that gives the command to study and the *only* one that reveals *how* to study (by rightly dividing).

34. Modern Versions

Q34—Is this the only problem with the modern versions?

A34—Well, that's another book . . .

For an in-depth study on the modern versions, check out *One Book Stands Alone* by the same author. It contains over 400 pages of comparative analysis of this issue.

The law and the gospel do not go in company. They are by nature as far apart as life and death. The one is the ministry of death, the other the life.

The law is the whip-lash of judgment.

The gospel is the silver bell ringing the anthem of love. The law brings a work to do. The gospel brings a word to believe.

The law is the reflex of one side of God's nature; the reflex of his terrible holiness, his exact justice. It reveals what man is not. He is not holy. He is not righteous. He is not accepted before God. It reveals what man is. He is a sinner, a hopeless sinner, a hopelessly lost sinner.

The gospel is the good news that the law has been honored, the claims met, and God satisfied: the good news that Jesus honored the law in life, met the penalty in death, and at God's right hand, a risen man, is witness of God's eternal satisfaction.

I.M. Haldeman, *How to Study the Bible*, p. 495.

18
What Must I Do?

God commands that we worship Him in Spirit and in truth. However, everyone has his own opinion concerning what constitutes worshipping God in this fashion. The first step, after becoming a Christian, involves joining a local church that preaches and teaches the word of God without changing it. Doing so enhances a person's chances of scripturally worshipping God. Yet, too many people get the "cart before the horse." Spiritually speaking, they try to run before they learn how to walk.

> *John 4:24* *God is a Spirit: and* **they that worship him must worship him in spirit and in truth.**

All of the information in this book, and indeed all the books that have ever been written, will profit you nothing if you are not first a child of God. The *person* of salvation is the Lord Jesus Christ and Him alone.

This book covers the Bible from Genesis through the book of the Revelation and back again. The information provided may seem useful, but will not profit you if you have never been saved *(Romans 10:9-13)*. In this final chapter, let us revisit the Church Age one more time. For a moment, forget all the confusion in the world, and gain the assurance *(I Thessalonians 1:5)* that you have this one issue settled. How does a person insure that heaven will be his home?

Almost anyone, when asked, will tell you that he desires to go to heaven when he dies. Many individuals assume that heaven will be their home as long as they try to be good people and live a good lives. Living a good life is a commendable endeavor, but certainly is not sufficient to earn a place in heaven. God gives four principles in the Bible that a person must understand and act upon in order to go to heaven.

First, you must understand . . . you are a sinner.

> *Romans 3:22* *...for there is no difference: 23 For all have sinned, and come short of the glory of God;*

Think about this: How many banks would you have to rob in order to comprehend that you are a bank robber? Only one, of course. The same principle holds true concerning sin. Committing even one sin should convince you that you are a sinner. For example, if you ever told a lie or simply disobeyed your parents as a child, you broke a biblical command and sinned. Therefore, you are a sinner. Every person is a sinner. You must first understand and accept the fact that you are a sinner *(Romans 5:12)*. The end of verse 22 refers to the fact that it does not matter whether one is a murder, prostitute or a "petty" sinner "for there is no difference...all have sinned."

Second, you must understand . . . the penalty for being a sinner.

> ***Romans 6:23*** *For the **wages of sin** is death; but the gift of God is eternal life through Jesus Christ our Lord.*

Wages are what a person has earned or deserves. Because of your personal sin, you have earned and deserve death. Death indicates a separation. There are two types of death. These are the *physical* death (the separation of the soul from the body) and the *spiritual* death (the separation of the soul from God). The preceding verse refers to eternal life (spiritual life) and, consequently, to an everlasting death—also spiritual *(**Matthew 25:41, II Thessalonians 1:8-9**)*.

When the body dies (physically), the individual experiences the *first* death. Following the judgment of the lost, the individual experiences the *second* death.

> ***Revelation 20:14*** *And death and hell were cast into the lake of fire. This is the **second death**. 15 And whosoever was not found written in the book of life was cast into the lake of fire.*

If *you* pay what you owe as a sinner, you must spend eternity in the lake of fire (hell), separated from God. Do not reject the truth and remain unrepentant.

Third, you must understand . . . what the Lord Jesus Christ has done for you.

> ***Romans 5:8*** *But God commendeth his love toward us, in that, while we were yet sinners, **Christ died for us**.*

The Lord Jesus Christ was not a sinner, yet He suffered death and separation from God the Father on the cross. The Bible says He did this for us!

> ***Matthew 27:46*** *And about the ninth hour **Jesus cried** with a loud voice, saying, Eli, Eli, lama sabachthani? that is to say, **My God, my God, why hast thou forsaken me?***

The Lord was buried and three days later arose from the grave. Why was this necessary? God requires payment for sin. The Lord Jesus Christ paid your debt and mine. He took responsibility for all of our sins while hanging on the cross *(II Corinthians 5:21)*, and God punished Him in our place to satisfy the debt that **we** owe *(Acts 2:27, 31)*. Praise God!

God draws the sinner to Himself. *No man can come to me, except the Father which hath sent me draw him: and I will raise him up at the last day. (**John 6:44**)* He offers the *gift* of eternal life through the *death and blood shed* by the Lord Jesus Christ. However, as with any gift, unless the receiver accepts the gift from the Giver, there is no benefit. This brings us to the fourth principle.

Fourth, you must understand . . . that by faith you need to accept what the Lord Jesus Christ has done for you.

> ***Romans 10:13*** *For whosoever shall call upon the name of the Lord shall be saved. 14 How then shall they call on him in whom they have not believed?. . .*

To call upon the name of the Lord, you must believe in Him. You cannot just believe on a mental or intellectual level. The word *believe* means to trust; to depend upon; to rely on. The act of believing involves a turning to Christ. A necessary complement to a true belief in Christ is repentance, for the Lord said, *"Nay; but, **except ye repent,** ye shall all likewise perish" (Luke 13:3).*

Repentance and belief are the two sides of a single coin. To repent is to turn from something. You must turn **from** believing and trusting in your own efforts, church membership or your own religion. You must turn **to** believing on the Lord Jesus Christ. Repentance is *not* the lost *sinner's* promising to clean up his life in exchange for salvation. It is certainly not contingent upon the promise of some future behavior. *(See the in-depth discussion on repentance at the end of this chapter.)*

The choice is now yours. You must either accept or reject the gift of God. There is no middle ground. Either you believe or you believe *not*. To believe on the Lord Jesus Christ is to accept the facts that you are a sinner; that you owe the sin penalty; and that the Lord Jesus Christ died on the cross to pay the debt you owe. Believing on the Lord Jesus Christ means placing the matter of your eternal life in His hands, and not attempting to add anything to His complete and perfect salvation.

> *John 3:18* *He that **believeth** on him is not condemned: but he that **believeth not** is condemned already, because he hath not believed in the name of the only begotten Son of God.*

If you continue in *unbelief*, you are condemned because you *must* believe in order to be saved. You can choose to change your eternal destination today. Once you have accepted Him as Saviour, the peace and assurance of knowing that you have eternal life is yours.

> *1 Timothy 1:16* *Howbeit for this cause I obtained mercy, that in me first Jesus Christ might shew forth all longsuffering, for a pattern to them which should hereafter **believe on him to life everlasting**.*

If God is dealing with you about the matter of salvation, please take time right now to put your belief and trust in the Lord Jesus Christ as your Saviour.

If you have never before made a true profession of faith in the Lord Jesus Christ, we would like to hear from you. Please take time right now to contact the publisher or the author of this book that we may rejoice with you. We will also send you some additional information to enable you to live a victorious Christian life. The Lord Jesus Christ indicated that salvation is only the beginning when He spoke the following words:

> *John 10:10* *The thief cometh not, but for to steal, and to kill, and to destroy: **I am come that they might have life, and that they might have it more abundantly.***

The Lord Jesus Christ wants you to be saved (to have life). Once you are saved, He wants you to serve Him (that is, to have life more abundantly). You cannot serve without salvation; you cannot have salvation without accepting His payment for your sin. If you would like more information or further study materials, contact the author or publisher for a list of other materials available including a verse by verse study of the scripture.

If by "ways" of salvation is meant different content of faith, then dispensationalism does teach various "ways" because the Scriptures reveal differing contents of faith in the progressive nature of God's revelation to mankind. But if by "ways" is meant more than one basis or means of salvation, then dispensationalism most emphatically does not teach more than one way, for salvation has been, is, and always will be based on the substitutionary death of Jesus Christ.

Charles C. Ryrie, *Dispensationalism*, p. 121.

A study of repentance

Repent, repentance and other derivatives of this word are found in the Bible over one hundred times. Repentance is a change of mind that affects the individual. Thomas Adams once said, *"**Repentance** is a change of mind and **regeneration** is a change of the man."* Reformation is good; however, a man who turns from sin without turning to God has simply *reformed* his life without *regeneration*. New Years Day is a big day of **reformation**, but *not* a big day of repentance and regeneration. The day of one's salvation is the biggest day of repentance and regeneration.

Repentance is more of an attitude or condition of the heart, rather than an action or change of life. In order for repentance to bring a change of life repentance must lead the individual to conversion. The Conversion itself instigates the life change. However, we tend only to grasp the outward appearance and effects of repentance; consequently, most associate the repentance directly with the outward reality of the changed life. Our propensity to look on the outward appearance causes us to incorrectly define repentance as the visible life changes that we witness.

Repentance might be more correctly considered, not as the changing of one's life, but as the unconditional coming to Christ. We are saved by faith. *Repentance* is the desire to have my sin-problem solved by God. *Faith* is the means by which I appropriate God's forgiveness in the Person of Christ. Repentance will not necessarily change your lifestyle, but regeneration certainly will *(II Corinthians 5:17)*.

Some who espouse the view of *Lordship Salvation* teach that a lost person must make Jesus the *Lord* of his life. Those who teach that a lost person must turn from all of his sins and make Jesus Lord of his life are getting the proverbial "cart before the horse." A lost person has no capacity to accomplish this feat, nor has he the capacity to make any such decision. A repentant sinner simply acknowledges and accepts that **Christ is Lord.** That is why we are told to "believe on the **Lord** Jesus Christ." The title *Lord* indicates His deity; *Jesus* indicates His position as Saviour; and *Christ* indicates that He is the Messiah—the Anointed One. The thief on the cross, said, "**Lord**, remember me…" The thief accepted Him as *Lord*; he did not *make* Him *Lord*. This thief simply accepted Him for Who He already was and is—the **Lord** Jesus Christ. The Apostle Paul did not make Jesus Lord…he simply acknowledged that He was Lord *(Acts 9:5)*.

A person with a repentant heart need only seek for the cure—which is *believing* on the Lord Jesus Christ. The Bible's use of the word *repent* in relation to salvation is addressed to people that must turn from some falsehood that is keeping them from fully trusting in Christ. What must a person do to be saved? The only correct answer is to "believe on the Lord Jesus Christ." A lost person must repent of any other answer and belief before salvation can occur. The word *believe* in scripture only addresses those with a hungry heart already under conviction, no longer in need of repentance. It is for those that are already drawn to the truth, nothing holding them back from trusting the Saviour. The Philippian jailer is a prime example of **a repentant sinner** who was simply told to *believe*.

A. Repentance precedes belief. Peter realized that the Gentiles believed on the Lord Jesus Christ because God granted (gave) them repentance unto life.

*Acts 11:17 Forasmuch then as God gave them the like gift as he did unto us, **who believed on the Lord Jesus Christ**; what was I, that I could withstand God? 18 When they heard these things, they held their peace, and glorified God, saying, Then hath God also **to the Gentiles granted repentance unto life**.*

Peter mentions to his Jewish brethren that the Gentiles believed on the Lord Jesus Christ. The Jewish brethren glorified God because He granted *"repentance **unto life**"* unto the Gentiles. This is the first recorded instance of Gentiles being saved following the resurrection. Later in the same chapter we see some more believers preaching "the Lord Jesus" and the results are also given. *"And the hand of the Lord was with them: and **a great number believed, and turned unto the Lord" (Acts 11:21).** Some lost people see the drastic change in a new Christian's life and reject the Saviour because they are afraid of the changes that the Lord will do in their own lives. They must repent of this or they will remain lost for fear of God's anticipated expectations. They love their sin *(Hebrews 11:25)* more than they want the love of God in their lives. Praise God—His empowerment accompanies His expectations for the newborn Christian.

B. The Apostle Paul tells us that God now commands everyone, everywhere to repent.

Acts 17:29 Forasmuch then as we are the offspring of God, we ought not to think that the Godhead is like unto gold, or silver, or stone, graven by art and man's device (worshipping of images and idols). *30 And the times of this ignorance God winked at; but **now commandeth all men every where to repent**:*

The city of Athens is wholly given to idolatry *(Acts 17:16)*. They think that the preaching concerning Jesus and the resurrection involves simply another strange god *(Acts 17:18)*. The Apostle Paul tells them to repent of those things driving a wedge into their understanding and acceptance of the one and only true God. God may have been more tolerant of image worship and serving of idols outside the Jewish nation, but now commands everyone to repent. They are to repent of their image worship and ignorance. They are to change their mind about serving idols and turn to the truth so that they can accept the true God.

As pagan countries and people groups are evangelized by the gospel, true repentance from their pagan forms of religion is absolutely essential. The word *repentance* may never be articulated, but a true convert from paganism to Christianity must turn from trusting in the established gods of his old religion. One cannot simply formulate his own version of Christ around the established image and idol worship of the people.

*Acts 17:31 Because he hath appointed a day, in the which he will judge the world in righteousness by that man whom he hath ordained; whereof he hath given assurance unto all men, in that he hath raised him from the dead. 32 And when they heard of the resurrection of the dead, **some** mocked: and **others** said, We will hear thee again of this matter. 33 **So Paul departed from among them.** 34 Howbeit **certain men clave unto him, and believed**: among the which was Dionysius the Areopagite, and a woman named Damaris, and others with them.*

Notice what Paul, the soul winner, does. He does *not* try to lead a bunch of *un*repentant *un*believers to Christ. He tells the group that they must repent because one day God is going to judge the world in righteousness by Jesus Christ (verse 31). *Some* were interested in hearing Paul's message again and *others* were not (verse 32), so he departed from the group as a whole (verse 33). The Bible says that certain of the men and a few women clave to him **and believed** (verse 33). These are the only ones who were saved, because they repented of trusting in their idolatry and believed on the Lord Jesus Christ. Paul didn't try to persuade the mixed multitude to repeat the "sinner's prayer." He allowed those under conviction to determine for themselves who would remain lost and who would come to Christ. Only the repentant sinner will draw closer to the soul winner and come away with Christ in his heart.

C. God is not willing that anyone perishes, but that each person comes to repentance.

Every lost person is trusting in something—organized religion, works and good deeds or some other false hope. A person must repent of trusting in these things in order to correctly place trust in the Saviour.

II Peter 3:9 The Lord is *not slack concerning his promise, as some men count slackness; but is longsuffering to us-ward,* **not willing that any should perish but that all should come to repentance**.

Again, God is not willing that any should perish. He wills for everyone to come to Him. The Apostle Paul in the next passage says that God's goodness, forbearance and longsuffering serve to lead a person **to** repentance. God's very nature should impress upon every sinner the need to turn and receive the free gift of salvation.

Romans 2:4 *Or despisest thou the riches of his goodness and forbearance and longsuffering; not knowing that* **the goodness of God leadeth thee to repentance?** *5 But after thy hardness and* **impenitent heart** *treasurest up unto thyself wrath against the day of* **wrath** *and revelation of the righteous judgment of God;*

Although God's attributes do work to lead a person to repentance, a person can remain with an unrepentant heart. Remaining impenitent means that such a person will treasure up for himself wrath, to be revealed on the day that God's wrath and His righteous judgment are revealed. The need for repentance is addressed to the lost.

Christians are not appointed to wrath *(I Thessalonians 5:9);* therefore, verse 5 must refer to the need for repentance in a lost person's life. The lost person is still a child of wrath by nature *(Ephesians 2:3)*. Also, notice the contrasting pronouns used—the *we* of *Romans 2:2* contrasted with *them* and *thou* used elsewhere in *Romans 2:1-5*. Paul contrasts what the Christian knows about the judgment of God against the lost who treasure up wrath unto themselves. Paul's commission and that of every Christian is to take people from darkness and the power of Satan to light and to God.

Acts 26:18 *To open their eyes, and to turn them from darkness* **to light**, *and from the power of Satan* **unto God, that they may receive forgiveness of sins**, *and inheritance among them which are sanctified by faith that is in me.*

Paul's commission (and ours) is to take people from the darkness *to light* and from the power of Satan *unto God* so that they can *receive forgiveness of sins*. This is salvation. Forgiveness of sins comes to the person that moves from the darkness and the power of

Satan unto the light and power of God. Once Paul understood this, he busied himself in the work of preaching the gospel. We should do the same.

*Acts 26:19 Whereupon, O king Agrippa, I was not disobedient unto the heavenly vision: 20 But shewed first unto them of Damascus, and at Jerusalem, and through-out all the coasts of Judaea, and **then to the Gentiles**, that they should **repent** and **turn to God**, and **do works** meet for repentance.*

Notice that Paul's preaching began with the Jews and then moved on to the Gentiles. He preached the same gospel to both groups. He said they needed to repent first; then turn to God; and lastly, do works meet for repentance. Some erroneously claim that repentance *is* works because this passage includes both terms. Repenting and turning to God (two different instructions) are involved in the message of salvation. Next, converts were to do works meet for repentance. These works were *result* or *fruit* of salvation. Repentance is of no value unless it turns a person to God. Paul commends those at Thessalonica because they repented. Their repentance was outwardly revealed by their turning to God from idols *(I Thessalonians 1:9)*.

It is inconceivable how anyone could miss the need for repentance when he reads Paul's words to the pagans of Iconium.

*Acts 14:12 And they called Barnabas, Jupiter; and Paul, Mercurius, because he was the chief speaker. 13 Then the priest of Jupiter, which was before their city, brought oxen and garlands unto the gates, and would have done sacrifice with the people. 14 Which when the apostles, Barnabas and Paul, heard of, they rent their clothes, and ran in among the people, crying out, 15 And saying, Sirs, why do ye these things? We also are men of like passions with you, **and preach unto you that ye should turn from these vanities unto the living God**, which made heaven, and earth, and the sea, and all things that are therein: 16 Who in times past suffered all nations to walk in their own ways.*

Paul preached to these *lost* people caught up in idolatry that they should *turn from these vanities to the living God.* There can be no doubt that the message to the lost must include the absolute need for a repentant mind and heart. Obviously, they were headed in the wrong direction—thus Paul gave the admonition to *turn*. Jesus said He is the way *(John 14:6)*. There is no straddling the fence with God. In this case, Paul and Barnabas knew what was keeping these lost sinners from the Saviour. What is keeping you from trusting in the Lord? These idol worshippers rejected the preaching of Paul and Barnabas and stoned Paul, leaving him for dead *(Acts 14:19)*. They loved their idols so much that they attempted to kill the messenger.

D. The Lord Jesus Christ said that eternal damnation will follow if a person refuses to repent.

*Luke 13:3 I tell you, Nay: but, **except ye repent, ye shall all likewise perish**.*

The preceding passage clearly contrasts repentance with perishing. In order not to perish (that is, not to burn in hell forever), God requires each person to repent. The penitent thief on the cross displays a great example of repentance which brings forth salvation. The thief initially joins with the other thief in mocking the Saviour.

*Matthew 27:41 Likewise also the chief priests **mocking him**, with the scribes and elders, said, 42 He saved others; himself he cannot save. If he be the King of Israel, let him now come down from the cross, and we will believe him. 43 He trusted in God; let him deliver him now, if he will have him: for he said, I am the Son of God. 44 **The thieves also, which were crucified with him, cast the same in his teeth.***

One thief repents; that is, he changes his mind concerning his sin and the Saviour. There would be no salvation for this man had he not repented.

*Luke 23:39 And one of the malefactors which were hanged railed on him, saying, If thou be Christ, save thyself and us. 40 **But the other answering rebuked him, saying, Dost not thou fear God**, seeing thou art in the same condemnation? 41 **And we indeed justly; for we receive the due reward of our deeds**: but this man hath done nothing amiss. 42 And he said unto Jesus, **Lord, remember me when thou comest into thy kingdom.** 43 And Jesus said unto him, Verily I say unto thee, To day shalt thou be with me in paradise.*

Christ saved the penitent thief. Another great example of repentance is the Philippian jailer in Acts chapter 16. His demeanor clearly reflects his thoughts concerning the gospel and Christ's messengers. Repentance is never mentioned; however, the fruits of repentance are quite evident. The jailer's initial actions reveal that he has no concern for these men, their message or their Messiah.

*Acts 16:24 Who, having received such a charge, **thrust them into the inner prison, and made their feet fast in the stocks.***

The prison guard initially cared nothing for these men of God. However, a mere five verses later in the chapter, note how this same jailer had repented and was now concerned about the message he had evidently heard them preach and sing while in his jailhouse. Paul and Silas had only to tell this jailer to *believe* since he had already been clearly stripped of all hope apart from Christ. The jailer's simple question reveals a heartfelt desire to trust in what he had already heard.

*Acts 16:29 Then he called for a light, and sprang in, and came **trembling**, and **fell down before Paul and Silas**, 30 And brought them out, and said, Sirs, **what must I do to be saved?** 31 And they said, Believe on the Lord Jesus Christ, and thou shalt be saved, and thy house. 32 And they spake unto him the word of the Lord, and to all that were in his house. 33 And he took them the same hour of the night, and washed their stripes; and was baptized, he and all his, straightway. 34 And when he had brought them into his house, he set meat before them, and rejoiced, believing in God with all his house.*

What is repentance?

Obedience is the opposite of rebellion. Repentance is the correction of the rebellion. Either a person repents, or he continues in his rebellion. The Bible says that rebellion is as the sin of witchcraft *(I Samuel 15:23)*. Repentance is the precursor to pardon (salvation). A.W. Tozer said, "The idea that God will pardon a rebel that has not given up his rebellion, is contrary to scripture and common sense."

What happens to a person with a rebellious heart who asks Jesus to come into his heart? Absolutely nothing, except maybe that he or she gains a false sense of assurance. Such a person may repeat the words of the prescribed "sinner's prayer," but he will not be saved as long as he clings to his rebellious heart. Such individuals make a *profession* but have no *possession*. They do what they are told with no conviction.

Allowing the "rule of first mention" to define biblical terminology, Genesis chapter 6 provides a great foundational definition of repentance. Clearly, this passage illustrates that repentance is not a work to perform in order to attain salvation.

> ***Genesis 6:5*** *And **God saw that the wickedness of man** was great in the earth, and that every imagination of the thoughts of his heart was only evil continually. 6 And **it repented the Lord** that he had made man on the earth, and **it grieved him at his heart**. 7 And the Lord said, **I will destroy** man whom I have created from the face of the earth; both man, and beast, and the creeping thing, and the fowls of the air; for it **repenteth** me that I have made them.*

There are four aspects of repentance communicated in the previous passage:

1. Repentance is a realization of the exceeding sinfulness of sin *(verse 5)*. "God saw that the wickedness of man was great in the earth."

2. Repentance is a change of mind and heart attitude which leads to a change of actions *(verse 6) (Exodus 32:12)*. The situation in the world repented the Lord and it grieved Him at His heart; He therefore determined to destroy man. The Lord changed His mind about making man. This change of mind resulted in a change of actions—the flood. **The lost sinner can repent of sin, but has no power apart from the indwelling Spirit following salvation to put into action his newfound understanding.**

3. Repentance is accompanied by sorrow for sin *(verse 6)*. Repentance is not the sorrow, but is generally accompanied by it. "It grieved Him at His heart." The initial repentance at salvation is not simply sorrow for what you have done. However, it may include a sorrow for what you are *(Matthew 27:3)*. Biblical repentance is not simply experiencing sorrow for sin. Instead, biblical repentance means to sorrow because you are a sinner.

   Job repented when he saw himself as God saw him. This is true repentance. To abhor oneself is not to repent; instead it can indicate a true understanding of being a sinner. The repentance followed the realization of his sinfulness.

   Job 42:6 *Wherefore **I abhor myself, and repent** in dust and ashes.*

4. Repentance is a turning to God that can be identified by its consequences: the fruit of repentance (a change of action) *(Galatians 5:22-23)*. Repentance is not the change of action. However, change of action is an indicator of true repentance. One can see the changed action as a result of the repentance.

   For instance, the Lord's repentance of Genesis chapter 6 (discussed earlier) reflects a change of action. He says I will destroy the wickedness—I will get rid of it by destroying men from off the face of the earth. The repentance drives God to this decision and the actions which follow.

Now our attention is directed to the four aspects of repentance in further detail. First, repentance is recognition of the exceeding sinfulness of sin. Second, repentance is a change of mind. Third, repentance may be accompanied by a sorrow for sin. Fourth, repentance is a turning to God.

I. Exceeding sinfulness of sin

Sam Jones said that David was a great *sinner*, but an even greater *repenter (II Samuel 12:13, 24:10, 24:17)*. He also said that repentance constitutes the *ABCs* of salvation; hence, a person never ceases to need repentance even after he has trusted the Lord as his Saviour. Regardless of the person's repentant behavior following salvation, the person remains saved; however, the individual should continue to have a repentant heart.

The preaching of the Lord Jesus Christ brings about true repentance. It brings true conviction. Today, many preachers are not preaching about sin and the wickedness of sin as the Lord Jesus did. For example, when the Lord spoke of His preaching, this was His perspective:

*John 7:7 **The world** cannot hate you; but me it hateth, because I testify of it, that **the works thereof are evil.***

When the word of God is truly preached it will give the hearer a knowledge of sin. The knowledge of sin will show the individual his sinful condition and will bring conviction. This conviction of sin is the primary precursor to salvation.

*Romans 3:20 Therefore by the deeds of the law there shall no flesh be justified in his sight: for **by the law is the knowledge of sin**.*

*Romans 7:7 What shall we say then? Is the law sin? God forbid. Nay, **I had not known sin, but by the law**: for I had not known lust, except the law had said, Thou shalt not covet.*

*Romans 7:13 Was then that which is good made death unto me? God forbid. But sin, that it might appear sin, working death in me by that which is good; **that sin by the commandment might become exceeding sinful**.*

If the lost fail to appreciate the true nature of sin—they will also fail to grasp why Christ had to die for them and their sin. The Lord promised to send a Comforter to comfort His followers. However, this same Comforter serves another purpose. He reproves the world of sin, righteousness and judgment. In other words, He promotes repentance.

*John 16:7 Nevertheless I tell you the truth; It is expedient for you that I go away: for if I go not away, **the Comforter** will not come unto you; but if I depart, I will send him unto you. 8 And when he is come, he **will reprove the world of sin, and of righteousness, and of judgment**: 9 Of sin, because they believe not on me;* (unbelief)

As a lost person hears the message of the gospel, God's Spirit convicts him of his sin. The Holy Spirit gives him a desire to repent and turn from his sin and to trust in the Lord Jesus Christ. Repentance is not the act of turning from sin; however, it is the catalyst that causes the turning from sin.

II. Change of mind—not an act

Repentance is *not* the act of trying to stop sinning. When God tells people to repent He is not commanding them to do something absolutely impossible. It is impossible for a lost man to stop sinning so God certainly would not make this a prerequisite of salvation. Repentance precedes belief; however, repentance is not a work that produces salvation. The following verses clearly show that a person cannot stop sinning. If repentance were more than the change of mind, then God would be requiring the impossible of a lost person.

*Romans 3:11 There is none that understandeth, **there is none that seeketh after God**.*

*Romans 5:6 For when we were yet **without strength**, in due time **Christ died for the ungodly**.*

*Romans 5:8 But God commendeth his love toward us, in that, **while we were yet sinners, Christ died for us.***

*Romans 5:10 For if, **when we were enemies**, we were reconciled to God by the death of his Son, much more, being reconciled, we shall be saved by his life.*

*Romans 7:18 For I know that in me (that is, **in my flesh,) dwelleth no good thing**: for to will is present with me; but how to perform that which is good I find not.*

*Romans 14:23 And he that doubteth is damned if he eat, because he eateth not of faith: **for whatsoever is not of faith is sin.***

*Matthew 7:18 A good tree cannot bring forth evil fruit, **neither can a corrupt tree***

If repentance is a work, then a lost person would be bringing forth a "good fruit." Repentance is a change of mind. One cannot believe God without repentance. The next passage differentiates between *repenting* and the act of *going*.

*Matthew 21:28 But what think ye? A certain man had two sons; and he came to the first, and said, Son, go work to day in my vineyard. 29 He answered and said, I will not: but afterward **he repented, and went**. 30 And he came to the second, and said likewise. And he answered and said, I go, sir: and went not. 31 Whether of them twain did the will of his father? They say unto him, The first. Jesus saith unto them, Verily I say unto you, That the publicans and the harlots go into the kingdom of God before you (chief priests and elders). 32 For John came unto you in the way of righteousness, and ye believed him not: but the publicans and the harlots believed him: and ye, when ye had seen it, **repented not afterward, that ye might believe him. (Repentance** precedes belief.)*

In the preceding passage, repentance is not the act of going. Otherwise, the passage would be interpreted: "he went (repented), and he went . . ." Repentance is a surrender of the will to the Lord Jesus Christ *(II Peter 3:9)*. If a person becomes convicted of his sin and follows it through to salvation, a consecrated life to the Lord will naturally follow.

The repentance (change of mind) affects the heart and the heart affects the will. A simple change of mind can fall short of a change of action; however, a biblical repentance includes both. The next example reveals that the hearers were in a state of unbelief.

*Mark 6:6 And he marvelled because of their **unbelief**. And he went round about the villages, teaching.*

In verse 6, the Lord marvels because of their *unbelief*, and Christ sends forth His disciples preaching that men should repent (verse 12). Why? They needed to repent of their unbelief (verse 6). Can a person be saved in a state of unbelief?

Mark 6:12 And they went out, and preached that men should repent.

Another example of repentance concerns Esau. Esau sought repentance from his father Isaac. He attempted to get Isaac to change his mind. Note that had Isaac changed his mind, his actions would have demonstrated his repentance (or changed mind).

Hebrews 12:16 Lest there be any fornicator, or profane person, as Esau, who for one morsel of meat sold his birthright. 17 For ye know how that afterward, when he would have inherited the blessing, he was rejected: for he found no place of repentance, though he sought it carefully with tears.

A biblical repentance involves a change of mind that culminates in a decision to act, followed by the act itself. Esau sought repentance from his father. He wanted him to change his mind about the birthright and blessings upon his brother. Because Isaac did not repent, his actions did not change.

Genesis 27:38 And Esau said unto his father, Hast thou but one blessing, my father? bless me, even me also, O my father. And Esau lifted up his voice, and wept.

Some would try to equate repentance with penance. Repentance is *not penance* for penance is the false notion of being able to engage in self-punishment for the reparation or forgiveness of sin and attainment of salvation.

III. Accompanied by sorrow for sin

Repentance is accompanied by a sorrow for sin. The next verse speaks of a broken heart and a contrite spirit.

Psalm 34:18 The Lord is nigh unto them that are of a broken heart; and saveth such as be of a contrite spirit.

A contrite spirit is one filled with remorse. In fact, contrite is defined as a "sense of guilt and the desire for atonement." The Apostle Paul makes a distinction concerning the two types of sorrow—godly sorrow and worldly sorrow. New Years resolutions and too many jailhouse conversions best typify the sorrow of the world. However, our apostle distinguishes between being sorry for what you have done and true biblical repentance.

II Corinthians 7:10 For godly sorrow worketh repentance to salvation not to be repented of: but the sorrow of the world worketh death.

This passage teaches the following truths:

- A person is saved only one time. Godly sorrow is not to be repented of.

- This godly sorrow that works repentance to salvation cannot be repeated.

- Repentance is not merely sorrow for sin since the verse mentions two kinds of sorrow.

- Many people weep over sin without repentance, as evidenced by their returning to the same sin *(Genesis 27:38—Esau).*

IV. Turning to God

The Apostle Paul is the pattern for the Church to follow *(I Timothy 1:16)*. Paul says to consider what he says and the Lord will give us understanding in all things *(II Timothy 2:7)*. The Christian is told to follow Paul, just as Paul follows the Lord Jesus Christ *(I Corinthians 11:1)*. For this reason, we need to pay particular attention to Paul's position concerning repentance. What did Paul preach about repentance? Paul preached the following truth to Jew and Gentile alike.

> *Acts 20:21 Testifying both to the Jews, and also to the Greeks,* **repentance toward God, and faith toward our Lord Jesus Christ.**

Paul preached repentance toward God and faith toward our Lord Jesus Christ. Some hyper-dispensationalists claim that the events of this verse occurred during the early part of Paul's ministry (his missionary journeys), but notice what Paul says three verses later.

> *Acts 20:24 But none of these things move me, neither count I my life dear unto myself, so that I might finish my course with joy, and the ministry, which* **I have received of the Lord Jesus, to testify the gospel of the grace of God.**

The Apostle Paul says that he received this truth from the Lord Jesus Christ and calls it the Gospel of the Grace of God. **The *Gospel of the Grace of God* is "repentance toward God, and faith toward our Lord Jesus Christ!"** No wonder so many people seem to be making a profession without taking possession. The "converts" who ask Jesus to come into their heart without true repentance are made twofold more children of hell *(Matthew 23:15)*. They are told that they are saved, when they simply prayed a prayer with no heartfelt conviction.

Judas Iscariot's actions following the crucifixion of the Lord are a good example of repentance without turning to God (belief in God).

> *Matthew 27:3 Then* **Judas,** *which had betrayed him, when he saw that he was condemned,* **repented himself,** *and brought again the thirty pieces of silver to the chief priests and elders, 4 Saying,* **I have sinned** *in that I have betrayed the innocent blood. And they said, What is that to us? see thou to that. 5 And he cast down the pieces of silver in the temple, and departed, and went and hanged himself.*

Judas died and went to hell *(Acts 1:25)*. Repentance is of no value unless the repentance turns a person to God. *"For they themselves shew of us what manner of entering in we had unto you, and how ye* **turned to God from idols** *to serve the living and true God;" (I Thessalonians 1:9)*.

The results of repentance

One result of a true biblical repentance is that all heaven rejoices.

> *Luke 15:7 I say unto you, that likewise joy shall be in heaven over* **one sinner that repenteth,** *more than over ninety and nine just persons, which need no repentance.*

Repentance does not cause one to merit forgiveness. Repentance is instead a condition for receiving forgiveness. Repentance prepares a man for pardon, but it does not entitle him to the pardon. The thing that brought repentance to the Corinthians was a letter (scripture) that Paul wrote to them.

*II Corinthians 7:8 For though I made you sorry with a **letter**, I do not repent, though I did repent: for I perceive that **the same epistle hath made you sorry**, though it were but for a season. 9 Now I rejoice, not that ye were made sorry, but that **ye sorrowed to repentance**: for ye were made sorry after a godly manner, that ye might receive damage by us in nothing.*

Sin must be addressed by the sinner before he can be saved. Wise Christians are concerned about souls and soulwinning *(Proverbs 11:30)*. What is the answer to a person that asks, "You mean all I must do is ask Jesus to save me, and I am saved?" The wise answer is as follows: "That depends on what you believe. If you repent from believing on *anything* and *everything else* but the Lord Jesus Christ and believe only on Him, then yes, you can be saved by believing on the Lord Jesus Christ."

What if the person continues: "You mean I can keep doing what I am doing (engaging in drug dealing, stealing, child molesting, homosexuality, etc.) as long as I ask Him to save me"? Sin should be addressed with this individual before asking for some type of decision. If a person's desire is to live and remain in sin, he really does not understand what the Saviour has done for him. This individual must repent and place his trust in Christ. A person desiring to hold on to his sin might repeat the "sinner's prayer," but certainly has not believed on the Lord Jesus Christ.

Once a person has believed on the Lord Jesus Christ, there will be an evident conviction of the sin in his life. If he has no Holy Spirit conviction of sin, there may have been a profession, but there certainly is no possession. There may be no indwelling of the Spirit and thus no salvation.

Romans 8:16 The Spirit itself beareth witness with our spirit, that we are the children of God:

No one should simply trust in some act performed for salvation. This includes avoiding the false trust of having "asked Jesus to come into your heart." Not one passage in the Bible tells anyone to ask Jesus to come into his heart in order to be saved. This choice of words is a simple euphemism created by man. While these may have been chose with the best of intentions, their widespread use has many people making a profession of salvation but remaining lost in sin.

Being saved is not merely saying a prayer. Salvation has never been only this—and it never will be! Soul winners offer the Lord Jesus Christ to the lost. He can take away the sin; can change the heart; and can make the believer a new creature. Ask the lost man if he wants this kind of Saviour. Ask him if he wants the Saviour who can change him and take away his sin and sinful desires.

Too many people have been taught to get the lost to bow their heads at all costs. They have been taught to say to the lost, "Just bow your head, close your eyes, and let's pray." Too many sinners bow their heads and say the "sinner's prayer" without any inward conviction and belief on the Lord Jesus Christ. Consequently, they may make a profession, but have no possession of salvation.

Satan has convinced churches that repentance is a work. As a result, many individuals are busy preaching that which has no power to save and no foundation in the scriptures. These churches have become as guilty as the scribes and Pharisees of whom the Lord spoke. Those witnessing may be saved, but the false assurance they provide is condemning scores to an eternity without God!

Appendix A
The Two Witnesses

Six reasons why the two Witnesses in the book of the Revelation are Moses and Elijah:

1. Moses and Elijah were the two who appeared at the mount of transfiguration *(Matthew 17:1-3)*. They witnessed Christ's Kingdom prior to its coming. The message that they will preach will be about the Kingdom during the Tribulation. Their message will be extremely poignant since they have already witnessed the Kingdom. *(Matthew 16:28)*.

2. *Revelation 11:4* refers to the two olive trees, as does *Zechariah 4:3.* Then *Zechariah 4:14* says these figurative olive trees (or branches) are the two anointed ones, **that stand by the Lord of the whole earth.** Elijah and Moses are both referenced as having stood with the Lord.

   Elijah: *I Kings 17:1* quotes Elijah as saying, "As the Lord God of Israel liveth, **before whom I stand . . .**"

   Moses: *Exodus 34:5* And the Lord descended in the cloud, and **stood with him there . . .**"

   Although point #2 does not, in itself, prove that the two Witnesses are Moses and Elijah, it adds to the evidence presented.

3. *Revelation 11:5* refers to fire that proceeds out of the mouths of the two Witnesses to devour their enemies.

   Both Moses and Elijah are two Old Testament examples of God's allowing fire to consume their enemies.

   Elijah: *II Kings 1:9-13* tells of the fire that Elijah called down from heaven to consume his enemies.

   Moses: *Numbers 16:31-35* tells about the earth opening to swallow up the followers of Korah and the fire that came down from the Lord and consumed the 250 that offered incense.

4. *Revelation 11:6* points out that:

   a. They have power to shut heaven that it rains not in the days of their prophecy (forty-two months or 3 ½ years).

      Elijah: *I Kings 17:1* says that Elijah prayed to stop the rain, and that it would not rain except according to *his* word. *James 5:17* says that it did not rain for the space of *three years and six months during that time.* This span of time equals exactly one-half of the Tribulation period.

b.   They have power over waters to turn them to blood and to smite the earth with plagues.

Moses: **Exodus 7:19-20** Moses uses the rod of God to turn the waters of Egypt into blood. This is in addition to the other plagues he had power to initiate: the frogs, lice, flies, murrain, boils, hail fire, locusts, darkness and death of the firstborn.

5.   *Malachi 4:3* includes the phrase "in that day." This day refers to the Day of the Lord and Malachi chapter 4 ends with a curse *(verse 6)*. In verses 4 and 5, God mentions Moses and Elijah. He says more specifically that He will send Elijah the prophet before "the coming of the great and dreadful day of the Lord."

6.   The two Witnesses are Moses and Elijah. The devil disputes over the body of Moses in *Jude 9,* presumably because of the significance of Moses' return as one of the two Witnesses.

Some claim that Enoch will be one of the two Witnesses. Enoch is not one of the two Witnesses. Enoch was raptured (caught away) prior to the worldwide judgment of the flood and is a picture of the Rapture of the Church prior to the worldwide judgment of the Tribulation. Praise God for His pictures and types that make the truth clear. Enoch's rapture prior to the worldwide judgment gives a clear picture of the doctrine of the Pre-tribulation Rapture of the Church. Many people fail to study the pictures and types and thereby miss the clear representations of doctrinal truths found throughout the Bible.

"The basis for salvation in every age is the death of Christ; the requirement for salvation in every age is faith; the object of faith in every age is God; the content of faith changes in the various dispensations. It is this last point, of course, which distinguishes dispensationalism from covenant theology, but it is not a point to which the charge of teaching two ways of salvation can be attested. It simply recognizes the obvious fact of progressive revelation. When Adam looked on the coats of skins with which God had clothed him and his wife, he did not see what the believer today sees looking back on the cross of Calvary. And neither did other Old Testament saints see what we can see today."

Charles C. Ryrie, *Dispensationalism Today* (Chicago: Moody Press, 1965), p. 123-124.

Appendix B
The Works of the Law

The Old Testament is full of examples of the role of works in the life of the follower of God. Any Bible teacher who claims that the Old Testament does not involve *works* does not have a sufficient grasp of God's word. Even the New Testament repeatedly references the Old Testament "***works*** of the law." Consider, for example, multiple references contained in the following verse:

> ***Galatians 2:16*** *Knowing that a man is not justified by **the works of the law**, but by the faith of Jesus Christ, even we have believed in Jesus Christ, that we might be justified by the faith of Christ, and not by **the works of the law**: for by **the works of the law** shall no flesh be justified.*

The law *is* works! However, this does not mean that the works of the law could eternally justify even one soul under the Old or New Testaments. If the works of the law were sufficient to eternally justify a sinner, the Lord Jesus Christ's sacrifice would have been unnecessary. There would be no need for Him to have died in our place for our sin if man could be justified in any way apart from Christ's sacrifice.

Israel's problem was not a lack of works, but a lack of faith. They sought to be justified by the works of the law *without faith*. In fact, Jesus rebuked the religious leaders of His day for their failure to keep the weightier matters of the law. The Pharisees wanted to do works to be seen by others, rather than out of the appropriate heart attitude and motivation.

> ***Matthew 23:23*** *Woe unto you, scribes and Pharisees, hypocrites! for ye pay tithe of mint and anise and cummin, and have **omitted the weightier matters of the law**, judgment, mercy, and faith: these ought ye to have done, **and not to leave the other undone**.*

The Lord does not tell these leaders of Israel to ignore *the works,* but instead tells them that they were correct in *not* leaving them undone. He instructed these religious leaders to do *both* matters of the law—judgment, mercy and faith *as well as* the tithe of their possessions. However, Paul admonishes anyone today desiring to live "of the works of the law." He warns us of the curse that accompanies the law. The law requires complete and total adherence.

> ***Galatians 3:10*** *For as many as are **of the works of the law are under the curse**: for it is written, Cursed is every one that continueth not **in all things which are written** in the book of the law to do them.*

Paul writes this warning to discourage anyone from thinking that he should incorrectly attempt to place himself under the law and its works. Why would anyone desire to be under a curse? The problem with the law was not a problem with the law itself, but with *man's inability* to abide by *the works of the law*. Man's flesh was weak, thus the law was weak through the flesh.

> ***Romans 8:3*** *For what **the law** could not do, in that **it was weak through the flesh**, God sending his own Son in the likeness of sinful flesh, and for sin, condemned sin in the flesh:*

The law could never justify anyone due to the weakness of man's sinful flesh. Because of man's propensity to sin, God instituted the sacrificial system. The animal sacrifices were brought to sanctify and temporarily purify a man's flesh. However, these sacrifices were intended simply to make the individual temporarily blameless concerning the law. **The animal sacrifices had no purifying effect on the soul. Only the shed blood of the Lord Jesus Christ could redeem the *soul*.**

> ***Hebrews 9:13*** *For if the blood of bulls and of goats, and the ashes of an heifer sprinkling the unclean, sanctifieth to the **purifying of the flesh**:*

Paul's preaching emphasizes the distinction between the sacrifice of the Lord Jesus Christ and the sacrifices required under the law. Paul preached concerning the justification which could not come by keeping the law.

> ***Acts 13:38*** *Be it known unto you therefore, men and brethren, that through this man is preached unto you the forgiveness of sins: 39 And by him all that believe are justified from all things, from **which ye could not be justified by the law of Moses**.*

Paul exclaims that it is by the blood of the Lord Jesus Christ that believers "are justified from all things." Keep in mind that the law's inadequacies were not a problem with the *law* itself, but a problem of *man's* inadequacies. The actions of the Pharisees are a prime example of the Jews' mentality and propensity to pervert God's ways. They sought to be justified by keeping the letter of the law. This is not what God demanded or expected of His people. The Jews were to keep the *spirit*, not simply the *letter,* of the law (or that which is explicitly delineated).

> ***II Corinthians 3:6*** *Who also hath made us able ministers of the new testament; not of the letter, but of the spirit: for **the letter killeth**, but the spirit giveth life.*

The Pharisees, like many other religious people, were only concerned with keeping the letter of the law. They ignored its true intent. This fact is easily demonstrated in the following three poignant examples:

1. After the Jews had betrayed and crucified the Lord Jesus Christ because of envy *(Mark 15:10),* they were concerned about breaking the law by allowing His body to remain on the cross on the Sabbath day!

> ***John 19:31*** *The Jews therefore, because it was the preparation, **that the bodies should not remain upon the cross on the sabbath day, (for that sabbath day was an high day,)** besought Pilate that their legs might be broken, and that they might be taken away.*

Imagine the hypocrisy of putting an innocent man to death and yet being concerned about abiding by a legal directive as insignificant in comparison? This gross hypocrisy should shock the reader's sensibilities. The Jews were trying to abide by the *letter of the law* while ignoring the greater sin.

2. The same was true concerning the Jews' dealings with Judas Iscariot. The religious leaders paid Judas to betray an innocent man. Yet, when he returned the tainted money to them, they wanted to abide by the law.

*Matthew 27:6 And the chief priests took the silver pieces, and said, It is **not lawful** for to put them into the treasury, **because it is the price of blood**.*

The Jews became "spiritual" and concerned about doing "right." In their own minds, the Jewish leaders could justify paying to betray an innocent man, but wanted to insure that they were not guilty of breaking the *letter* of the law. They could break the law in secret, as long as they followed the more overt aspects of the letter of the law.

3. These same religious leaders sought out **false** witnesses *(Matthew 26:59)* to testify against the Lord. Yet, they wanted to abide by the letter of the law when it came to deciding what to do with the "blood money." People are no different today when they think they can do some religious good deed to atone for their past indiscretions.

The book of Romans reiterates Israel's omission of one of the weightier matters of the law: that of *faith*. **Israel sought justification by the works of the law and not by faith.**

*Romans 9:31 But Israel, which followed after the law of righteousness, hath not attained to the law of righteousness. 32 Wherefore? Because **they sought it not by faith**, but as it were by **the works of the law**. For they stumbled at that stumblingstone;*

The Bible says that without faith it is impossible to please God *(Hebrews 11:6)*. This fact is true whether considering either the Old or New Testament. Faith was a key ingredient *under the law*. One need only read Hebrews chapter 11 to see the importance of faith in the life of the Old Testament saints. For example, Hebrews 11 mentions incorporates the phrase "through faith" in verses 3, 11, 28, 33, 39; and "by faith" in verses 4, 5, 7, 8, 9, 17, 20, 21, 22, 23, 24, 27, 29, 30, 31. Israel wanted to live by the works but lacked the faith which God expected.

The LAW and the CHURCH

It must be repeated once again—absolutely no one gets to heaven apart from the grace and mercy of God. To claim otherwise is to diminish the importance of Christ's sacrifice and even nullify His work on the cross. If it were possible for obedience to the law to eternally justify a person, the Bible says that God would have given such a law.

*Galatians 3:21 Is the law then against the promises of God? God forbid: **for if there had been a law given which could have given life, verily righteousness should have been by the law.***

Righteousness does not come by keeping the law. It comes from trusting in the One Who kept the law. Some skeptic reading this verse might reply: "If God is truly omnipotent, why couldn't God give a law for man to keep in order to be justified?" Understanding this point is crucial. Does the fact that God could *not* give such a law reveal an impotent God in some way? Or should we direct our attention toward the part of God's creation incapable of fulfilling any such law? Paul wrote that there was no problem with the law. It is holy.

*Romans 7:12 Wherefore **the law is holy,** and the commandment holy, and just, and good.*

There was never anything wrong with the law or God's commandments (or His expectations). The problem has always resided with man. Man could never be eternally righteous by keeping the law and simultaneously retain a freewill to love and to serve (or despise and reject) his Maker. The problem with the law was man's inability to fulfill it in all points.

*James 2:10 For whosoever shall keep the whole law, and yet **offend in one point, he is guilty of all.***

A lawbreaker is not someone who breaks only the most serious statutes, but someone who breaks *any* part of the law. For this reason, God instituted certain sacrifices that could temporarily make the individual *blameless*. For example, consider the cases of Zacharias and Elizabeth in *Luke 1:6*, and the Apostle Paul in *Philippians 3:6*. These all were blameless in the law because they fulfilled the necessary sacrifices prescribed for having broken the law.

*Luke 1:6 And they were both **righteous** before God, walking in all the commandments and ordinances of the Lord **blameless**.*

The Bible says that the law with its sacrifices could never make the sinner perfect. If the sacrifices ever accomplished this feat, the individual's conscience would be purged of sin and there would be no further need for future sacrifices.

*Hebrews 10:1 For **the law** having a shadow of good things to come, and not the very image of the things, **can never with those sacrifices which they offered year by year continually make the comers thereunto perfect.** 2 For then would they not have ceased to be offered? because that the worshippers once purged should have had **no more conscience of sins.***

If the Old Testament sacrifices ever completely purged the penitent sinner of his sin then he would have ceased offering them. Sin would never again have pricked his conscience. The passage continues by informing us that the sacrifices were acceptable to God for another reason. The purpose of the sacrifices was not to take away the sins. These particular sacrifices were instituted to bring to remembrance the individual's sins annually.

*Hebrews 1:3 But in those sacrifices there is a **remembrance** again made of sins every year. 4 **For it is not possible that the blood of bulls and of goats should take away sins**.*

What the animal sacrifices could not do, the blood of Jesus could completely accomplish. John the Baptist identified Christ as the Lamb of God. John pointed to Him as the sacrificial Lamb of God who would one day die to take away the sins of the world.

*John 1:29 The next day John seeth Jesus coming unto him, and saith, **Behold the Lamb of God, which taketh away the sin of the world**.*

Only Christ as the perfect sacrificial Lamb could eternally atone for sin *(Romans 5:11)*. **Eternal righteousness** could only come from a *complete* fulfillment of the *entire* law. This is something that only one Man ever attained. *"For we have not an high priest which cannot be touched with the feeling of our infirmities; but was in all points tempted like as we are, **yet without sin" (Hebrews 4:15)**.* The weakness of the law rested in man, and *not* with God. Thankfully, the fulfillment of God's law rested with God and *not* with man.

*Romans 8:3 For **what the law could not do**, in that **it was weak through the flesh*** (man's sinfulness), *God sending his own Son in the likeness of sinful flesh, and for sin, condemned sin in the flesh:*

Some might ask, what is the purpose of the law today if not to justify the sinner? The Apostle Paul explains that the law serves as the lost person's schoolmaster (or teacher). The law points out the sinner's inability to reconcile himself to his Creator and his dire need to trust in God's Son by faith. By magnifying our sin, the law points us to Christ as our only hope for redemption.

*Galatians 3:23 But before faith came, we were kept under the law, shut up unto the faith which should afterwards be revealed. 24 **Wherefore the law was our school-master to bring us unto Christ**, that we might be justified by faith. 25 But after that faith is come, we are no longer under a schoolmaster.*

The Bible goes on to point out that the Christian is no longer under a *schoolmaster (Galatians 3:25)* and no longer *under the law (Romans 6:15)*. Some skeptics think this teaching offers the Christian a license to sin. For this reason, the salvation passages are generally quickly followed by verses explaining one's need to work.

Works in the Church Age

The Christian's faith is tested through his obedience to God's word. The fact that we are Christians means that we are supposed to work for God *(I Corinthians 3:9)*. We are certainly not saved BY works, but we are saved TO work. Paul wrote that he hoped that the followers of Christ had not received the grace of God in vain.

*II Corinthians 6:1 We then, as workers together with him, beseech you also that ye **receive not the grace of God in vain**.*

There is only one way *not* to receive the grace of God in vain—and that is to WORK! What good is a Christian who receives Christ as Saviour and then simply lives unto himself? None at all. Therefore, Paul also writes that we are to be fruitful in every good work following salvation.

*Colossians 1:10 That ye might walk worthy of the Lord unto all pleasing, **being fruitful in every good work**, and increasing in the knowledge of God;*

Those Christians who have not received the grace of God in vain are the ones who realize that they were saved TO work. In order to walk worthy of the Lord, Christians are to remain fruitful. These are indisputable truths. In fact, those who fail to maintain good works are the ones deemed unfruitful.

*Titus 3:14 And let ours also learn to **maintain good works** for necessary uses, **that they be not unfruitful**.*

The Christian's bearing fruit is a simple concept. What good is a mature fruit tree that bears no fruit? A Christian who fails to reproduce is no better than a barren fruit tree. God saved us and we are to bring others to a saving knowledge of Christ. We are to be fruitful by maintaining good works.

Salvation and works!

God intended for the most often quoted salvation passages to lead a person to work for Christ following salvation. Consider these three examples of what is meant by works following salvation. Verses 8 and 9 of Ephesians chapter 2 address salvation as a gift from God. Verse 10 addresses the natural progression which is to follow salvation—working for one's newfound Saviour.

> *Ephesians 2:8 For **by grace are ye saved through faith**; and that not of your-selves: it is the gift of God: 9 Not of works, lest any man should boast. 10 For we are his workmanship, **created in Christ Jesus unto good works, which God hath before ordained that we should walk in them.***

God ordained (or decreed) that Christians would work for Him as His *ambassadors (II Corinthians 5:20)*. We are to represent Him in this life and enjoy the fruits of our labors in the next. There is no other reason for God to save a person's soul and then leave him on this sin-sick planet. Titus also addresses salvation in verse 11 and the works that are to follow in verse 14.

> *Titus 2:11 For **the grace of God that bringeth salvation** hath appeared to all men, 12 Teaching us that, denying ungodliness and worldly lusts, we should live so-berly, righteously, and godly, in this present world; 13 Looking for that blessed hope, and the glorious appearing of the great God and our Saviour Jesus Christ; 14 Who gave himself for us, that he might redeem us from all iniquity, and **purify unto himself a peculiar people, zealous of good works.***

The same grace that saves the lost also teaches Christians to deny ungodliness and worldly lusts. Grace teaches that a Christian is to live soberly, righteously and godly in this present world. As we work, verse 13 says we are to be looking forward to Christ's imminent return. The next chapter of Titus reveals the same principle. Salvation is not by works, but a fruitful life certainly is!

> *Titus 3:5 **Not by works** of righteousness which we have done, but according to his mercy he saved us, by the washing of regeneration, and renewing of the Holy Ghost;...8 This is a faithful saying, and these things I will that thou affirm con-stantly, **that they which have believed in God might be careful to maintain good works**. These things are good and profitable unto men.*

Many religious people think that they must do good works in order to obtain salvation. As logical as this may *sound* God's ways cannot be comprehended through our finite levels of reason. Religion says DO; Christianity says DONE. Only by accepting what Christ has DONE are people enabled by God to DO the good works that He expects.

Everyone judged according to work(s)

Works and salvation—these are interrelated concepts that confuse the vast majority of people. The fact that both the **Great White Throne Judgment** and the **Judgment Seat of Christ** mention being judged for one's *works* confuses those with a cursory understanding of the scriptures. For those questioning why and how works will play a role at these two judgments, the answer is rather simple. Both judgments involve the judgment of works, but neither judgment affects the predetermined destination of the soul.

The Great White Throne Judgment

In the book of Revelation, John writes that he saw in heaven a great white throne. As the dead stand before this throne, the book of life and the "books" are opened. As anyone with basic

Bible knowledge understands, the *book of life* contains the names of all those *not* cast into the lake of fire. The "books" on the other hand contain a record of the *works* of those standing before this judgment throne. One can only imagine this awesome spectacle.

> ***Revelation 20:11*** *And I saw **a great white throne**, and him that sat on it, from whose face the earth and the heaven fled away; and there was found no place for them. 12 And I saw the dead, small and great, stand before God; and the books were opened: and another book was opened, which is the book of life: and the dead were **judged** out of those things which were written in the books, **according to their works**. 13 And the sea gave up the dead which were in it; and death and hell delivered up the dead which were in them: and **they were judged every man according to their works**. 14 And death and hell were cast into the lake of fire. This is the second death. 15 And **whosoever was not found written in the book of life was cast into the lake of fire.***

The book of life is opened at the same time that the books of works are opened. Whether an individual is cast into the lake of fire (verse 15) is determined by one thing—whether or not his name is found in the book of life. Whether a person's name is found in the book of life is determined long before he reaches the Great White Throne for judgment. Otherwise, Paul certainly would not have referred to those *whose names are in the book of life.*

> ***Philippians 4:3*** *And I intreat thee also, true yokefellow, help those women which laboured with me in the gospel, with Clement also, and with other my fellowlabourers, **whose names are in the book of life.***

It is inconceivable how anyone could honestly teach that a man's works, as recorded in the "books," will determine his eternal destiny. The Apostle Paul makes reference to those already in the book of life before the time of judgment, and John references those that are *not* in the book of life.

> ***Revelation 13:8*** *And all that dwell upon the earth shall worship him* (the beast of verse 1), ***whose names are not written in the book of life*** *of the Lamb slain from the foundation of the world.*

According to John, no one that worships the Beast during the Tribulation has his or her name in the book of life. The Great White Throne Judgment will simply demonstrate the fact that these people's names are not found in the book of life.

> ***Revelation 17:8*** *The beast that thou sawest was, and is not; and shall ascend out of the bottomless pit, and go into perdition: and **they that dwell on the earth shall wonder, whose names were not written in the book of life** from the foundation of the world, when they behold the beast that was, and is not, and yet is.*

Revelation chapter 20 reveals the destination of all those who do not have their names in the book of life. That ultimate destination is the lake of fire. The works judged at the Great White Throne will determine the degree of eternal punishment that a person without Christ receives *(Matthew 10:15)*. The absence of one's name from the book of life will determine his eternal destination. In contrast to the Great White Throne Judgment, the Judgment Seat of Christ will involve *strictly* those individuals whose names *are* found in the book of life.

The Judgment Seat of Christ

The purpose of the Judgment Seat of Christ is to judge the life's work of every Christian. Therefore, only the redeemed through the precious blood of Jesus Christ will appear at this judgment.

This judgment determines the Christian's reward or loss for the life lived following salvation. It reveals which type of works the individual produced—works deserving of reward or works of no eternal value and reward. It cannot be overemphasized that the Judgment Seat of Christ is also a judgment for *service (I Corinthians 3:8)*, and *not* a judgment to determine *salvation*. Salvation is settled long before anyone arrives at this judgment. Only those individuals who have believed on the Lord Jesus Christ *(Acts 16:31)* and received the full pardon for their sins will appear at the Judgment Seat of Christ. One's belief on the Lord Jesus Christ in this life removes condemnation in the next life.

> *John 3:17 For God sent not his Son into the world to condemn the world; but that the world through him might be saved. 18 **He that believeth on him is not condemned**: but **he that believeth not is condemned already**, because he hath not believed in the name of the only begotten Son of God.*

The individual who has *not* believed on the Lord Jesus Christ remains in a state of condemnation awaiting the end of this life. The Bible says the unbeliever is "condemned already." His name will not be found in the book of life at the Great White Throne Judgment.

The Bible repeatedly says that salvation is a *gift* to all those who believe *(Romans 6:23, Ephesians 2:8-9, 3:7, etc.)*; salvation is never referred to as a *reward* for service. Christ was punished (He died) in our place and for our sins *(I Corinthians 15:3)*. We receive the benefit of His work on the cross so that He may reward us for our work in the life to come.

> *II Corinthians 5:10 **For we must all appear before the judgment seat of Christ**; that every one may **receive the things done in his body**, according to that he hath done, **whether it be good or bad.***

Every Christian will receive a reward or else suffer loss for the things done in his body at the Judgment Seat of Christ. God is not mocked; Christians will receive the fruits of the things done in their bodies—whether they are good or bad! Only believers will be judged at the Judgment Seat of Christ. The unsaved will not appear at this judgment seat for they do not have the correct foundation, identified in the following passage as Jesus Christ.

> *I Corinthians 3:10 According to the grace of God which is given unto me, as a wise masterbuilder, I have laid **the foundation**, and another buildeth thereon. But let every man take heed how he buildeth thereupon. 11 For other **foundation** can no man lay than that is laid, **which is Jesus Christ**.*

Only Christians have the necessary foundation of Jesus Christ; therefore, only the work of a Christian will be judged at this judgment. The Bible says that "*every* man's work" shall be made manifest at the judgment seat. The work will be judged when the fire reveals its true properties.

> *I Corinthians 3:12 Now if any man build upon this foundation gold, silver, precious stones, wood, hay, stubble; 13 **Every man's work** shall be made manifest: for the day shall declare it, because it shall be **revealed by fire**; and the fire shall try*

every man's work of what sort it is. *14 If any man's work* abide which he hath built thereupon, he shall receive a reward. *15 If any man's work* shall be burned, he shall suffer loss: but he himself shall be saved; yet so as by fire.

It is important to recognize that the Judgment Seat of Christ is a judgment of the quality or nature of works but is *not* a judgment upon the individual himself. There is absolutely no indication that the saved individual will be harmed or punished should his life's work go up in flames. The fire simply reveals the sort of work the man performed—whether good and enduring works, or bad and temporal works. What is this fire? The Bible indicates that fire undoubtedly refers to the word of God. Jeremiah likens God's word to fire and Jesus states that it will be His word that judges in the last day.

> *Jeremiah 23:29 Is not my word like as a fire*? saith the LORD; and like a hammer that breaketh the rock in pieces?

> *John 12:48 He that rejecteth me, and receiveth not my words, hath one that judgeth him: **the word** that I have spoken, **the same shall judge him in the last day**.*

The Bible also relates the Son of God to the fire of judgment in the book of Revelation. When it refers to Him as the one *"...who hath his eyes like unto a flame of fire..." **(Revelation 2:18)**.* One can only imagine being eye to eye with the Saviour. Christ will sit on the judgment seat, but He may *not* be the only one present when the individual is judged. Paul defines a man's work in the Lord as those whom he has influenced during his life.

> *I Corinthians 9:1 Am I not an apostle? am I not free? have I not seen Jesus Christ our Lord? **are not ye my work in the Lord?***

The same holds true for us. Our work is not some building we build or even the ministry into which we pour our lives. Our work is people! It is everyone that we have influenced and affected, whether for good or for bad. Just because a Christian's standing—that is, his ultimate place in heaven— is guaranteed does *not* mean that he will not have to give an account of how he has lived his life following salvation. In fact, the opposite is true. Every Christian will give an account for his life.

> *Romans 14:10 But why dost thou judge thy brother? or why dost thou set at nought thy brother? for **we shall all stand before the judgment seat of Christ**. 11 For it is written, As I live, saith the Lord, every knee shall bow to me, and every tongue shall **confess** to God. 12 So then **every one of us shall give account of himself to God**.*

What will the Christian have to confess before God? Of what will he be required to give an account? Those claiming that Christians need only be concerned with loss of rewards at the Judgment Seat of Christ never consider that the Bible also points out that we will *receive* for the wrong we have done. The Bible says that we are joint-heirs with Christ IF...*(Romans 8:17, II Timothy 2:12).* This passage makes reigning with Christ contingent upon suffering for Him IN THIS LIFE.

> *Romans 8:16 The Spirit itself beareth witness with our spirit, that we are the children of God: 17 And if children, then heirs; heirs of God, and joint-heirs with Christ; **if so be that we suffer with him**, that we may be also glorified together.*

The book of Romans tells us that we are the children of God; because we are His children, we are heirs. However, our inheritance is conditioned upon how we conduct ourselves as His children. In other words, our inheritance is directly related to suffering in this life. (Suffering as a Christian does not necessarily mean that we must be stretched on the rack and tortured. It can simply refer to the kind of suffering which takes place when a godly Christian works in a wicked workplace.) The next passage from Second Timothy promises that our inheritance, or lack of inheritance, will *not* interfere with our living with Him for eternity. We are spiritually crucified with Him in this life *(Romans 6:6, Galatians 2:20)* and will eternally live with Him in the next.

II Timothy 2:11 It is a faithful saying: For if we be dead with him, we shall also live with him: 12 If we suffer, we shall also reign with him: if we deny him, he also will deny us: 13 If we believe not, yet he abideth faithful: he cannot deny himself.

All Christians will live with the Lord eternally; however, not all Christians will receive the reward of the inheritance. A refusal to live godly and suffer reproach in the present life for the cause of Christ will negate any heavenly inheritance. How does one suffer for Christ in this life? It is not a difficult concept to understand. Americans can suffer simply by trying to live right in this evil world.

*II Timothy 3:12 Yea, and all that will **live godly** in Christ Jesus shall **suffer persecution**.*

If a person lives in a godly manner, he will suffer in this life. Our willingness to suffer for the cause of Christ will determine the extent of our reward and reign in the next life. However, those who do not serve and suffer in this life will not *merely* lose rewards in the next life…they will *receive* something as well. This fact has absolutely nothing to do with any punishment or Christian "purgatory," for neither concept is at all biblical. Christians are promised the reward of the inheritance or warned that they will receive for the wrong that they have done.

*Colossians 3:23 And whatsoever ye do, do it heartily, as to the Lord, and not unto men; 24 Knowing that of the Lord ye shall **receive the reward of the inheritance**: for ye serve the Lord Christ. 25 But he that doeth wrong shall **receive for the wrong** which he hath done: and there is no respect of persons.*

The Bible clearly teaches that the Judgment Seat of Christ for an unfaithful Christian is not just a matter of losing or missing out on rewards. Christians will receive something, too. What might that something be? Can we know what heaven will be like? The Bible says that future things are revealed to Christians by God's Spirit, Who knows all.

*I Corinthians 2:9 But as it is written, Eye hath not seen, nor ear heard, neither have entered into the heart of man, the things which God hath prepared for them that love him. 10 **But God hath revealed them unto us by his Spirit**: for the Spirit searcheth all things, yea, the deep things of God.*

Many preachers who base their teaching on verse 9 have endorsed the view that we cannot know or understand the things yet to come, including matters concerning heaven. However, it is incorrect to apply the truths of verse 9 to Christians today. To do so is to take the passage out of its context.

Verse 9 says that man has not seen, heard or understood future things prepared for him; however, verse 10 begins with the conjunction *but*. Therefore, the truths following this conjunction have a completely opposite application from the facts that precede it. Although the things prepared for man have not been previously revealed, we can know some things about God and the things He has prepared for us…even the deep things of God! Yet, the Old Testament saint could not see or understand what we can now see and comprehend.

Before we consider the things of heaven, some groundwork must be clearly established. Each of these truths concerns light. The Bible says Christians are the light of the world; yet the world is anti-light. The world (those that are in it) hates the light of the Bible, the light of God and the light of the Christian. Yet, these are their only hope.

WORLD: *John 3:19 And this is the condemnation, that **light is come into the world,** and men loved darkness rather than **light**, because their deeds were evil. 20 For every one that doeth evil hateth the **light**, neither cometh to the **light**, lest his deeds should be reproved. 21 But he that doeth truth cometh to the **light**, that his deeds may be made manifest, that they are wrought in God.*

The Bible says that we receive light by Jesus Christ. If you do not have the light of God in your life, you are obviously without light.

Those in the world can receive true light from three places: the Lord Jesus Christ, the word of God and through the life of a godly Christian. Light came into the world by the Lord Jesus Christ when He walked this earth in human form; today it comes into the world through the word of God and the obedient Christian. Lost people will generally avoid each of these three because the light shines on their sin and they love darkness, rather than light.

Lost people and backslidden Christians who hate the light will avoid the word of God. They will avoid the Son. They will avoid you if you are truly reflecting the light of God and the truth of the gospel. If a Christian doesn't live a godly, separated life, the world and the devil will treat him as one of their own. Satan will convince you that everything is fine because he impersonates the light.

SATAN: *II Corinthians 11:14 And no marvel; for **Satan** himself is transformed into an **angel of light**.*

Satan appears as an angel of light because he wants to convince the lost person or backslidden Christian that no changes in his manner of living are necessary. But the false light is evident because it appeals to the flesh, and not to the Spirit within the believer. This is sensual and devilish, and Satan is behind it all.

Joseph Smith, the founder of Mormonism, is an excellent example of the operations of the angel of light. Smith said an "angel of light" appeared to him and gave him the book of Mormon. Satan, posing as the angel of light, set in motion the deception to help begin one of the largest cults in the world.

Millions have since followed this false light to the condemnation of their souls and the worthlessness of their works. All of this deception and untruth could have been avoided had Joseph Smith been a Bible-studying, Bible-believing Christian. The previous verse from Second Corinthians 11 would have revealed to him the false light and satanic nature of his meeting with the angel. A deceived person will believe that anything that looks spiritual must be of God.

For every good thing, there is an opposite or opposing evil or bad. This opposite (false light) can be identified by the fact that it will generally appeal to one's flesh. For instance, the Mormon cult teaches (or taught) that you can have more than one wife, that you can become a god, and that you can be baptized to save the dead. Each of these teachings appeals to the flesh.

Satan can impersonate the light, but he cannot fool the Christian who learns his Bible and stays in contact with God through prayer. When Christians are confronted with false light, their spirits will be affected in such a way as to reveal that the influence at hand is not from God. This is the case only when a Christian's relationship with God is right. When there is sin interfering with that critical relationship, spiritual discernment will be lost and a "spiritual" appeal to the flesh will be alluring.

John chapter 9 tells us about the real light...our Lord and Saviour Jesus Christ. Satan is the false light, and Jesus is the true light.

JESUS: *John 9:5 As long as I am in the world, **I am the light of the world.***

Jesus was the light of the world when He was here in bodily form. Men marveled at Him. They knew that no man had ever spoken like this Man *(John 7:46)*. He taught with authority *(Matthew 7:29)*. The religious leaders of His day hated the light because of the crowds that came to hear Him speak. They wanted to smother the light.

Today, these same religious leaders have put out the light by changing the true and perfect word of God. When the true authority (God's word) is followed, it puts the preacher, the priest and the religious leader under its authority. It is in authority over them and over all. The light from God's word reveals the sin of unbelief or infidelity concerning His word and His way. This is why men love darkness and change the word.

*John 8:12 Then spake Jesus again unto them, **I am the light of the world**: he that followeth me shall not walk in darkness, but shall have **the light of life**.*

The author received a special blessing while viewing a missions video called *EE-Taow*. The mission organization that produced this video emphasizes presentation of the gospel to tribes that have never before been exposed to the gospel. The video records the presentation of the gospel to this tribe and the events thereafter. After the conversion of almost the entire tribe, many of the surrounding tribal villages wanted the missionaries to come and speak to them. The stated reason for the other tribes' desire to hear the truth was because they looked into the eyes of the tribal people (who had been saved) and saw "light in their eyes."

These tribal people have more sense than most of our educated, civilized—but lost—Doctors of Divinity today. These tribal people knew that the light comes from the word. Jesus is the light of the world and the only way to receive this light is through the word of God.

THE WORD: *Psalm 119:130 **The entrance of thy words giveth light**; it giveth understanding unto the simple.*

The reason there is so little light today is because people don't even know where to find the word of God. There are hundreds of different versions of the Bible on the market and more coming out every year. (See the author's work entitled *One Book Stands Alone* for an in depth study.)

You will not get the shining light from all of the modern versions; their foundations are flawed and too much has been perverted in them. Is there some light in the other versions? Sure, the same light you would expect from the "angel of light." If God has His word, you can be assured that Satan has his counterfeits.

Jesus said that so long as He was in the world, He was the light of the world. Today, Jesus gives the light through the word and it is to shine through every Christian's life. If you are saved, you are to be the light of this world.

LIGHT/WORKS: *Matthew 5:14* ***Ye are the light of the world****. A city that is set on an hill cannot be hid. 15 Neither do men light a candle, and put it under a bushel, but on a candlestick; and it giveth light unto all that are in the house. 16* ***Let your light so shine before men, that they may see your good works,*** *and glorify your Father which is in heaven.*

Your light is a direct reflection of your good works. The Christian must always be pointing up…always pointing toward the cross of the Saviour. People see the light through our lives, and our good works reveal this light. Jesus, the word and Christians offer the only hope for those in the world to see the true light. Satan wants to "knock your lights out." If he can't knock your lights out, he at the very minimum desires to install a spiritual dimmer switch.

As we have seen, every Christian will be rewarded at the Judgment Seat of Christ according to his works. The Bible says in Second Corinthians 5 that we will receive the things done in this body. The greater your work, maybe the brighter your light-to-be?

WORKS/JUDGMENT: *II Corinthians 5:9 Wherefore we labour, that, whether present or absent, we may be accepted of him. 10 For we must all appear before the judgment seat of Christ; that* ***every one may receive the things done in his body,*** *according to that he hath done, whether it be good or bad. 11 Knowing therefore the terror of the Lord, we persuade men; but* ***we are made manifest unto God****; and I trust also are made manifest in your consciences.*

A light that is manifest can be seen. A light that is hidden or a light that is darkened cannot be seen. We are the light of the world. The world is to look at the Christian and know that there is hope. We are to shine forth the truth of the word, the Lord and the gospel. Without each Christian doing his part, the darkness will continue to overtake the light.

At the Judgment Seat, we will receive "the things done in our bodies." The more you live by the Book, the greater your light will shine now...and the greater your light will be in heaven. When we look in the books of Revelation and Daniel, this statement will become crystal clear.

For now, remember that you (the Christian) are the light of this present world. You are commanded to let the light (Jesus/the word) so shine through you that men may see your good works and glorify God.

The judgment is yet to come when we will stand before God the Son. While on earth we are told to put on the Lord Jesus Christ—to put on the armor of light. We have no light of our own; we walked in darkness before we were saved. We are to light up this world for Jesus Christ. Our light is a direct reflection of how much Jesus shines through us. What do people see when they look at you? Do they see the light?

THE ARMOR: *Romans 13:12 The night is far spent, the day is at hand: let us therefore cast off the works of darkness, and let us **put on the armour of light**. 13 Let us walk honestly, as in the day; not in rioting and drunkenness, not in chambering and wantonness, not in strife and envying. 14 But **put ye on the Lord Jesus Christ**, and make not provision for the flesh, to fulfill the lusts thereof.*

Armor is a protective covering. Without a protective covering, you are exposed to the fiery darts of the wicked without protection. Not only are you to put on the armor (a conscious decision), but you are also told to cast off the works of darkness (anti-light). If people can't see Jesus in your life, it is because your works of darkness have dimmed the light that should be shining through your life.

Jesus is the light. We are told to put on the armor of light and to put on the Lord Jesus Christ. The effect is the same in either case…illumination! Because Jesus is in us, He should be shining through us and be seen by others. If people do not see Jesus (the light) in your life, it is because of a lack of faithfulness on your part.

Take some advice from Ephesians chapter 5. This passage instructs Christians how to walk as children of light.

WALK: *Ephesians 5:8 For ye were sometimes darkness, but **now are ye light in the Lord; walk as children of light***:

Christians are told to walk as children of light, not as children of this world and not as children of disobedience. We must understand the importance of letting people see the light in our lives. Our walk will have eternal consequences—it could determine whether or not we light up heaven.

At the Judgment Seat of Christ, Christians are going to receive an inheritance. Do all children receive the same inheritance? No! Those that live a life pleasing to the Father will be the only ones to receive any inheritance. This inheritance is directly associated with light.

INHERITANCE: *Colossians 1:12 Giving thanks unto the Father, which hath made us meet to be partakers of **the inheritance of the saints in light:***

Because of Jesus we have the opportunity to partake (or take part) in the inheritance. We are told in Second Corinthians chapter 5 that we will receive the things done in our bodies. This will be our inheritance. What we do on this earth will determine what our inheritance will be. Every child of God has an inheritance based on the fact that he is a child of God, but those who have their works burned up will suffer loss—the loss of the inheritance that was rightfully theirs because of Jesus. This is not a punishment; it is simply a loss of something that they had received because of their position as a child of God.

The Bible says if we live godly, we will suffer persecution *(II Timothy 3:12)*. If we suffer, we will reign *(II Timothy 2:12)*. If we fail to live godly and avoid the spiritual suffering, we will be denied the reign rightfully ours *(Romans 8:17)*. This is the suffering of loss—it is not a punishment. Not everyone is going to be equal in heaven. The Bible says Christians are to be *"Laying up in store for themselves a good foundation against the time to come, **that they may lay hold on eternal life" (I Timothy 6:19)***. Our foundation for salvation is Jesus Christ, but we are to be laying our own foundation for future reward through what we do and how we live.

We now need to examine two concepts: the glorious gospel of Christ and the glory of God as sources of light on this earth.

> **LIGHT/GLORY OF GOD:** *II Corinthians 4:3 But if our gospel be hid, it is hid to them that are lost: 4 In whom the god of this world hath **blinded the minds** of them which believe not, lest **the light of the glorious gospel of Christ,** who is the image of God, **should shine unto them.** 5 For we preach not ourselves, but Christ Jesus the Lord; and ourselves your servants for Jesus' sake. 6 For God, who commanded the **light** to shine out of darkness, hath shined in our hearts, to give **the light of the knowledge of the glory of God** in the face of Jesus Christ. 7 But we have this treasure in earthen vessels, that the excellency of the power may be of God, and not of us.*

We have something in our earthen vessels (our bodies)—it is the "light of the knowledge of the glory of God." What is the glory of God? There are two aspects of the glory of God. First, it is just that...God's glory or His fame and attributes. Secondly, it is *man* according to First Corinthians. Every saved man is the image and glory of God.

> **MAN/GLORY OF GOD:** *1 Corinthians 11:7 For **a man** indeed ought not to cover his head, forasmuch as he **is the image and glory of God**: but the woman is the glory of the man.*

Man is the "glory of God." And the woman is the glory of the man. Generally, the spiritual level of the home follows that of the husband. For this reason, Acts chapter 16 says *"...Believe on the Lord Jesus Christ, and thou shalt be saved, **and thy house.**"* If the spiritual maturity of the husband is nonexistent, generally that is the way the house goes. The husband –and not the wife's pastor/priest or guru— is to be the spiritual leader of his own home.

Now, let us return to the subject of heaven for a moment. Who is the glory of God? The MAN! Verses 1 and 2 reveal the context of Revelation chapter 21.

> **GLORY OF GOD/LIGHT:** *Revelation 21:1 And I saw a new heaven and a new earth: for the first heaven and the first earth were passed away; and there was no more sea. 2 And I John saw the holy city, new Jerusalem, coming down from God out of heaven, prepared as a bride adorned for her husband.*

The context is the destruction of the heaven and earth and their creation anew. John saw the New Jerusalem coming down from God. The Bible says the glory of God lights up New Jerusalem.

> *Revelation 21:22 And I saw no temple therein: for the Lord God Almighty and the Lamb are the temple of it. 23 And the city had no need of the sun, neither of the moon, to shine in it: **for the glory of God did lighten it**, and **the Lamb is the light thereof**.*

The glory of God could be just that...God's glory... or it could be **the man** as defined in *I Corinthians 11:7*. Notice that the Lamb (Jesus) and the glory of God illuminate the Holy City— New Jerusalem. Remember *II Corinthians 5:10* said that we will "receive the things done in this body." Maybe only those that allow the Lord to light up this earth through them will light up the New Jerusalem in the future.

Will man light up heaven? Daniel chapter 12 answers this question. But before we go there, we will consider the next chapter of Revelation. It connects the light with the Christian's reign.

GOD GIVES LIGHT: *Revelation 22:5 And there shall be no night there; and they need no candle, neither light of the sun; for **the Lord God giveth them light**: and **they shall reign for ever and ever**.*

How does the Lord God give the light? Who will reign with Him for ever and ever? Will Christians who are rewarded for their works on earth reflect the light that God gives them? The Lord connects the light with those who will reign with Him.

Revelation chapter 21 says that the Lamb is the light also. We are going to receive a body fashioned like Jesus' body. If He lights up heaven, won't we as well? The answer? Maybe!

*Philippians 3:21 Who shall **change our vile body**, that it may **fashioned like unto his glorious body**...*

Christ was the light of the world when He was in the world. We are to be the light of the world today. In heaven, we will all be changed and have a body like the body of our Lord and Saviour, Jesus Christ. The Lamb (Jesus) will light up heaven, and so will the glory of God. Man is the glory of God, and our glorified body is like Jesus' body. He will light up heaven, and so will we…IF we receive an inheritance that the Son makes us worthy to receive.

The Bible says that there will be no need for the sun, moon or stars for light in heaven. God is going to "give them light" and "they shall reign for ever and ever." Our vile body shall be changed like His glorious body. The next two passages equate the glory with the shining face of Moses and the change to take place in the body of a Christian.

*II Corinthians 3:7 But if the ministration of death, written and engraven in stones, was glorious, so that the children of Israel **could not stedfastly behold the face of Moses for the glory of his countenance**; which glory was to be done away: 8 How shall not **the ministration of the spirit be rather glorious**? 9 For if the ministration of condemnation be **glory**, much more the ministration of righteousness exceed in **glory**. 10 For even that which was made **glorious** had no **glory** in this respect, by reason of the **glory** that excelleth. 11 For if that which is done away was **glorious**, much more that which remaineth is **glorious**.*

*II Corinthians 3:18 But we all, with open face beholding as in a glass **the glory of the Lord**, are **changed into the same image from glory to glory**, even as by the Spirit of the Lord.*

The children of Israel could not look on the face of Moses after he had been with the Lord. Why? *Exodus 34:29* says that the *"skin of his face shone…"* when he came down from the mountain after speaking to God. If God did this to Moses (prior to the cross and the death of Jesus), the glory that will shine from the Christian will be much greater (see verse 9 above). It will "exceed in glory."

The next passage of scripture discusses the glory of the sun, moon and stars and likens them to the resurrection. Read these verses carefully and notice first the question everyone should be pondering. What type of body will the Christian receive?

*I Corinthians 15:35 But some man will say, **How are the dead raised up?** and with **what body** do they come?*

This is the issue: what type of body will the Christian have following the resurrection? Of course, each will have a glorious body, like that of our Lord. However, the connection goes much further than this. The answer to the questions of how the dead are raised and with what body follows:

*I Corinthians 15:41 There is **one glory of the sun**, and another **glory of the moon**, and another **glory of the stars: for one star differeth from another star in glory**. 42 **So also is the resurrection of the dead**. It is sown in corruption; it is raised in incorruption: 43 It is sown in dishonour; it is **raised in glory**: it is sown in weakness; it is raised in power: 44 It is sown a natural body; it is raised **a spiritual body**. There is a natural body, and there is a spiritual body.*

The bodies are likened to the glory of the sun, moon and stars. Will everyone shine alike? The Bible obviously does not and would not teach that. Verse 41 above says that one star differs from another. There will be no need of the sun, moon and stars in heaven because the resurrected bodies will provide the necessary light. If the Christian allows the Lord to light up this earth through his life, he will have the opportunity to light up heaven as well. If Christians will in fact light up heaven, will everyone light it up? No!

*Galatians 6:7 Be not deceived; God is not mocked: for whatsoever a man soweth, that shall he also reap. 8 For he that soweth to his flesh shall of the flesh reap corruption; but **he that soweth to the Spirit shall** of the Spirit **reap life everlasting**.*

Now look at Daniel chapter 12 to connect a few more pieces of the puzzle.

SOME SHALL SHINE: *Daniel 12:1 And at that time shall **Michael** stand up, the great prince which standeth for the children of thy people: and there shall be a **time of trouble**, such as never was since there was a nation even to that same time: and at that time thy people shall be delivered, every one that shall be found written in the **book**. 2 And many of them that sleep in the dust of the earth shall awake, some to **everlasting life**, and some to shame and **everlasting contempt**. 3 And they that be **wise shall shine as the brightness of the firmament; and they that turn many to righteousness as the stars for ever and ever**. 4 But thou, O Daniel, shut up the words, and seal the book, even to the time of the end: many shall run to and fro, and knowledge shall be increased.*

In order to understand when this is happening and what is taking place, we must look at some of the key words in the passage:

verse 1
Michael—the archangel
time of trouble—Jacob's trouble...the Tribulation
the book—the book of life

verse 2
The two judgments after the resurrection:
everlasting life—the redeemed
everlasting contempt—the lost

verse 3

There are two categories of light:

the wise and *those that turn many to righteousness*—(discussion follows)

for ever and ever—all eternity *(Revelation 2:5)*

So...who are the *wise* of verse 3? Proverbs reveals their identify—they are soul winners.

Proverbs 11:30 *The fruit of the righteous is a tree of life; and* ***he that winneth souls is wise***.

The wise are plainly identified as those who win souls. Who is going to be shining as the brightness of the firmament? Soul winners will be. Christians that think they are getting away with their backslidden ways are not. When their work burns up and the only thing left is a smoldering heap, it will be too late to change the outcome.

Because of the ingratitude for God's salvation and negligence of His holy justice, there is going to be inequality in heaven. Some will shine and some will not. The *wise* (soul winner) will shine as the firmament. Those who live a life which *turns people to righteousness* will shine as the stars. Barnabas and Paul at Lystra are good examples of Christians turning people to righteousness. We read in Acts of their telling some idolaters to turn to the living God (that is, to turn to righteousness).

Acts 14:15 *And saying, Sirs, why do ye these things? We also are men of like passions with you, and* ***preach unto you that ye should turn*** *from these vanities* ***unto the living God***, *which made heaven, and earth, and the sea, and all things that are therein...*

The Bible says that Paul and Barnabas told these people to turn to righteousness. Because of their lives, they both will shine as the firmament and as the stars. Both will shine for ever and ever. Will you light up heaven?

In light of the fact that the life we now live will determine our position eternally, how should we live here and now? What manner of persons ought we to be? There will be some that will shine and some that will not. Your light in heaven will be directly proportional to the light that you allow God to shine through you while you are on this earth.

Christian, will you light up heaven...or suffer loss?

Additional thought:

While editing a book on the etymology of the Chinese language, the author recognized an amazing connection between the stories found in the book of Genesis and the subject at hand. While reading the manuscript, it became evident that God clearly provided a witness of Himself and His word in this 5,500-year old language. The Chinese language consists of characters rather than letters combined to form words. It provides a profound illustration of God's mercy and grace for those that know the Bible story. For example, the Chinese character (or pictograph) for the word ***create*** has the component parts of *dust, mouth, talk* or *tell,* and *walk.*

Of course, the scriptural connection is evident to those that have a basic appreciation of the Bible. Genesis states that God *created* Adam from the dust of the ground and breathed into him the breath of life. The component parts of the Chinese character *create* reveals the Genesis account of creation. Furthermore, the character for ***garden*** (symbolizing the Garden of Eden) contains the symbols for *dust, mouth* and *two people*. This reflects the Chinese ancestors' understanding of the Genesis account of Adam and Eve being created from the dust of the ground and being placed in the Garden. The symbol for **righteousness** consists of the component parts of *Lamb* (*is under*) *I* or *me*. Could all of these characters (and the many others like them) be simple coincidences? Or do these facts reflect the Genesis account of creation and the sacrificial Lamb that would bring God's righteousness down to man?

These profound truths found in the Chinese language are used by missionaries to show Chinese men and women that the word of God was part of their ancestry long before it came into the Western world. Perhaps the most striking such example is the etymology of the Chinese symbol for **naked**.

Adam and Eve were created, of course, without clothing. Why were they not ashamed? Most people familiar with the creation story imagine that there were two totally naked bodies walking around in the Garden of Eden. However, let's see what the Bible says and what the Chinese characters depict. Some people would find it hard to believe that the Chinese language could truly further illuminate the plain truths of scripture. The Psalmist writes, *Bless the LORD, O my soul. O LORD my God, thou art very great; thou art **clothed** with honour and majesty. Who **coverest thyself with light as with a garment... (Psalm 104:1-2)***.

Notice that the Bible says that God is covered with light as a garment. Since Adam was made in the image of God, his covering could very well have matched God's own covering. Adam and Eve were not ashamed because they were clothed in righteousness (light or glory). Since they were created in the image of a glorious God, they were conceivably clothed with the same type of glorious garment.

Interestingly, the Chinese character for **clothed** consists of three smaller characters. They reveal a *man* made from *dust* with the *appearance of bright light* coming out of him. We usually think that Adam and Eve had bodies just like our own; however, the Chinese character seems to shed additional light on our understanding. Their bodies had glorious light for a covering; sin caused them to lose this light. The Chinese word for **naked** shows no light rays. The Apostle Paul tells us that we presently have a vile body that will one day be changed *(Philippians 3:21)*. We lost the covering of light in the Garden, but will one day regain it.

Ever wonder what kind of body you will have in heaven? Your life here on earth will determine how you will be clothed in heaven!

> **"The gospel of the kingdom was the good news that the promised King was soon to appear on the scene to offer the promised kingdom. In such usage the gospel of the kingdom was not primarily soteriological but eschatological in concept. The gospel of the kingdom did not offer a way of salvation, but rather offered the hope of the fulfillment of Israel's eschatological promises, which contained within them the fulfillment of the soteriological hopes..."**
>
> J. Dwight Pentecost, *Things to Come* (Findlay: Dunham Publishign, 1953) p. 272.

"The word Gospel is so familiar, its general definition as 'good news' so well understood, that its application is supposed to be uniform. When therefore we read of the Gospel of the Kingdom, the Gospel of God, the Gospel of the Grace, the Glorious Gospel, and the Everlasting Gospel, it is taken for granted that they all refer to one and the same thing. The similarity is impressed upon the average mind by the word Gospel. But however the word Gospel may make for similarity it is a mistake to imagine that the word covers one subject. On the contrary the several designations of the Gospel are of themselves the indications of marked distinctions which the Spirit impresses on us to observe.

The Gospel of the Kingdom is the good news of the Kingdom to be set up in Israel with Jerusalem as the Capital, when the Lord Jesus shall come the second time as Messiah, as Son of David...

The Gospel of Grace is the good news that Christ died for our sins, and rose again for our justification; this is peculiarly the Gospel that is to be preached in this age.

The Everlasting Gospel is the good news of that era of time which is called the Age of Ages, the Millennial era; the good news that the King of Righteousness has come and seated in Jerusalem as the King of nations, as the Prince of the Kings of the earth.

In recognizing these varied Gospels we get vistas of truth heretofore unopened and behold the keys with which many statements of Scripture otherwise dark are unlocked to our comprehension."

I.M. Haldeman, *How to Study the Bible* (NY: Charles C. Cook, 1904), p. 31.

Appendix C
Sickness and Disease

Another of the signs used by God and frequently misunderstood today is that of physical healing. The misconception that God cannot (or will not) cause sickness must be addressed. Many erroneously conclude that all sickness originates with the devil. Thus, they further conclude that God's will for a person never includes sickness. Searching the scriptures helps the student of the Bible to arrive at correct position on this matter. Consider the three following biblical truths concerning illness and healing:

1. Not all sickness is a result of sin, unbelief or being out of God's will. Jesus' own words concerning the blind from birth, referenced in John chapter 9, should prove this truth.

   *John 9:1 And as Jesus passed by, he saw a man which **was blind from his birth**. 2 And his disciples asked him, saying, Master, **who did sin**, this man, or his parents, that he was born blind? 3 Jesus answered, **Neither hath this man sinned, nor his parents**: but that the works of God should be made manifest in him.*

   This particular man was born blind so that the works of God could be seen by all. God was glorified because of this illness.

2. The Lord can cause the sickness and death of a child because of the sin of his father.

   *II Samuel 12:13 And David said unto Nathan, I have sinned against the LORD. And Nathan said unto David, The LORD also hath put away thy sin; thou shalt not die. 14 Howbeit, because by this deed thou hast given great occasion to the enemies of the LORD to blaspheme, **the child also that is born unto thee shall surely die**. 15 And Nathan departed unto his house. And **the LORD struck the child** that Uriah's wife bare unto David, and **it was very sick**.*

3. God can cause an incurable disease.

   *II Chronicles 21:14 Behold, with **a great plague will the LORD smite thy people, and thy children, and thy wives, and all thy goods**: 15 And thou shalt have **great sickness by disease** of thy bowels, until thy bowels fall out by reason of the sickness day by day.*

   Continuing in verse 18:

   *II Chronicles 21:18 And after all this **the LORD smote him in his bowels with an incurable disease**. 19 And it came to pass, that in process of time, after the end of two years, his bowels fell out by reason of his sickness: so he died of sore diseases. And his people made no burning for him, like the burning of his fathers.*

These three passages clearly illustrate that it is a false teaching to claim that God wants *everyone* healthy. The will of God, even for a Christian, may include sickness. However, some preachers still attempt to use the scripture to prove that *all* sickness occurs as a result of being out of the will of God. Here are seven biblical reasons for sickness:

Seven reasons for sickness

1. For God's glory *(John 11:1-4)*

2. Because of sin *(Romans 1:27)*

3. Rejection of the truth *(II Chronicles 26:18-21)*

4. Caused by others *(Philippians 2:25-30)*

5. To teach humility *(II Corinthians 12:7-10)*

6. To teach a lesson *(Acts 13:11)*

7. God's testing and glory *(Job 2:3, 5-8)*

Two more points to consider:

The *last days* are likened to the period of time when Pharaoh's magicians did their work. The description of the last days begins in verse 1 of the following passage. The description continues through verse 8, which mentions two of the Pharaoh's magicians (Jannes and Jambres). These two magicians withstood Moses by duplicating the signs and miracles of God. **The same atmosphere will be prevalent in the last days.**

> *II Timothy 3:1 This know also, that **in the last days** perilous times shall come. 2 For men shall be lovers of their own selves, covetous, boasters, proud, blasphemers, disobedient to parents, unthankful, unholy, 3 Without natural affection, trucebreakers, false accusers, incontinent, fierce, despisers of those that are good, 4 Traitors, heady, highminded, lovers of pleasures more than lovers of God; 5 Having a form of godliness, but denying the power thereof: from such turn away. 6 For of this sort are they which creep into houses, and lead captive silly women laden with sins, led away with divers lusts, 7 Ever learning, and never able to come to the knowledge of the truth. 8 **Now as Jannes and Jambres withstood Moses, so do these also resist the truth**: men of corrupt minds, reprobate concerning the faith.*

Second Timothy clearly describes the last days and the condition of the world today. The book of Exodus gives the actual account of Jannes and Jambres working their enchantments. They resisted the truth—God's word is truth.

> *Exodus 7:11 Then Pharaoh also called the wise men and the sorcerers: **now the magicians of Egypt, they also did in like manner with their enchantments**. 12 For they cast down every man his rod, and they became serpents: but Aaron's rod swallowed up their rods.*

God uses signs, and Satan's workers duplicate them. That which is a sign from God can also be used as an enchantment from Satan. Later in the same chapter of Exodus, we see the result of these false "signs and miracles." The people's hearts hardened against the will of God.

*Exodus 7:22 And the magicians of Egypt did so with their enchantments: **and Pharaoh's heart was hardened**, neither did he hearken unto them; as the LORD had said.*

There are many indications to prove that we are living in the "last days." The result is that the people's hearts have been similarly hardened. There has never been a spiritually colder time in the modern era. The truth no longer seems to matter. The "if it feels good, do it" philosophy runs rampant. Recent elections and scandals reveal that a strong economy ($) is all that matters. Self-gratification and the love of money are the two predominant ruling forces today.

Although sickness may be God-ordained, the following verse is nevertheless a good prayer. However, just because a person does not have good health does not mean that he is out of the will of God.

***III John 2** Beloved, I wish above all things that thou mayest prosper and **be in health**, even as thy soul prospereth.*

As is evident from the scripture, God can and will use sickness in order to reveal His will and glory. Any person or group who claims that God's will *never* includes sickness simply does not know the Bible. One must be cautious not to believe something just because it seems logical to the natural man. Sometimes the most logical conclusions are nothing more than Satan's lies *(Isaiah 55:8)*.

***I Corinthians 2:14** But the **natural man** receiveth not the things of the Spirit of God: for they are foolishness unto him: neither can he know them, because they are spiritually discerned.*

Glossary of Terms

apostles' doctrine—The standard of conduct applicable to the early Acts believers *(Acts 2:42)*. A primary article of this doctrine included claiming no ownership of any personal belongings *(Acts 4:32)*.

ascension—A reference to the Lord Jesus Christ's bodily ascension into heaven following His resurrection *(Acts 1:9, Mark 16:19)*.

baptism—(1) There are at least seven different types of baptism in the Bible. (2) *Believer's baptism* is one of the two ordinances of the local church *(I Corinthians 11:2)*. It is the immersion of the believer in water, *following* salvation, testifying to the believer's identity with his Lord Jesus Christ. Believer's baptism is *not* an instrument of grace (not a means to salvation), but pictures the gospel—the death, burial and resurrection of the Lord Jesus Christ. (3) Another type of baptism is the new believer's baptism by the Holy Spirit of God into the Body of Christ *(I Corinthians 12:13)*. This is a spiritual baptism not involving water or human assistance.

Body of Christ—Also known as the Church. It includes all believers in the Church Age regardless of denominational or church affiliation *(Colossians 1:18-24)*.

bondage—Taking away a person's liberty during the Church Age by "requiring" the administration of the Old Testament ordinances such as circumcision, the observing of certain days, abstaining from meats, etc. *(Galatians 4:9)*.

Church, The—See the Body of Christ. Not a reference to the Roman Catholic Church as an institution.

Church Age—The period of time when God saves a person through simple faith and seals the believer with the Holy Spirit until his body is redeemed *(Ephesians 1:13, 4:30)*. Paul's thirteen epistles, bearing his name as the first word, primarily cover this period of time. This period will end with the catching out of the saints (Rapture of the Church) *(I Thessalonians 4:13-18)*. Paul is the spokesman for this age *(II Timothy 2:7)*.

church, local—(In the New Testament) A church is any number of souls united together for the purpose of evangelizing the world with the Gospel of the Grace of God. They meet together for preaching, fellowship, and administering the two ordinances of the local church (baptism and the Lord's Supper). A pastor holds the main office of bishop over the church.

circumcision—(1) The Jewish custom of cutting away the foreskin of the male children *(Genesis 17:9-14)*. This Old Testament ordinance is no longer required during the Church Age *(Galatians 6:15)*. (2) The term is also used to represent the Jews as a group *(Galatians 2:7)*. (3) Under the New Testament, it refers to the operation of God made without hands—the cutting away of the flesh from the soul *(Colossians 2:10-14)*.

Conscience, Age of—The second dispensation of the Old Testament. The period begins in Genesis chapter 4 and ends in chapter 8. The knowledge of evil (sin) awakened man's conscience. During this period, man was to do all known good and to refrain from all known evil. His conscience was to be his guide. The worldwide flood during Noah's day ended this age and began the next (the Age of Government).

dispensations—The different plans for different periods of time in God's dealings with man *(I Corinthians 9:17)*. In each dispensation, God reveals something new about Himself. Each dispensation is a distinctive economy in the outworking of God's purpose and plan. It reveals God's purpose, plan or attributes, man's test and ultimate failure, and God's judgment. When applied in this fashion, the Bible is divided into at least nine dispensations with each period unique from the others. However, Eternity Future is timeless and could be considered ageless.

doctrine—Sound teaching based on the word of God. One is saved by believing the right doctrine and is to separate himself from those who teach false doctrine. The Bible is basically a history book that gives the doctrine for each age. An indicator of the last days will be a turning away from *sound* doctrine *(II Timothy 4:3)*.

endure to the end—A Tribulation Period requirement. One that endures to the end will not take the Mark of the Beast *(Matthew 24:13, Hebrews 10:26)*.

eternal security—The result of the spiritual birth upon salvation. Eternal security has a beginning, but no end. The Holy Spirit's indwelling of the believer at his acceptance of the Lord Jesus Christ as Saviour seals his eternal destiny *(Ephesians 1:13)*.

Eternity Future, Age of—The period following the Age of the Kingdom when the new heaven and earth are created and the old ones are destroyed by fire. This period follows the Millennial reign of the Lord Jesus Christ. Man is pure, free from sin and able to worship and serve God perfectly forever.

Faith of Jesus Christ—Refers to the faith that saves the believer and the faith by which he also lives *(Galatians 2:16)*.

gospel—Good tidings or good news *(Isaiah 61:1, Luke 4:18)*. The Gospel of the Grace of God presents the Lord Jesus as Saviour because of His death, burial and resurrection. This gospel is the only means whereby a person can be saved. It differs from the Gospel of the Kingdom *(Matthew 4:23)*.

Gospel books—The books of Matthew, Mark, Luke and John are commonly referred to as the Gospels. Each of these books has a distinct emphasis, but the four of them collectively cover the earthly ministry of the Lord Jesus Christ and His twelve apostles.

Gospel of the Kingdom—The gospel presented to the nation of Israel by John the Baptist, the Lord Jesus Christ, and the twelve apostles *(Matthew 4:23)*. This gospel is found in the four Gospel books and differs from the Gospel of the Grace of God *(Acts 20:24)*.

Government, Age of—The third dispensation of the Old Testament. The period begins in Genesis 9 and ends in chapter 11. Man was now to govern himself and the animal world by exercising judgment and justice for any shedding of man's blood. This governmental authority extended over his fellow man. The Tower of Babel and then the calling out of Abraham end this age and initiate the Age of Patriarchs.

Great White Throne Judgment—The judgment prior to the establishment of the new heaven and earth. The unsaved will be resurrected to this judgment and will join the Tribulation and Millennial saints *(Revelation 20:11)*. This judgment follows the Millennium, but occurs prior to the formation of the new heaven and new earth.

hyper-dispensational—also referred to as ultra-dispensational. A term applicable to the practice of dividing the Bible in excess, or beyond God's method of dispensational Bible study. The most prominent example involves dividing the Bible to eliminate the application of the two Church Age ordinances to the local church—water baptism and the Lord's Supper.

Innocence, Age of—The first dispensation of the Old Testament. The period begins in Genesis 1 and ends in chapter 3. Man is in a state of innocence concerning evil. God places man (Adam) in a perfect environment (the Garden of Eden). The Lord gives only one command concerning the Tree of the Knowledge of Good and Evil. Nevertheless, man fails; thus ends the Age of Innocence and begins the Age of Conscience.

Jew First—Refers to the gospel presentation during the early part of Paul's ministry covered by the book of Acts. He endeavored to reach the Jew first and then to the Gentile peoples.

Jews Only—The presentation of the Gospel of the Kingdom during the Lord's earthly ministry and shortly thereafter. This presentation was made by the Lord, His apostles and the disciples *(Matthew 15:24)*.

Kingdom, Age of—The eighth dispensation which follows the Age of Readiness. It will last one thousand years and the Lord Jesus Christ will rule on this earth with a rod of iron. Satan will be in the pit and unable to deceive man for the first time since the Garden of Eden. At the end of this age, Satan will be loosed for a short time and allowed to deceive the multitudes. God will then instantaneously destroy them all with fire out of heaven.

Law, Age of—The fifth dispensation of the Old Testament. The period begins in Exodus 20 and ends in the early part of each of the four Gospel books. God's commands are given in great detail along with a variety of punitive and corrective actions to be taken when any of the laws was violated. In His mercy and grace, God also provided an elaborate system of sacrifices and offerings to allow a person to remain blameless under the law. The age ends with the coming forth of John the Baptist; however, the law is not abolished.

legalism—Unlawful application of the Old Testament ordinances to the local church, especially circumcision and the Levitical dietary laws *(Galatians 6:13)*.

liberty—Applicable to the Church Age Christian because he is made free from the Old Testament ordinances *(I Corinthians 8:8)*.

Lord's Supper—One of the two ordinances of the local New Testament church clearly delineated in *I Corinthians 11:20-24*. It is named *supper;* therefore, appropriately administered during the evening services. Should not be performed in any ritualistic fashion, but as often as the Lord leads the church to do so.

Mark of the Beast—A physical mark, used for purposes of commerce, that must be avoided by everyone during the Tribulation Period *(Revelation 19:20)*.

Millennium—Term indicating the thousand-year period of Christ's future reign on this earth before the Great White Throne Judgment. Satan will be bound during this time and unable to deceive the nations. At the end of this period he will be loosed for a short time and then be immediately consumed by fire *(Revelation 20:3-9)*.

Missionary Epistles—Four of Paul's epistles that have particular and peculiar application during his Acts missionary journeys. These books begin in Romans and end with the book of Galatians. Some of the unusual features of these epistles include the practice of going to the Jew first and performing miracles, signs and wonders.

mystery—Designation for the unrevealed Gospel of the Grace of God *(Ephesians 6:19)*. The mystery was supernaturally revealed to the Apostle Paul following the cross. Prior to the cross, this gospel was spoken, but not revealed *(Luke 18:31-34)*.

New Testament books—The books of Matthew through Revelation. The New Testament did not actually begin until after the death of the Testator—the Lord Jesus Christ *(Hebrews 9:16)*. Although the New Testament actually begins toward the end of the four Gospel books, to avoid confusion, the division is made between Malachi and Matthew to avoid confusion.

Old Testament books—The books of Genesis through Malachi. Although the Old Testament does not actually end until sometime in each of the four Gospel books *(Hebrews 9:16)*, for ease of understanding, the division is made between Malachi and Matthew.

Patriarchs, Age of—The fourth dispensation of the Old Testament. The period begins in Genesis 12 and ends around Exodus 19. God calls out a man willing to obey His commands. His name is Abram, later changed to Abraham. God promised blessings to and through Abraham. The blessings were passed down through his seed beginning with his son, Isaac. God gave Abraham and his seed a sign—that of circumcision. God closes the Age of Patriarchs and begins the Age of the Law with Moses.

Paul—The apostle known as Saul before God changed his name *(Acts 13:9)* shortly following his conversion in Acts 9. The Lord revealed the Gospel of God's Grace, which had remained a mystery prior to that time, to Paul *(Ephesians 3:3)*. The Church is commanded to follow him as he followed the Lord Jesus Christ *(I Corinthians 11:1)*.

Paul's Epistles—Thirteen books bearing Paul's name as the first word in each book. These books begin with Romans and end with Philemon.

Pentecost—One of the seven Jewish feast days. See question #19 in chapter 17 of this book.

Peter—One of the twelve apostles who preached the Gospel of the Kingdom and primarily ministered to the Jews. Like the Lord, his primary ministry involved going to the Jew *(Matthew 15:24, John 20:21)*.

Prison Epistles—The nine books written by the Apostle Paul (Ephesians through Philemon) that have particular application following his Acts ministry.

proselyte—A convert to Judaism *(Acts 2:10)* prior to the Church Age. Also used in a generic sense to refer to a Christian convert.

Rapture—(1) The actual word is not found in the Bible, but denotes the "catching out of the saints" as revealed in *I Thessalonians 4:13-18*. The Church Age will end with this event. (2) The Bible also includes a Rapture of the Tribulation saints.

Readiness, Age of—This age begins with John the Baptist and ends at the Second Coming of the Lord Jesus Christ. The primary purpose of this time is to ready a people for the return of the Lord. The Church Age parenthetically divides this age into two distinct parts. The first period ends when the Church Age begins. Following the Rapture of the Church, the Age of Readiness resumes until the Lord's return.

remnant—The Jewish population to which Paul preferentially ministered—presenting to them the Gospel of the Grace of God—during his Acts missionary journeys. Once the Jewish remnant was reached in any area, God began treating Jew and Gentile alike *(Romans 11:5)*.

right division—The true method of Bible study. This is the practice of obediently following the biblical command *(II Timothy 2:15)* to divide (not rearrange) the Bible into different periods. These periods of division are based on the primary person speaking in the scriptures and the main group(s) being addressed. Right division is the application of dispensationalism to Bible study. Due to the ever increasing rise of the cults and perversion of truth, God seems to have revealed its necessity during these last days.

Roman's Road—A collection of verses from the book of Romans used to show a lost person his need to repent of his sins and trust in the Lord Jesus Christ as Saviour.

salvation—Occurs at a point in time when a lost sinner accepts Jesus Christ as Saviour. It is the redemption of a person from the eternal damnation of hell. The Lord Jesus Christ provided the only means whereby a person can be saved from the penalty of sin either before or after the cross. The application of His shed blood is the only means by which a person is admitted into heaven with a holy God. Although the "content of faith" may differ through the various ages, the shed blood of the Lord Jesus Christ is one constant throughout every period.

scriptures—(1) Denotes the books of the Old and New Testaments. The word of God found complete in the sixty-six books of the King James Bible for English-speaking people. (2) Also the individual verses within the same.

Second Coming—The bodily return of the Lord Jesus Christ to the earth following the end of the Tribulation Period, when He sets up His visible, earthly Kingdom for one thousand years. Also referred to as the Second Advent.

semi-chronological—The Bible as set forth and arranged by God, especially as applied to the New Testament. The New Testament follows this format more than the Old Testament since the New Testament saint is commanded to rightly divide the scriptures.

signs of an apostle—A sign is a token; a representation; or a witness *(Genesis 1:14)*. A sign is also a miracle performed as evidence of the truth of the message being presented *(Exodus 4:8, Acts 2:22)*. The signs of an apostle were given in Mark chapter 16 and designated as such in the book of Corinthians *(II Corinthians 12:12)*.

spiritualizing—The act of applying scripture in a non-doctrinal manner. It is the opposite of applying the passage in a literal sense.

spokesman—A person chosen by God to present His message to the world or to a group of people chosen to receive it during a particular age or time period.

transition—The period of time moving from one dispensational age to the next. The book of Acts is an excellent representation of a transition book and period.

Tribulation or Great Tribulation—A period of seven years when the Anti-Christ will be revealed and the Lord will pour out His wrath upon all of the inhabitants of the earth *(Revelation 6:17)*. This will occur just prior to His Second Coming and will follow the Rapture of the Church. It will be a time when Israel will be preparing to receive her Messiah and persecution against God's people will be executed worldwide. The Tribulation saint will be required to faithfully endure to the end of this very difficult period.

Two Witnesses—The scriptures indirectly identify these two Tribulation preachers as Moses and Elijah *(Revelation 11:3)*. (See Appendix A for a discussion pertaining to their identity.)

unconditional security—See Eternal security.

witnessing—The act of proclaiming the good news of the Lord Jesus Christ including the fact that He died on the cross for our sins and paid the sin debt owed by every sinner.

works—The Gospel of the Grace of God *(Acts 20:4)* emphasizes that true salvation is a free gift of God's grace through faith alone *without works*. Any addition (of works) to the Gospel of Grace is cursed of God *(Galatians 1:6-9)*. Following salvation, faith *produces* good works in every believer. However, the *fruit* of salvation *(Galatians 5:22)* should not be confused with the *root* of salvation which is grace *(Ephesians 2:8-10)*.

Index

A

A.D. 100 88, 117, 120, 129, 131, 132, 136
Aaron 73, 124
Abel 173
Abimelech 181
Abraham 141, 178, 179, 180
  believed God 179
  blessings as stars 178
Abraham's Bosom 170
Abram 177
abundance of the revelations 66
Acts 72, 80, 83, 196, 204
  introduction 7
  overview 10
Acts chapter 13, 18, 28 102–103
Adam 172, 226
Agabus 141, 209
age, components of each 170
Age of Conscience 173–175
  defined 252
  judgment on body 177
Age of Eternity Future 193
  defined 252
Age of Government 175–177
  defined 252
  judgment on soul 177
Age of Grace 150, 152
Age of Innocence 171–173
  defined 253
  judgment on man's spirit 177
Age of Kingdom, defined 253
Age of Law, defined 253
Age of Patriarchs, defined 254
Age of Patriarchs/Promise 177–181
Age of Readiness 185–188
  defined 255
Age of the Church 188–191, 191
Age of the Kingdom 192
Age of the Law 183

Agrippa, King 92
all things common 53, 83
ambassadors for Christ 192
Ananias and Sapphira 53, 84, 133, 197
angel of light 140
angels 192
animals 93, 175
another Gospel, 76, defined (Scofield) 168
Anti-Christ 134, 136
Antioch of Pisidia 130
apostle 138–140, 145
  requirements 139
Apostle of the Gentiles 62, 137, 140
Apostle Paul 254
  against baptism? 201
  establishing the believer 74
  appointed a preacher, apostle and teacher 63
  baptized his converts 201
  central figure of N.T. (Haldeman) 72
  charge to the rich 52
  Charles C. Ryrie 20
  chosen vessel 62
  command to follow him 79
  commission 216
  doctrine of the Church (Haldeman) 73, 127
  first name in books 17
  fulfilling the word of God 67, 73
  gospel gone into all the world 54
  gospel received by revelation 67
  his preaching 43
  hold the traditions 74
  in bonds 90
  in Christ before me 166
  introductory scriptures 18–19
  judge the secrets of men 76
  Minister of Jesus Christ 64
  missionary epistles 87
  ordained a preacher and an apostle 63
  our foundation 64

Apostle Paul (continued)
    our pattern 65
    persecuted the Church 166
    preached the faith once destroyed 166
    present the church 78
    previously Saul 17
    prison epistles 88
    prisoner of Jesus Christ 90
    reveals the mysteries 24
    revelation of the mystery 74
    salutation in all epistles 29
    snake bit 128
    synagogue first 91
    Trophimus left at Miletum sick 130
    who Paul is 61
apostles 137
    eleven 119
    false 140
Apostles and Prophets 137
apostles' doctrine 83, defined 251
apostleship of the circumcision 107
application of Right Division 83
appointed 63
ascension 120, 251
Ashtor 101
Asia Minor 102
    forbidden to preach 130
astrology 104
at this present time 93
attributes of God unchanged 169, 171

B

Babel 176
Babylonian feast 101
baptism 87, 104, 161, 186, 198, 201, 202, 206
    defined 251
    denied by Bullinger (Ryrie) 161
    infants 202
    John's 203
    of repentance 186
    ordinance of the church 80
    unquenchable fire 206
baptismal regeneration 202
baptize with the Holy Ghost 206
baptized into one body 190
barbarians 128, 129
Barnabas 138, 141
basis for salvation, death of Christ (Ryrie) 226
Baxter, J. Sidlow, Kingdom of Heaven 43

Beast 49, 134, 135
Bible study
    all scripture 2
    literal interpretation 79
    primary group addressed 3
    right division approach 1
    what if 171
biblical numerology, number seven 6
bishop 137, 144
blasphemy 102
Body of Christ 6, 18, 137, 190, 251
    broken down middle wall 167
    Hebrews 34
    when began dividing point (Ryrie) 166
bondage 96, 150, 153, 162
    defined 251
    not entangled again 162
    what is 161
Book of James 47–54
Book of John, gospel 113
Book of Mark, gospel 113
Book of Matthew, gospel 114
breaking bread 207-208
Bullinger, began church after Acts (Ryrie) 161
burning bush 206

C

call no man your father 148
capital punishment 37
carnal Christianity from spiritualized teachings 79
casting out devils 119, 138
catching out of the saints 4
ceremonial law 159
Certified Public Accountant 154
Chafer, Lewis Sperry
    dispensations 150
    kingdom teachings 52
    on salvation 116
    position in Christ 109
    teachings of Christ 113
chains 67, 104
    Paul's journey to Rome 89
charismatic 197
Christ sent me not to baptize 201
Christmas 101, 162
Church
    began at Pentecost (Ryrie) 166
    Body of Christ 6, 251
    built on foundation of Apostles 167

Church (continued)
   Gentiles fellowheirs 167
   revealed by Paul (Pettingill) 19
   same body 167
      Paul persecuted 166
      yet future in Matthew (Scofield) 9
Church Age 4, 6, 18, 19, 117
   defined 251
   introduction 8
   Revelation 4:1 208
church in Bible, small section (Haldeman) 104
Church patterned after Acts 196
circumcision 76, 95–96, 107, 159, 162
   defined 251
   gospel of 85, 107
   of Timothy 94
   of Titus 95
clergy 147
collection 83
commission 202
communes, found in Acts 80, 84
communism 84
confusion, God is not the author of 82
conscience 173
   weak brother's 164
   seared 97
consider Paul's sayings 81
content of faith
   changes (Ryrie) 226
   scripture teaches (Ryrie) 213
continents 176
contradictions 200
   reconciling the 33
converts 223
conviction 220, 224
Corinthian Church 139
Cornelius 68, 93
covenant
   Abrahamic 180
   Noahic 174
covenant theology
   distinguished (Ryrie) 226
CPA 154

D

Damascus 67, 139
David 247
   anointed with Spirit 55
   sin with Bathsheba 150

David's prayer, take not spirit (Haldeman) 125
deacon 137
deadly wound 134-135
declare the gospel 18
dietary laws, Jewish 96
dispensation 68
dispensation of the grace of God 108
Dispensational Ages
   New Testament 185
   Old Testament 169
dispensational study, key to Bible (Haldeman) 149
dispensationalist 80, 149
dispensations 169, 185
   consistent interpretation (Ryrie) 155
   defined 252
   Isaac Watts 184
   sheds light on Bible (Chafer) 150
   Spirit indwelling (Rice) 194
doctrine, defined 252
doctrines of devils 160
dual baptisms 199

E

early and latter rain 50–51
Easter 101, 162
Egypt 122
Elijah 225
end of the law for righteousness 155
endure to the end 252
Enoch 226
Ephesians, beginning of prison epistles 88
epistles of Paul, develop Church doctrine (Scofield) 77
establish the law 152
establish their own righteousness 155
eternal security 252
Ethiopian eunuch 199
Eutycus 207
Evangelist 137, 143
Eve 172
Everlasting Gospel 46, 192, 246
   defined (Scofield) 168
eye for an eye 36
Ezra, mercy and grace 150

F

faith 57, 98, 121, 125, 189
   defined 118
   gift from God (Spurgeon) 61
   His 57

faith (continued)
  of Jesus Christ 57
  personal 118
faith of Jesus Christ 189, 252
  boldness and access 59
  justified by 59
  promise of 59
  righteousness comes through 58
faith of the Lord Jesus Christ 59
false brethren 96
false prophets 135, 142
feast days under the law 205
fellowcitizens with the saints 167
fertility 101
fire 135
  of Acts 2 206
flood 174
follow Paul 79
followers of me 18
foundation 64, 144, 145
fulfill the law 158
fulfilling the word of God 67

G

garden economy 173
Garden of Eden 171
Gentiles 17, 18, 40, 61, 68
  wild olive tree 167
  Christ refused (Haldeman) 194
gibberish 128
Gideon 124
giving to God's works 38, 83
godly sorrow 222
God's plan for man changes 35
God's unchanging character 34–35
good tidings 186
  gospel defined 107
Gospel 76, 105, 186, 202
  declared by Paul 71
  defined 107, 252
  defined (Scofield) 168
  differing types (Haldeman) 246
  four forms of (Scofield) 168
  hid from the twelve 26
  hid to the lost 25
  hidden from all men 68
  in trust 71
  my 54
  of the circumcision 76

Gospel (continued)
  of the uncircumcision 76
  preaching in all the world 54
  taught to Paul by none 67
  understood none 110
Gospel books, defined 252
gospel of the circumcision 85, 107
Gospel of the Grace of God 11, 19, 42, 44, 105, 223
  Christ died for us (Haldeman) 246
  defined (Scofield) 168
  hidden from the twelve 45
  how of Christ's death 23
Gospel of the Kingdom 26–27, 42, 76, 108-109, 135, 187, 246
  defined 252, (Scofield) 168
  John R. Rice 27
  John R. Rice, future application 29
  not soteriological (Haldeman) 245
  present and future (Scofield) 168
gospel of the uncircumcision 85, 107
Gospels 3
  defined 7
  overview 9
government 175
grace 150
  defined 170
  in the epistles (Scofield) 15
grace of God, displayed (Ryrie) 20
graffed in among them 167
Great Commission, The 12
Great Tribulation 4
  defined 256
Great White Throne Judgment 4, 192
  defined 253
Greek language, utilized to change Bible 161

H

Haldeman, I.M.
  Christ to lost sheep 194
  Church occupies small part of Bible 104
  Church revealed to Paul 77
  dispensational truth key 149
  doctrine of Church, committed to Paul 73
  gospel is good news 246
  indwelling Spirit 125
  kingdom postponed 127
  law and gospel 210
  Paul is central figure in N.T. 72

healing 94, 119, 129, 187, 247
    first 123
    included in the Kingdom Gospel 28
heaven
    individual's righteousness insufficient 154
    only through the blood 26
Hebrews
    authored by 29
    future application 33
    message of 28–32
    millennial rest 31
    twice mentions church 32
heresy 116
High Priest 21
his faith 183
history of the signs 122
holy city 193
holy days 159, 162
Holy Father 148
Holy Ghost, received through prayer 197
Holy Ghost fell on them 198
Holy Spirit
    indwelling (Haldeman) 125
    pattern for receiving 200
    sealed until redemption 55
Hosea, early and latter rain 51
Hyper-dispensationalism, defined 149, 253
hyper-dispensationalist 89, 150-152, 158, 164-165
    eliminates baptism 80
hyper-divide 89, 149
hyperdispensationalism, roots of 87

I

idle tales 111
idolatry 100, 223
immunity to poison 138
impenitent heart 216
in Christ, none under law (Chafer) 109
incurable disease 247
infidel 85
inheritance 86
innocence 171
iIntroduction to Paul's epistles (Scofield) 77
Isaac 178
Isaac Watts, dispensationalist 184
Israel
    broken off 47, 91
    cast away 29
Israel's problem 227

J

Jannes and Jambres 248
James 179
    authorship date 48
    patience 50
    rich condemned 51
    timing of book (Scofield) 48
Jew first 40, 62, 86, 87, 91, 117, 131, 253
Jew first principle 92
Jews only 39, 61, 93, 253
Jews require a sign 117, 121
John the Baptist 185, 186, 206
    his preaching 42
John's baptism 198
Jones, Jim 84
Joshua 14
Judas Iscariot 110, 141
judge the secrets of men 76
judgment and justice 175
Judgment Seat of Christ 234–245

K

King David 183
King James Bible 2, 210
King Saul 56, 183
kingdom 7, 27, 186
    not from hence 37
    Paul preached 195
    postponed 127
Kingdom Age 4
    tribulation teachings (Chafer) 52
Kingdom Gospel 26–27, 186
Kingdom of God, spriritual properties 195
kingdom of God 109, 195, seek first 187
Kingdom of heaven,
    spiritual properties 196
    at hand 27
    future, historical, visible (Baxter) 43
knowledge 132, 133
Korah 73
Koresh, David 84

L

laity 147
languages 177
laughing revival 142

law 150, 152, 155, 183, 186, 204
   According to the glorious gospel 158
   and the church 229
   animal sacrifices 228
   applicable portions 162
   brings the knoweledge of sin 220
   debtor to do the whole law 163
   effect of the cross 155
   establish 159
   if a man use it lawfully 158
   mine own righteousness 154
   of righteousness 154
   righteous person 154
   schoolmaster 58, 60, 183
law and the gospel, description (Haldeman) 210
law and the prophets 141
legalism 153, 253
letter of the law 229
Levitical Law 97, 99
liberty 99, 150, 153, 253
   biblical not license to sin 163
   limitations while the world stands 164
light237-244
   Chinese characters 244
little wine 130
live peaceably 37
location sensitive 102
looked forward to the cross 25-26, 170
   Adam not (Ryrie) 226
   How God saved 170
   scripture does (Scofield) 77
Lord Jesus Christ
   His preaching 42
   sent to Israel 22
Lord's Supper 87, 104, 105, 161, 208
   defined 253
   denied by Bullinger (Ryrie) 161
   frequency 207
   ordinance of the church 80
Lordship Salvation 214
Losing the Spirit of God 55
lying wonders 134

M

Mark of the Beast. 51
meats, nothing unclean 98
Melchizedek 40
mercy 150
   defined 170
   taken from Saul 56

Miletum 130
millennium 4, 6, 8, 11, 253
minister 64
missionary epistles 87, 165, 254
missionary journeys 10
missions, God's heartbeat 12
modern versions 199, 210
Mormons 140
Mosaic Law 101
Moses
   14, 73, 79, 122, 123, 124, 181, 182, 206, 225
Mount Sinai 183
murmur 182
my Gospel, defined (Scofield) 168
mystery 23–24, 44, 108, 110, 254
   committed to Paul (Scofield) 44
   given to Paul (Rice) 45
   hidden in God (Haldeman) 77
   hidden wisdom 70
   now revealed 69
   revealed by Paul (Scofield) 77
   revealed to apostles and prophets 144
   revelation of 71, 74

N

nailed to the cross 101,160
Nathan 247
natural man 249
neither Jew nor Greek 47
New Covenant, Jeremiah 31 34
new heaven and earth 193
new Jerusalem 193
New Testament
   course of 33
   dispensational ages 185
   true beginning 1
Noah 14, 21, 174
   preacher of righteousness 175
   found grace 174
none of the princes 110

O

offering 64, 83
Old Testament 8
   defined 7
   Dispensational ages 169
   for ensamples and examples 165
   for our learning 165
   vail done away 25

Old Testament books 254
one body by the cross 167
ordained 63
ordinances 105, 159, 208
    abolished 159
    blotting out 101
    freedom from the 163
    of the law ended 159, 162
    of the churches 80

P

Paradise, located in heart of earth 170
parenthetically, Church Age insert 188
Passover 181, 205
pastor and teacher 137, 143, 144
patience of Job 49
patience of the saints 49
pattern 65, 82
Paul 138, 204, 209
    first word in epistles 62
Paul in Roman prison 90
Paul only 210
Paul's citizenship 209
Paul's epistles, defined 254
penance 222
Pentecost 84, 205, 254
    Jewish Feast Day 72
Pentecost, J. Dwight, Gospel of the Kingdom 245
Pentecostal experience 205
People's Temple 84
perfected 131
    defined 88
Peter 17, 66, 69, 79, 93, 127, 145, 204, 254
    apostleship of the circumcision 107
    following him 202
    looking forward to the cross 25
    message of the Kingdom 108
    no earthly possessions 53, 84
    Paul hard to understand 77
    rebuked Lord 114
    set aside (Haldeman) 127
    shadow healing 127
    sheet with animals 68
    speaking to Jews in Acts 2 205
    wondering in himself 111
Pettingill, William L.
    truth of church, revealed by Paul 19
Pharaoh 122, 181
Pharaoh's magicians 248

Philip 143, 196
Philippian jailer, repentance 218
present distress 94
priest, no mention in Paul's epistles 146
prison epistles 88, 254
progressive revelation
    dispensationalism recognizes (Ryrie) 226
    God's nature (Ryrie) 213
prophecy 132
    shall fail 142
prophet 137, 142, 145
purpose of the law 157

R

Rapture 192
    catching out of the saints 4
    defined 254
reaching the Jewish remnant 91
Readiness Age 4
    overview 11
rearrange, versus rightly divide 88
reformation 214
regions beyond 131
relief unto the brethren 85
remnant
        40, 93, 102, 117, 128, 130, 131, 136, 209
    defined 255
    reaching the Jewish 91
repent 215
repentance 200, 213, 214–222, 221, 223
    accompanied by sorrow for sin 222
    city of Athens 215
    defined (Adams) 214
    exceeding sinfulness of sin 220
    Gentiles granted repentance 215
    he repented and went 221
    idol worship 215
    leads to conversion 214
    Philippian jailer 218
    repented the Lord 219
    results of 223
    sinner's prayer 216
    thief 217
    unrepentant unbelievers 215
    what is 218
repentant sinner 214
restore kingdom to Israel 196
resurrection
    shine as brightness of firmament 243
    what body 243

revelation 106, 132
reverend 147
Rice, John R.
    dispensations 194
    Gospel of the Kingdom 27, 29
    mysteries given to Paul 45
    Scofield Reference best 184
right division 115, 121, 255
righteousness, Christ's 154
Righteousness of God 58
ritualism 207
rod 124, 122, 192
Roman's Road 22, 255
Rome 128, 131, 142
rule of first mention 219
Ryrie, Charles C
    Apostle Paul and grace 20
    basis for salvation 226
    Bullinger's teachings 161
    dispensationalism compared 166
    dispensationalism, unites parts into whole 155
    Isaac Watts 184
    ways of salvation 213

S

sabbath day requirements 36
Sabbath days 159, 162
sacrifices 184
Salvation and works 231
salvation 255
    believing on the Lord 214
    through the blood 78
    ways of (Ryrie) 213
    work of God (Chafer) 116
salvation of Israel, based on Christ's death 116
Sam Jones 220
Satan 133
Saul, Ananias laid hands on 197
save money for posterity 86
Scofield Reference Bible
    best in world (Rice) 184
    doctrine of the church 9
    doctrines of grace 15
    Gospel, four forms of 168
    Intro to Paul's epistles 77
    introduction to James 48
    mystery committed to Paul 44
scripture given by inspiration 149
scriptures 255

Second Advent 4
Second Coming 11, 27, 255
    introduction 4
second death 212
seducing spirits 97, 160
seeking 187
semi-chronological 2
    defined 255
seminaries
    spiritualized method of teaching 79
serpents 119, 138
Seventh Day Adventist 159
shipwrecked 128
sickness, seven reason for 248
sign 121, 128
    first 123
    latter 123
sign of circumcision 180
signs 91, 92, 99, 117, 118, 125, 127
    confirming the word 139
Signs and Wonders
    Old Testament 117
    false 133
    New Testament 127
signs of an apostle 119, 120, 138
    defined 255
Silas 141
Simeon 141
sinner, scripturally defined 211
sinner's prayer 219, 224
Smith, Joseph 140
snake handling 122
snakebite 128
sodomites 104
sold their possessions 83
sought it not by faith 154
Spain 89
special meats 96, 159
Spirit
    David prays to keep 56
    departed from Saul 56
Spirit baptizes 191
spiritual death 212
spiritualized method of teaching, seminaries use 79
spiritualizing, defined 255
Spokesman, of the Old Testament 13–14
spokesman 82
    defined 255
    introduction 13

spokesman (continued)
   of the book of Acts 17
   of the Church Age 17
   of the Gospels 15
   of the Millennium 16–17
   of the Readiness/Tribulation 15–16
   primary today 79
Spurgeon, C.H., faith as a gift 61
Stephen's message 43
stumblingblock 99
supernatural knowledge 132
synagogue 92, 95

T

teachings of Christ
   threefold division (Chafer) 113
televangelist 84, 157
television 127, 129
The Great White Throne Judgment 232–233
they remembered his words 111
thief on cross, repentance 217
time is short 94
time-sensitive 92, 93, 102
timing of Romans 89
Timothy 94–95, 129
tithing 40
to the Jew first 87
to the twelve tribes 47
tongues 91, 94, 104, 119, 121, 123, 132, 138
   defined 203
   unknown 203
tongues are for a sign 121
tower 176
transition
   7, 10, 61, 92, 93, 97, 100, 108, 198, 204
   defined 255
transition record 102
tree 171
Tribulation 8, 11, 15, 49, 134, 192, 206
   rich condemned 51–53
Trophimus 130
try the spirits 121, 142
turn the cheek 37
turning points 102
Twelve Apostles, their preaching 43
two olive trees 225
Two Witnesses 54, 192, 225–226
   defined 256
   introduction & identity 16

U

ultra-dispensationalism
   related with dispesationalism (Ryrie) 166
   begin church after Pentecost (Ryrie) 161
unbelief 122
uncircumcision 76
   gospel of 85, 107
unclean animals 68, 97, 99
   Cornelius 93
unconditional security 256
under the law 153
understanding in all things 19, 81
unknown god 204
unknown tongues 204

V

void 152, 153

W

Waco, Texas 84
walk, learn how to 75
washings of Hebrews
   not baptism 80, 161
water baptism 161
water become blood 123
weak and beggarly elements 100
weak brother 97
while the world is standing 99
Wicked 134
wild olive tree 167
witnessing 87
   defined 256
wonders 117, 128
word, committed to Paul 72
work 86
work or eat 39
works
   defined 256
   everyone judged by works 232
   in the Church Age 231
works of the Law 227–244
worship, in Spirit and truth 211

Z

Zacharias 184
zodiac 104

Scripture Index

GENESIS

1:14	254
1:28	171, 175
2:15	171, 173
2:16-17	171
3:6-7	172
3:16-17	172, 173
3:16-19	172
3:21	150, 172
3:22-24	172
4:3	173
4:4	173
4:5	173
4:7	173, 174, 175
4:15	175
6:5	174
6:5-7	219
6:7	174
6:8	150, 174
6:14	21
6:18	174
6:22	174
7:1	174
7:23	174
8:15	175
8:20	175
9:1-2	175
9:3	175
9:4	175
9:5-6	175
9:21-22	176
10:25	176
11:4	176
11:6-9	176
12:1	177
12:2-3	178
12:7-8	178
14:18-20	40
15:5	178
17:1-2	180

GENESIS (continued)

17:5	178
17:7	180
20:9-14	250
20:7	141
22:1-2	178
22:11-12	178
22:12	180
22:15-18	179
27:38	222

EXODUS

1:8	181
1:11-14	181
2:22	254
2:24-25	181
3:2	205
3:14	122
3:20	122
4:1	122
4:2-3	122
4:5	122
4:6	123
4:8	123, 254
4:9	123
4:10	123
4:17	124
4:22	32
4:31	178, 181
5:2	124
5:21	181
6:9	181
7:11-12	248
7:19	206
7:19-20	226
7:22	249
10:1-2	125
12:26-28	181
14:10	181
14:11-12	181

EXODUS (continued)

15:24	182
16:2	182
16:7-8	182
18:8-12	182
19:3-8	182
21:23-25	36
29:33-37	183
32:12	219
34:5	225
34:29	242

LEVITICUS

4:20	21, 183
4:26	14, 183
4:31	183
4:35	183
5:6	183
5:10	183
5:13	183
5:16	183
5:18	183
6:7	183
11:46-47	97
12:3	96
19:6	200
20:10	151
24:11-14	36
27:30-32	41

NUMBERS

15:32-36	36
16:1-3	73
16:31-35	225
16:35	73
23:10	183

DEUTERONOMY

13:6-10	36
15:12	29
21:18-21	36

JOSHUA

1:1-2	14
8:31	14

JUDGES

3:9	15
3:15	15
6:37-40	124
21:25	14, 152

I SAMUEL

6:14	1
15:23	218
16:7	170, 179
16:13	55
16:14	56, 183
18:12	183

II SAMUEL

7:15	56
12:13	151, 220
12:13-15	247
23:4	51
24:10	220
24:17	220

I KINGS

8:32	154
17:1	225

II KINGS

1:9-13	225

II CHRONICLES

6:23	154
8:16	131
21:14-15	247
21:18-19	247
26:18-21	248

EZRA

9:8	150
9:13	150

JOB

2:3	248
2:5-8	248
42:6	219

PSALMS

1:5-6	154
14:1-3	169
22:22	32
22:23-28	32
34:18	222
51:11	1
51:10-11	56, 183
68:9	51
78:41	122
104:1-2	245
111:9	147
119:130	238
130:7	172
147:5	178

PROVERBS
11:30 .... 224, 244
16:18 148
18:12 148
21:3 175

ISAIAH
9:6-7 175
55:8 249
61:1 .... 107, 186, 251
66:23-24 16

JEREMIAH
17:9-10 170
17:10 179
23:29 235
31:31-34 34
31:3 100
36:32 37

EZEKIEL
18:21 154
18:24 154
18:24-32 183
18:31 183

DANIEL
2:44 196
12:1-4 243

HOSEA
6:2-3 50

AMOS
8:11 115

HABAKKUK
2:4 .... 57, 183, 189

ZECHARIAH
4:3 225
4:14 225

MALACHI
3:6 169
4:3 226

MATTHEW
1:1 1
2:6 48
3:11-12 206
3:13-15 186
3:13-17 199
4:17 .... 27, 42, 186
4:18 186
4:19 79
4:23 .... 27, 76, 105, 187, 251

MATTHEW (continued)
5:14-16 239
5:17 141
5:17-20 186
5:38-39 37
5:39 101
5:42 .... 38, 39
6:5 148
6:10 196
6:33 187
7:12 141
7:13 192
7:18 221
9:35 .... 27, 76, 105
10:5 .... 12, 68, 93
10:5-7 .... 40, 43
10:6 62
10:15 233
10:16 38
10:19-22 52
10:22 74
11:13 .... 62, 141
12:32 30
15:24 .... 22, 40, 48, 62, 63, 76, 93, 252
15:26 92
16:4 122
16:21 71
16:21-22 114
16:28 225
17:1-3 225
17:23 71
19:28 78
20:19 71
21:28-32 221
22:36 141
23:1-6 184
23:6-9 147
23:14 76
23:15 .... 223, 224
23:23 .... 184, 227
24:3-4 135
24:11-14 135
24:13 .... 31, 50, 251
24:14 .... 28, 54, 105, 187
24:14-21 30
24:21 135
24:44 .... 7, 186, 188
25:10 .... 7, 188
25:31-46 192
25:34 31

MATTHEW (continued)

25:41	212
26:59	229
27:3	219
27:3-5	223
27:6	222, 229
27:24	108
27:41-44	218
27:46	212
28:19	12

MARK

1:14	46
1:14-15	28
1:44	21
3:29	102
6:6	221
6:12	222
8:31-32	68
9:9-10	113
10:30	30
15:10	228
16:6	119
16:14	119
16:14-18	139
16:14-20	118
16:15	12
16:15-20	202
16:17	118
16:17-18	119
16:19	120, 250
16:19-20	119, 139
16:20	125, 205

LUKE

1:5-6	184
1:6	230
1:13-17	184
1:17	7
4:18	107, 251
8:32	25
9:1	45
9:1-2	109, 187
9:6	45, 109, 187
9:44	81
12:31	187
12:40	7
13:3	212, 217
15:7	223
16:16	186
16:22-23	180

LUKE (continued) ....

16:26	78, 170
18:30	30
18:31-33	109
18:31-34	26, 44, 191, 253
18:34	68, 110
21:24	85
23:39-43	218
23:43	78, 119, 170
24:6-8	111
24:9-11	111
24:11	25
24:12	25, 68, 70, 111
24:29-30	208
24:35	208
24:44-46	112
24:51	10

JOHN

1:17	150
1:29	230
3:18	58, 213
2:17-18	234
3:18	58, 213
3:19-21	237
4:22	181
4:24	211
5:39	1
6:4	205
6:15	188
6:44	212
6:70	108
7:7	220
7:46	238
8:12	238
8:32	91
9:1-3	247
9:5	238
10:10	213
10:28	190
11:1-4	248
11:4	127
12:48	235
13:34	169
14:6	217
14:28-29	114
15:1	234
15:2	230
15:4-6	234
15:9-12	232
16:7-9	220

JOHN (continued)

17:11 148
17:12 .... 26, 110
18:10 .... 25, 70
18:36 37
19:31 228
20:8-9 114
20:21 .... 76, 93, 253

ACTS

1:6 .... 85, 196
1:9 .... 10, 120, 250
1:20-22 139
1:25 223
1:26 188
2:4 80
2:5 205
2:6 .... 128, 203
2:8 203
2:10 .... 39, 253
2:11 203
2:14 .... 17, 188, 205
2:22 205
2:27 .... 119, 212
2:31 .... 119, 212
2:36 205
2:38 .... 1, 80, 200, 202, 250
2:42 .... 83, 208
2:44 80
2:44-45 .... 53, 83
2:46 208
3:6 .... 53, 84
4:32 .... 72, 80, 250
4:32-35 .... 53, 84
5:3 133
5:5 .... 53, 80, 84
5:10 .... 53, 84
5:15-16 127
6:2 188
7:37-38 32
7:38 190
7:58 53
8:12-17 196
8:35-38 199
9:3 67
9:5 214
9:8 67
9:15 .... 24, 62, 68
9:17 139
9:17-18 197

ACTS (continued)

9:20 92
10:5 93
10:8-10 68
10:13 93
10:20 .... 68, 93
10:44-48 .... 128, 198
10:46 .... 80, 93, 203
11:17-18 214
11:19 .... 68, 93
11:21 215
11:27-28 141
11:29 85
12:4 101
13:1 141
13:9 253
13:11 248
13:14 .... 91, 130
13:15 145
13:27 146
13:38-39 228
13:44-46 103
13:45-46 130
13:47 192
14:1 91
14:3 128
14:12-16 217
14:14 138
14:15 244
14:19 217
15:7 17
15:7-12 68
15:25 125
15:28-29 107
15:32 .... 125, 141
16:1-3 95
16:6 130
16:24 218
16:26 67
16:29-31 188
16:29-34 218
16:30-33 201
16:31 234
16:34 201
17:1 91
17:10-11 151
7:16 215
7:18 215
17:23 204
17:29-30 215

ACTS (continued)

18:1	209
18:4	91
18:5-6	103
18:8	201
19:1-7	80
19:3	203
19:3-5	80
19:3-6	198
19:4	203
19:5	203
19:10	54
19:6	80, 200
19:8	91
19:21	209
19:37	190
20:4	255
20:7	207
20:10-12	207
20:16	130
20:21	60, 223
20:24	27, 105, 223, 251
20:25	195
21:4	209
21:8	143
21:10-13	209
21:18-26	209
21:27	209
21:29	130
21:39	210
22:16	198, 202
22:27	210
23:6	210
24:14	116
24:27	209
26:16	67
26:18	216
26:19-20	92, 217
27:33-35	208
28:4-5	128
28:6	129
28:20	89, 104
28:26-28	103
28:30-31	195

ROMANS

1:10	89
1:13	89
1:16	40, 62, 86, 87, 91, 92, 117, 128, 165
1:17	57, 189

ROMANS (continued)

1:20	174
1:25	104
1:27	248
1:29	230
2:2	216
2:1-5	216
3:10	155, 169
3:11	221
3:20	220
3:21-22	189
3:22	211
3:23	23, 60, 169
3:24	172
3:31	152, 153
4:1-3	179
4:11	180
5:1	163
5:6	221
5:8	23, 212, 221
5:10	221
5:11	22, 231
5:12	169, 211
5:18	153
5:20	31, 57
6:6	236
6:14	57, 58, 80
6:14-15	153
6:15	231
6:23	23, 171, 212, 234
7:7	220
7:12	229
7:13	220
7:18	221
8:3	59, 228, 231
8:4	157
8:9	197, 200
8:11	190
8:15	31
8:16	200, 224
8:16-17	235
8:17	235, 240
8:23	55, 180
9:17	132
9:31-32	154, 229
10:1-4	155
10:3	173
10:4	155
10:9-10	72

ROMANS (continued)

10:9-13	211
10:12-13	47
10:13	23
10:13-14	212
10:14	60
11:1	93
11:5	40, 91, 93, 254
11:7	93
11:13	39, 40, 43, 62, 137, 167
11:15	29
11:17	29, 47, 117, 167
11:20	91, 209
11:25	24, 61
12:3	59
12:5	166
12:17-18	37
13:4	37
13:8	60
13:8-10	157
13:12-14	240
14:1-5	97
14:10-11	235
14:14-23	98
14:17	195
14:23	221
15:4	104, 165
15:16	18, 64
15:20-23	131
15:22-25	89
15:25	85
16:7	166
16:17	60
16:25	24, 66, 74, 76
16:25-26	54, 83, 165
16:26	146

I CORINTHIANS

1:14-17	80, 201
1:17	104, 201
1:17-18	46
1:18	72
1:21	72
1:22	91, 121, 125
2:3	206
2:7	70
2:7-8	45, 110
2:8	70
2:9-10	236
2:14	80, 249

I CORINTHIANS (continued)

3:1	139
3:8	234
3:9	231
3:10	65, 77
3:10-12	64
3:10-15	234
3:13-15	64
3:16	190
4:1	24, 122
4:1-2	66
4:3-4	110
4:16	18, 80
4:20	195
5:9-11	239
6:7	38, 164
6:20	147
7:23	147
7:26	94
7:29	94
8:8	252
8:8-13	99, 164
8:14	23
9:1	126, 235
9:1-2	139
9:17	169, 251
9:20	94
9:22	210
10:6	165
10:11	165
10:27-28	100
10:28-30	163
11:1	37, 70, 74, 92, 105, 108, 167, 223, 253
11:1-2	80, 160, 208
11:2	250
11:7	241
11:20	252
11:23-34	80
12:12-13	190
12:13	190, 250
13:8-10	132, 143
13:10	131
13:11-13	132
14:2	203, 204
14:4	203
14:13	204
14:14	204
14:19	203
14:22	91, 121, 122

I Corinthians (continued)

14:27	204
14:29-33	142
14:33	66, 82, 96, 204
15:1	18
15:1-4	23, 43, 45, 64, 65, 71, 105
15:1-6	191
15:3	234
15:5-9	140
15:9	60, 166
15:9-10	148
15:22	166
15:34	192
15:35	243
15:41-44	243
15:51	24
16:1-3	83

II Corinthians

1:21-22	191
1:22	180
2:7	24
2:7-8	23
3:6	228
3:7-11	242
3:14	25
3:14-16	69
3:18	242
4:3	23, 25, 26
4:3-4	66
4:3-7	241
4:4	39
5:7	98, 117, 122, 140
5:10	64, 234, 241
5:17	214
5:20	192, 232
5:20-21	147
5:21	60, 154, 155, 180, 212
6:1	231
7:8-9	224
7:10	222
9:6-8	41
10:16	131
11:2	78
11:4	142
11:13-15	140
11:14	140, 237
12:4	170
12:7	65, 66
12:7-10	248

II Corinthians (continued)

12:11-12	120
12:12	119, 138, 254
12:14	84, 86
12:15	66

Galatians

1:4	39
1:6-7	105
1:6-9	255
1:8	76
1:11-12	10, 29, 45, 67, 105, 106, 191
1:13	60, 166
1:16	10, 29
1:23	60, 166
2:1-2	107
2:1-4	96
2:4	162, 163
2:6	10, 30
2:6-8	107
2:7	76, 85, 250
2:9	76
2:11	17
2:11-14	76, 93, 100
2:16	59, 72, 155, 183,, 189, 211, 227, 251
2:20	57, 59, 60, 236
2:21	154
3:3	10
3:8	132
3:10	227
3:13	58
3:14	59
3:19	183
3:21	183, 229
3:22-23	59
3:23	153
3:23-25	231
3:24	165, 183
3:24-25	156
3:25	231
3:28	34, 47, 94
4:9	250
4:9-10	100, 162
4:21	57, 153
5:1	163
5:1-4	162
5:3	14
5:6	96
5:13	161
5:13-14	157

GALATIANS (continued)

5:14 60
5:18 .... 23, 57, 153
5:22 255
5:22-23 219
6:7-8 243
6:13 252
6:11 67
6:15 .... 96, 250

EPHESIANS

1:3 24
1:4 .... 32, 59
1:9 24
1:10 169
1:13 .... 24, 55, 180, 191, 200, 250, 251
1:22 6
1:22-23 190
2:2 70
2:3 216
2:6 24
2:8-9 .... 60, , 234, 255
2:8-10 232
2:10 156
2:11-14 48
2:13-15 159
2:13-18 167
2:14 33
2:19-20 167
2:20 145
3:1 90
3:1-3 44
3:1-4 68
3:1-5 191
3:2 169
3:2-3 108
3:3 .... 29, 253
3:3-5 24
3:4-5 144
3:4-6 166
3:5 .... 44, 69, 107, 115
3:6-9 69
3:7 234
3:9 24
3:9-10 110
3:12 59
4:1 90
4:3 48
4:9 119

EPHESIANS (continued) ....

4:11 143
4:11-12 137
4:12-13 131
4:30 .... 55, 56, 180, 191, 250
5:2 146
5:8 240
5:30 1
5:32 24
6:12 82
6:19 .... 24, 253
6:20 90

PHILIPPIANS

1:7 90
1:13-16 90
2:25-30 248
3:4-8 94
3:6 .... 60, 166
3:8-9 183
3:9 .... 58, 154
3:20-21 180
3:21 .... 56, 242, 245
4:3 233
4:6-7 42
4:9 .... 18, 78, 82

COLOSSIANS

1:5-6 54
1:10 231
1:12 240
1:18-24 250
1:18 .... 6, 62, 166, 190
1:23 54
1:24 .... 6, 62, 70, 166
1:25 .... 73, 169
1:26-27 24
1:27 57
2:2 24
2:8 104
2:10-14 250
2:12 1
2:13 191
2:13-17 101
2:14-16 .... 80, 160
2:20-23 .... 80, 101
3:1-3 24
3:23-25 236
4:3 .... 24, 90
4:18 91

I THESSALONIANS

1:5 211
1:9 .... 217, 223
2:4 71
4:1 .... 18, 59, 75
4:13-18 .... 4, 250, 253
4:17 44
5:9 216
5:23 177

II THESSALONIANS

1:6-9 210
1:8 170
1:8-9 212
2:7 .... 134, 136
2:8-9 134
2:9 117
2:14-15 73
3:10 .... 39, 86
3:17 29

I TIMOTHY

1:8 152
1:8-11 158
1:9 183
1:16 .... 65, 213, 222
2:4 170
2:7 63
3:1 137
3:9 24
3:10 137
3:16 .... 24, 125, 149
4:1-3 .... 147, 160
4:1-4 96
4:4 164
5:8 .... 38, 84, 85
5:23 130
6:17-19 52
6:19 240
6:20 104

II TIMOTHY

1:7 31
1:11 63
1:13 81
1:16 91
2:7 .... 19, 20, 81, 83, 115, 133, 149, 165, 202
.... 222, 250
2:8 76
2:9 91
2:11-13 236

II TIMOTHY (continued)

2:12 .... 235, 240
2:15 .... 2, 17, 20, 57, 85, 88, 115, 136,
.... 149, 202, 210, 254
3:1 .... 30, 74, 116
3:1-8 248
3:12 .... 236, 240
3:15 165
3:16 .... 20, 165
3:17 131
4:2 202
4:2-4 74
4:3 .... 104, 251
4:5 144
4:7 78
4:17 19
4:20 130

TITUS

1:1-3 72
2:11-14 232
2:13-14 191
3:5 .... 72, 232
3:8 .... 156, 232
3:14 231

PHILEMON

9-10 91

HEBREWS

1:1 .... 13, 28
1:2 30
2:3-4 29
2:3-5 28
2:5 30
2:9 119
2:12 32
3:1 21
4:1-11 31
4:3 31
4:12 132
4:15 230
5:13 74
6:4-6 .... 31, 49, 235
6:5 30
7:19 183
7:24-27 146
8:8 34
9:9-12 80
9:10 161
9:12 172

HEBREWS (continued)

9:13 .... 183, 228
9:16 253
9:16-18 7
9:17 1
9:22-28 169
10:1-2 230
10:5 29
10:11-12 .... 22, 146
11:25 215
10:26 251
10:29 234
10:34 29
11:1 .... 118, 125
11:6 229
12:2 58
12:16-17 222
12:23 32
13:8 .... 34, 169
13:11 29
13:3 29
13:23 29
13:24 29

JAMES

1:1 47
1:2-4 50
1:10-11 51
1:17 169
2:6-7 51
2:10 230
2:20-24 179
5:1-3 52
5:7 50
5:7-9 50
5:10-11 49
5:17 .... 50, 225

I PETER

1:16 59
3:15 33
3:17 116
3:21 202
4:17 170

II PETER

1:16-19 132
1:20 72
1:21 13
2:5 175
3:1-2 145

II PETER(continued)

3:8 31
3:9 .... 170, 216, 221
3:10-12 12
3:15 77
3:15-16 .... 70, 77

I JOHN

4:1 142
5:16-17 151

II JOHN

12 132

III JOHN

2 249

JUDE

9 226

REVELATION

1:4 29
1:10 30
2:1 192
2:8 192
2:11 29
2:12 192
2:18 .... 192, 235
3:1 192
3:7 192
3:14 192
3:17 84
4:1 208
6:7 51
6:17 255
7:3-4 48
7:4 .... 16, 47, 54, 192
10:7 24
11:2-3 .... 49, 50
11:3 .... 16, 54, 192, 255
11:4 225
11:5 225
11:6 225
11:15 32
13:3 135
13:4-5 51
13:4-7 49
13:7 135
13:8 233
13:12 134
13:13-14 .... 135, 206
13:16-18 51
14:1 16

REVELATION (continued)

14:3-4	192
14:4	16
14:6	192
14:6-7	46
14:8	46
14:11-12	49
16:4	142
17:8	233
19:6	32
19:15-16	16
19:20	192, 252
19:21	192
20:1-3	192
20:3-8	253
20:4	192
20:6	4
20:11	252
20:11-15	233
20:14-15	212
21:1	4, 177
21:1-2	241
21:22-23	241
21:22-27	193
22:3-5	193
22:5	242
22:20	194